Avenues of Participation

PRINCETON STUDIES IN MUSLIM POLITICS

Dale F. Eickelman and James Piscatori, editors

Avenues of Participation

FAMILY, POLITICS, AND NETWORKS IN URBAN QUARTERS OF CAIRO

• *DIANE SINGERMAN* •

PRINCETON UNIVERSITY PRESS

PRINCETON, NEW JERSEY

Library of Congress Cataloging-in-Publication Data

Singerman, Diane.
Avenues of participation : family, politics, and networks
in urban quarters of Cairo / Diane Singerman.
p.   cm. — (Princeton studies in Muslim politics)
Includes bibliographical references (p.   ) and index.
ISBN 0-691-08654-0 (CL)
1. Political participation—Egypt—Cairo.   2. Family—Egypt—
Cairo.   3. Households—Egypt—Cairo.   4. Informal sector
(Economics)—Egypt—Cairo.   I. Title.   II. Series.
JS7782.S55   1995   323'.042'096216—dc20   94-19060   cip

The jacket photo and photos on pages 26 and 28 courtesy of
John Waterbury. All other text photos are by the author.

This book has been composed in Laser Sabon

Princeton University Press books are printed on acid-free paper and meet the guidelines for
permanence and durability of the Committee on Production Guidelines for Book
Longevity of the Council on Library Resources

Printed in the United States of America

1   3   5   7   9   10   8   6   4   2

TO MY MOTHER, PHYLLIS SINGERMAN,
• *AND TO THE MEMORY OF MY FATHER,* •
SOL SINGERMAN

• C O N T E N T S •

· L I S T   O F   T A B L E S ·

THE STUDY OF politics in Muslim societies has been dominated by elites and formal institutions. All too often observers of these, and other, societies assume that power exclusively resides in such state institutions as the bureaucracy, the military, and the intelligence services. Prodded by the theoretical work of scholars sensitive to political, sociological, and anthropological concerns, regionally focused work is beginning to emphasize the politically significant activities of nonelites and to recognize that an evaluation of the civic order depends on a more complex calculus of actors, interests, and values than has previously prevailed.

By concentrating on the popular (*shaʿbi*) quarters of Cairo, Diane Singerman provides just such a rich analysis in this volume. The minutely observed story she tells is of an inventive people who, because of the demands of everyday life in an overly bureaucratized and largely authoritarian society, evolve networks that facilitate access, or provide alternatives, to the formal resources of the state; these do not, however, displace the formal power of the Egyptian state. Here are a people who rely on the ties of family or neighborhood to plant a sympathetic word or financial favor with normally unreceptive bureaucrats; who mitigate the effects of underemployment by holding supplementary jobs in a vigorous informal economy; who establish savings associations to provide credit to individuals who would not otherwise qualify in the rigid, formal banking system; who resettle to outlying areas of the municipality and thereby force the government to accord them *de facto* autonomy. Despite the high degree of illiteracy, the urban quarters of Cairo are mixed in composition and are not exclusively lower class. Indeed, the common sense of economic and political discontent and the enterprising roles of women detailed by Professor Singerman disturb the customary image of the Muslim masses as a subdued, fatalistic political underclass.

Two conclusions are particularly suggestive for the study of what we call Muslim politics—that is, the competition and contest of both symbolic production and control of the institutions, both formal and informal, which serve as symbolic or normative arbiters of society. First, Professor Singerman demonstrates that the distribution and redistribution of goods and services occur in the context of broadly shared values and assumptions. As her empirical findings amply indicate, individuals in the *shaʿbi* quarters of Cairo respond to material interests, whether it be the need to accumulate marriage trousseaus, avoid the predatory tax collector, or gain a quality education unavailable through the state sector. It is equally clear that Islamic doctrine does not simply determine the popular politics of Egypt; considerations of class, education, and family are often the critical factors at work. Moreover, as Professor Singerman demonstrates in a comparative perspective, informal patterns of participation are not unique to Islamic societies. Yet Muslim politics in Egypt is played out against the background of an underlying framework that, while subject to contextualized nuances, is common to Muslims across the world.

As it does elsewhere in the Muslim world, the family, for instance, emerges as the repository of social—and Muslim—values in Egyptian society. Much political action that unfolds is connected with the prior imperative to defend the family as a kind of Islamic microcosm and to advance its welfare. In addition, one reason why the *gamʿiyyat*, or informal banks, are so popular is that Muslims are able to fulfill their financial needs while assuring themselves that they are participating in an Islamic venture that does not engage in *riba* or usurious practices. Moreover, the high value placed on education among the Cairenes is indicative of the Muslim ethos, which encourages full development of the faculties given by God, and many private voluntary organizations, such as health clinics and day-care centers, regard the collection of the *zakat*, or Islamic alms, for social welfare purposes as religiously enjoined.

Second, Professor Singerman demonstrates that the usual dichotomized distinctions between the "public" and the "private," "above" and "below," in political analyses are tenuous. The former is generally thought to be the realm of the state and "high politics"; the latter, the realm of the family, women, and the nonpolitical or at best "low politics." This volume, and the volumes to follow in this series, argues that such distinctions ignore the near-constant interpenetration of networks that evolve in the social and political life of Muslims, without, however, ignoring or underestimating the resources and capabilities of entrenched elite interests or étatist institutions. Precisely because the family is so esteemed, it becomes a natural vehicle by which economic and social relations are organized and regulated in societies such as Egypt, and its normative structure provides a standard by which individuals may assess the Islamic credentials of the government. Displeasure wtih the increase in marriages of Egyptian men to foreign, often non-Muslim, women, for example, turns into a political criticism of the government's "open door" (*infitah*) economic policy with its unwelcome rise in consumerism and foreign tourism. Incidents of rape become a political indictment of the goverment's inability to protect its citizens and to provide an effective moral lead. Moreover, the concerns of the family with the morality and with the appearance of the morality of its younger members (in matters of dress, comportment, and association) intersect—at times overlapping, at other times clashing—with the larger concerns of secular-minded liberals, the official religious establishment, and Islamist protest groups.

In the pages to follow, the Muslim politics of the popular quarters of Cairo cohere into patterns of both cooperation and conflict over evolving values and interests, of commitment to and contest over symbols and contextualized symbolic understandings. In the face of closed avenues to meaningful political participation, alternative political institutions emerge. These include the mosque, but also family-based economic enterprises, informal banks, and private voluntary organizations. There is no doubt that Islamist groups benefit from the evolution of such an alternative political system, for it stands as a powerful counterpoint to the state's self-ascribed monopoly to designate the rules of the political society. These groups also advance their goals by deriving financial rewards from the informal economy and by expressing the underlying popular criticisms of government. Yet the politics of the *sha'b* also suggests that to look for an apparent winner or loser in Muslim politics is to perpetuate the elementary "us against them," elite versus counterelite bias of political analysis. The Cairene scenes that unfold in this book constructively provide greater vibrancy and subtlety.

Dale F. Eickelman
James Piscatori

something about political science and Egypt when I was a graduate student there. The instruction and advice of Abbas al-Tonsy and Zeinab Taha at the Center for Arabic Study Abroad were also extremely helpful. This research could never have been accomplished without the support and encouragement of my Arabic professors along the way who have had to listen to my mutilations of the language, beginning with David Powers, Avram Udovitch, and Andras Hamori at Princeton University, Amin Bonnah and Adnan Haydar at Middlebury Summer Language Program, and, among others, Zeinab Taha, Abbas al-Tonsy, Nabila al-Asuity, and Wahid Sami at the American University in Cairo. I am indebted to them all. Discussions on literature and gender politics with Muna Abu Sinna of Ain Shams University still resonate today. A community of scholars and researchers in Cairo and the United States, including Ann Lesch, Barbara Ibrahim, Richard Lobban, Huda Zurayk, Margot Badran, Rebecca Copeland, Marsha Pripstein Posusney, Clarissa Burt, Ahmed Taha, and Ragui Assaad offered important encouragement and advice over several years.

During the course of this study I was extremely fortunate to work with Frederic Shorter of the Population Council. He is the model of a scholar and researcher, whose gracious and generous support knew no bounds. In Cairo I also met Homa Hoodfar, whose experience as an anthropologist and whose wise counsel and friendship I was to rely upon again and again. With Homa I have benefited greatly from an ongoing exchange of ideas and research with Arlene MacLeod, Kathryn Kamphoefner, Nadia Khouri-Dagher, and Nawal Hassan. Without the assistance of Nawal Hassan, the Director of the Centre for Egyptian Civilisation Studies, this project would not have materialized. She provided essential assistance at the outset of my fieldwork, offering her Centre as a library and base for my research in central Cairo and sharing her experience as a dedicated ombudsman for people in *sha'bi* communities. I would also like to thank Professor Ibrahim el-Muelhy and Madame Yusriyya at the Centre for their intellectual and personal hospitality. In Cairo, Sylvia Mitchell and Lou Ann McNeill of the USAID Information Center provided gracious assistance.

Living in Cairo has increased my understanding of interdependence and mutual support. Since I arrived there several people have become "fictive kin," and these bonds have continued even after leaving each other's company. Bob Vitalis has been an extremely important friend as well as colleague and critic. Karen Glasgow and Khadry Sobhi Mahmoud have offered not only their friendship and assistance but the engagement of experienced and critical minds. George Marquis tried to sort out my Arabic and was a very appreciated editor. While writing much of this book, discussions with Sylvia Gruner helped clarify my thoughts, and her presence restored imagination and vitality to Cambridge. Linda Suter not only improved my writing with her editing skills, but she has been an immense source of support and wisdom since I have known her (I am forced to use superlatives, despite her advice). In Cambridge I would also like to acknowledge the friendship and

• A C K N O W L E D G M E N T S •

DURING THE COURSE of this study I learned of the support that familial and informal networks provide during good and bad times. Throughout the recent past I relied upon networks of professional, emotional, and financial support which rival the size of the community I studied in Cairo. I have exploited them as assiduously as any black marketeer or marriage broker. While these relationships have not proven to be nearly as reciprocal as is typical in Cairean networks, in the future I hope they will be. I also hope readers will tolerate the length of these acknowledgments, for this book is not only a product of individual effort, but when I consider the assistance of some of the people mentioned here it takes on more of the shape of a collaborative project.

This study would not have materialized without the support of several important advisers at Princeton. In the very beginning, John Willis encouraged me to study Arabic and pursue my interest in Near Eastern Studies. L. Carl Brown provided direct and indirect encouragement throughout my studies at Princeton, as the Director of the Program in Near Eastern Studies. My primary adviser, John Waterbury, patiently allowed my ideas to gel, while offering essential suggestions and practical advice both in Princeton and Cairo. His dedication to his students, quiet support for their work, and his knowledge of the Middle East is remarkable. Nancy Bermeo set my research within a larger comparative context and provided critical structural and methodological advice. Samir Khalaf's sociological approach and understanding of other Middle Eastern societies provided a broader perspective for this research. Throughout my graduate work at Princeton, I came to depend upon Mildred Kalmus for far more than advice and assistance. Anne Norton, Manfred Halpern, Atul Kohli, Elizabeth Petras, Julie Mostov, Peter Gran, Bob Vitalis, and Homa Hoodfar have also offered important advice at various stages of this project. And I am very appreciative of the comments from my readers at Princeton University Press as well as of the editorial support and encouragement I received from Jennifer Matthews, Walter Lippincott, and Margaret Case at Princeton University Press and from my copyeditor Roy Thomas.

Equally important throughout the past several years were my colleagues at Princeton. Muna Zaki, Margaret Koval, Steve Cowley, and Nathan Brown are owed many thanks. Rachel Kranton graciously answered frequent distress calls about economic issues raised by my research. Carolyn Makinson has always provided just the needed balance of logic, clarity, and support since the beginning of graduate school. Her reading of parts of this book provided somewhat of a breakthrough.

Gail Gerhart, Walid Khezziha, Robert Bianchi, and Tim Sullivan, present and former members of the American University in Cairo faculty, taught me assistance of Anne Steurnagel, Maggie Browning, Rebecca Foote, Denise Spellberg, Matthew Gordon, Stefania Pandolfo, and Harriet. Since the early days of graduate school I have always been able to look to Eva Bellin for intellectual and professional solace, humor, friendship, and spirit, no matter if we were in Princeton, Cairo, Vermont, Washington, D.C., or, more often, on the phone. This endeavor has been easier due to her friendship.

This book is based upon the experiences of a group of people who invited me into their homes and lives in a most gracious and generous way. Time and again they offered me their hospitality, tolerantly withstood my ignorance and questions, and opened their homes to me. To the family that offered me a room in their house, I cannot possibly thank them enough. While being an outsider should have been a difficult position, somehow my presence became routine and expected. While I am sure I have misinterpreted many things, and misunderstood others, I hope I have conveyed the deep admiration and respect I have for my friends in Cairo and their dedication to their families and communities. Through them I have learned much more about Egypt than would have been possible in any other manner. Although they remain anonymous, each and every one of them was incredibly hospitable to me, for which I am deeply appreciative. Most of all, to AB and her family and ʿAlaʾ, *shukran gaziilan*.

I would also like to thank the Fulbright Commission, the Social Science Research Council, the American Research Center in Egypt, and the Department of Politics, Near Eastern Studies Program, Council on Regional Studies, and the Center for International Studies at Princeton University, the Department of History and Politics at Drexel University, and Dean Neil Kerwin and the School of Public Affairs at the American University for logistical and financial support for various stages of this research. In addition, I would like to thank my able research assistants at the American University—Ryan Rusek, Matt Baker, Quintan Wiktorowicz, and Candace Walsh—for their contributions to this book.

Tragically, three people who were not only deeply important in my life but who played such a significant role in this project have died in the recent past. AB, the matriarch of the family I lived with in Cairo, who was such a unique person—dedicated to her family, incredibly resourceful, determined, and generous—could no longer withstand her health problems. Though her memory lives on with her family and her fictive kin in the United States, Cairo has lost a most impressive and wise leader. I met Chuck Raht shortly after I first arrived in Cairo in 1980, and we became fast friends. Luckily he stayed in the Middle East for several years so that I could remain his sidekick. Chuck not only influenced my outlook on life in many ways but was always there with humor, encouragement, and gentle pointed words at the appropriate moments. Several years later Kevin Rimmington was incorporated into Cairo's fictive kin networks along with his constant good humor and cups of tea. He edited many versions of this book, from London or Cairo, even as he became ill. I cannot really convey how much these two friends are missed by myself and everyone who came to know them and how thankful I am that I ran into Chuck in the courtyard of the AUC dormitory so many years ago.

Finally, my siblings Leni, Janet, and Robert Singerman have been a never-ending source of support. There is little to say that conveys the sense of my appreciation to them, Terry Post, Court Fulton, Cleo Sofie Post, Ben and Deena Fulton. Mickey Lewis and Sol Lewis have always spurred me on with humor and love. From Cora Reed I first learned to listen to stories and to value the lives and experiences of others. Paul Wapner reappeared in my life at a time when I least expected to find such a find and, following my promise to friends in Cairo to worry about marriage after I had completed my Ph.D., I quickly married him. He has shown me that it is possible to finish a book while enjoying life. My kinship networks have now been enriched with the inclusion of the Wapner/Thiele clan as well. Finally, this book is dedicated to my parents, Phyllis and Sol Singerman, who sparked my tendency to question the obvious from an early age and then allowed me to pursue my interests, even if that meant sacrificing some of their own. Although I have heeded his advice to eat fish, my father is not here to see the fruits of his wisdom and encouragement, and he is sorely missed.

THE SYSTEM of phonetic transcription used in the following chapters has been chosen for reasons of accuracy and simplicity to represent spoken Egyptian Arabic in readable form for an English-speaking audience. The grammatical structure and phonological rules of colloquial Arabic and classical Arabic differ in some aspects, and various transliteration systems have been used by scholars to better capture the nuances of colloquial Egyptian Arabic. Since I conducted my research primarily in colloquial Egyptian Arabic (outside of my use of written Arabic sources), I believe the system that I have adopted here best reflects those nuances.

Ideally, a one-character symbol for each corresponding consonant sound in Egyptian colloquial Arabic should have been used, however, due to printing limitations, this was not possible and two-letter symbols have been used to represent the sounds of غ and ش, perhaps causing some confusion. As well, I have used *one* symbol ['] to transcribe the qaf [ق] (when it is not pronounced in colloquial Egyptian Arabic), the hamza [ء], and the glottal stop, because in spoken Egyptian Arabic these sounds are indistinguishable to the ear in most cases. In order to represent Egyptian colloquial phonetically, i.e., the terms as they *sound*, it is necessary to include the glottal stop in this transcription system. The glottal stop is part of the sound system of Arabic, although Arabic orthography has no symbol to represent it.

The symbols used for vowels are those adopted by Virginia Stevens and Maurice Salib in *A Dictionary of the Spoken Arabic of Cairo* (Cairo: American University in Cairo Press, 1986) and El-Said Badawi and Martin Hinds in *A Dictionary of Egyptian Arabic* (Beirut: Librarie du Liban, 1986). In this transcription system, a consonant symbol is doubled to indicate that the length of that consonant is double that of its single counterpart. In the orthography of the Arabic script, this doubling of consonant length would be represented by the use of a *shadda*. The situation of vowel length, however, is not so straightforward. While it would be accurate to say that doubled vowel symbols of *aa*, *ii/ee*, and *uu/oo* correspond to the Arabic script counterparts ا, ي, and و, respectively, it is not always the case that single vowel symbols correspond to Arabic-script short vowel markers (*fatHa, kasra, Dumma*). For example, the word *dallaala* is transcribed as *dallalaat* in the plural, with the second vowel sound shortening in length due to a phonological rule of the Egyptian colloquial language. There is no corresponding "change" in the orthography, and thus it should not be inferred that the transcription *dallalaat* reflects anything more than the *phonetic* representation of the word, as it exists in the Egyptian spoken language.

Rather than use this transliteration system for proper names, place names, and frequently translated Arabic words, I have generally used their conventional spellings found in English-language sources.

Consonants:

Transliterated English	Arabic
ʾ	ق, ء, and the glottal stop
b	ب
t	ت ث
g	ج
H	ح
x	خ
d	د ذ
r	ر
z	ز ذ
s	س ث
sh	ش ث
S	ص
D	ض
T	ط
Z	ظ
ʿ	ع
gh	غ
f	ف
q	ق
k	ك
l	ل
m	م
n	ن
h	ه
w	و
y	ي

Vowels:

The six vowel symbols used are:

a   approximately the same as *a* in English *back* or *a* in British *class*, but never elongated

e   approximately the same as *e* between the vowel sounds in English *tin* and *ten*

i   approximately the same as *i* as in English *win*

o   approximately the same as *o* in standard English *pop*

u   approximately the same as *u* as in English *put*

Vowel length:

aa   approximately the same sound but slightly longer than the *a* in English *mad* or *palm*

ee   approximately the same as in English *mate*

ii   approximately the same as in English *seat*

oo   approximately the same as in English *note*

uu   approximately the same as in English *pool*

Avenues of Participation

THE VOICES, experiences, and political activity of men and women from the lower strata of society are largely unrepresented in political analyses. Those who do not participate in private or state-sanctioned formal organizations such as interest groups, labor unions, and political parties, and who do not join protest movements or clandestine organizations that directly challenge the established political order, remain "unaccounted for" and "uncounted." Under authoritarian regimes the political participation of ordinary men and women is even more circumscribed as repression and fear work to intimidate their voices and their leaders. As power is concentrated in fewer hands—a charismatic ruler, a bureaucratized military, a president for life, a monarch, or an ethnic minority—the machinations of the elite become the natural object of study. The power of the popular sector, the majority of the nation, is assumed to be "neutralized." They have either been brutally repressed, co-opted, or have grown apathetic and acquiescent, socialized into accepting elite domination.

This study argues against this view. Far from being unimportant, politically apathetic, or acquiescent, popular classes under authoritarian regimes engage in a range of activities that have political import and aggregate power for collective benefit. While elites may succeed in excluding them from the formal political arena through repression or co-optation, they often fail to stop them from forming alternative, informal political institutions to further their interests. Informal activities, whether economic or political, are those that escape licensing, regulation, and even enumeration by the state and thus have an illegal or quasi-legal status. Informal networks and informal institutions seek to avoid the notice of the state, even as they extract as much as possible from its distributional mechanisms. In Egypt, the subject of this study, it is illegal to hold a meeting with a group that is not registered by the Ministry of Information. The state attempts to control and regulate every common mechanism that people use to further collective interests, such as unions, meetings of every kind, political parties, newspapers, voluntary associations, interest groups, demonstrations, books, radio, and television. Those who consciously resist the state or who engage in strategies that conflict with statist objectives are rarely free of fears and anxieties about possible retribution.

This study does not argue, naively, that popular classes are somehow more important or powerful than formal elite institutions and the state, but rather that they are part and parcel of the overall political dynamic in a nation and cannot be left out of political analyses without misrepresentation. Whenever there is an outbreak of political expression despite authoritarianism, whether in the form of a demonstration, a strike, sabotage, dissident writing, interest group activity, or a social movement, analysts scramble to understand those in the popular sector and their demands. Visible and direct resistance is noticed, yet these same political forces predate and postdate demonstrations whether they are visibly apparent or not. My point is that popular political activity is always taking place, reorienting collective forces and revising political ideologies. It does not simply emerge, suddenly, at peak moments such as demonstrations but is only the end result of a political process.

To understand the dynamics of political change, we must widen our investigation of the locus of politics and revise our stereotypes about its institutional shape. As James Scott argues, "So long as we confine our conception of the political to activity that is openly declared we are driven to conclude that subordinate groups essentially lack a political life or that what political life they do have is restricted to those exceptional moments of popular explosion."[1]

Constituencies that are intentionally excluded from formal political participation by a ruling power are not only repressed by their governments but discounted and ignored by reigning typologies of politics. Prevailing definitions of political participation suffer from an obvious bias toward influencing the elite, governmental institutions and formal, legal associations. Verba and Nie defined political participation as "the activities aimed at influencing the selection of government personnel and/or the actions they take."[2] Huntington and Nelson broadened the definition to include any attempt at influencing government decision-making in general.[3] Nelson further suggested, more recently, that violent and nonviolent extralegal protest activities should be recognized as political participation in authoritarian or nondemocratic nations. "Participation is simply the efforts of ordinary people in any type of political system to influence the actions of their rulers, and sometimes to change their rulers."[4] While this revised definition now includes a wider range of political action, it only recognizes citizens as politically active if they directly engage the political elite or rulers. Alternatively, Adams's notion of participation as a "structural, dialectical condition of society" recognizes and understands power struggles and communal conflict within and between communities, neighborhoods, provinces, ethnic groups, and religious groups.[5] An interactive notion of the political process captures the participation of less visible members of the community and refutes, or at least modifies, claims that they are apathetic, alienated, or repressed.

Equally important, each society manifests political activity in different ways, depending on an ever-changing variety of factors, and political scientists need to be more aware and sensitive to the creative mechanisms people use to further their aims. We need even greater self-conscious sensitivity when we study societies other than our own and are outsiders to the nuances of rule, representation, production, resistance, expression, and distribution. In nations where few legal avenues of political participation are accessible to the vast majority of citizens, opposition to the state can involve great personal and professional risks. Because of these risks, people learn to express their political beliefs in subtle and creative ways. Often the structure and discourse of this political arena has gone underground, or is too subtle or symbolic to capture the notice of scholars or politicians who are more interested in the powerful and schooled in the political dynamics and traditions of their own societies.

Egypt offers vibrant evidence for revising the boundaries of political research as well as our notions of the political, public, and private spheres, and the avenues by which a variety of constituencies participate in politics. Egypt presents an example of politics despite authoritarian rule in an area of the world where so many stereotypes about passivity, fatalism, repression, corruption, fanaticism, and terrorism still reign, barely removed from the surface of supposedly expert and scholarly analysis. Such stereotypes have remained fixed, particularly in Western minds, with little attention to the structures of power (both national and international) under which citizens live. The *sha*ᶜ*b* (the common people or the popular sector in Egypt), only recently written back into history through the efforts of social and labor historians, students of peasant politics, and feminist scholars, still are portrayed largely as the objects of political rule rather than as the architects of political change and struggle.

EGYPT AND POPULAR POLITICAL EXPRESSION

The impetus for this study arose from questions about the locus of politics and the meaning of political participation under repressive conditions. I focused my questions on a particular country, Egypt, while I attended graduate school there and continued to consider them after I returned to the United States and entered a doctoral program. Two related questions about Egyptian politics fused my comparative interests with a concern for the politics of the excluded. Despite my familiarity with the wide range of scholarship on Egypt, I was still puzzled about the participation of men *and* women from the popular sector, particularly considering the populist rhetoric and agenda of the Free Officers' Revolution, which brought Gamal Abdel Nasser to power in 1952. While there are classic works on elite politics in Egypt, its political economy, class formation, interest groups, the bureaucracy, and the military, the politics of the common people or the *sha*ᶜ*b* have received little attention. Their political demands, actions, and grievances remain of secondary interest to elite analysis. It has been anthropologists, historians, and sociologists who have told us about the politics of the common people while the "high politics" of the elite (including interest group politics) remained the domain of political scientists. However, if one truly wants to consider state-society relations, it seems only natural to try to link up these two arenas of interests since dynamic political forces do not mirror our self-conscious construction of disciplinary boundaries. Since the nature of power is constantly shifting as constellations of interests rise and fall, it seems odd that political scientists are closely attuned to the role of elites yet pay far less attention to the other pole in the power dynamic: the popular sector.

Like the inattention to popular classes in Egypt, there was a second perplexing question that fueled this research: why is it that many ethnographic and anthropological studies depict women as important community figures who exert influence over the management of the household and wider social networks,[6] yet the classic works on Egyptian politics and political economy barely allude to them? Where does all that power go? Does it dissipate at "higher" levels of power and authority in Egypt? Despite the recent proliferation of research on women in Egypt and their participation in political and economic life, the macro analysis of "high politics" remains androcentric and gender blind.[7] By examining the dynamic interaction of both men and women in extrasystemic, informal political processes, I hope to present an alternative view of politics which locates power in a wider range of structures and institutions, in which both men and women participate. In short, I hope to complicate the story of power, interest, and participation in Egypt.

"Leaving out" women from political analyses in Egypt replicates the invisibility of the popular sector, more generally. If women do not riot, are not powerful members of interest groups, unions, political parties, or representative institutions, there is no real reason to consider them as political actors. If they do not appear as a significant force in the institutions that Western social scientists categorize as political, then they must not be engaged in politics. In other words, if they are not present in the public arena, we can only argue that their power must derive from social institutions or the family, clear territory of the private realm. This approach to politics in Egypt mirrors the research on political participation in the United States which defined women's activities and their organizations as private or social activities, thus rendering them invisible until the path-breaking work of such feminist political activists and political theorists as Carole Pateman challenged the very categories and gender-blind assumptions of political analysis.[8] Redefining the "public" and "private" realms then becomes a crucial step in reinterpreting the dynamics of Egyptian politics.

In a classic example of the centrality of this issue to the way we think about politics,[9] Myron Wiener conflates politics and the public realm when he argues that political participation is "any voluntary action, successful or unsuccessful, organized or unorganized, episodic or continuous, employing legitimate or illegitimate methods *intended* to influence the choice of *public* policies, the administration of *public* affairs, or the choice of *political* leaders at any level of *government*, local or national."[10] This definition suffers from two major conceptual problems (which I will elaborate upon in the first chapter). First, Weiner places undue emphasis on the intentionality of political behavior, like many political scientists who consider it a key variable in identifying political behavior. Yet understanding the "intentions" of people, whether elites or the common people, is a slippery slope.[11] Do women who create parallel, illegal distribution markets of subsidized food commodities intend to influence state policy or are they merely interested in profit and providing food for their families? Does prayer only become political when people attend mosques whose leaders are known opposition figures? Is fulfilling the Muslim obligation to give charity to the poor (*'iz-zakaah*) a routine religious duty or does it become political if the funds are used to convert Christians or publish tracts calling for the imposition of Islamic law? Is engaging in the informal economy a self-interested rational act that maximizes utility or is it an explicit strategy to evade the repressive and fiscal power of the state? Is wife-beating a private affair or domestic violence and a violation of human rights? Is a woman merely self-interested and materialistic when she demands an expensive engagement gift or is she supporting the power and rights of women? Where do informal political and economic activities fall in this typology if people who design informal networks never would suggest that they are intentionally influencing the choice of public policies, the administration of public affairs, or the choice of political leaders at any level of government? The important variable in this discussion is not whether a man or woman "intends" to act politically but whether his or her actions, individually and cumulatively, actually influence the political order, the distribution and redistribution of public goods and services. The following chapters will argue that individual strategies to accumulate savings, provide an education for a child, or migrate abroad, when repeated thousands of times, influence the macro allocation and distribution of scarce resources and public goods, as well as political and economic phenomenon in the nation. Everyday decisions add up incrementally to create the boundaries and interests of the political and economic order.

Too often, a neat distinction is drawn between political and apolitical behavior, the former consciously directed at collective behavior to influence public decisions and the latter merely individual, self-interested behavior directed toward private ends. However, to separate political behavior from personal self-interest is misguided, considering the complex motivations that influence behavior, particularly among people who live daily with scarcity and cannot afford to misjudge their options. As Scott explains in his discussion of peasant politics,

> To require of lower-class resistance that it somehow be "principled" or "selfless" is not only utopian and a slander on the moral status of fundamental material needs; it is, more fundamentally, a misconstruction of the basis of class struggle, which is, first and foremost, a struggle over the appropriation of work, production, property, and taxes. "Bread-and-butter" issues are the essence of lower-class politics and resistance. Consumption, from this perspective, is both the goal and the result of resistance and counterresistance. It is precisely the fusion of self-interest and resistance that is the vital force animating the resistance of peasants and proletarians. When a peasant hides part of his crop to avoid paying taxes, he is both filling his stomach and depriving the state of grain.[12]

The needs, desires, and political preferences of the *sha'b* are inextricably linked to their material condition, and they develop informal methods and strategies outside the framework of formal institutions to fight their "bread and butter" issues. However, to reduce politics to mere self-interest and cost-benefit analysis in the tradition of rational choice scholarship veers too far to the other extreme. Though I pay particular attention to the bargaining among individuals within the family unit and the costs of visible collective action among the popular sector in Egypt and I examine one of the central questions of rational choice theory (i.e., political participation), I have a problem with the definition of both "action" and "collective" in the rational choice paradigm. Action suggests visibility, and visibility is dangerous under repressive political conditions. One of the important ways in which informal institutions further the interests of their constituents in Egypt is that they are not "active" and open but are instead invisible and subterranean. Almost all of the activities that I discuss as political and collective in this study would not be recognized as collective action by rational choice theorists and many Western social scientists, in general. One of the primary purposes of this work is to recognize and analyze political activity that does not directly oppose the state or its elite but lies between individual actions and organized, visible, legal collective action, within the context of Egyptian politics and society. As Charles Taylor argues, it can be disastrous to the study of comparative politics if we interpret all other societies in the categories of our own. The indefensible result of such an approach is that theories of political development place "the Atlantic-type polity at the summit of human political development."[13]

Furthermore, the underlying assumption of methodological individualism in rational choice theory (that all social phenomena are comprehensible as an outcome of actions of individuals) denies the mediating political role of an institution such as the family in Egypt and simplifies the complexity of political and social forces.[14] Egyptian society is not "a collection of undifferentiated and unrelated individuals" but a society where individuals go to great efforts to enhance their relations to others, at times even creating fictive kin in their efforts.[15] Individual interests are always balanced against the larger consideration of familial interests, and often they are subordinated to the interests of the family. At the same time, families and individuals do not exist in an isolated context: they are influenced by other structures of power, ideals, and culture, which cannot always be neatly linked to individual preferences and behavior.

In trying to understand collective action and the role of institutions in politics, Robert Bates has argued that rational choice theorists have overlooked the ways in which the elite in developing countries have designed and structured political institutions to serve their needs. My characterization of the politics of the *sha'b* in the following chapters must be seen within the context of the structures of power in Egypt, which are largely devoted to maintaining the power of those who rule. In the language of rational choice theory, I argue that the *sha'b* understand the high costs of participating in formal politics and thus develop other institutions to serve their needs. While I have not concentrated on detailed explanations of the ways in which elites manipulate political and economic institutions in Egypt (because so many scholars have already demonstrated this), I will suggest that the less visible, informal institutions that foster types of collective action which serve popular interests are of equal importance to already organized and visible collective institutions.[16]

The second deficiency of Weiner's conception of participation is that it conveniently ignores the fact that elites devote considerable public resources to construct constrained arenas for formal politics and use their legal systems, institutions, and security forces to enforce their limited vision of politics, thus excluding many subordinated constituencies from political life. Elites structure politics so that most people cannot participate in the system or their participation is not much more than a charade. Furthermore, elites attempt to convince citizens that their dominant position is not only necessary but "natural." Timothy Mitchell argues that

> producing and maintaining the distinction between state and society is itself a mechanism that generates resources of power. The boundary of the state (or political system) *never marks a real exterior*. The line between state and society is not the perimeter of an intrinsic entity, which can be thought of as a free-standing object or actor. It is a line drawn internally, *within* the network of institutional mechanisms through which a certain social and political order is maintained.[17]

The Egyptian elites' drawing of a particular state-society construct has excluded an entire institutional dimension of Egyptian politics, which nevertheless influences the nature and structure of Egypt's social and political order. My use of the term "informal politics" not only suggests a specific type of extrasystemic activity but it alerts us to the authoritarian and repressive conditions under which a broad range of people live as they nevertheless pursue their own interests and cooperate and struggle with others to build a better political order and a different version of "the good." Unfortunately, we are far more able to trace the particular lines of a state-society construct drawn by the elite rather than one drawn by the *sha'b*. While the efforts that elites invest in the system to naturalize power are enormous and costly, the best strategies and intentions of the elite can occasionally be unraveled or weakened by alternative visions from below. The challenge of tracing the constructions and visions of subordinate groups is complicated by their absence from the public or official transcript.[18] While historians are continually confronted with the lopsided nature of the written historical record, political scientists interested in contemporary politics have a better chance to understand the alternative preferences and visions of the popular sector because here the architects of challenges to the dominant order are, simply stated, still alive. This study is an effort toward rendering visible the political community and institutions of the *sha'b*.

In the politics of everyday life among the popular sector in Egypt, men and women are deeply involved in forging collective institutions that serve common public and private needs. Through their informal political institutions, women and men both create public space and invade what is conventionally considered the public arena as they connect individuals and communities to state bureaucracies, public institutions, and formal political institutions. As Chapter 3 details, they organize informal networks that weave in and out of the bureaucracy, the offices of politicians, religious institutions, private charitable and voluntary associations, workplaces, households, markets, schools, health clinics, the extended family, and the neighborhood in order to fulfill individual and collective needs. These networks are pervasive, flexible, and efficient. The range of classes, occupations, age cohorts, and kinship groups represented in specific networks is wide, since incorporating people with different characteristics, high and low status, and a variety of resources and contacts into the network increases their effectiveness. While these institutions may not look the same to us as formal political institutions, they are bound by what I have called "the familial ethos," or rules and norms that are supported by the popular sector. They are intentionally designed to serve collective needs, and they penetrate the public sphere. The first chapter will discuss the links between the familial ethos and political participation. Because informal networks link the household and extended family to bureaucratic offices, politicians, the marketplace, and public services and institutions, I argue that the household is incorporated into the public realm. Thus, there is a much grayer area between private society and public politics in Egypt, particularly within *sha'bi* communities, which depend upon networks more than other segments of the population.

Informal networks not only have an institutional dimension but are seen as legitimate in the eyes of their constituents. In many developing nations, "communal sanction is as definitive for informal associations as legal recognition is for formal ones."[19] In some of these nations, communal sanction is even more legitimate than legal recognition since the latter may taint an organization bearing the imprimatur of an unpopular and weak state. Again, the role of informal institutions must be seen within the context of authoritarian politics in Egypt where the boundaries between individuals, groups, and state authority are still highly contested, and many citizens may not see formal and governmental institutions as legitimate.

The "success" of informal institutions to gain power or their ultimate ability to displace the elite is not the focus of this research. My arguments are not about resistance to the state or the possibilities for revolution in Egypt but about noticing and analyzing the institutional mechanisms that excluded groups create to further their claims and interests.[20] My intentions are interpretative rather than predictive. I am trying to move away from a state-centric model of politics, and emphasizing resistance rather than participation does not allow one to escape from this state-centric paradigm since the assumed target of resistance remains the state and its elite. While I maintain that the context of formal politics in Egypt is crucial to understanding informal political institutions, this study is very much an examination of politics from the perspective of the popular sector. I did not proceed by asking men and women in densely populated neighborhoods about their views of elite politicians, the state, or their membership in political organizations. Rather, I focused on the political institutions these people utilized and created to pursue their various interests.

It is appropriate here to discuss in more detail the meaning of the *sha͑b* or what I interchangeably call the popular sector throughout this work. While the noun, the *sha͑b*, refers to a collective people, populace, or folk and has an implicit collective connotation to it, as an adjective *sha͑bi* demarcates a wide range of indigenous practices, tastes, and patterns of behavior in everyday life. The indigenous nature of things *sha͑bi* is key to an understanding of its meaning among Egyptians. Wealthier, more Westernized Egyptians use the term to distinguish themselves and their way of life from the more popular mainstream because, for one reason or another, they have departed from a lifestyle that they themselves would identify as more Egyptian. A similar but distinct adjective, *baladi*, is associated somewhat more with one's place of origin and lifestyles, or with practices that are associated with it. Egyptians use *al-balad*, the noun, to mean country and nation, but the same word also means village or town. An *Ibn al-balad* is a son of the soil, a true, trusted, and sincere Egyptian salt of the earth with the best of positive connotations (the feminine equivalent is *bint al-balad*).[21] At the same time, *baladi* has more of a provincial connotation to it since the term is also associated with the countryside and its peasantry, even if, perhaps generations ago, rural families moved into urban areas in Egypt, maintaining the same values and traditions.

Though both of these terms generally describe behavior that is more common to lower-income communities in Egypt, it is not fitting to describe the *sha͑b* as lower class since there is class heterogeneity within *sha͑bi* neighborhoods. It is not uncommon for a destitute widowed woman to live next to a wealthy merchant family with international business partners and connections. Skilled workers, owners of artisanal workshops and factories, lower-level professionals and civil servants, and merchants and traders all live and work side by side. However, there is a relative sense that these men and women are disadvantaged in comparison to middle- and upper-class Egyptians. They generally lie between the poor and the middle class, and most of them struggle continually with economic scarcity as they seek upward mobility and fear returning to the ranks of the poor. While millionaires and wealthy people live in these neighborhoods because they may prefer the lifestyle or the proximity to their workplaces, kin, and neighbors, they are not numerous. What is more common, particularly in the decade of the 1980s, is to find families that have prospered enough to rise to the ranks of the solid middle class yet do not want to leave their communities behind.

More than a class dimension, a certain political aura surrounds the construct of the popular sector in Egypt due to the historical legacy of political exclusion, fueled by foreign rule and colonialism. From the conquest of Egypt by Alexander the Great in 332 B.C. to the Free Officers' Revolution in 1952, Roman, Greek, Persian, Byzantine, Arab, Ottoman, Mamluk, and British rule denied Egyptians self-government.[22] While the struggle against British colonialism in the nineteenth and early twentieth centuries was primarily nationalist (fueled by the slogan "Egypt for the Egyptians"), Egyptian nationalists also mobilized around the disadvantaged position of the majority of Egyptians in relation to the foreign occupiers and those segments of the elite that prospered under them. Voices were raised about the skewed income distribution in Egypt, the plight of landless and poor peasants, and the lack of basic services and social welfare for the urban and rural poor. Finally, after the 1952 revolution the "people" ruled under the leadership of General Naguib and, later, Col. Gamal Abdel Nasser. Government would protect and promote popular interests, and the colonial and feudal past would be swept away by the new regime. To some extent, Nasser was successful at changing Egypt's social, political, and economic order while enhancing the international role of a newly independent nation. As Joel Gordon argues, "By uprooting the old landed class and the foreign community, affecting a modest redistribution of their property, and extending educational opportunity to all Egyptians, Nasserism destroyed the rigid class system that separated pasha from peasant, hastened a transition to industrialism, and gave Egypt sovereignty over its resources."[23]

While the early Nasser government instituted redistributive policies such as land reform, rent control, public education, subsidies of basic goods, and so forth, the real and perceived threats from opposition voices (the ancien régime as well as the Muslim Brotherhood and leftist parties) pushed the government to deny freedoms of association and expression to its citizens. The regime was plagued by the tensions between promoting development and Arab nationalism, on the one hand, and continuing the revolution. However, mass political participation and inclusion in the political process was soon sacrificed to the competing desire for regime maintenance. As Gordon says, "Few Egyptians today contend that Nasser ruled with anything but dictatorial powers."[24] The record of "politics without participation" during the Nasser era has been extensively documented by many foreign and Egyptian scholars, and it will not be reiterated in any detail here.[25] Nasser created a succession of three mass political parties to "refine a system that maintained rigid control of the polity behind a facade of popular participation."[26] While he offered Egyptians far more influence in the government and the state than the Egyptian monarchy and the British colonial forces had, Nasser and his more recent successors (President Anwar Sadat and

Husni Mubarak) have relied upon organized labor, elections, professional groups, political parties, and the bureaucracy more as instruments of control and co-optation than of participation. Under the regime's notion of politics, a process where one candidate runs for office is called an election and institutions originally created by the regime are called political parties.[27] Public affairs are those issues that the government allows to be discussed in the media without threat of government censorship. Usually, the autonomous behavior of legal organizations is immediately seen as a threat to the regime, and opposition from unlicensed organizations is rarely tolerated. Either Egyptians play by the rules of the government's game or they are labeled terrorists. The middle ground of "loyal opposition" is, unfortunately, very narrow. Since most opposition parties are in fact creations of the state, the legal opposition is oddly and uncomfortably dependent on the government and restricted from developing truly autonomous financial and organizational support by a complex variety of mechanisms. It is not that Egyptians accept the government's self-serving and expedient notion of politics. Rather, many committed and courageous men and women pursue their political agendas through fettered political parties, state-licensed unions, clandestine organizations, and underground movements. Other men and women still manage to forge collective informal institutions that serve their interests in a less visible and far less risky way.

This pattern of elite domination and extrasystemic challenges from below is not limited to Egypt or the Middle East. The *sha'b* in Egypt are similar to the *pueblo* or *lo popular* in Latin America who share collective identities that stand above class cleavages. These collective identities, under specific political circumstances, can be the basis for significant political mobilization and the emergence of social movements as common people demand to be treated as citizens. The history of the popular sector has received far more attention in Latin America than in the Middle East due to its role in populist projects in the pre–World War II era, trade union movements, guerrilla and revolutionary movements, and much more recently, in urban social movements, liberation theology, and redemocratization campaigns, which brought civilians back to power throughout Latin America in the late 1980s. The popular sector seeks additional power and its fair share of public resources since it is still economically oppressed or disadvantaged, unlike the middle and upper classes who have prospered through dependent development and the growth of the state. Daniel Levine suggests the meaning of "popular" in Latin America "rests not on popularity (something favored by many), but rather on a sense of what constitutes the populous—the central defining characteristic of the population. At a minimum, 'popular' thus involves some notion of subordination and inequality, pointing to 'popular' groups or classes."[28] In Latin America "popular" is usually associated with the poor and their ideas, beliefs, and practices as well as the "kinds of ties that bind them to institutions of power, privilege, and meaning."[29]

All of these sectors are disadvantaged in comparison to a minority composed of the middle and upper classes. *The notion 'popular' thus becomes associated with democracy in the sense that popular interests represent the interests of the vast majority in developing societies.* The sense of being disadvantaged, or that other groups in society are in some way 'privileged,' forms a basis for distinctive popular cultures and common experiences.[30]

As reservoirs of national identity and the Egyptian character, then, the *sha'b* have a sense of their authenticity and believe that they embody the values and beliefs of the nation. From their bonds of national identity and an underlying commonality of interests, political communities can emerge. They are not the only ones who share this view of their authenticity and their role in maintaining a national identity. Because they are a majority and a relatively disadvantaged one, they can claim certain goods and services from the state whose initial legitimacy rested on its commitment to "the people."[31]

The ability of those in the popular sector to make claims on the state and to organize and fulfill their private and public interests is facilitated by a wide range of institutional structures. Despite the intentional and systematic efforts of elites to exclude men and women from formal political participation in Egypt, the *sha'b* have created and carefully maintained an institutional structure that strengthens their collective life. Though dissimilar from Western institutions and largely invisible to those in power, informal political institutions pervade Egyptian society. Just as governments throughout the Middle East have established institutions to serve elite interests and maintain their power, the *sha'b* have their own institutional framework, which serves their interests. The *sha'b* have found the controlled, co-opted institutions of the state to be of limited utility. They are consumers of the benefits of state services and public goods, but they can do little legally and directly to influence the nature of the elite or the course and direction of government policy. Like any political constituency they have reacted to the realities of their situation by altering the nature of collective life. Like the rise of new social movements in Europe in the 1960s, "Changing the boundaries of the political . . . entail[ed] changing the nature of associational life in general."[32] With a different, informal, less visible associational life, the popular sector in Egypt will continue to change the boundaries of Egyptian politics.

The institutional structure of the *sha'b* is composed of informal networks, institutions, and associations by which people engage in collective life. These institutions are designed to promote economic well-being, to reproduce the family, to secure basic needs such as food, employment, and education, to arbitrate conflict, and to encourage the political, social, and cultural norms of the community. It is difficult to notice the institutional life of this community without first understanding the community's basic needs and material struggles. The following chapters elaborate both upon these goals and the institutions the *sha'b* have devised to realize them. For example, Chapter 2 examines the objective of reproducing the family. While this goal might not seem to be political in nature, to the *sha'b* and to most Egyptians, both urban and rural, the struggle to marry off the younger generation is the largest economic struggle they face in their lifetimes. While marriage does not compete with screaming headlines on new economic projects, Palestinian autonomy, regional political alliances, or "high politics," it is one of the most important issues around which "low politics" is centered. My unexpected focus on the struggle to reproduce the family came about after living with people in this community for several months and finally coming to some appreciation of the struggles they faced. The objective of reproducing the family receives such extensive attention in several chapters because it was, to some extent, the key to understanding many other issues and the ways in which people reacted to domestic and international policy changes. Ignoring the material, social, and cultural struggle to reproduce the family makes it very difficult to understand why gender and sexual relations are so sensitive in Egypt, why housing costs are so high and yet so many apartments lay vacant, why migration is so critical to younger Egyptians, and why people riot over increases in the cost of bread and other commodities. A bread riot is not only a protest over prices or a government but a threat to the goal of reproducing the family. Raising the price of bread directly affects the ability of young people and their families to save money, and savings are directed, almost entirely among certain age cohorts, toward the goal of marriage. Marriage is a deeply held normative preference in Egypt (as self-expression or individual rights might be in other societies), and it allows young people to engage in affective and sexual relations after a closely supervised adolescence. Through marriage, one generation transfers its assets to another, and a couple gains some autonomy by creating a new household. In Joseph Gusfield's terminology, marriage is a "deep structure" that influences and is influenced by many different facets of Egyptian life.[33]

If marriage and reproducing the family is such a critical issue in Egypt, we should expect constellations of power to form around it. It is not therefore surprising that Personal Status Law, which regulates marriage, divorce, child custody, and inheritance, has been one of the most deeply contested and sensitive issues for a wide range of political forces in Egypt, at different historical moments. Nor is it surprising that Islamic theologians, jurists, and activists have historically seen gender relations as a critical political issue and the cause of justifiable concern for society and the polity. Reproducing the family is a public issue in Egypt, and it has a deep material and ideological connection to everyday life. Because it is such a shared concern for the *sha'b*, they have devised institutions such as informal networks and informal savings associations (described in Chapters 2 and 3) to help realize their needs.

Here, however, I want to pause to introduce an important caveat to my argument. By using the term the *sha'b* I run the risk of creating a homogeneous version of "the people"—which is far too simplistic and not at all reflective of the differences among such an aggregate group. My intention is not merely to describe the lifestyle or values of the *sha'b* but to portray the ways in which men and women in *sha'bi* communities forge collective institutions and shared understandings that become poles around which interests are articulated and negotiated and conflicts resolved. I do not attempt to characterize the nature of Egyptian "authenticity" or wish to present a monolithic and indefensible portrayal of common values and behavior among the *sha'b* but rather to expose the organizational grid and institutional structure of this community, which represents a large constituency within Egyptian politics.

My understanding of the popular sector is based on detailed fieldwork in a small community in central Cairo. By that, I refer to four contiguous districts whose histories and growth date back to the medieval period when the victorious Fatimid rulers of Egypt built a new walled, exclusively royal city in A.D. 969 and named it al-Qahira (which still remains the Arabic name for Cairo). These districts include al-Darb al-Ahmar, al-Gamaliyya, Bab al-Sha'riyya, and al-Musky. Within the details of everyday life, however, one can recognize issues and debates which concern the wider constituency of the popular sector in urban Egypt, even if these differ from the typical concerns of elite politics. An understanding of the roots of these debates and the fault lines within *sha'bi* communities leads one to understand the nature of their political participation and the advantages and disadvantages of the political institutions they create to further their interests.

Too often in research and analyses about Egypt and the Middle East there are many assumptions about prevailing values and ideals but far less understanding of the ways in which ideals are so deeply contested locally. In the following chapters I present many accounts of disputes within households, the family, and the community. Many of these arguments (which sometimes escalated into physical fights) centered around crucial material, social, and ethical issues. Men, women, and children sought to protect their rights and their interests within the context and confines of the household, the extended family, the community, and the state. Blanket characterizations of the Egyptian family as patriarchal and authoritarian are challenged by the level of contestation, negotiation, and bargaining that is endemic to these communities. As Chapters 1 and 2 will explore, intrahousehold politics are far more competitive and confrontational than is generally represented.[34] While many of the accepted norms and roles for kin, gender, and age cohorts within the family and community have been socially constructed over the years, as constructions they are constantly evolving and there are still wide variations from the "ideal." I recount these disputes because they reveal so much of the debates within this community, and it is the contestation over ideals, rights, and resource allocation that serves as the basis for change in any society. Though some may wonder whether I have drawn an overly contentious picture of the *sha'b*, debates serve to both shape and reinforce public norms and private behavior in the community, and they are not repressed. Public discourse not only serves to educate younger members of the community on proper behavior but it diffuses problems and tensions, and it is an important component of participation in the affairs of the community. Secrecy within the family and community is seen as being far more dangerous. While the family that I lived with was somewhat renowned for its propensity to argue (and for some of those fights to become violent), much of the decibel level and the violence was theatrical and indicated the seriousness of an issue. As any resident of Cairo would know, fights between people after traffic accidents or an exchange of insults may become fairly heated and boisterous. A crowd usually gathers out of curiosity as well as to control tempers and figure out an honorable and fair solution to the problem, yet these disputes rarely become violent.[35] Though disputes were common among the *sha'b*, so was the ability to resolve them and diffuse tensions. These arbitrative and judicial mechanisms are deeply embedded within the community and are an important component of its institutional life. Recounting these conflicts will not, I hope, overshadow the warmth and cooperation among families but rather should highlight the tradition of negotiation, arbitration, and conflict resolution within *sha'bi* communities.

THE CONTEXT AND APPROACH OF THE STUDY

In order to understand the nature of the struggles within this community and its fault lines, I adopted a methodology of participant/observation and lived with a family in a densely populated neighborhood in central Cairo that dates back to the medieval period. Without this foundation in the everyday life of the community, it would have been impossible to recognize and understand their political activity. Methodologically, one has to invest time in understanding individual problems before one can identify shared concerns and community dilemmas. Publicly and privately recounted stories, experiences, struggles, fights, and debates gradually sensitize an observer to the politics of the community.

I began with the perspective that scarcity, values, and priorities vary from one community to another as do preferences for the role and structure of "good government." Having lived in Egypt previously, I did not assume that Western political experience is replicated elsewhere or that familiar institutions in Egypt worked in ways that they would in Western democracies with vastly different economic, political, historical, and cultural traditions. Many of the issues and the institutions that constitute political life in the United States work themselves out very differently in Egypt. Too often it seems our a priori and ethnocentric assumptions about politics distort our research and our conclusions unless we learn the basic characteristics and fault lines of a specific constituency. Through an inductive approach and deep empiricism I hope to encourage broader notions of politics that travel better and lead us out of ethnocentric and elite-laden assumptions about politics and political participation.

People from these communities are not part of the intellectual elite of the nation; they are rarely the subject of historical or contemporary analyses and even more rarely are they the authors of the few primary or secondary sources on these communities. While historians and other scholars have had to creatively use legal and state archives to reconstruct the lives of peasants and the urban popular classes in Egypt from earlier periods, I was fortunate to be able to interact with people whose hospitality runs very deep and who revere storytelling and the memory of their past.[36] Repeatedly I was impressed by the acute memories of men and women who could recall family histories and economic details with great precision. They interpreted marriages, political changes, and family crises within the context of their particular community, their network of kin, colleagues, neighbors, bureaucrats, and so on. One factor related to another, which related to yet another factor, and the complicated stories and relationships between people were explained in detail because personal interactions mattered so much within the community. Connections between people provided resources, assistance, information, and even marriage partners.

Rather than examining what Geertz has called divergent data, which "one gets from polls, surveys, or censuses, which yield facts about classes of individuals not otherwise related,"[37] and using a family, neighborhood, workplace, or institution to define my research, the networks of several early key informants grew to form the outline of the *sha'bi* community I studied. This approach and the data that result from it, referred to by some as "snowball sampling," has both advantages and limitations. It is largely composed of

> descriptions, measures, observations, what you will, which are at once diverse, even rather miscellaneous, both as to type and degree of precision and generality, unstandardized facts, opportunistically collected and variously portrayed, which yet turn out to shed light on one another for the simple reason that the individuals they are descriptions, measures, or observations of are directly involved in one another's lives: people, who in a marvelous phrase of Alfred Schutz's "grow old together."[38]

My entry into the community might be described as dating from 1985 when, after several months of trying to find a family to live with, I finally succeeded in moving into the area I had targeted as an appropriate research site. My fieldwork, however, built upon three previous years of residence in Egypt, including two years as a graduate student at the American University in Cairo (AUC) between 1980–1982 and a year as a student in the Center for Arabic Study Abroad (CASA) program, also at AUC. Or, perhaps, I could argue that my departure point began when I naively followed the advice of a professor who insisted that an undergraduate interested in studying Africa needed to learn Arabic in order to understand the history of Islamic Africa.

Like a trusting disciple I began studying Arabic though I was unclear where this interest would lead. Shortly after graduation, upon the advice of another professor who warned against launching a career on the Middle East without first spending time there, I applied for and was granted a fellowship for graduate school at AUC. Those two years in Egypt were crucial since they gave me time to study Egypt and its history, and learn how to survive and, at times, even prosper. During this period my academic and social world expanded gradually beyond AUC students and professors, the resident academic and professional expatriate community.

When I returned to Egypt for the third year of residence to study at CASA, my contacts and friends outside of AUC increased. A friend would meet a family in a *sha'bi* neighborhood and I would accompany her to a Friday meal and then return again and again, thanks to the generous and widespread hospitality of Egyptians. When a professor took our class to a conference on women in Egypt, I befriended a young woman from Sayyida Zaynab, a slightly more middle-class neighborhood, and visited her frequently. I began to be able to speak with and interact with Egyptians who knew little or no English. During this year I developed a better feel for the geography and social dynamics of the city and focused upon a few neighborhoods where I thought I could find a family to live with and yet be close enough to some of the academic institutions and libraries that I frequented in Cairo. When I met people who knew, lived in, or worked in these neighborhoods, I would talk with them about everyday life in these communities and try to maintain contact with them.

To begin my research, I explained to friends and colleagues that I wanted to study Egyptian families and *sha'bi* neighborhoods for a doctoral dissertation and asked their help in finding an appropriate site for my research. One local merchant from central Cairo whom I had known for a year had a wealthier business associate in an area that I had thought might provide an excellent research site. This wealthier grocer shared an apartment building with his relatives which was located just across the street from his large grocery store. He suggested that they could empty one of the apartments they used as an office and I could live there, underneath his own apartment. It soon became clear that living in an apartment under the protection of this male merchant (who had a reputation as a local Casanova) would not be a good idea since people would assume that I was one of his new girlfriends and this would damage my reputation in, and accessibility to, the community. Finally, through the critical efforts of another intermediary, I was introduced to a woman who lived and worked in the area I hoped to live in and who was willing to rent her parlor room to me. When she found out my other option she insisted that I drop those plans and move in with her, later explaining that she had been trying to protect me from the wealthy merchant because he was not to be trusted. She had a relatively large four-room apartment on the top floor of an old building primarily inhabited by her extended family. As a widow with three unmarried children still at home (really two since one of her sons was a bus driver with long hours who was rarely at home), there was room for me in the salon or formal guest room common to most Egyptian apartments. (And because she kept important papers and items of value in this room, it was always locked and off limits to the family anyway.) When the families of her four married daughters would visit nearly every week, the apartment could hold an impressive number of relatives.

I refer to this widow anonymously and do not cite the specific neighborhood of my research out of respect for the privacy of the people who were kind enough to share their experiences candidly with me and open up their homes and workplaces. Some of the stories I recount here are very personal matters, while others involve delicate negotiations between community members and officials or politicians. Other stories recount illegal activities or, at least, irregular activities. At an early point in my research I decided not to name particular persons or to identify my research site out of concern that somehow this book might jeopardize or embarrass the very people who welcomed me into their homes, looked after me, and tolerated my constant stream of questions.

While I understand that this anonymity may decrease the comparative utility of my conclusions, I did not conceptualize or execute a geographically focused study. Although I obviously needed to situate myself in a particular neighborhood, I did not investigate any one neighborhood systematically and get to know all its resident or workers; as I mentioned earlier, I allowed the associations of several early informants to shape and limit my study. However, I consciously strove to broaden the geographical reach of my study to see, in fact, if geography made a difference. This turned out to be an easy task since networks and family contacts among the *sha'b* today extend far beyond where they live or work.

The Greater Cairo Metropolitan area—composed of all of Cairo Governorate on the east bank of the Nile (including the inhabited islands); most of Giza Governorate, which is on the west bank of the Nile; and some of Qalyubia Governorate, which lies to the north, toward the beginning of the Nile delta—has grown dramatically through natural internal growth, migration from the countryside and the residential settlement of former agricultural and desert areas, and marginal public land on the outskirts of Cairo. In 1960 the population of Metropolitan Cairo equaled 4,530,000; by 1976 its population reached 7,471,000, and by 1986 urban sprawl had reached 9,754,000. Interestingly, while its population grew significantly, Metropolitan Cairo's share of the total Egyptian population rose only modestly: in 1960 it comprised 17.5 percent of Egypt's population; in 1976, 20.4 percent; and in 1986 the percentage actually decreased to 20.2 percent.[39] However, the central districts of Cairo cannot expand very easily since they have been largely hemmed in by other densely populated areas.[40] Thus, when younger couples need to buy apartments or land in order to marry, they can rarely find affordable housing in the areas where their families have lived and so join their age cohorts, migrants from outside Cairo, and some upwardly mobile families in newly settled areas which now ring Cairo and are fast becoming major urban areas in their own right. As more men and women find employment outside their immediate neighborhoods as well, people's networks extend beyond their residential area.

The recent geographic expansion of networks mandated by changing residential patterns and demographic pressures has altered the distinctive features and cohesiveness of urban quarters in Cairo. Previous studies of central Cairo have noted that the boundaries of quarters were far more spatially defined as late as the 1960s.[41] Nadim suggested that the *harah* [alley] culture of densely populated, older neighborhoods of Cairo, "generate[s] a type of social behavior which demarcates the *harah* people as distinct."[42] To understand the particular nature of urban quarters, one has to return to the city's historical and administrative development, and therefore I rely here upon Janet Abu-Lughod's explanation of the development of urban quarters from the earliest days of the Fatimid dynasty in the tenth century:

> The original plan of the Fatimid suburb was regular and rectangular in the extreme. In addition to the extensive palaces, gardens, cemetery, mosque and market squares, all of which were concentrated within the centermost core of the walled enclosure, there were ten to fifteen *Haraat* (pl.) or quarters in which members of the ethnically organized military units of Muʿizz [the fourth Caliph or leader of the Fatimid dynasty] were installed. Physically, a *Hara* (sing.) is a subsection of a city. Having only limited access, usually through a street terminating in an open square, it is equipped with walls and gates which can be closed at night and, in addition, barricaded completely during times of crisis. Socially, the *Hara* is a group of persons usually unified by ethnic and/or occupational characteristics as well as by vicinal ties, and segregated physically and socially from other subgroups of the city. Politically it is often a unit of administration and control. As the commercial life of al-Qaahira [Cairo] diversified, and as occupational groupings came to dominate more and more of the essential loyalties and identification of the nonmilitary classes, the original *Haraat* and those established both north and south of the first walls were adapted to the requirements of craftsmanship and trade. Whereas the nomenclature of the earlier *Haraat* showed a preoccupation with ethnic and tribal affiliations, the names of later *Haraat* sometimes revealed the dominant occupational or commercial functions of the areas.[43]

The guild system, where each trade and profession maintained a corporate structure headed by a *shaykh* and supervised by the *muhtasib* (who was the agent of the municipality authorized to supervise the guilds and the morality of the marketplace), only served to enhance the distinctive, homogeneous character of certain quarters.[44] The devolution but not eradication of the social, occupational, and religious system of spatial segregation in Cairo is a subject that unfortunately cannot be addressed in any detail here, yet I would argue that due to largely socioeconomic, demographic, and political consequences of the Open Door Economic Policy (ʾil-ʾinfitaaH) instituted by President Sadat in 1974 and the Camp David Accords signed in 1978, urban Cairo is becoming far more heterogeneous and far less geographically defined.

More recently, as people are forced out of older neighborhoods, they take the *harah* culture (as Nadim labeled it earlier) with them. The ideas, norms, institutions, and preferences of their former communities infuse these newly settled areas, although the physical setting and social organization of the community may differ markedly. A *harah* culture that is now defined more by socioeconomic conditions and cultural preferences is less geographically distinct but increasingly pervasive throughout Cairo and other urban areas of Egypt. During the course of my research I made visits to homes or workplaces in twenty-three different neighborhoods, and many of my contacts were concentrated in ten largely contiguous neighborhoods. Informal networks and political institutions among the *sha'b* did not vary by residential affiliation within areas that shared a similar socioeconomic profile. If I had included a more middle-class, slightly suburban area in the study (such as Dokki or Muhandisiin), I would have expected greater internal variation. The same concerns, the same methods of fulfilling needs, and the same structural constraints of daily life in Cairo were shared by residents of various lower-income, densely populated neighborhoods. It is only the character and membership of networks which change as neighbors or colleagues rather than relatives become the central force of networks in newer residential areas.

Janet Abu-Lughod's classic and comprehensive study of Cairo labels the area that I call central Cairo "Medieval Cairo Unreconstituted."[45] Since many of the people in my community either lived or worked in this general area, in the following few pages I attempt to give the reader who is unfamiliar with Cairo a few visual images to frame the successive chapters. This begins by first noting that the richness of central Cairo is in its complexity, vibrancy, and historical heritage. Originally designed to fulfill the royal needs of the new Fatimid dynasty, this area is now populated by a distinctly nonroyal mass, except for the esteemed presence of al-Azhar University (the Islamic university founded in 970 A.D.), its faculty and theologians. What is most compelling is the synergy of buildings, commerce, monuments, dress, industry, education, entertainment, and modes of transport whose origins range across centuries. Within the former walls of the royal city and just outside them are majestic mosques, schools, minarets, and markets dating back to the tenth century. With the help of my more historically oriented colleagues, I can almost date the historical growth of the city simply by looking across its skyline: the very thin, pointed, unadorned minarets of the Ottoman period; the minarets of the Mamluk period, with several well-defined sections; and the simpler, squatter, less sculpted shape of Fatimid and Ayyubid minarets. There are hundreds of mosques in this area, ranging from the cavernous mosque of Husayn, which serves as the government's official mosque and attracts dignitaries and common people at all hours and reli-

1. Workers transport fabric through a market just next to the covered "Street of the Tentmakers" in Darb al-Ahmar, whose distinctive architecture dates back to the medieval period.

gious holidays, to tiny mosques that local businessmen or residents have established, sandwiched between workshops and stores. These mosques contain little more than a place to perform ablutions before praying and plastic mats for prayer. When the congregation increases on Friday, more mats are spread out onto sidewalks and roads, as a sheikh or imam reads the weekly sermon.

In certain parts of al-Musky in central Cairo, the most recent fashion trend for women, *zayy al-Islami*, or Islamic dress, fills large, expensive boutiques where women can purchase modestly subdued ensembles of long-sleeved shirts, long skirts, and head coverings, similar outfits in brighter, more fashionable styles, or quite elaborate and almost glitzy Islamic formal wear (with gilded and sequined matching head coverings as well) appropriate for weddings at the fanciest five-star hotels. Other women purchase yards of black, often shiny, translucent fabric to use as *milaaya laff*, the cloak that women wrap loosely around their clothes and head when they venture outside. Many women and men still choose fabric from the hundreds of stores that specialize in the trade and order all their clothes custom-made by tailors. Al-Gamaliyya and al-Musky, and parts of al-Darb al-Ahmar, have always been the heart of Egypt's garment district, selling textiles both wholesale and retail. Despite the profusion of imported and domestic ready-to-wear garments in Egypt since the Open Door policy, jeans, Korean shirts, and Brazilian shoes fill the boutiques next to seamstress' shops.

In Khan al-Khaliili, the shops that are geared to foreign tourists sell very stylish Egyptian handmade leather shoes for $45 and fine briefcases for hundreds of dollars. In Bab al-Shaʿriyya, long the center of the shoemaking trade (a very important industry in Egypt), young apprentices and skilled artisans produce shoes for the equivalent of $3 to $4. The streets are filled with young men with dozens of shoe boxes slung across their backs, delivering daily production to the numerous shoe stores in the area and the major retail shoe district in downtown Cairo around Midan Taʿlat Harb and Qasr al-Niil street. (Cairo's streets not only destroy new shoes more quickly, but shoe shopping is one of the major affordable entertainments for fashion-conscious Egyptians. In contrast, clothes, either handmade or ready-made, are far more expensive.) Pickup trucks, motorcycles, taxis, private cars, donkey- and horse-drawn carts, bicycles, and large trucks careen around these neighborhoods through very narrow alleyways and clog the few very congested thoroughfares that penetrate the heart of Cairo. When walking in these areas, one always has to have a sixth sense to stay out of the way of traffic and throngs of people. (Actually only one major road, Shaariʿa al-Azhar, bisects the area from east to west. The other major artery, Shaariʿa Muaz al-Diin Allah, is a narrow road running north-south between Bab al-Zuwalah and Bab al-Nasr. Shaariʿa Port Saʿid, the western border of the medieval city, bisects al-Musky and Bab al-Shaʿriyya and runs north-south.)

The commercial and industrial diversity of the area is equally fascinating as exclusive jewelry stores in the tourist area border jewelry stores that cater to the *shaʿb*, who buy and sell gold not as much for its decorative or status value but because gold is a form of savings which can be easily sold during financial crises (see Chapter 2). Women purchase henna to enrich and color their hair from the spice market where commodities are sold in bulk and buy imported cosmetics from abroad at neighboring boutiques and pharmacies. For a few Egyptian pounds in Bab al-Shaʿriyya, traditionally a stronghold of the metals trade, women can purchase cheap aluminum *tabliyyas*, round tables with short, squat legs, which families gather around to eat. In other areas of the same district, furniture shops sell sets of elaborately gilded formal salon furniture (labeled Louis Faruq, for its French and royalist influ-

2. Small shops, many of them selling fabric and clothes, dominate one of the main yet very narrow thoroughfares running through central Cairo. On either side of this road lay densely populated residential areas and industrial workshops that manufacture goods for local shops. The dynamism and vibrancy of central Cairo means that pedestrians must always be on the lookout for trucks, cars, horses, and motorcycles.

ences) for thousands of pounds. On other streets itinerant men offer their services to households to clean and restuff pillows, mattresses, and furniture with good Egyptian cotton. One of the consequences of economic liberalization in the past decade has been a profusion of locally produced and imported goods on the market, feeding a tremendous consumption urge, which the government and economic analysts, depending on their perspectives, both condemn and promote. Suffice it to say here that these densely populated neighborhoods in central Cairo are at the center of this consumption and production boom, where the least expensive as well as some of the most expensive items are available for purchase (though the most exclusive shops are concentrated in wealthier neighborhoods, new skyscrapers, or luxury hotels). Consumption is not only the right of the wealthy anymore, and the allure of expensive or imported items is as apparent in Gamaliyya as it is in Zamalek (a much wealthier area where many foreigners also live). What differs in central Cairo is that far fewer residents can afford the items on display.

One of the more distinctive characteristics of Cairo's neighborhoods and economies is the mixed use of space. Commercial areas, residences, and even industrial plants coexist—at times, with difficulty. The workshops that

3. This man and his young apprentice are beating and fluffing cotton from an old lumpy mattress. A *minaggid* (upholsterer) will also sew and fill new mattresses and pillows for a couple's trousseau or a family's couches. They circulate through neighborhoods and, with their distinctive melody from the street, advertise their services to local women. Mattresses then become a renewable resource. While not a particularly lucrative profession, these self-employed men earn a steady income. (*Photo by John Waterbury*)

4. In central Cairo, small shops sell both local and imported spices and herbs for an array of cosmetic, medicinal, spiritual, celebratory, and nutritional needs. Here homeopathic pharmacists service the local population and others who come from around Cairo for their knowledge, advice, and wares. Though not as numerous as before, the spice market is concentrated in central Cairo and sells commodities in bulk which are no longer readily available elsewhere.
(*Photo by John Waterbury*)

make cheap aluminum products, produced in Gamaliyya and Bab al-Shaʿriyya, and sold largely in the latter district, emit a constant din from men hammering out designs on tables and trays. While there are some newer buildings and small alleyways solely devoted to industry or artisanal workshops, most economic activity—from professional occupations and service establishments to print shops, lemon wholesalers, chicken-griller manufacturers, machine shops, and shoe factories—fill the ground level or first floors of residential buildings. Many of the smaller establishments, and some of the larger ones, are family enterprises and rely on nearby labor and supervision from family members. Government employees and others can return from their primary jobs in the early afternoon, eat a meal, and start their second job in one of these establishments near their homes. As Chapter 4 discusses in more detail, 48 percent of my economically active "sample" (262 of the 350 men, women, and children in the larger community) had a secondary source of income. (Throughout the following chapters I use the term *sample* only occasionally and somewhat loosely, largely when describing the economic activities of members of the community I studied, since that data is more quantitative.) Other enterprises distribute their manufactured goods to outlets in the same neighborhood or rely on complementary industries and services nearby. Textile factories in the area produce fabric which is sold in local stores or fashioned into ready-made garments in local factories and sweatshops. The machinists in Bab al-Shaʿriyya can copy many types of imported machinery, which they then sell locally along with the dyes that the aluminum industry relies upon to produce cheap consumer goods. Local bakers and self-employed residents produce the sweets and candy that is consumed by the children who visit the area during major religious festivals. Central Cairo is characterized by the complementarity of many commercial and economic activities that depend on the mixed-use character of the neighborhood. However, it also suffers from many adverse effects of its mixed-use character, including industrial and noise pollution, industrial accidents, traffic from commercial activities, pervasive child labor, and so on.

Yet trying to describe this area visually brings up the very question of the efficacy of visibility in understanding such basic issues as the socioeconomic profile of the area, its social organization, and the nature of commerce and industry. Tourists who visit the area are impressed by its monuments and vitality, but bemoan the insufficient attention that the Ministry of Antiquities devotes to preserving Egypt's historical and cultural heritage. The concentration of people, the competition for residential and commercial space, and very high property values place enormous stress on mosques and homes dating back centuries. Yet some of the factors that visually connote deterioration are actually signs of the area's vitality and the reconstitution of space for contemporary needs. Many residential buildings seem to be falling down when they are actually undergoing reconstruction. Steel rods and unfinished brickwork dot the area's skyline as people build additional floors onto already existing buildings as a way to create additional housing for their

5. This typically small workshop not only manufactures simple, inexpensive metal products but sells them as well both for the wholesale and retail trade. As the standard of living increased in the 1970s and 1980s, many new workshops were opened and artisans introduced new consumer products to local markets. The din from these workshops (which are usually concentrated in specific streets and alley-ways) can be overpowering as machines and apprentices bang out the metal or hammer very simple decorations into their products. (*Photo by John Waterbury*)

married children or other tenants. This construction only proceeds when people have the money to finance the additional floors, and stops, often in midstream, when their savings run out, or a wedding is canceled. At the same time that this construction may serve some of the housing needs of people, new construction can also weaken or destroy the building and even adjacent structures. Many people still live in nineteenth-century buildings, and the fear of collapsed houses is a constant and sensible concern.[46] Most residents can recount stories of apartment walls crumbling, bathrooms flooding, and local buildings collapsing, often killing people and wounding dozens.

In a similar vein, the visual assessment of the socioeconomic status and wealth of area residents can be very misleading. As explained later in Chapter 4, fear of taxation (a new apartment, a car, or jewelry can be used as evidence by tax collectors for charges of tax evasion) and the shortage of housing are only two of the factors encouraging people to remain in the same homes they lived in when first married. Since there are few financial incentives and little government pressure on landlords to maintain their property (such as rent control laws) or for communities to band together to

6. From this view of Cairo's skyline, one can see the ways in which space is exploited to the fullest extent. Since many neighborhoods lay within mixed commercial and industrial areas in central Cairo, residents are subject to the pollution, dust, and noise from local industries.

7. The view from the apartment where I lived, looking down into the common courtyard of an adjacent building. In each one of the shuttered doors below, a separate family lived in one room. The small building on the left served as the common bathroom and water supply. Since their living quarters were very small, they used the courtyard as additional living space. A local cat suns herself on the roof of this building where garbage from our building and others was thrown.

8. Another view outside our apartment: a woman goes up to her roof to check on something she left there "in storage." The steel rods sticking up out of concrete pillars are very common in Cairo and suggest that the owner of the building is still not finished adding floors to it. The building on the right is obviously a much older building with wrought-iron balconies. Even though their roofs may be covered with litter or look unfinished, land and construction costs are extremely high in densely populated neighborhoods, and only people with considerable financial resources can afford to build today.

clean up and improve their neighborhoods (notably the government's limitations on freedom of association and the formation of autonomous organizations), many structures are covered with the omnipresent dust that blows off of the adjacent desert and settles over everything, rarely getting washed away in Cairo's very dry climate. The age of many buildings and the construction boom of recent years give the area a chaotic or deteriorating air. Many people, particularly foreigners, assume that local residents are poor and the area is a slum, when in fact real estate is quite expensive. But one does not see the wealth and economic differences between families until one ventures inside homes and factories. As noted earlier, a destitute family may occupy a single room on the ground floor of a building while a wealthy grocer or machinist may live on the top floor. One would be more likely to notice a family using the street to complement their single-room lodgings on the ground floor than to see the well-dressed, educated middle-class daughters of a merchant inhabiting an upper-floor apartment. Even though new buildings quickly take on the brownish dusty exterior of the area, they are valued at tens of thousands of pounds, if not much more (for more specific information on housing costs, see Chapters 2 and 3).

At the same time, it is also difficult to trust visual assessments of family income when one is inside a household since some households display huge televisions, new video recorders, and expensive furniture while other families who are actually much wealthier do not display their wealth conspicuously, often out of fear of tax collectors or due to a preference for a more modest and less materialistic lifestyle. While some residents certainly live in poverty, a significant number of residents are lower class, lower-middle class, and fewer attain the ranks of the solid to upper middle class. Within these communities there are also millionaires who have extensive legal and illegal investments; although they could move to fancier and more Westernized neighborhoods or suburbs, they prefer to stay in the area, with all its advantages and disadvantages, in order to remain near their workplaces, their friends, and their relatives.

To understand the economic dynamics of central Cairo, and perhaps most of Egypt, one cannot rely on appearances as well. Many economic activities are part of the informal economic sector since they are unrecognized, unenumerated, and unregulated by the government. Civil servants who moonlight are part of this economy as are self-employed peddlers, food sellers, and accountants who do not report their income to tax authorities, and women who manage informal savings associations. This sector incorporates shoemakers who produce shoes off the books and do not register their workers for social security benefits, manufacturers who hide their property and their machinery from tax authorities, and women who raise chicken and geese in their homes. The informal economy provides an alternative and far less visible sphere of employment, production, and investment opportunities for the *sha`b*. In fact, 28 percent of the economically active population in this community was engaged in the informal sector as a primary economic activity and 40 percent as a secondary economic activity. Sixty-two percent of the community was engaged in informal economic activity in at least one of their primary, secondary, or tertiary economic activities. Chapter 4 examines the structure and consequences of the informal economy's extensive role within this community. One has to acknowledge this new character of *sha`bi* communities in order to understand Egypt's larger political economy, particularly if recent national surveys are correct in their estimates of the size of this sector. The results of the 1986 Survey of Employment, Wages and Hours of Work Bulletin indicate that the informal sector (defined somewhat problematically in this survey as fewer than ten workers per establishment) accounts for 43 percent of all nonagricultural private-sector employment.[47]

A final note about visual images of public and private arenas in Egypt reinforces an argument I introduced earlier. While women are seen walking, shopping, and chatting on the streets in central Cairo, and can be seen working in many schools, institutions of various types, stores, and even in factories, they are very rarely seen in local cafés or restaurants. Far more men than women are employed in certain local industries in the area, such as metalworking, shoemaking, commodity bulk trading, and the gold market.

The visual image of social and occupational settings is that Egypt is a highly gender-segregated society. However, when one ventures inside homes where large families frequently visit each other, there is far less sexual segregation. Among outsiders, sexual segregation is more pronounced than among insiders—one's family and its extended networks of relatives. Many decisions affecting people's daily lives and their future are made within the household, and it is here that both men and women negotiate to pursue their interests. I do not mean to suggest that sexual segregation in social settings is meaningless, but only that people should not assume that what is visually apparent from public spaces has the utmost meaning within a community.

Situating my research from within the household provided a much more complex picture of the everyday lives of men and women in these areas. Within the structure of the household I could incorporate both men and women into my analysis, and speak of a political community that is inclusive of both genders, unlike so much of the research on politics in Egypt. The household is where public facades of gender segregation and the submissive role of women break down as men and women engage each other to ensure the prosperity of the family and their own individual needs.

Once I met people and visited them in their homes, I found that my access to the community expanded dramatically. The evidence for the following chapters is drawn from the day-to-day events in the household where I lived and from visits to relatives, colleagues, neighborhood stores, offices, schools, and the various workplaces of the people I met or was introduced to by several key male and female informants. Each day I made choices about visiting people in their homes or workplaces or about accompanying someone on an errand or remaining in my adopted home, always hoping that neighbors or relatives would visit and interesting topics would arise. During this initial period I focused primarily on understanding conversations, especially the issues that arose and the relationships among the people I was meeting.

From nine independent introductions the group of people I interacted with, interviewed, and came to know eventually grew to 350 men, women, and, to a lesser extent, children.[48] I have characterized these 350 people (197 males and 153 females)[49] as a community because of their associations and networks with each other (though at other moments in this work I refer to them as my "sample," largely when I describe and analyze the economic character of the community). Even though these initial contacts did not know each other, some of their associates knew, or knew of, people whom I had met through others. Since many of the initial contacts lived in contiguous neighborhoods, it is not very surprising that they knew of men and women in surrounding areas. Each initial contact introduced me to other relatives, colleagues, neighbors, and friends. These people then provided other contacts to their associates. Typically, for circumstantial reasons, one family would be particularly welcoming and informative, and I would spend more time with them. On other occasions, a person would become interested in my study and take it upon him or herself to introduce me to others and encourage people to answer my questions.

One of the most important members of the community, from the family I lived with, introduced me to over ninety-two people and was the secondary contact to more than thirty-two other men and women (i.e., through the people she introduced me to, I met others). Another neighbor introduced me to members of his extended family but, more importantly, provided a crucial contact to members of the local business and merchant community. This same young man was serving in the army after attending a higher vocational institute and, without my knowledge or direction, administered a survey I had composed to several members of his army platoon (more on the survey below). While not all of these young men were from Cairo, their experiences offer interesting comparison to the Cairo data.[50] More than thirty other men and women in the sample were associated with the workplace of a key person in the study. Approximately forty members of the sample were neighbors of the household where I resided; I met them as I circulated in the neighborhood or was introduced to them across balconies and through open windows.

The connections between some of the families in the sample were further strengthened through marriage. One cluster of relatives, related by marriage, accounted for eighty people within thirty-eight different households. Since I came to know these 350 people through introductions from others, I often met various members of a single household and several households within an extended family. At the same time, many individuals in the sample (110), who most likely also had large extended families, were not related to others in the sample, simply because I had not met their relatives. When I was introduced to individuals through their networks with colleagues, neighbors, or local merchants, I did not always meet their relatives as well. Individuals typically interacted with only certain members of their extended family, and I rarely met all the members of an extended family. In total, I visited sixty-one homes within this community and met many other individuals at their workplaces, in the market, on the streets, or sometimes during public occasions.[51]

In order to understand the political economy of this *sha'bi* community, I constructed a subsample of the economically active population from the larger group of 350 individuals. Included in the economically active sample were 172 men and 120 women.[52] According to the United Nations' system of national accounts and balances, the economically active population "comprises all persons of either sex who furnish the supply of labour for the production of economic goods and services . . . during a specified time-reference period."[53] In my study the reference period was a full year from September 1985 to August 1986. By living in households and visiting people in their homes and workplaces, many economic activities came to light that were not usually captured by a national census due to methodological and administrative problems. In my sample the production of economic goods and services included "all production and processing of primary products, whether for the market, for barter or for own consumption, the production of all goods and services for the market and, in the case of households which produce such goods and services for the market, the corresponding production for own consumption."[54] In Chapter 4 the range of activities in the community encompassed by this definition is illustrated.

After five months into my fieldwork, I embarked on another strategy to collect and systematize my data. I wrote an extensive questionnaire, in colloquial Egyptian Arabic, to guide my research by focusing on the critical issues that constantly arose in the community. The main headings of the survey included: personal background and status; education; employment/earning a living; housing; financial services; fights and legal disputes; organizations; political activity; government services/benefits; and citizen obligations. Each section included detailed questions about the processes necessary to realize particular needs and the nuances of issues such as arbitration or public propriety. Except for the young army conscript whom I referred to above who read the questionnaire, understood its purpose, and then administered it to his fellow recruits in his army platoon, no one else saw the survey in written form since I intended to administer the questionnaire orally. I began these tape-recorded interviews with some of the more important members of the community. However, I found that it was too ambitious to expect people to answer thirty pages of questions patiently. People were rarely alone or free to sit quietly for several hours. Interruptions would occur constantly as they greeted visitors, attended to their children, washed clothes, or prepared meals. Not surprisingly, personal histories were often reconstructed in a favorable and somewhat more ideal light during these more formal interviews. After a few months of frustrating attempts to tape-record structured interviews that seemed to provoke only partial accounts of important issues or experiences, I returned to the much richer methodology of participant/observation, relying on my memory and note-taking to record conversations, experiences, and events during the course of the next several months. During the normal course of daily life, when a debate broke out or a fiancée was found, I could follow the situation and later ask those involved details that I did not understand or to elaborate upon the background and significance of the issue. This approach yielded far richer data than if I had asked a single participant to recount the dynamics of the matter.

In addition to using secondary source material to support the historical and theoretical arguments in the following chapters, toward the end of my year of fieldwork I also collected newspaper articles about the same issues that had come up continually in the course of daily conversation in the community and that were the focus of my written survey (referred to previously). While this was not an extensive component of my research, the articles that I found on marriage, housing problems, the black market, or education (in a cursory examination of the most popular newspapers and magazines) supported my sense that these issues were not only of concern to the particular community I studied but, as national media coverage indicated, they also concerned a much larger cross-section of Egyptians.

While the methodology of participant/observation and open-ended interviews yields rich information and patterns of behavior, one does not have the benefit of standardized data for each member of a sample. Particularly for the purposes of the chapter on the informal economy (Chapter 4), uniform data for a set of specific questions would have been helpful, but on the other hand I learned a great deal about many issues through my more ethnographic approach which would not have come to light in structured, formal interviews. For example, through observation and an understanding of the internal workings of the household, I gained important insight and data about the economic contribution of women to the household and community. Women themselves do not typically identify their financial contribution or informal employment to outside interviewers, and as we shall see later in Chapter 4, the proportion of women participating in the labor force in my community was much higher than national figures suggest. In the same vein, formal interviews and surveys would not have produced the detailed information on either informal networks or the informal economy analyzed in Chapters 3 and 4.

Collecting material and coming to know a community is a slow process, and the nature of the relationship between informants and the researcher is critical. This relationship is a two-way street, and one's own background and the way one initially presents oneself to the community is critically important. I explore some of these issues here because it is foolish to believe that my background did not have an effect on my interaction with people and the very ability to conduct this research in the first place. Without the enhanced political and economic alliance between Egypt and the United States following the Open Door policy and the Camp David Accords, I would not have gained the research clearance from security authorities or perhaps the financial support from American funding institutions to launch this research project. But aside from the international alliances that set the stage for my presence in Egypt, more personal characteristics also were factors, to varying degrees, during the course of my research.

Almost the first three questions most Egyptians ask a foreigner is where they are from, whether they are married, and their religious status. It was obvious I was a woman and fairly obvious through my dress and accent that I was a Westerner, probably an American, but most Egyptians assume Westerners are Christian although I am Jewish. From the beginning of my residence in Egypt I decided not to hide my religion. When I first arrived in 1980, President Sadat was still in power, the Camp David Accords had been signed only two years earlier, thus ending Egypt's state of war with Israel, and both governments were encouraging normalized relations. There were a sizable number of Jewish students in exchange programs at AUC, and Jewish tourists were visiting Egypt again. Depending on who I was talking to, when I would tell people that I was Jewish a discussion about Israel and

Zionism might ensue or people would suggest that we all share the same God and that Jews are people of the book. As a secular Jew my experience in Egypt was perhaps different than other observant Jews since I was not affected by the difficulties and challenges of worshiping in one of the few remaining Egyptian synagogues with the extremely small and almost exclusively octogenarian Egyptian Jewish community (though I did attend Passover Seders in Cairo). In addition, my views on the Arab-Israeli conflict and Israeli politics were not distressing to most Egyptians. When I first arrived in Egypt I was often engaged in debates about the Arab-Israeli conflict and the foreign policy role of the United States, but like many long-term residents in Egypt, it became annoying to have to constantly restate my views to new people once I told them that I was Jewish and to be tested by those who suspected my politics. On occasion, in taxis or during fleeting social occasions, I would say I was Christian to avoid an all too familiar discussion. In a similar way, when I was feeling moody or tired I might tell a taxi driver that I was married and Italian to avoid another query on marriage and gender relations in the United States.

Before I concluded final arrangements to move into the widow's apartment, I felt that she should know that I was Jewish, in case that would cause her or her family any difficulty or raise suspicions in the neighborhood. She was surprised that I had brought up the issue and wondered why anyone would inquire about my religion, since it was really none of their business. Then she said that even if my religion annoyed some people for whatever reasons, they would never say anything to me since I would be living with her well-respected family, which had deep, honored roots in the neighborhood. Finally, she mentioned that she had attended a Jewish intermediate school (which remained functioning until the 1960s) and told fond stories of her teachers. She then began to praise the Jewish merchants who had lived in the area before most Jews left Egypt following the 1948, 1956, and finally 1967 wars with Israel. A neighboring area was called "the alleyway of the Jews" (originally Haarat Zuwaylah, later renamed Harat al-Yahuud) because Jews had lived in central Cairo under the physical protection of Egypt's rulers, since the royal city of walled Cairo had been built by the Fatimids in 969.[55] Some Egyptian private voluntary organizations in the area still had faint ties to the Jewish organizations that had catered to their community before most Egyptian Jews left the country. During my year of fieldwork people were curious about my religion and my experience as an American Jew in Egypt, but I never encountered a single instance of hostility.

My status as an unmarried woman (I was nearly thirty by the time of my fieldwork) was somewhat more complicated and schizophrenic. Having lived in Egypt for three years previously, I was very aware of social norms and the nuances of public and private behavior. An unmarried woman is referred to as a *bint* or girl in Egypt, and it is expected that since she is not married she is a virgin. It is an insult to call an unmarried female a woman, *sitt*, even if she is fifty or sixty years old. When I began my fieldwork I identified myself as a *bint* since I was unmarried. My demeanor and "good morals" was commented on by my Egyptian family, and I was used as a model when people would spot tourists, particularly women, who ventured into these neighborhoods wearing short sleeves, skirts, and shorts.

However, unlike an anthropologist living in a village, my fieldwork was conducted in the middle of a dynamic, metropolitan city, and it was possible to move back and forth with some ease between the neighborhood, libraries, research centers, and houses of friends. As the recipient of a Fulbright grant, I was able to rent a room in the Fulbright Commission's guest flat in Zamalek, a much wealthier area of Cairo, where I always kept my computer, books, and personal belongings. This room offered some privacy and the solitude to sift through my research. I would stay for a week or five days "in the field" and then return to my room for a day or two if I needed to be alone for a while, see other friends, attend a lecture or seminar, or meet colleagues. I would tell my Egyptian family when I was going and when I would return and was always allowed a great amount of flexibility, even returning to their home late at night. Because of the close quarters in central Cairo and the familiarity of residents and merchants with each other, these areas are some of the safest in the city.

My Egyptian family also understood that, as a researcher and a doctoral student, I had colleagues and advisers to see and that I had American friends as well, some of whom visited me in their home. Perhaps they also understood that I needed to be alone occasionally and to study. It was my doctorate that provided the excuse as to why I was not married even though I was almost thirty. Most Egyptians have a deep respect for education, and they accepted the fact that I needed to be devoted to my studies rather than a man and a family, which marriage supposedly entails. I took this "dissertation excuse" to the extreme and denied that I had any boyfriends or much interest in them. To everyone's repeated inquiries about my unmarried status, I replied that after I finished my doctorate perhaps I might consider marriage. Because I would be living in a home with two unmarried sons, meeting new people constantly and circulating within a community with conservative norms about propriety and gender relations, I thought it more appropriate not to share my social life (which was not as dormant as I had suggested) with them. I tend to agree with Nikki Keddie that American women and other Westerners are usually far more reluctant to talk about their private lives than are Egyptian women who discuss social and sexual dynamics quite openly (if they are married).[56] I have known some unmarried American women who have been very candid about their love life with people from these neighborhoods, without encountering the expected stereotypical negative reactions. Yet on the other hand, as a newcomer to the community who would circulate in and out of homes and workplaces, I decided to adopt the role of an unmarried girl dedicated to my education.

As a newcomer to the community who knew very little, I was dependent on people's loquacious nature and goodwill to teach me about what mattered in their lives. Despite my best intentions to be patient, a timetable—my own research agenda and the expectations of my supervisors—always weighed heavily on me. On the other hand, I had very little control over the course of events, the personalities of people I became intimately involved with, and the serendipitous factors that ultimately defined my research. I was constantly on my best behavior, trying to make some sense of a new environment and understand rapid-fire colloquial Arabic while members of the household and relatives checked me out.

From this position as an aberrant interloper in the community I gradually became more than an "observer" and little by little became someone whose presence seemed normal, who was even occasionally asked my opinions on family debates, and who eventually became embroiled in certain family dynamics. At the same time, I was always an American, a foreigner who most people understood would return to her family and her university. On some occasions I seemed to bring a certain status to my Egyptian family and would sometimes be shown off at gatherings and brought to meet the more important associates of this family and others. At the same time, particularly during the beginning of my stay with them, I almost had a childlike status (i.e., I didn't understand many basic things in life—the educational system, complicated stories, the ration system, the stages of an engagement, how to feed geese or cook most Egyptian food, what to joke about or not to joke about, and so on). The role of a curious student allowed me to ask many questions and gain their patience, very naturally. They, like almost all Egyptians, were not only pleased that I could understand them and gratified that I wanted to master Arabic but were very tolerant of my mistakes—unlike the very rude reception that foreigners in the United States often receive if they have difficulties with English. As time elapsed and my familiarity with the language, issues, and figures in the community increased, and people came to know me better, my presence seemed more natural and routine. Occasionally, since I understood the complexities of certain situations or enmity between individuals, my actions were more constrained than they were earlier. If the family broke off relations with a potential suitor, that meant I could not contact him either. When "my" part of the family fought with another branch, I was expected to support their position. Slowly I found myself liking certain families and individuals more than others, and occasionally I would develop friendships with certain people that rattled some members of my family. Although I would not argue that my presence in the community was seen as normal, they did encourage me to stay in Egypt and hoped that I would marry an Egyptian, which only reinforced some of my own ambivalence about returning to the United States. Like most anthropologists, leaving my friends and community after my research was complete had a very unreal feeling to it. Although I knew that this moment would be difficult, leaving people behind and separating oneself from their lives (even knowing that letters, phone calls, and visits would continue) was quite difficult and somewhat numbing. It seems coldly utilitarian to reduce the humanity, the personalities and character of people, to the dictates of completing a research project. Life never stands still, and from abroad you learn about the deaths of people you were very close to and the births of children, but you are not really part of the community until you return and are again welcomed with such warmth and hospitality.

The patience and consideration of this community can perhaps only be partially reciprocated by recounting the record of their participation and trying to convince people to no longer ignore them. The last chapter of this study returns to the question of political participation and political exclusion. It argues that the *sha'b* have turned exploiting the government into a fine art. People in the community who had a particular talent for dealing with bureaucrats, or a wide range of connections to elite politicians and officials, were sought after and valued. Individuals repeatedly stated that the government was something to "take from," an outside, external force to be patronized and exploited. *Siyaasa*, defined in English as politics, clearly referred to the government or the realm of formal politics, and since the formal, legal channels of participation for the *sha'b* were very few, they participated by demanding their fair share of public goods and services and consuming an even greater share of subsidized goods and services through the black market.

The Egyptian government's policies of political exclusion have gone hand in hand with their public commitment to provide for the basic needs of the population. Because it limits and controls mass political participation, the government maintains its legitimacy by providing goods and services to the population. In essence, the government has reduced the realm of politics to distribution. Chapter 5 describes the *sha'b*'s interaction with private voluntary organizations and elite politicians, both of which serve as points of distribution for government goods and services at the local level. From their end of the bargain, the *sha'b* participate in formal politics by consuming goods and services. As members of a predominantly lower-income community, they are extremely sensitive and conscious of any changes in prices and values of commodities, whether publicly or privately distributed. The consequences of this distortion of formal politics leaves the government with very few options. It must maintain its increasingly costly financing of subsidized goods and services or bear the protests of the *sha'b*. While the government and many upper-middle-class commentators condemn the growing consumerism and its associated decadent values in Egypt, they are not prepared to relinquish the reins of power and thus they are caught by their own predicament. It is within this context that my arguments about the role and importance of the family and informal networks are set. I do not argue that the family and informal institutions are the only avenues of political participation in Egypt, but for this particular *sha'bi* community they were a critical component to furthering their interests.

This community showed none of the traits of Almond and Verba's passive participants in a "parochial" or "subject" political culture. People were active participants in a political community that had shared meaning, rules, and priorities.[57] To ignore this vibrant community is to distort the dynamics of state-society relations in Egypt and to underestimate the political awareness of vast segments of the Egyptian *sha'b*. Recognition of this community's priorities and its political vision is the first step toward understanding its ambivalent relationship with the state and its political and bureaucratic representatives. At the same time, an understanding of the politics and political participation of the *sha'b* suggests that the state is linked to its citizens by informal as well as formal political institutions. This imposes burdens and benefits for both the *sha'b* and the state. While the *sha'b* are constantly aware of the power and resources of the Egyptian state since they interact with various representatives of the bureaucracy on a weekly, if not daily basis, the state must also step gingerly when new policies affect the *sha'b*'s interests. As national and international constraints and new challenges confront the government, and it attempts to redefine its relationship with its citizens, the informal institutions and political preferences of the *sha'b* may gain greater visibility and weight in the dynamics of national politics. Moreover, independent of whether the *sha'b* ever make it into the formal limelight, they will always be under the surface, partially structuring, defining, and ordering Egyptian collective life. But first, it is necessary to lay out in successive chapters the nature of those institutions and the community norms and socioeconomic conditions that support them.

The Family, Politics, and the Familial Ethos

IN URBAN QUARTERS of Cairo, *'id-dallalaat* (female peddlers) organize extensive networks of women who collect ration cards from neighbors and kin, bribe local employees of government food cooperatives, and endure raucous crowds outside cooperatives in densely populated areas in order to obtain a large volume of government-subsidized and distributed food.[1] These generally illiterate female brokers then resell their products at a profit to people in *sha'bi* communities whose demand for the goods is not satisfied through official channels.[2] These shrewd businesswomen are sought after in the community because they have access to scarce commodities, even though people express ambivalent feelings about the integrity of their activities.[3] *'Id-dallalaat* realize there is little likelihood of selecting or removing the "men at the top," but they know how to exploit the government, organize the community, and personally profit in the process. Through their activities in the community, they end up influencing government capacity more than elites like by sabotaging the distribution networks, which are a cornerstone of the government's legitimacy. At the same time, they are subject to arrest and harassment by the police and supervisors of the Ministry of Food Supply.[4] They prudently devote attention to the structures that rule them: the bureaucracy and its local institutions, the market, and the family.

This chapter and the next focus on one of those structures that disproportionately influences various aspects of political, social, and economic life in *sha'bi* communities: the family. I refer to both families and households throughout this study, though they are not synonymous terms. A family, in the largest sense, is a group that shares a common ancestry. As Eickelman points out, however, "Whatever the actual groupings of people who feel obliged to one another through 'family' relationships, these groupings act in cultural terms which have a biogenetic reference."[5] Larger historical, economic, and cultural forces shape the meaning of the term *family* and the nature of relationships of individuals within a family unit. The structure of families varies from country to country, from urban to rural areas, from the 1960s to the 1980s. In this study I emphasize the nature of the family as a collective structure and have been unable, unfortunately, to adequately address the historical evolution of family structure in Egypt, its cultural meaning or genealogical structure. A smaller grouping than the family, the household in urban Egypt is generally composed of smaller units of the nuclear family which reside in an autonomous residence. Among the *sha'b*, numerous households consider themselves part of much larger families, and they devote great effort to maintaining their relationships with a wide range of kin. Because nonkin may become part of a household, recent scholarship has defined the household more as an economic unit than a mere association of closely related kin. Wood emphasizes the collective nature of the household when he defines it as "a group that ensures its maintenance and reproduction by generating and disposing collective income."[6] My preference for the use of "family" rather than "household" in this chapter reflects the *shaʿb*'s usage of two words with very nearly equivalent meanings of "family"—*ʾahla* and *ʾusra*. *ʾAhla* and the slightly more formal *ʾusra* are used somewhat interchangeably though the latter seems to be used more commonly to refer to an individual's nuclear family or household unit. While people make a distinction between their nuclear and extended family, because they are situated in a larger association of kin, it is that association which figures so prominently in structuring community life. A recent analysis of the composition of households in Cairo, using 1980 census materials, found that 90 percent of Cairene households were of the nuclear (a couple and their children) or extended nuclear type (where one additional person resides with a couple and their children).[7] At the most fundamental level, the family serves its members by providing material and political security, by formulating the obligations and responsibilities of family members to one another, and by supporting family members in the local neighborhood, the larger community, and in their dealings with the state and its bureaucracy. Within these communities, the family provides a structure and a context through which resources are allocated and distributed, disputes are arbitrated, and behavior is closely monitored. In short, the family serves as a political institution for the *shaʿb*.[8]

The family receives detailed attention here because it means so much to *shaʿbi* communities in a very concrete sense. One of the overwhelming interests of the community is protecting and enhancing the integrity of the family. Though not the *only* concern of the community, creating and sustaining a family absorbs the material, political, and social resources of individuals and groups. While market forces and government initiatives clearly have a great impact on these communities, the *shaʿb* closely follow the consequences of these changes on the position and resources of the family and judge state and political elites accordingly.

A "familial ethos" fashioned by the *shaʿb* supports channels of arbitration, conflict resolution, economic assistance and cooperation in the community, and the reproduction of the family (or marriage and children). Clifford Geertz describes an ethos as "the moral (and aesthetic) aspects of a given culture, the evaluate elements. . . . A people's ethos is the tone, character, and quality of their life, its moral and aesthetic style and mood; it is the underlying attitude toward themselves and their world that life reflects."[9] Although Geertz sets an ethos in a distinctly cultural context, while I would not diminish its cultural meaning, an ethos is also a product of economic and political dynamics, and my arguments about the significance of the familial ethos have to be placed within a context of financial insecurity, considerable government intervention in the economy, and a tradition of political exclusion in Egypt. An ethos of cooperation, arbitration, and association with trusted individuals, which promotes a certain code of morality and propriety, is situated within the realities of everyday life among the *sha'b*. The Egyptian government, through its legal system, executive power, and its intervention in the economy, also promotes its own vision of justice, development, "the good," and propriety. Its public relations efforts attempt to influence values and norms in Egypt as well, so that a certain tension between communal norms and "official" norms and priorities pervades daily life within *sha'bi* communities. "Politics, power and control are not of necessity coterminous with the state," as Chazan argues, and communities that are oppressed both politically and economically struggle to control resources and to promote their authority and their vision of "the good."[10] A community's understanding of "the good," of justice, and of fairness, based on a widely shared consensus of values and norms, can obviously serve as the foundation of a wider-reaching political and philosophical outlook. There is a convergence between the familial ethos at the local level and the way in which the *sha'b* judge national events and politics and envision a better Egypt. A communal philosophy can set the parameters for theory construction and praxis. Sheldon Wolin explains how creating alternative norms and visions has an implicit political dimension that ultimately sets the ground for challenges to the prevailing order.

> The politics of founding or theory destruction refers to the critical activity of defeating rival theoretical claims. Theoretical founding has both a *political* dimension and *politics*. The former is the constitutive activity of laying down basic and general principles, which, when legitimated, become the presuppositions of practices, the ethos of practitioners. The point of engaging in the politics of theory is to demonstrate the superiority of one set of constitutive principles over another so that in the future these will be recognized as the basis of theoretical inquiry. Thus the founder's *action* prepares the *way* for *inquiry*, that is, for activity which can proceed uninterruptedly because its presuppositions are not in dispute.[11]

The familial ethos in *sha'bi* communities, then, is quite powerful. It orders individual lives, sets parameters of behavior in the community, and shapes the political vision of many Egyptian citizens. Like all structures, the family is not wholly benevolent or harmless and the familial ethos is deeply contested within the community. It is an ideal shaped by an ever-changing variety of new material, social, and political forces. But men, women, and children understand the power and authority of the family and the meaning of the familial ethos as well as they understand the power and authority of the state and its underlying principles. The family is bound as much by unity as it is by discord; by cooperation, as by competition. The sections of the chapter on the familial ethos are divided by these dualities.

The conclusion of this chapter argues that informal networks incorporate the household and extended family into the public realm. As informal networks penetrate the realm of the household and extended family, they strengthen the ability and capacity of the *sha'b* to pursue their objectives and notions of propriety, justice, and "the good." Networks connect the realm of the household and extended family to the bureaucracy and local private and public institutions. Thus, the boundaries of public and private arenas are permeable and offer political space for influence from below. We must recognize informal networks as avenues of participation for the *sha'b* and incorporate this level of collective institutions into our analyses of both Egyptian "high" and "low" politics. In Egypt the *sha'b* have fashioned informal institutions to reclaim political space that has been denied to them.

THE PUBLIC/PRIVATE DICHOTOMY AND POLITICAL PARTICIPATION

I am suggesting that notions of political participation be broadened to encompass a wider spectrum of the citizenry, one that includes formerly "silent" constituencies or those that create alternative institutions to satisfy their political needs. The family and informal political institutions have been excluded from discussions of political participation due to a specific construct of the boundaries between what constitutes "the public" as opposed to "the private."[12] Throughout Western political history, beginning with Aristotelian definitions of public and private realms, women and slaves inhabited the realm of the private household (*oikos*) and men dominated the public world of politics (*polis*).[13] In the classical age the *oikos* was not only the sphere of reproduction but also of production, which gave the household economic importance, a role that has since diminished with the rise of capitalism. Men strove to avoid the *oikos*, or sphere of "unfreedom," which was "downgraded and demeaned systematically by powerful public voices, including those of Plato and Aristotle."[14] Elshtain warns against an uncritical adoption of these categories.

> The matters that were hidden and private in Greek society have remained surprisingly concealed in subsequent treatments of Greek society by political thinkers who have carried forward into later epochs not simply the categories public and private but much of the original content infused into those categories, thus enshrouding Greek misogyny, imperialism, and the exploitation of slaves behind the same ideological distortions deployed self-servingly by the Greeks.[15]

This digression into classical political theory is hesitatingly broached to make a simple point: the basic dichotomy between public and private conceals or distorts the participation of women and slaves (the working class in contemporary times) from public discourse, debate, and political activity. Discarding definitions and systems of classification that exclude far more than half of humanity from the political realm is essential. Yet political scientists continue to rely on this dichotomy when they limit the locus of politics to specific understandings of public institutions. Our definitions lead us to conclude that women or lower-class men are unimportant and politically inactive—because they are not visible players in those institutions we have identified as "political"—rather than encourage us to investigate and recognize the less obvious and informal realms of political action and participation. Rassam argues, "Far from being simply the 'domain of women', the family/household in the Middle East is the basic socio-economic unit and the arena where the public/private differentiation dissolves."[16] Despite the evidence that many men and women in popular quarters of Cairo are not members of political parties, unions, or interest groups and avoid formal political involvement or activism, they organize networks within the community that work to satisfy their basic economic, social, and political needs and desires in context with other interests in Egypt. Redrawing the boundaries of the public and the private is one of the most classic contests over resources, power, and legitimacy in any society. Charles Maier argues that "some of the most striking political interventions have been either to reduce private power, or to roll back accumulated public authority on behalf of rights of privacy or property."[17] Again, because the contest between public and private authority and achieving a popular balance between individual, collective, and state authority is still an ongoing struggle in Egypt, the *sha'b*'s commitment to the familial ethos provides a normative basis for their interests.

PATRIMONIALISM, THE FAMILY, AND PARTICIPATION IN A MIDDLE EASTERN CONTEXT

In the ideology and practice of liberal politics, individual self-interest is mediated by institutions that serve the collective good. Individual spirit, ambition, and independence are valued and honored in the political culture of Western liberalism. In other societies, where the cult of the individual is less pronounced and individual rights are not protected by enforced legal codes, the political system and the political culture reflect alternative norms and preferences. In the Middle East the family, rather than the individual, continues to be the more relevant unit of society. However, negative connotations surround the family in analyses of Middle Eastern politics and society as patrimonial politics, nepotism, and corruption are blamed on the familial ethos, without any regard for the structure of national and international politics and political economy in the region.

Bill and Leiden devote extensive attention to the role of family and kinship in Middle Eastern polities. Their characterization of Middle Eastern politics relies heavily on group analysis, and kinship and family remain one of the most important groups, cutting across class lines and vertical and horizontal cleavages.

> The family, which is the basic unit and building block of groups in the Middle East, retains characteristics that render it more rigid and formal than most factional and nonassociational groups. . . . Since family networks are virtually impossible to rupture or break, they provide the element of permanence needed to offset the impermanence of the other informal groups. Family groups are the linchpins of the system of group interaction in the Middle East.[18]

Their analysis begins and ends with a discussion of political development and modernization in the Middle East. They argue that political institutionalization must accompany political development to allow for access and communication between ruler and ruled although "the political elite . . . enjoy(s) the prerogative of action and regress."[19] The personalistic, face-to-face relationship between ruler and ruled is an inherent part of the political tradition of patrimonialism and patriarchy in the region. While these personalistic ties link together individuals from various groups and may account for individual success stories or a rapid rise to power of a small clique, they counteract class solidarity and a sense of class consciousness. The latter, they argue, propels modernization and political development.

> The traditional social system refuses to be torn, and the basic power and authority relations that make up this system are extraordinarily difficult to uproot. Since class conflict, often the agent of transformation, is neutralized, change involves chipping away at pieces of the mosaic. This modifying change seldom disturbs the underlying network of power relations that is the basis for the group and class structure of Middle Eastern societies.[20]

Despite their cogent analysis of the importance of family and kinship groups to politics in the Middle East, Bill and Leiden echo the normative biases of modernization theorists. There are two particular problems in their analysis which are all too common in analyses of Middle East politics. First, their notion of political participation is quite similar to other elite-centric definitions: "Political participation is a process whereby individuals engage in activity that impinges directly upon the *national* power and authority structure of society."[21] Their definition of participation denies the political resources and experience of nonelites, even though they carefully document the national influence and power that traditional leaders and families attain.

Second, they claim that patrimonial rule, which is "little more than an extension and expansion of the patriarchal system," dominates Middle Eastern politics.[22] Paradoxically, Bill and Leiden provide evidence in their book of the power and influence of women in the family and in the polity. They argue that social scientists have overemphasized the "formal, public, and institutional aspects of political behavior" at the expense of the private and informal aspects overlooking "precisely those individuals who dominate the private and informal aspects."[23] Their use of patriarchy as the basis of their understanding of Middle Eastern politics, however, suffers from a reified, ahistorical, ideal notion of patriarchy. Disregarding their own insightful analysis of the informal power of women, they argue: "In patriarchal or patrimonial societies, the patriarch is the main social and political reality. He is the model, the guide, the innovator, the planner, the mediator, the chastiser, and the protector. The community wraps itself around the leader, who governs through a constantly expanding web of personal relations. Within the family, which is the basic social unit in the Middle East, the father is the unrivaled leader."[24]

Like other scholars, Bill and Leiden treat the family and the household as an undifferentiated "black-box" where the commands of the father are unquestioningly obeyed.[25] The family has few internal dynamics, the family itself does not change, and external socioeconomic and political forces have little influence. To be fair, perhaps the absolute authority of the father in Middle Eastern families has declined since their research was completed due to the increase in female employment, education, changes in migration opportunities, and the growing commercialization of the economy, but their argument is posed in unchanging terms that rest on ahistorical cultural arguments. More persuasively, Rassam argues that "everywhere in the Middle East, we see the erosion of the extended patriarchal family and the emergence of the individual, both male and female, as an independent actor on the social scene. The domination of the young by the old and of women by men is no longer taken for granted."[26]

In *sha'bi* communities men, women, and children in the household actively compete with one another for scarce resources and defend their interests and rights with all their strength.[27] As will be demonstrated later in this chapter, the household does not always act as a wholly cooperative unit[28] but is characterized more distinctly by what Sen has called "cooperative conflict."[29] Intrahousehold politics is far more competitive and confrontational than is generally believed.[30] While many of the acceptable norms and roles for family members are socially constructed by tradition and ideology, time does not stand still, nor do popular ideals.

On another level, the problem is even more complicated. Western political scientists generally believe what Arab men tell them about the family: that men are all-powerful. The same political scientists dispute claims that Arab governments are omnipotent, thus resisting the persuasive influence of state propaganda machines, yet they are willing to believe claims of male authority within the household. The lack of fieldwork conducted by male researchers and their problem of gaining access to households perpetuates stereotypes and generalizations. A distorted picture of the patriarchal family supports orientalist views of Middle Eastern women as subjected, oppressed, and invisible. To project a strictly patriarchal view of intrahousehold politics throughout the Middle East which is based on either cultural or economic arguments only obscures the real dilemmas facing rulers and the ruled and the possibilities for change.

Khalaf offers a more consistent argument about the role of the family in both communal and elite politics. In Lebanon kinship culture and filial piety provided the basis for communal solidarity and social welfare. However, this structural and cultural basis of community destroyed the unity of the nation when national elites ignored demographic trends and refused to change out-of-date formulas for parliamentary representation. In other words, it was not the family and filial piety that tore Lebanon apart, but the tradition of political exclusion in Lebanon serving to maintain elite interests: "The very factors that account for much of the viability, resourcefulness, and integration of the Lebanese are also the factors that are responsible for the erosion of civic ties and national loyalties. . . . In short, the factors that enable at the micro and communal level, disable at the macro and national level. This is, indeed, Lebanon's predicament."[31]

The central role of the family in Middle Eastern society has been recognized by scholars throughout social science disciplines. Anthropologists and sociologists have continually stressed the legitimacy and tenacity of kinship links—whether embodied by the clan, the tribe, or simply the extended family.[32] "If the Koran is the soul of Islam, then perhaps the institution of the Muslim family might be described as its body."[33] Familial networks are not anachronistic remnants from an era when dynastic rule was the predominant system of government, but a continuing positive resource that binds individuals together and protects them from external interference or unanticipated political and economic change.[34]

Sayigh observed that "membership in kin-based groups is the individual's chief guarantee of security and access to resources—hence the necessity for strong group maintenance mechanisms. Arab 'familism' (or 'tribalism') must be viewed, not as a cultural trait, but as a very ancient adaptive response to insecurity; group cohesion is as important for survival under state oppression as it is for survival in the absence of the State."[35] Sayigh places the family in a specifically political, not cultural, context. Individuals in precarious environments, pressured daily by economic and political exploitation, rely upon the family as a political resource.[36]

Joseph has also argued that individuals use the family to provide political security in their daily struggle with limited resources and political and economic uncertainties in urban, working-class districts of Beirut. "Family affiliation . . . provides the urban working class individual with a social idiom, identity, loyalties, voting power, brokerage, mediation and physical protection."[37] Largely excluded from the politics of elite competition for places within the party and state bureaucracy, the family has become the basis for a political community for lower-class men and women—one that is effective, bound by a common set of moral and ethical precepts and obligations, and responsive to the demands and priorities of its members.

Broadening the locus of politics to various arenas of power and authority within the community is not meant in any way to deny the power and penetration of the Egyptian state and bureaucracy. Considering informal networks or the family as an informal political institution does not preclude the importance of political elites, public or clandestine political parties, or interest groups. However, because the *sha'b* and other segments of the population are excluded from formal channels of participation, these informal avenues of participation remain particularly effective. In the Middle East, where generally authoritarian regimes ruled by male leaders dominate the political landscape, women and lower-class men are generally excluded from the *polis*. The reasons behind this popular exclusion obviously vary from one nation to the next but can be reduced to an aversion to sharing the resources and power of national office (as discussed briefly in the Introduction).

The argument that the family is a crucial resource in the Middle East is obviously not new. I am suggesting, however, that we take this piece of common knowledge and place it in a political context. The family not only sees to the material and social needs of a community but fills a political vacuum as well. I am arguing that the family is an important avenue of participation that complements or parallels the formal political sphere. Those men or women with strong ties to local politicians or a local branch of the National Democratic Party (the official party of the regime) certainly exploit those ties. Others use their influence within an office of the state bureaucracy to further personal and familial interests. Still others use their accumulated wealth to influence public officials. However, many people with or without access to local, provincial, or national elites use informal institutions to further their interests, and to gain influence in their community.

While the power of the Egyptian state was felt daily by this community, and men and women sought assistance from state bureaucrats and politicians, people focused their energy, efforts, and resources toward furthering familial interests and priorities. Individual constituent members of the family competed under some circumstances and forged alliances in others to gain access to scarce resources. Prominent family members made distributive decisions and enforced proper behavior and codes of conduct within the family and the community. An underlying commitment to familial unity forged particular patterns of relationships and norms of behavior that bound individuals and collective units such as households and families to each other and to the community. As a family elder said, when called in to arbitrate a particularly renting conflict between three brothers who lived and worked together, "A few words [*kilmateen*] should not be allowed to destroy the family. It is impossible for family members to go their own way [*mish mumkin yib'a kulli waaHid fi-Hallu*]." The familial ethos represents far more than a desire to promote individual interests.

THE FAMILIAL ETHOS

The *sha'b* possess a common worldview of the rights and responsibilities of individuals within the household and the proper boundaries of family authority and power within the larger community. People constantly articulate and defend the importance of family within the community and within the nation. Ideal notions of proper family relations and authority patterns pepper the conversation of men and women in their homes, on the streets, and at their workplaces. In the media and in Parliament, images and arguments concerning the importance of family in contemporary Egypt or warnings related to its demise are a recurrent theme.[38]

It would be foolish to represent this worldview as a "traditional" or "backward" orientation that restricts the interaction of men and women to their kin in isolated micro units of the household or extended family. Rather, men and women promote shared perspectives among members of their community, binding them together. Cooperation, trust, and mutual dependence make sense in a context where financial scarcity, political exclusion, and incomplete information are everyday realities. Communities cannot exist as a cohesive group without a sense of underlying norms and shared understandings of how people should live their lives, and how societies should be structured. Horizontal associations among a wide range of networks are even more critical in polities where vertical linkages among different groups are intentionally discouraged. Relying on family, on colleagues, on neighbors brings support to people who need it, and those people understand that they benefit as a community by furthering systems of support.

While the familial ethos was supported in theory by broad segments of the community, discrepancies between theory and practice were common. These discrepancies do not complicate the story, but rather make it more realistic and credible since they reflect typical contradictions and ambiguities in daily life and in the polity. At times men or women would pursue selfish interests while defending their actions as altruistic. Others would attack elderly parents or supposedly honored people in the community one day and condemn other people for similar offenses the next. When people were asked very direct questions of what was right or wrong, their answers, at times, contradicted recent behavior. In a similar sense, forces that were responsible for uniting families under certain circumstances divided families in others. These observations are not surprising but serve as reminders of the importance of ideals in the life of a community and the ways in which they are contested daily.

Bonds of Unity

The predominant goal of families is to maintain the integrity of the household unit despite personal differences or external threats. In times of crisis, when the integrity of the household or the family is threatened, members of the extended family, trusted neighbors, or colleagues are called upon to arbitrate disputes. Their ultimate goal is to preserve the family unit while accommodating individual feelings and interests. Although family conflicts are common, there are accepted protocols for resolving them.

The pervasiveness of arbitration channels provides critical evidence for my argument that the family fulfills political as well as social and economic needs in the community. The power of individuals within households, households within extended families, individuals within extended families, and extended families within the community is constantly renegotiated and redefined according to changing circumstances. Although people may insist publicly that a specific type of behavior is expected from a man or woman at a given point in his or her life (as will be demonstrated below and in the following chapter), the community actually tolerates a broader spectrum of behavior and action. However, competition and conflict often surround the renegotiation of power and position, and interestingly, this frequently occurs in public. The choices of staying in school or leaving it to work in a family workshop, of having children early in marriage or waiting a year or two, of marrying someone still in school or postponing the wedding until after graduation are all examples of issues that are publicly discussed and contested. Repeated by the thousands, these decisions influence political, economic, and social trends in the nation and the sensitivity of the *sha'b* to the government's policies and programs.

Since one of the community's most important goals is the preservation of the household unit, many of the following examples involve marital disputes which if left unresolved can lead to the disintegration of the family. Even if the sources of serious tensions are intimate issues, a husband and wife will seek the arbitration of their families. A wife who feels wronged or exploited will return to her parental home (*beet 'ahlaaha*) to seek protection from physical, verbal, or economic abuse.[39] Her parents or other relatives will then intercede on her behalf to resolve the problem, whatever its cause. Often, one side of the family may not wait to be invited to intervene and will act quickly to protect a son's or daughter's interests. While returning to one's parents' home after an argument is far more common among women, men will seek or at least listen to the counsel of their family when facing major marital problems.

In one instance, the pregnant wife of a public-sector employee returned to her mother's home with her three young children in tow. They were all very somber and remained in the more formal attire that people generally wear when "going out." (*Libs il-xuruug* are only worn when people are either working, socializing outside the home, attending school, or visiting each other. As soon as most Egyptians return home or visit people they are familiar with, they change into more comfortable and less expensive clothes such as *galaliib* [pl.], housedresses, and pajamas.) Even the youngest son, only two years old, sensed the gravity of the situation and was uncommonly quiet and subdued. The woman explained to her mother that she could no longer endure beatings and abuse from her husband since her health and the health of her unborn child was at risk. "A divorce would be preferable to this hellish marriage," she insisted.

The threat of divorce, despite her inability to initiate one, was raised to communicate the severity of their disagreement.[40] If her family failed to resolve the problem and the couple divorced, the daughter and her three young children would have to move back to her mother's home, thereby adding an additional burden to this woman's household. The daughter demanded the mother's intervention because she blamed her for causing the couple's disagreement in the first place. Earlier in the year, the mother had asked her daughter's husband to lend a considerable sum of money to her son in order to purchase a taxi. Now the husband demanded to be repaid, but since the taxi had broken down, neither the son nor his mother could repay the loan.

The young wife was also angry at her husband for inviting his male friends to their apartment to watch pornography on a recently purchased video cassette recorder. The wife had returned home on several occasions to find her children playing unsupervised in the busy street in their good clothes, while her husband watched pornographic films with several young men, some of whom she had never met.[41]

Shortly after the married daughter had come to her mother's apartment with her children, an uncle who lived on the ground floor yelled up to warn them that her husband and a male friend had arrived.[42] It was clear that they had not only come to defend the husband's position but also to participate in resolving the disagreement. The husband's friend was now their neighbor, but he had also grown up with the wife in a different, older neighborhood. The friend who had come to speak on behalf of the husband in an effort to *yiSaliH-hum maʿa baʿd*, or reconcile the two, reminded those present that he had known the wife from birth, long before he had become a friend of her husband's, and thus could not merely take the position of the husband. The wife dismissed the bonds of long association, explaining to the family that this old friend was one of the men whom she had found watching pornography in her apartment.

In an effort to placate his wife, the husband proposed selling the VCR, if that would satisfy her. She responded by saying that it was not necessary to sell it, but for him merely to stop renting pornographic films and inviting strangers to her apartment. The uncle tried to calm down both husband and wife, and finally the mother agreed to repay some of the outstanding debt to her son-in-law. The husband promised not to invite strangers to their apartment. Exploiting the audience and family council to the fullest, the wife brought up other unrelated complaints about her marriage including the husband's minimal financial support of the household and the way his family treated her. These new complaints were not taken very seriously, but the immediate crisis concerning the outstanding loan and the pornography had been diffused. Through the intervention of neighbors and relatives, their marriage was salvaged. In the end, the couple began teasing and joking with each other.

Another young woman, newly married at the time, was in the habit of returning to her parental home after serious disagreements with her husband. Her family, after hearing her complaints, usually concluded that she was in the wrong and advised her to return to her husband. After one particularly serious argument, she and her husband visited her parents. While there, and without creating a public scene, she said that she was ill and did not feel up to returning to her own home. The husband knew that she was not ill but angry with him, yet rather than admit his guilt in this matter and apologize so that she would return home with him, he accepted her decision to remain with her parents. As he was leaving, however, he gave his wife £E20, regardless of the marital spat, saying, "Don't I still have the responsibility to provide for you?" Despite his daily visits to his in-laws, she refused to go back to their home unless he apologized to her. Eventually her father spoke to the husband and told him that, on this occasion, he was in the wrong. The husband finally apologized and told his wife that if they had a serious argument in the future, *la qaddar allaah* (God forbid), he would leave so that she could remain in their home.

Within the community, people make themselves available (others might say, interfere) as arbitrators in domestic disputes to ensure that couples remain together and households are not dissolved. When such crises occur, they have negative repercussions not only on the individuals directly involved but on the relations between members of the extended family and members of the community, such as neighbors and friends. The high cost of marriage remains another important factor that severely discourages separation and divorce. Even if they are suffering terribly in their marriage, the couple knows they would have enormous difficulty accumulating another £E7,000–15,000 to finance a second marriage.[43] Arbitration mechanisms, whether familial or governmental, are apparently fairly successful since the national divorce rate of 2 percent is extremely low compared to many other nations (the rate is 2.9 percent in Cairo Governorate, 1.5 percent in Giza Governorate).[44]

To maintain the integrity of the household unit, the family must protect its position within the community. The question of honor and respect permeates discussions within the community. It is important for both individuals and families that others respect them since respect increases one's status and position within the community. While this is not something one can demand from others, people consciously and unconsciously promote their reputations in the community. Some families may not earn much money, but because of the respect that the community gives them they are sought after to arbitrate disputes, give advice, find suitable mates for other people's children, and so on. Individuals are seen as members of a family, and the respect given or withheld from an individual reflects upon his or her household and extended family.

Parents rear their children to conform to communal norms that regulate interpersonal relationships, and men and women consider it their duty to ensure that their relatives conform to these norms. As a result of this, the male *and* female relatives of an unmarried girl will carefully monitor a woman's movements to ensure that she is not having an illicit relationship with a man. However, the boundaries of an "illicit" relationship are somewhat ambiguous and can include flirting or secretly meeting with unrelated males. What is very clearly known to young people is that they are certainly not to engage in sexual relations with each other. Many young women, when walking to school, working, or shopping, interact with young men in an entirely acceptable fashion. Furthermore, within many households, male relatives and friends of the family visit regularly, and since some of those relatives are eligible mates, social interaction within the household may be more flirtatious and serious than it could be outside the home with unrelated men and secret admirers. Once a young woman is formally engaged, her fiancé is allowed to visit the house quite often, since the relationship is recognized as legitimate and unfolds in public. While the household is not accessible to strangers and even to certain neighbors or colleagues, it is part of the public domain for relatives within an extended family. When relationships are monitored within the household few problems occur, but if a young couple evades supervision by meeting secretly they risk family and community censure for being dishonorable.

The cost of illicit sexual activities for men and women is unequal. Although people do not actively supervise the sexual liaisons of men, either young or old, their illicit activities, if discovered and publicized, can erode their status in the community or adversely affect their marriage prospects. But for young women the costs of illicit sexual activity can be much higher, and arguments about a woman's morality, honor, and virginity are one of the common causes of domestic violence in the community.[45] Even younger brothers or cousins participate in arguments about the behavior or actions of their older sisters or cousins. Such constant surveillance can be a source of great tension for a young woman, but intervention by respected members of the community usually serves to control people's behavior and diffuse potentially serious conflicts.

In one serious incident, a teenage girl was visiting her girlfriend, who was also the sister of her brother's fiancée. She was allowed to stay overnight with this friend because their families were soon to be related by marriage and their houses were across the street from each other. The girl's brother visited his fiancée almost every day and was often present when his younger sister was there. One night, when she and her brother were visiting, a cousin of his fiancée insulted the brother by saying, *ya roH 'ummak* (most closely, you are your mother's end all and be all). Usually a term of endearment, in the context of this conversation the phrase questioned the maturity and manhood of the young man because it suggested that he had been spoiled and dominated by his mother. Phrases that refer to one's mother as *'umm* instead of *waalida* are usually impolite and disrespectful in Egyptian society. However, when friends are joking, these insults are not taken seriously. In formal situations, and in particular in mixed company, the use of this genre of expressions is not only insulting but embarrassing—because a man must defend his honor and his mother's by responding to the insult.

In this case, the fiancé's sister immediately got up to leave, explaining to her girlfriend that the cousin had been impolite. By not tolerating such behavior and publicly demonstrating that she was not used to hearing such remarks, it was understood that she was defending her family's reputation, even if the cousin had not intended to insult her family. Her brother warned her not to recount the details of this incident to their mother because he knew she would be insulted and that the incident would damage even further the already delicate relations between the two families. Relations had been strained for some time because each family had wanted a "better match," but both families had reluctantly acceded to the wishes of their children, who by now were deeply in love.

The young woman returned home and said nothing to her mother about the insult. However, when her brother arrived, he immediately began hitting her, having assumed that she had told his mother of the cousin's insult. The mother had no idea why they were fighting and tried to separate them. When the mother insisted on knowing the cause of the fight, the full story came out.

The next day, the prospective bride's entire family came to pay a formal visit; they were all very subdued. Trivial conversation was exchanged until the end of the visit when it became clear that they had come to apologize for their cousin's behavior. They explained that he had been impolite in the past and had caused similar problems with other members of their family. He had referred to several women as *ya mara*, an Egyptian colloquial term meaning a woman of ill-repute, the usage of which is both vulgar and disrespectful. The young man had argued in his defense that in Iraq, where he had worked intermittently, the term was not offensive, but naturally he knew its connotation in Egypt and was therefore reprimanded by his family. At the same time, the fiancée's family condemned the brother's violence against his sister, agreeing with the daughter that she was right to have left their home after her mother had been insulted.

The mother explained that she did not ordinarily allow her daughter to sleep over at anyone else's home, but had trusted the mother of her son's fiancée. Wasn't the mother of her future daughter-in-law responsible for the character of her guests, when she was entrusting her daughter to her care? Each party appealed to a common sense of honor and propriety, or the familial ethos, to defend their behavior—and it was obvious, since the family had come to apologize, that they accepted responsibility for the behavior of guests in their home. A few words from a black sheep in the family had almost caused the dissolution of a lengthy betrothal. Although the marriage of the engaged couple eventually took place, the daughter was never allowed to stay over at her girlfriend's home again and rarely went to visit her after this incident. Even after the marriage of this couple and the birth of their child, the relationship between the two families remained delicate and lukewarm.

In general, people are concerned not only with the reputation of families within the community but also with the reputation of individuals within the extended family. Parents rear their children to respect their elders, whether these are parents, grandparents, elder brothers or sisters, or cousins. In *sha'bi* communities, older siblings are often given substantial domestic responsibilities such as cleaning, cooking, marketing, or child care. Younger children use the title of '*abla*, which denotes respect when referring to older women in authority, whether they are sisters, teachers, or respected unmarried women in the community. A parental role for older siblings in Egypt is not uncommon since older men typically marry younger women and many children thus grow up in a single-parent household, with various connections to the extended family.[46] Although there are not as many families with siblings from several generations in this community as there were in the past, the youngest child of a woman can be the same age or younger than some of her grandchildren. When younger children do not respect their elders, people usually condemn their behavior.

As an example, one day a nineteen-year-old and her married forty-year-old eldest sister became embroiled in an argument that led quickly to fighting. Their mother, tired of these arguments in her home, complained that her youngest daughter was disrespectful and uncontrollable and nothing had been the same since she had first hit her eldest sister several months earlier. By disrespecting her sister, even if the eldest sister was overbearing and self-centered, the youngest daughter had transgressed the norms of acceptable behavior. Now the youngest sister seemed all too ready to strike her eldest sister. She eventually suffered the consequences of her actions: the eldest sister effectively sabotaged her sister's engagement by interfering in the courtship and convincing their mother that the fiancé did not show enough respect to their family. The principles of the familial ethos were used against the youngest sister and then legitimized the eventual breakup of this engagement.

In a similar incident, an older brother had refused to speak with his younger brother for months after the younger brother had insulted him. Because the older brother was away for several weeks at a time in the army, this dispute had lingered longer than usual. Had he been at home, and the conflict continued, older members of the family would have intervened more quickly.

Arguments between brothers, or men in general, are often more violent than fights between men and women. In one episode, Tahir, a young man now married with a family of his own, financially supported his father's second wife and his three younger halfbrothers. (Tahir's mother had run away from her husband, and he had married a second wife who was only fifteen at the time. His father, who was in his mid-fifties, had died ten years later, leaving his second wife a widow at twenty-five.) As a deaf-mute, the stepmother was limited in her ability to support herself and her three sons after the husband's death, although she functioned quite well in her household and within the community. While disabled people do not have considerable access to sophisticated medical technology or educational training programs, many are incorporated into the community and marry and establish households. Their relatives and the government assist them, and usually they are not isolated or marginalized. In my community several disabled people lived with relatives in semi-independent households.

Tahir employed two of her sons in his workshop. One of them had failed to come to work for several days, and Tahir finally went to find him at the mother's home. The confrontation between the two brothers quickly grew violent as blows were exchanged and Tahir broke medicine bottles over his half brother's head. He also brandished a knife, threatening his younger half brother, and although the younger one was able to gain control of the knife twice, he did not use it to stab his older half brother. Even in the heat of the battle, the younger brother still could not transgress the norm of respect for an older brother who had acted as his surrogate father. Rather, relatives living in the building summoned an older male in the family to break up this particularly violent fight. This story was recounted to others, and it brought respect to the younger brother because he had demonstrated self-restraint. At the same time, despite the violence of Tahir's methods, the community endorsed his attempt to discipline a younger half brother.

Later Tahir heard that his half brothers had not defended their mother when a young man who shared their apartment had pulled her to the window and threatened to throw her out of the building for not paying her share of the electric bill.[47] Only her youngest son had come to her defense. Tahir immediately went to find his "worthless" two older half brothers to punish them for not protecting their mother and for sleeping through the entire scene. Violence, threats, and appeals to their honor were all perfectly reasonable means for Tahir to keep his family together.

Bonds of Discord

While men and women work to ensure ideal notions of family unity and empowerment, they also compete for the resources of the household. At times, competition for money or affection, for example, can be quite destructive, tearing apart the household or causing enduring rifts between members of households and the larger extended family. But people would not struggle unless something important was at stake. Arguments, when acted out over and over again, to the extent that they seem trivial to the outside observer, provide arenas for men and women to claim their fair share of the scarce resources of the household, and guide the manner in which the household, or family, as a collective unit represents itself in the community.[48] However, as mentioned before, there are standard channels for conflict resolution within the community, and individuals with reputations as skilled arbitrators are utilized by their relatives, neighbors, or colleagues.

One illiterate young woman in the neighborhood assisted her family in the wholesale fruit trade, rising at five in the morning to help her elderly father and older brother auction off their produce outside their small store. According to this young woman, her eldest sister was trying to hurt her father and steal his store and land. She even suggested her sister would go so far as to kill their father to gain control of his land and property. Whether she was being melodramatic, or actually had evidence of her sister's malicious intentions, was difficult to determine. In her support, the family had a lengthy record of intrafamily violence, which included the father's murder of his own brother and, more recently, the suicide of her favorite brother by self-immolation after a particularly violent and humiliating fight with another brother. A third brother had just broken his wife's arm after she had put her hands on her hips during an argument and looked him up and down derisively, an action he interpreted as being extremely disrespectful. At least one brother was being kept somewhat out of trouble, as he languished in a military jail, charged with attempted desertion from the army. People in their neighborhood explained this family's reputation for violence by referring to their rural roots, as well as to their involvement in the fruit trade. The wholesale fruit trade can be quite profitable in Egypt, and some of these merchants are said to be involved in illegal commerce and the drug trade. Such incidents from this young woman's family history thus gave some credence for suspecting her sister.

Despite her deep suspicion of her close relatives, this young woman was engaged to marry one of her cousins, whose own nuclear family was far more educated than hers. He had graduated from high school and worked as a public-sector clerk in the Ministry of Justice in addition to his familial responsibilities in the lemon market. Her father approved of the match although he argued over many of the wedding expenses with his relatives. The cousin's family was less violent, better educated, and aspired to a more middle-class lifestyle. Thus she chose to marry into a part of the family that offered some hope of upward mobility and less violence, while still being in a position to protect her father from the constant plots of her other relatives.

When intrafamily violence becomes too threatening or destructive to the family as a whole, other members of the family, colleagues, or neighbors will intervene to protect individuals and the family's reputation. When one mother could not stop a particularly violent dispute between two of her children still living at home, neighbors came to her rescue and took her to the home of one of her married daughters. The married daughter and her in-laws would not let her return home until her other children had agreed to stop fighting. They blamed the children for ruining their mother's health. She was often ill, and after particularly vicious fights her heart would beat furiously and she would experience difficulty in breathing. These attacks, while seemingly severe, served as a tactic to divert the combatants from their conflict and to redirect attention toward her. On the other hand, she often became so embroiled in the fights and participated so vociferously that it was also likely that these respiratory attacks were induced by her own conduct during these heated arguments. During and after an attack, relatives or neighbors would condemn the behavior of the children and appeal to their concern for their mother's health to stop fighting—a strategy that unfortunately rarely worked.

When outsiders, even if they are relatives, need to be called to mediate disputes, the reputation of the household suffers somewhat because members of the community are reluctant to establish networks (marriage, financial, marketing, political) with a family that has a reputation for constant bickering. Rather, people would comment on the inability of these families to resolve conflicts with *siyaasa* (politics, diplomacy) and *'a'l* (reason), and grown men and women would be condemned as *'iyaal* (children) for their inability to resolve family disputes calmly.

Within large extended families, which include married children who have set up independent households, competition between each household can also serve to bind the family together. Nuclear families within the extended family will try to compete with each other to earn the respect of elderly matriarchs or patriarchs who almost always live with the family of a daughter or son, rather than alone or in a nursing home. Community elders maintain an active political, social, and economic role until death (they rarely live to the point of incapacitating senility or illness), and their offspring will frequently seek their approval and respect. The family as a larger unit benefits from these attempts to seek approval if married children devote greater resources to the family. For example, one son will suggest that he build an apartment building to house his family and the families of his siblings to earn the respect of his father. A daughter might search the neighborhood and extended family for suitable mates for the rest of the family while another one may be an expert procurer of subsidized food, which she distributes to the extended family.

At the same time, competition for the respect and affection of these matriarchs and patriarchs can be divisive as well. In one case, a matriarch lived with an unmarried daughter in her own apartment. Her eldest son, second daughter, and two younger sons lived with their spouses and children in an apartment building in another neighborhood. Their proximity produced an atmosphere of intense competition between the daughters-in-law and the second daughter. At each birthday or on some national or religious holidays, they would note who spent more time at the matriarch's apartment, who cooked more food, or who bought the most expensive gifts for the grandchildren. Eventually, in order to alleviate some of the financial pressure of competition, the women met together and agreed to limit the value of the birthday presents they bought for the children and exchanged among themselves.

As in all societies, marriage affects family relationships, and competition and jealousy can arise. One of the most sensitive and common sources of friction in Egypt is the mother, son, and daughter-in-law triangle, lionized and mythologized in Egyptian humor, popular literature, and films. For several years after the marriage of a son, particularly an eldest or only son, the bargaining power of individual family members is renegotiated. The mother must adjust to the daughter-in-law's competing demands for financial and emotional support, and the daughter-in-law must simultaneously earn the respect of her mother-in-law, retain her relationship with her own family, and establish a relationship with her new husband. Anticipating these problems after the marriage of a favored son, relatives and neighbors mediate the couple's delicate steps to create a new household while maintaining dependent links and emotional ties to their respective families. Some couples live with their in-laws until the birth of a first child, if they cannot afford a new home or younger siblings or elderly parents need care. An analysis of complex households found that 12 percent of the wives in a 1980 survey of Cairo lived with their own mother and 23 percent with their mother-in-law. Neither mother nor mother-in-law was present in 65 percent of the households. Complex households (one couple with additional persons or multiple couples with or without additional persons) comprised 18 percent of the total sample of 2,103 Cairo households.[49]

A more destructive aspect of intrafamilial competition can arise when the matriarch or patriarch of the family dies. Inheritance disputes will occasionally leave families bitterly divided as previous enmities and disputes surface after a death, particularly if it was the extended family's peacemaker who died. In an environment of scarcity, families will dispute wills or file suit against their relatives if they think they are being cheated out of their share of an inheritance, no matter how large or small. Islamic inheritance laws divide property among heirs in specific proportions, resulting in joint ownership of land, housing, workshops, and businesses in this community. Therefore families must cooperate to maintain the financial viability of property or a business enterprise, or the already limited resources of the family will be immobilized by tedious courtroom and family battles.

Under Islamic inheritance laws and Egyptian law a widow is entitled to the support of her husband's male relatives. Inheritance can be an extremely important source of security for both sexes, but for those women who do not earn cash and whose ability to save is therefore limited, an inheritance can provide one of the few sources of personal financial security.[50] After the early death of her husband, one widow took her husband's brothers to court when they tried to deprive her of her inheritance. She successfully sued them again after they failed to support her children, which was their duty as her husband's next of kin. Every month she faithfully went to the post office to pick up the £E2 (approximately $1.40) the court had awarded her for the support of her two children. This sum was grossly inadequate and hardly covered a day's expenses for them, but she exploited every piaster of support that was available (100 piasters equal one Egyptian pound). In order to win even this extremely small sum from her husband's relatives, she had found it necessary to pursue her case for several years in the court system. Needless to say, she never spoke to these relatives again and became very angry if any of her children or other relatives had anything to do with them. There was so little contact that when her son met one of his uncles by chance, in the uncle's official capacity as a schoolteacher, they did not recognize each other.

Even as various parties to an argument take each other to court, or engage in a physical fight, they protect the larger financial and social interests of the family and remain engaged and connected to each other, if only through discord. Fighting over economic interests, such as inheritance, or over the family's reputation is perfectly acceptable and expected behavior because people understand the familial ethos and mediate conflict according to its rules.

Bonds of Dissolution

In times of crisis, when a household or a marriage is dissolving, the familial ethos continues to inform, regulate, and moderate the behavior and reactions of men and women. Resources and responsibilities are rearranged between members of the household and the extended family, according to the norms of the familial ethos. Although the ideal goal of family unity or prosperity can no longer be met, the community negotiates other alternatives, which, ideally, protect and provide for family members. After the death of a head of household of either sex, the community supports family members in their struggle to reestablish a viable household. When a woman is divorced by her husband, she relies on the community and her immediate relatives for help in supporting her children, finding a new husband (if she and her family agree that remarriage is the proper option), and protecting her property and right to child support and alimony from her former husband.[51] When illness in a family affects the earning potential of a mother or father, or incapacitates a woman from fulfilling her responsibilities in the household, others in the community volunteer to assist the family, and in some cases relatives will even move into the household to help. However, there are examples in *sha'bi* neighborhoods of a woman being widowed and receiving little support from relatives or friends and neighbors. Divorced women, especially if they lose their right to remain in their home, can face difficult economic and social problems. They must struggle to survive and are vulnerable to many forms of exploitation.

Through remarriage, polygyny, or the merging of two households into a complex household, men and women combine scarce resources to overcome their precarious economic or social positions. (The term *polygyny* describes the practice of having more than one wife at a time, while the more familiar term *polygamy* refers to a marriage where a spouse of either sex may have more than one mate at the same time. Under Personal Status Law in Muslim societies, *only* men may marry four wives.) The most important goal of individuals is to ensure enough support to maintain a household and its members. In the majority of cases, this means that children must be supported, and strategies are centered around that requirement. People share a common commitment toward supporting the family, which is maintained even under the most difficult circumstances.

By their refusal to remarry, widows can place financial claims on their husband's relatives for support and thereby maintain independent households. Many people believe that a new husband will treat his wife's children from a previous marriage poorly and, if the woman is still able to bear children, will favor the couple's new children. Occasionally, potential suitors will insist that a mother relinquish custody of her children to her former husband's family, particularly when the woman is divorced rather than widowed. Women and men commonly express the opinion that remarriage after bearing children is *Haraam*, or forbidden, although there is no legal prescription against it. When one husband died leaving his forty-year-old wife with seven children to support, she refused to remarry. Every year, when this widow's brothers returned from their jobs in the Gulf countries, they would bring her fabric and other presents, gifts she saw as part of their obligation to support her family.

In another family a young woman with three children was widowed when her husband suffered a sudden heart attack. Since she was so young, her older brother encouraged her to remarry. However, her older sister, who was herself twice divorced, forbade her to remarry, supposedly for the sake of the children. The older sister had remarried after her first marriage but was soon divorced again. These two sisters lived near each other, and the widowhood of the younger sister provided support for the older sister's position as a single head of her household. The young widow waited for six years before she finally married a widower who expected to have more children with his new wife. However, unlike her older sister's second husband, she argued her new husband would treat her children well since he brought several children of his own into the marriage.

When children are orphaned by the death of both parents, they are typically cared for by older siblings or other relatives. Relatives contribute to support the household if the children are older, or welcome them into their own households. However, poor families cannot usually offer financial assistance, since they are barely able to meet the expenses of their own family. Unless it is a situation where all the children are extremely young, elder siblings will try to maintain the household. The children who are old enough to work join the labor force. In these neighborhoods it is possible for very young children, over the age of five or six, to find employment as apprentices in manufacturing workshops, bakeries, or warehouses.

Small manufacturing workshops that pervade commercial areas of the inner city and some outlying new residential areas are common sources of employment for very young workers (between the ages of ten and sixteen). Most of these children work because they must support themselves, or elderly parents, or must contribute to the upkeep of a single-parent household (usually headed by a female). In a study surveying 2,432 owners and employees of 531 manufacturing enterprises in *sha'bi* neighborhoods, Meyer discovered that one out of five workers was younger than fifteen, while 6 percent had not reached the age of ten.[52] In the aluminum manufacturing industry, a significant employer in central Cairo, one study found that 34 percent of the labor force is comprised of boys under the age of fifteen and 12 percent of the labor force is between the ages of five and nine.[53]

On occasion, girls are also compelled to support themselves and their families. Young women who are orphaned or who have elderly parents to support may contribute to the daily expenses of the household and must finance the considerable costs of their marriage by themselves. Even if she does not need to support the household, a young orphaned woman would be primarily responsible for her wedding expenses. In one instance, a young woman in the neighborhood was supported by her older brother after their parents died. Her uncles, who were very poor, could not offer support to her and her siblings. Both she and her older brother were trying to save for their respective marriage expenses; the young woman held two jobs and also earned occasional income as a seamstress for clients in her neighborhood.

When a man divorces a woman who has no experience in the formal or informal labor market, she must find a way to support any children that remain in her custody.[54] If she has never attended school, or after years of not using her skills is functionally illiterate, she often must seek employment in some of the lowest-paid and lowest-status positions—for example, servants, cooks, janitors, factory workers, or petty traders in local markets. One woman, who had no relatives in Cairo, was divorced by her husband and awarded custody of only one of her seven children. Although still fairly young, she had few marketable skills but finally found a job as a janitor and messenger at a charitable organization through the influence of a kind neighbor who worked for the same organization. She earned extra money by shopping for neighbors or colleagues from work, walking small children to and from school and a day-care center, and delivering messages. She was a shrewd woman, but very poor, and at times tried to evade paying for her share of the communal breakfasts at work. Usually people tolerated this behavior because they understood that this woman was very *maskiina* (not only poor but someone who has had a very hard life and is basically a good person) and was only trying to provide for her daughter. The staff of the organization she worked for had registered her in their literacy program so she could earn a diploma that would entitle her to work in an unskilled public-sector position, thus giving her important benefits she would not receive in a low-paying private-sector job. Eventually, however, her pilfering and demands for small tips, or *ba'shiish*, aggravated too many people and she was unceremoniously fired. Later she was to be found in the informal economy selling chick peas on the sidewalk near her home in a public housing project.

At times, an individual's strategy for maintaining his or her household can be the seeds of another household's destruction, or at least disarray. Polygyny is one of the rarer marital arrangements in Egypt and other Muslim societies which often produce tension and competition for resources and affection. In a sample survey of Cairo, Amman, and Beirut, less than 1 percent of the households was found to include polygynous marriages (though the incidence of polygyny in rural households was slightly higher).[55] Within my community in central Cairo, there were only three people who were involved in polygynous relationships, although I knew some details about a fourth polygynous relationship from people in an entirely different community. In two of these cases, the second marriages were kept a secret from the first wives. Both of the women in the second marriages were widows (one had been divorced from a second husband after being widowed in her first marriage and so this was her third marriage). In the third case, a man married a second wife because his first wife had been unable to conceive. The fourth case represents a growing cause of polygyny among returning male migrants to Egypt who have money burning their pockets. One poor young man from a *sha'bi* neighborhood had married a woman from his neighborhood and left shortly thereafter for Kuwait. Every few years he would return for a brief visit. When he finally returned to Egypt permanently, he wanted to (and could afford to) marry a second, younger, more educated woman, who would bring him more status than the first wife who shared his humble background.

In the most complicated case, a widow had become friends with a neighbor's husband as the two commuted together to work over a period of five years. The couple moved away from the neighborhood, but the widow (who was only in her late thirties and who supported three children) continued to see this man while commuting to work. She had been widowed for five years, and eventually they decided to marry secretly and legally. According to customary law, *'il-gawaaz 'il-'urfi*, the only requirement for marriage is that the couple sign a wedding contract also signed by a witness. The man always kept the contract with him in his wallet. In the first few years of their secret marriage, the couple would spend time together in a rented furnished flat in a distant part of town where they would not be recognized. Only the closest friend of this woman knew of her remarriage; her children, while perhaps suspicious of their mother's absences, were unaware of it. Not wanting to lose the support of her deceased husband's relatives may have been another reason that the woman also kept the marriage a secret. The man, in his mid-forties, did not inform his first wife of the marriage, which he was under no legal obligation to do, at that time.[56]

After four years of leading a double life, they decided to tell her children and some friends and colleagues about the marriage. When her neighbors found out about the marriage, one of them sent an anonymous note to the first wife, who immediately ran to the second wife's neighborhood to discover if the note was true. She was enraged and devastated by her husband's duplicity and her friend's betrayal and tried to force him to divorce the second wife. He responded by threatening to divorce her instead. Having little recourse, she accepted the marriage but demanded more financial support so that he would not have any money for his second wife. The first wife quickly became pregnant and gave birth to a boy, even though her other children were in secondary school and university. Each wife, in attempts to protect her own interests, made incessant demands on this man.

Unable to tolerate the pressure any longer, he finally divorced the second wife. He clearly did not have the courage to face his second wife since he sent her written notification of the divorce through the mail. She insisted that her husband had not acted "like a man" and should not have tolerated the pressure from his first wife. Soon, however, the man returned to the second wife, only to separate from her again six months later.

From the perspective of a second wife who is widowed or divorced and supporting children with very limited resources, polygyny may be a more attractive alternative than being a single parent. Through polygyny, a women may (or may not) gain some of the financial, emotional, and sexual advantages of marriage without losing control of her household. Often an older woman who might enter into this type of marriage has lived independently for many years and is not eager to give up her autonomy. However, many members of the community consider women who enter into polygynous relationships "home wreckers" since these relationships, if discovered, can cause lasting emotional pain to the first wife and her children as well as diverting economic support from the first household to the second.

In the second case of polygyny in the community, a woman who was widowed and then divorced from a second husband married an older man employed as a driver for a hospital administrator. Every few weeks her new husband would tell his first wife that he was driving his boss to a distant province and then spend a few days with the second wife and her young daughter from the second marriage. He was also a former neighbor of his second wife, but he managed to keep his second marriage completely secret. Though not frequent, it is not entirely uncommon in Egypt for a first wife to discover when her husband dies that he has been married to another woman and has had other children. In these situations, the inheritance and pension must be divided between two families, and needless to say, these circumstances can be extremely painful for those who have been kept in the dark for so many years.

While the incidence of polygyny has decreased significantly in recent years, it still is practiced in *sha'bi* communities, although many people consider it anachronistic. The community does not look favorably upon men who take second wives when they become wealthy or who keep their second marriage a secret from their family, but it is more acceptable for men to marry a second wife if they have not been able to have children. Women, in this situation, sometimes prefer polygyny to a divorce from their husband (divorce is a not uncommon response to fertility problems in marriage). The man in my community who had taken a second wife because his first wife could not bear children insisted that his wives were friends and that they were satisfied with this arrangement. His first wife, whom he said he still loved, was his cousin, and divorcing her would have probably destroyed family harmony.

In all these cases, however, there is a financial disincentive for a man to take a second wife, since it is very expensive to support even one household in Cairo, especially within a low-income community. Women in polygynous marriages usually insist on separate households, which increases the cost of polygyny. Shortly after the man mentioned just above married a second wife, she gave birth to twins and he was forced to take a second job to meet the financial demands of two households.

In sum, polygyny exists, but does not flourish in *sha'bi* communities. Primarily, people resort to polygyny as a way of "shoring up" households. In my community widowed and divorced women became second wives in an effort to strengthen and improve their financial and social situations—without forfeiting the independence and autonomy of their status as head of a household. Infertile women tolerate polygyny as a way of maintaining their marriages, their financial position, and their standing in the community.

Polygyny is also a way for men to legitimize sexual relations with other women because marrying more than one woman is far more publicly acceptable than having an adulterous affair. From the woman's point of view, the offspring of such a union are legitimate and have full rights of inheritance. Furthermore, marriage forces the man to support the woman and her children. If a young girl knowingly marries a man with another family, she will demand that normal protocol be followed and that he fulfill all the financial and social traditions surrounding marriage. If an older woman who is divorced or widowed enters into a polygynous marriage, she too will insist upon a certain amount of social and financial support. While some married women may have adulterous affairs at great risk, unmarried women are far more likely to insist on marriage. Revelation of illicit sexual affairs would almost certainly tarnish any woman's reputation and position in her community, but it would be far worse for an unmarried woman (who, as earlier noted, is assumed to be a virgin) since even gossip or evidence of an affair would "ruin" her chances for a good marriage in the future and perhaps result in a violent attack on her from her family and male relatives.

Unfortunately, one woman's strategy for "shoring up" her household and fulfilling her emotional needs through polygyny may be extremely painful and difficult for another woman's family (the first wife). In many cases, when a man marries a second wife, for whatever reasons, the first wife and family is neglected. These women, while officially married, are better characterized as permanently separated, since they receive minimal financial support for their children from their husband and no longer engage in conjugal relations. Additionally, because they are not divorced they cannot remarry. Thus, although it is legal, this latter type of polygynous relationship is universally condemned for eroding the familial ethos in the community.

Bonds of Tradition

The familial ethos is reinforced and encouraged in the community by many traditions that celebrate events in the life course of families. Births, graduations, engagements, weddings, and funerals become occasions for members of the family to renew their commitment and bonds with each other. Relatives and families visit each other very frequently, exchanging news, advice, and services. Close family ties encourage the interdependence of the community, which serves to reinforce the familial ethos in *sha'bi* communities. The interdependence of the community, based on the principles of the familial ethos, also encourages men and women to abide by its norms. As families and individuals interact, the rules of the game are more widely and persuasively articulated, and people rely upon the familial ethos for financial support, emotional gratification, and for mediation and conflict resolution. If these are the rules of the game and an individual ignores those rules, he or she may suffer from community opprobrium or rejection. When finding a job, a fiancé, a home, or interacting with the bureaucracy, these people will not have access to the same set of resources and information as another respected community figure who lives comfortably with the familial ethos and works to encourage community cooperation, mediation, information-exchange, and informal networks. The everyday life of people, lived out through many rituals, celebrations, and social interaction, reinforces the norms of the familial ethos by encouraging interdependence, reciprocity, and what Eickelman has called "closeness" (*qaraaba*) in his discussion of Moroccan society:

> "Closeness" carries contextual meanings which range imperceptibly from asserted and recognized ties of kinship to participation in factional alliances, ties of patronage and clientship, and common bonds developed through neighborliness. Closeness is constituted by compelling ties of obligations. Often closeness is expressed as a 'blood' tie, even when no demonstrable lineal ties exist, because however such ties are valued in practice, they are considered permanent and cannot be broken.[57]

Many of the guests at celebrations, funerals, or the simple Friday ritual of gathering together for a leisurely special meal, are related to one another. At large public events such as wedding processions, neighbors and colleagues are invited, but people generally associate with relatives. Those families who have few relatives in Cairo may develop close ties with local neighbors, but even families who live far apart travel frequently to visit their relatives.

These frequent visits are usually quite informal and not very ritualistic. The women may help each other to prepare the Friday meal, while the men leave for Friday prayers, and the children play in the street, on the roof, or in the apartment. Later, when the whole family is assembled, there will be an exchange of news or gossip and, often, a conference aimed at solving a prob-

9. The young boy in the middle celebrates his birthday with his extended family. Among the newly wealthy *Harafiyyiin* (the boy's father is a machinist), birthday celebrations are becoming far more common than they used to be, and more lavish.

lem faced by a relative or neighbor. On Fridays, other members of the family or neighbors may "pass by" to discuss a particular problem or recent event, knowing that the family will be together that day. The private sector of manufacturing workshops and local stores and markets all close on Sunday, rather than Friday, and skilled blue-collar workers (*Harafiyyiin*) usually work on Friday and relax with their families on Sunday. In one family with economic ties in the manufacturing sector, twenty-four people would stay overnight in the matriarch's apartment in order to spend their holiday together. While there is nothing unique about families spending time together throughout the world, in Egypt the frequency and regularity of visits is much greater. If part of an extended family stays away for several Fridays (or Sundays), it is interpreted as a sign of a serious trouble.

When foreigners are invited to an Egyptian home, they are often incorporated into the family within a very short time and are expected to visit regularly. At the end of a meal a visitor will be asked when he or she will come again. Usually, the host will insist that the guest visit the following Friday, if not before. When they see each other again, the welcome will be effusive, and they will be chastised for not having visited sooner. Attempts to leave are rebuffed and guests are told they must stay longer. The host will declare frequently to the guest *nawwart il-beet* (you have brought light to our house) or, more effusively, *nawwart maSr* (you have lighted up Cairo).

It is very important to show respect for one's guests, to offer them hospitality, and to make them feel extremely welcome. The most expensive and elaborate meals are prepared for important guests, and if they cannot stay for a meal they must at least have tea or something cold to drink. In Cairo today, it is current practice for children to be sent out to the local grocer to buy a cold soda as this beverage now constitutes the appropriate sign of a guest's importance. The host will also insist that the guest share a meal and complain later that he or she has not eaten enough. The hospitality of Egyptians is renowned and a source of pride.

When people judge the reputation of a family in the community, they often will recount in detail the quantity and quality of the food and drink offered to guests. The heritage of scarcity in this community still has a deep influence on people's judgments, and while generosity is commended people are very aware of the value of food, gifts, or even the cost of a cold drink. A multicourse meal with chicken, meat, pasta, rice, vegetables, pickles, tea, desert, fruit, and so forth, signifies that the guest is an honored and valued visitor to that household. Hospitality must be reciprocated, and the recipient of a huge meal will be expected to prepare a similar meal for the host when he or she next visits. The cost of entertaining visitors can become too expensive, which sometimes results in a refusal to share a meal at someone else's home, even when invited to do so, since the courtesy cannot be reciprocated. As Khouri-Dagher notes, the poorest families cannot afford to entertain visitors or exchange gifts and therefore do not participate in utilitarian familial and neighborhood networks within the lower-income community.[58] They are thus even more socially isolated and economically marginalized. Hoodfar has explained that maintaining one's social status in a community is costly and includes hidden expenses, which families must absorb.[59] Because generosity and hospitality increase one's position in the community and strengthen one's web of social, economic, and political networks, if people can possibly afford to they embrace these norms.

In addition to routine weekly visits, relatives have a stronger obligation to visit each other on important holidays and celebrations such as weddings, funerals, engagements, *subuuᶜ* (a traditional ceremony, held seven days after the birth of a child), or religious celebrations like the Islamic month of Ramadan when families gather to break the daily fast together. These events celebrate important rites of passage in Egyptian society, and the community reaffirms the importance of these events by its participation. Weddings, in particular, are very social occasions where members of the family, guests, and neighbors march in a traditional street procession (*zaffa*), dress up, eat special food, meet friends and relatives, and perhaps under certain circumstances even dance. Weddings provide a chaperoned setting for young men and women to meet potential suitors. Since weddings are usually held outside in a courtyard or alleyway, they are communal events (although only invited guests consume the available refreshments).

While the following chapter will discuss the family's intimate involvement in marriage, families also organize funerals, *subuuᶜ*, and Ramadan meals. When a Muslim dies, the funeral must be held within twenty-four hours, and a family of any means will set up a large tent in the street where the men (and women, at different times) gather to pay their respects for the deceased for three successive nights.[60] A sheikh reads the Koran, and when he is not there religious music is played on a tape recorder. At home, women mourners, dressed in black, gather to pay their respects and are served unsweetened coffee (the traditional drink for condolence calls). Once the funeral tent comes down, men also pay their respects at the deceased's home. Unless the family is very orthodox, women as well as men accompany the corpse to the familial plot in the cemeteries that surround the northern and southern walls of the old Fatimid city of Cairo. In these processions, the female relatives demonstrate their grief by ululating, as the procession passes through the surrounding neighborhoods.

At specific interludes following the death (the first four Fridays, and the 'il-'arba'iin or forty-day anniversary), the family will bake pastries and bring oranges, dates, and tea to the family tomb to commemorate the death. The women and men, sitting separately on these occasions, listen as a religious man reads the Koran, and relatives and friends pay their condolences. Members of the family alternate responsibility for baking and purchasing the other ritual food on this occasion. During the year, at specific points in the Islamic calendar (the tenth of Sha'baan, the first day of the 'il-'iid ik-kibiir, and so on), relatives will return to the tomb to pay their respects to the deceased and to share ritual foods and listen to recitals of the Koran.

On another important popular religious holiday in Egypt, *Muulid in-Nabi* (the birthday of MuHammad the Prophet), families visit each other and distribute sugar dolls to girls and knights to boys.[61] People also purchase traditional *Muulid* sweets from kiosks set up all over the city for relatives, friends, and employees. The price of these sweets has risen considerably in recent years to the extent that it is not unusual for a young man to spend £E30 ($21), approximately a quarter to a third of his monthly salary, on a box of candy for his fiancée. The fiancé of one young woman in the neighborhood insisted that his entire family accompany him when he delivered his expensive box of sweets to his future bride. The value of the sweets, and the fact that his family accompanied him to pay their respects to her family on this holiday, signified his esteem for her and her family. Even public-sector factories distribute these boxes of sweets to their employees. It has been rumored that managers occasionally suggest distributing cash bonuses instead of sweets on *Muulid in-Nabi*, but employees object too strenuously.

Some families who see each other several times a month will vacation together during the long summer school holidays. If a family can possibly afford a few days or a week along the Mediterranean or Red Sea, they will rent a small flat or bungalow. Many large public- and private-sector firms arrange summer outings and vacations for their employees. Self-employed *Harafiyyiin* or workshop owners usually close their workshops during important religious holidays, and if these fall in the summer they will take their families on a brief vacation, if finances permit. While this constant interaction between families on Fridays, celebrations, holidays, and vacations can lead to occasional conflict, people generally prefer to spend their leisure time with their most important associates: their relatives. The familial ethos is further strengthened by these social bonds.

CONCLUSION: AN ETHOS BEYOND THE HOUSEHOLD

A young woman who fights to marry a local boyfriend, a man who decides to marry a second wife, a separated couple that seeks the arbitration of an uncle, and a teenager who fights with an older half brother over his independence share a desire to further personal interests. To succeed they must convince others that their actions are reasonable and proper and that the family, as a whole, will not be adversely affected by an individual interest, since these conflicts impinge directly on political and economic dynamics within the household and the extended family. Individuals protect their position in the family to gain support, legitimacy, and power. A person's standing in the larger community is enhanced by an esteemed or secure position within the family. In a similar manner, a person who succeeds in the market or graduates from a prestigious university increases his or her status and position in the family. The relationship between family dynamics and power within the community is interdependent. The familial ethos is a basis for solidarity, a basis for membership in the larger collective body of the community.

The familial ethos informs these decisions and interpersonal relations within households and the community. A desire for unity, a current of competition, and a preference for maintaining tradition can all influence mundane and important issues. This ethos, however, influences far more than the resolution of intrahousehold conflict, power, and authority. People's values, their opinions, interests, and goals are not expressed solely within the walls of their homes. They resonate upwards throughout the community, the economy, and the nation as a whole. Interests that are important in maintaining the family are pursued within the larger community. Such issues as Personal Status Law (which regulates marriage, inheritance, divorce, and child custody), the social and economic structure of the household, proper sexual relations between men and women, drug use, domestic violence and violence among the young, childrearing practices, changes in civil codes to reflect more Islamic legal norms, the importance of motherhood, religious education, plus the issue of working women, fill the airwaves, television, pages of government, opposition, and Islamic newspapers and magazines, and official government reports as well as studies by domestic and international organizations. A consensus about the relationship between private, public, and governmental spheres has not been established in Egypt, leaving basic questions about individual and collective rights, representation, and the source of governmental authority (God, the President, Parliament, the people, the military, or foreign powers). Certainly, different interests in Egyptian society now have greater resources at their disposal to promote their various viewpoints, but as communities maintain and sustain their visions of a good society they enter the debate and negotiate over the future direction of the country.

I do not mean to suggest that the familial ethos is a static, monolithic set of preferences for all people, under all circumstances. Rather, it is one of the important influences on behavior and action within *sha'bi* communities, where the family retains strong economic, political, and social functions. It represents an ideal around which local disputes are contested and national disputes are contextualized. Bonds of unity, discord, dissolution, and tradition shape the lives of men and women in *sha'bi* communities and shape the preferences of this community and their ideals. Because the family is still very meaningful to the community, and because it organizes economic forces and political relationships in the community, the familial ethos influences individuals and groups when they deal with a broader spectrum of issues and problems. As the following chapter will discuss in more detail, when the goal of reproducing the family is threatened by changing economic conditions, a war, or legal reforms, people are deeply concerned and follow the implications of such changes. Both women and men are assertive watchdogs of possible challenges to the family and the community. As JoAnn Martin argues in her study of women's political participation in Mexico, the daily involvement of women in raising, housing, feeding, and providing for children "gives them a stake in political participation. As women they defend their political action from charges of self-interest by stressing their roles as mothers. Theirs is a morally justified politics. Their political work is done in the interest of community, the future of community members, not just the moment at hand."[62] I am not making a culturally defined argument about the familial ethos, but rather would suggest that men and women are, as Wolin would say, "laying down basic and general principles, which, when legitimated, become the presuppositions of practices, the ethos of practitioners."[63] When the *sha'b* promote the familial ethos, they are engaging in theoretical founding and demonstrating the superiority, legitimacy, and merit of their set of constitutive principles.

The political dimension of the familial ethos must be understood within the context of a tradition of political exclusion in Egypt *and* an understanding of politics, both among elites and political scientists alike, which excludes the family and informal political institutions from consideration because they are not part of the public realm. The following chapters, however, will demonstrate the ways in which informal networks incorporate the household into the public arena and assist the *sha'b* in pursuit of their material objectives and philosophical vision(s). Informal networks are one of the most important avenues of participation for this community. The backbone of informal networks—mutual reciprocity, trust, and shared interest—is built upon the principles of the familial ethos. As will be demonstrated repeatedly in the following chapters, people exert considerable calculated efforts to achieve common objectives and to connect their household to important officials or merchants, to elite politicians, and to people with a wide range of practical skills and resources. These networks begin in the household and interact with other constellations of power and authority, emanating from different settings throughout Egypt.

CHAPTER 2

Reproducing the Family

THIS CHAPTER explores and analyzes one of the most commonly shared interests in *shaʿbi* communities: reproducing the family. As argued earlier in the Introduction, before one can understand the politics of a community one must understand its particular structure, economy, collective institutions, and shared goals and preferences. I found that the objective of reproducing the family touched upon deeply held normative preferences, economic activities, cultural values, symbols, and the social structure of the community. Men and women designed collective institutions within the community to further this aim, thus enriching its collective life and its repertoire of political institutions. Understanding this need to reproduce the family within the community was essential to understanding much of the behavior and opinions of men and women—both at the level of "low" politics and "high" politics.

The goal of marriage and procreation (within the legal bounds of matrimony) vexes young men and women between the ages of sixteen and thirty-five, their parents, and the legions of relatives, friends, colleagues, and neighbors who play a role in the process.[1] Impending marriages affect career choices, education, employment, investment, migration, savings, and consumption patterns of men and women. Parents organize their savings and consumption strategies to be able to finance the marriage of their children, sacrificing their material comfort for the future of the family—not unlike parents in the United States who begin saving for a child's college education as soon as he or she is born. And young men and women often spend several years desperately trying to accumulate the necessary sums needed to finance a wedding. Marriage gives them a measure of autonomy, control over a new household, and public sanction to satisfy their emotional and sexual needs. With marriage and the birth of the first child, they complete the process of reproducing the family. Practically and normatively, it is extremely difficult to accomplish any of these goals outside the institution of marriage. Apart from students and conscripts, almost the entire population of Cairo resides with its family until marriage. The Koranic injunction in Islam that marriage is one-half of religion demonstrates its role in Muslim society. Marriage plays a similarly critical role for Christians in Egypt as well.

At issue, in this struggle, is the regeneration of the family unit itself. Through marriage, each generation transfers financial resources to the next and hopes to maintain the wealth, reputation, and status of the family. Individuals and families act collectively to amass the largest investment that they will probably make in their lives. The community collaborates to plan a marriage, and the resources of the two families involved are mobilized around this goal, often for several years. Perhaps prosperous merchants or traders will invest larger sums in commerce or industry, but for the majority of men and women in *sha'bi* communities, marriage remains the largest single capital investment. Most couples, when they marry, enjoy a higher material standard of living than they will ever experience again in their lives, as they move into a new or renovated apartment, wear new clothes from their trousseau, sit on new furniture, eat from new plates, and cook in new pots and pans. At the same time, marriage is not solely an excuse for consumerist and materialistic impulses, since monies are invested in valuable physical assets: housing, gold, and furniture.[2]

Apart from the important intergenerational exchange of resources, a young couple must also negotiate standardized and elaborate protocols before they finally consummate the marriage sexually. These practices are defined both by communal traditions and legal precepts in Islam and in the Egyptian legal system. To choose a spouse, families and the community use well-known criteria, based on the familial ethos, and continually monitor his or her behavior throughout the engagement period. The involvement of the community in arbitrating and mediating marriages will be addressed in the first two sections of this chapter.

Reproducing the family is not only a concern of individuals and families; throughout Egyptian society, questions of morality, sexuality, and reproducing the family are publicly debated in most oral and written forms of expression (literature, film, newspapers, poetry, television, and theater). Marriage, divorce, and child custody is regulated by Egyptian law, and conflicts are mediated by the court system. Recent changes in Personal Status Law in 1979 and 1985 have been hotly contested by Islamic activists, political parties, feminist groups, and women's associations. Regardless of the opinions of public figures, everyone agrees that these questions do matter to Egyptians.

Sexual practices and gender relations (discussed in the third section) at times are congruent with, and under other circumstances may transgress, the moral ideals and traditions of the community. Within *sha'bi* communities, and Egyptian society in general, there is a far wider spectrum of sexual behavior and gender relations than is routinely represented in the media, or by many Egyptians and foreign scholars. While the community tries to enforce notions of sexual propriety, honor, and respect, these are ideals that are contested locally by alternative practices and beliefs. There is far more diversity within these communities than meets the eye. Ideals are neither "traditional" nor unchanging, as a wide range of phenomena and shifting constellations of power and interest in Egypt transform or promote new and old models. Occasionally, certain incidents and phenomena, such as a sudden rise in the incidence of rape or the issue of female circumcision, become public and politically sensitive issues, which various constituencies in Egypt use to express opposition to the current regime or to the political and economic system, as a whole. Because of the controls on political expression and associational life in Egypt, it is far easier to attack the government through diatribes about declining morality and decadence than it is to launch a street demonstration, strike, or new political party.

The fifth and sixth sections of the chapter will describe and analyze the pattern of massive capital accumulation for marriage and its consequences for the political economy of *sha'bi* communities. Financing a wedding or purchasing a marital apartment is an economic transaction; however, when the entire community is mobilized and organized to establish new households, it must be seen as a collective need that is politically significant. Many of the informal institutions created within communities across Egypt are, in fact, designed to meet the goal of reproducing the family. These institutions organize the interests of the community and are useful for fulfilling objectives, outside of marriage as well. Thus, an unintended consequence of marriage politics in Egypt is a pervasive grid of institutions which organize and articulate the demands of the popular sector in a collective fashion.

Finally, the conclusion to the chapter argues that the massive investment of scarce capital in marriage influences the political economy of the nation in several ways. Informal savings associations, or *gam'iyyaat* (pl.), are extremely common in *sha'bi* communities (and throughout Egyptian society). Huge sums of money circulate within them and provide credit on a scale that competes with the formal banking system. *Gam'iyyaat* allow men and women to accumulate the savings needed to marry and to meet other significant financial needs. While families and communities benefit from this informal financial system, the government does not, since these sums remain outside the formal banking system and the reach of tax authorities. However, *sha'bi* communities benefit tremendously from these informal economic institutions. Unfortunately, these sums are not "counted" in Egypt's formal economy, which challenges the figures for a series of official economic indicators in Egypt, such as the national savings rate, private savings rate, and investment rates.

While *sha'bi* communities are committed and organized around the goal of reproducing the family, the government only indirectly addresses this need through its provision of certain services that subsidize some of its associated costs. At the same time, other government policies have significant intended and unintended consequences on the community's ability to afford marriages. Individuals make sensitive, detailed, and long-range allocational decisions in order to finance marriages, and small price increases or changes in migration or employment policies can upset carefully laid strategies. Thus, in addition to other factors, people react to, and judge, certain government policies vis á vis their effect on the goal of reproducing the family.

The *sha'b*'s economic resourcefulness, encouraged through informal institutions, has certain unintended consequences on state capacity and administration. For example, the demand for housing among newlyweds, returning migrants, and prosperous families has created sprawling, informal settlements on land surrounding Cairo. As people build their own homes, organize private services, and open unregulated, unlicensed, and untaxed businesses, certain pressures are placed on the state. If the government hopes to enforce its fiscal power in these areas, it must provide services. If it wants to control political and economic life in these new areas, it must invest in enforcement and administrative services. Negotiations between community leaders and bureaucrats to incorporate these communities into the administrative apparatus of the state are prolonged and sensitive because most of these residences are actually constructed illegally or sit on land that is not zoned for residential use. And while the nation may benefit from the infusion of informal investment in new housing, the government must respond to the unintended consequences of the accumulated desires of young couples to find affordable housing. Government funds and attention must be redirected toward these new densely populated areas, placing new pressures on an already overextended state, which has only tenuous links to these new areas.

CHOOSING A MATE:
SHABABIIK, SHABABIIK, ʾID-DUNYA KULLAHA SHABABIIK[3]

One Friday a carpenter from the neighborhood was called to replace the old, broken lock on a family's front door. Because the mother of the family had once been invited to share a meal with the carpenter's family, she caught up on news of his family—and in particular, recent marriages—while he replaced the lock. She then reciprocated by supplying him with information about the marriages in her own family, finally mentioning the upcoming engagement of her youngest daughter. At that point the daughter ended the conversation by telling her mother to stop pestering the carpenter since, "After all, didn't he come to fix our door rather than talk about marriages and engagements?" Similar scenes were often enacted throughout the community. When anyone met a relative, neighbor, or colleague that he or she had not seen for a while, vital information about local marriages would be exchanged. This unending concern for information about marriages provided an up-to-date account of unmarried men and women from the community (the candidate pool, so to speak). In addition, gossip about a recent marriage might reveal information allowing others to decide if a match with the same family would be prudent or attractive. Because marriage involves many sensitive financial, emotional, and sexual issues, disputes (which are not uncommon) often reveal internal family matters that otherwise might not be publicly aired.

The criteria used by the community to judge prospective mates for their children logically reflect its values and concerns. A man is judged according to his moral character, family reputation, wealth, occupation, and education, while a woman's moral character, politeness, family reputation, education, and resourcefulness are most crucial. Women are not expected to

10. The man in the undershirt in the window was the father of a young woman that the youngest son in my Egyptian family was interested in. During the summer, there was a constant stream of chatting and joking through the open windows even though the two families (and certainly not the young sweethearts) never visited each other in their homes. This relationship had the early markings of a *shababiik* affair, or a love affair that transpires over balconies.

support a family, but due to the high cost of living in Egypt both educated and uneducated women have had to join the labor force in larger numbers in order to do so. However, some men within my community refused to allow their wives to work, despite the latter's qualifications and interest. They believed that men should fulfill their traditional role as the sole bread-winner, and anything less would be humiliating. Women may carefully investigate whether a potential groom objects to her working before she marries. Disagreements over the issue of a wife's working can at times unravel engagements. However, many lower-middle-class families have come to depend on two cash incomes out of economic necessity, and thus a woman's earning potential can attract some suitors.

In Cairo the rate of endogamous marriage (within the kin group) is quite high (32 percent), and the same general framework for evaluating a potential mate applies to relatives as well. The rate of consanguineous marriages is higher for those women with less than a primary school certificate (35 percent) and lower for those with a primary school certificate and above (20.2). Interestingly, the average age of women who marry their relatives is one and a half years younger than the general population of married women.[4] As in all families, there are some young men and women who are well-liked and respected, and others who are not. However, a well-educated, sincere, prosperous cousin is usually more acceptable than a well-educated, sincere, prosperous young man from the neighborhood or the university. Consanguineous marriages in Cairo are often less expensive and less complicated since the parties know and trust each other and cooperate more effectively. At the same time, when cousin-marriages fail, the results can be disastrous since various parts of the extended family invariably become embroiled in the dispute. One such case was the cause of a noisy fight in the neighborhood: the mother of a young husband (who had married his cousin supposedly under pressure from his family) called the police to arrest her son, whom the mother accused of stealing money from her to finance his second marriage.

Among families with rural origins, the prevalence of endogamous marriages is even higher. As one young woman explained, she was marrying her *'ibn 'amm* (the son of her paternal uncle) because families from Upper Egypt wanted their daughters to marry within the family, and one's *'ibn 'amm* is the preferred match. Both the bride and groom (who was much older) were born and raised in Cairo but adhered to Upper Egyptian traditions.

Under different circumstances, one partner's rural traditions may clash with the urban origins of the other. One young woman brought her wedding plans to a halt when she discovered that she would be expected to live in one room of her in-laws' house, as is customary with extended families of rural origins. She argued that all her sisters had lived in apartments after they married and, not wanting any less than they had, she insisted on the same arrangement. Even though this family now lived in Cairo, they retained this custom of living together as an extended family under one roof and expected their sons to join them upon marriage. When her fiancé would not disappoint his parents' expectations, the engagement was broken off by mutual consent.

In *sha'bi* communities the examination of a young man or woman's moral character and suitability for marriage begins before the engagement is publicly announced and continues until the consummation of the marriage (the *duxla*). Despite the supposed importance of a suitor's character and reputation, the choice of a mate is often hasty and determined more by the financial resources at his disposal than his reputation. This practice is a typical example of the contradiction between theory and practice in these communities. Once a man commits himself to saving money for marriage and has enough cash at least for some of the initial costs, it is not very difficult to find a bride.

A young man sets his female and male relatives to search for a bride, or the family begins the search without his consent. When one young man had accumulated sufficient resources to begin thinking about marriage, a relative of his sister-in-law, who lived in a different neighborhood, arranged three interviews in a single day with young women in her neighborhood. He fancied a young woman he met in his last stop in the neighborhood and was married within three months. When the mother in another large family decided it was time that her eldest son married, she and her eldest daughter quickly arranged meetings with several families with eligible daughters. After disappointing formal teas with a few prospects, a younger brother suggested a young woman who lived in their same building as a candidate. He had only learned of her existence after knocking on their door to warn them of a fire in the building, and she had answered. Since this young woman's father had been working in Libya for many years, her upbringing had been very strict and the eldest son had never seen her despite living in the same building for years. The young man's family considered her seclusion and the traditional values of her family a sign of her good character. Shortly after the tea where the son met the woman briefly, the two neighbors were married.

Even more hurried matches are arranged when a worker who has been out of the country returns to Egypt. A migrant worker might marry within the span of a month-long holiday. Some of these men may have been engaged for a long time, while others may meet their brides during their vacation, and because they have returned to Egypt with a large sum of money they can marry within a month. Most people consider these marriages too risky, since the families do not have enough time to evaluate the character of the groom or his family. Occasionally, people liken these marriages to the sale of one's daughter, but usually the family of a migrant worker in this situation has been hard at work arranging all the details of the match long before the migrant returns. At times this situation hardly resembles a marriage, since the man immediately returns to his job overseas, only returning to Egypt for one month a year, sometimes for years on end.

"Selling" daughters to wealthy grooms in Gulf countries tempts some families from these communities, whose relatives work abroad and serve as intermediaries to arrange such marriages. For example, after a mother had suffered through one daughter's engagement to someone she did not really like, she considered a proposal from her brother who worked in Saudi Arabia to marry her younger daughter at an early age to a Saudi acquaintance of his. In the end, the mother decided against the marriage, despite the prodding of her wealthy brother.

This is a problem not only in *sha'bi* communities but throughout Egypt as well, and it has received considerable attention from the national media. In a long article, an opposition newspaper, *al-Sha'b*, investigated two troubling phenomena related to the rising cost of marriage: poor Egyptian girls who marry wealthy foreigners (largely older Arab men from wealthy Gulf countries), and poor or lower-middle-class Egyptian men who marry foreign women (largely Europeans). The article condemns tourist marriages, which have flourished within the last ten years, "because [their] sole objective is gratification and pleasure or, to be more precise, a fixation with pleasure, which Egyptian families have resorted to because of poverty, and pressure on a girl." In Giza province, a fifty-year-old foreign man married a seventeen-year-old girl for a dower of £E700 and two gold bracelets. (A dower, *maHr*, is the gift due from a groom to a bride as part of the financial arrangements of marriage. A dowry, *gihaaz*, consists of the items that the bride's family provides for the couple, which are explained below.) "The girl was from a poor family in a difficult social position, and she concluded that marriage to a poor young man would only increase her poverty. She wanted to live better and went to a woman who worked as a broker [*simsaar*] for this type of marriage." After she was married, her husband divorced her two weeks later and she returned to her family.[5] The article also describes another case where a 55-year-old man from Dubai married an eleven-year-old bride (which is illegal). The marriage lasted six months. This man was already married and had grandchildren her age.

The problem of Egyptian men marrying foreign women is also explained in economic terms. A young man who was interviewed explained: "In Germany the costs of marriage are a great deal easier than here. . . . In Egypt the dowry and the *shabka* [see note 11] and the like are so expensive. I am a young man from a modest background, and if I waited the marriage train would pass me by." Another young man married an Italian woman whom he had met in Egypt. "I don't regret this step because my salary here was not more than £E80, and how could I live and think about an apartment or marriage?"[6] At the end of the article, "experts" argued that many of these marriages ended in divorce, were contrary to Islamic law, and produced troubled children. The subtext of this article, in an opposition newspaper, blamed the government for this phenomenon since it associated such marriages with the rise of consumerism, the 1974 Open Door Economic Policy, and the government's efforts to promote foreign tourism. Dr. ʿAzat Karim, from the Unit on Family Research at the National Center for Sociological and Criminological Research, argued that "we must pay attention to the restrictions that our young men feel in his society, whether they are ideological, social, political, or economic, for these are the direct reasons behind these marriages."

In contrast to marriages that are hastily arranged, many in the community believe that if a man "tires" (*byitʿab*) in his struggle to marry, he will be a better provider and a more loving husband and father. Young men who have had to support their families and assume the role of breadwinner at an early age are particularly attractive to the parents of a young woman because they have already proved their maturity and responsibility. When a man has had to support his family and delay his own marriage because of a lack of capital, it is not uncommon for him to marry a younger woman. Under these circumstances, the family of the bride will not be overly concerned by the age difference.

In the past it was very common for brides to be much younger than their husbands. However, many in the community now see large age differences in a negative light, and in one proposed match between a 34-year-old man and a nineteen-year-old woman, part of the family used the difference in ages to argue against the marriage. In spite of this, there are a few cases where older men (particularly divorced men or widowers) have married much younger women. In one case, a middle-aged man living in Cairo for years returned to his village of origin after the death of his wife to marry a woman in her early twenties, thereby upsetting his children, who were about the same age as his new wife. Older women can recount many stories of marriages between much older men and very young women of thirteen or fourteen. Although the legal minimum age for marriage in Egypt is now sixteen, the law can be circumvented if a doctor examines a young woman and legally attests that she is over the age of sixteen. As birth registration and certificates become more common in Egypt, it is becoming harder to circumvent the minimum age for marriage.

The choice of a marriage mate places pressure most particularly on mothers, who are deeply involved in the selection process and experienced in the consequences of mate selection. Mothers often worry about the reputation of their daughters and its effect on their marriage prospects. Rumors of a daughter's relationship with young men in the neighborhood, stubbornness, or independence can adversely affect her reputation in the community. Young women (between the ages of fifteen and twenty-five) are usually not allowed to come and go as they please. When they go to school, to shops, private lessons, or their job, they are expected to travel with their girlfriends or relatives. If there is no one to accompany them, they should walk purposely and ignore the taunts and flirtatious comments from men, whether they know them or not. The men themselves would approve of such behavior. In reality, these excursions are used by some young women as opportunities to flirt with young men, or to meet others. However, in *shaʿbi* communities both parties know the limits of this flirtatious interaction, and women will seldom tolerate insulting or abusive behavior. While women often ignore harassment if they are in their neighborhoods or surrounded by people they believe will support them, they will occasionally answer back or even verbally and physically attack obnoxious or abusive men.

Aside from school, university, workplaces, or occasionally the mosque, there are very few places in these communities for women to congregate publicly. They do not frequent cafés, restaurants, or places of entertainment alone or with their girlfriends, and only when they are accompanied by male relatives or their fiancé (often chaperoned) do they *byuxrugu* (go out). Young women will occasionally make elaborate plans with their friends or boyfriends to meet each other secretly, but they are constantly aware of the risks involved and the price of discovery. These meetings typically involve a meal, a cold nonalcoholic drink, ice cream, or a long walk along the Nile since women are very wary of straying from public places, even in the company of their fiancé.

While concern over the "honor" (i.e., virginity) of a young woman is the motivating force behind the restrictions on most women, the community judges a woman on many issues such as her intelligence, resourcefulness, dress, makeup, the way she walks, whom she walks with, and when she comes and goes. It is far more important for a young woman to be *mu'ad-daba* (polite and well-mannered) than a young man. Even if a woman is much better educated than her fiancé and comes from a well-respected family, her character remains a critical factor in his family's acceptance of the match. One young woman was unacceptable to her admirer's family because of her flashy clothes and makeup. Her own family, on the other hand, rejected the match because of the low status and insecurity of his occupation. Since neither family approved of the match, the man eventually married a paternal cousin. While people also consider similar characteristics when judging young men, they are far more likely to dismiss the indiscretions of a young man than of a young woman.

If a daughter is forced to marry a man against her will, after having had a local "boyfriend," the family will limit her movements even further, and object to her leaving the house, unaccompanied. In one instance, a daughter was presented with a potential groom by her family, even though it was common knowledge that she liked a neighbor whose balcony faced their kitchen window. She had made a hole in the window's shutter so that she could see her "boyfriend" coming and going. When her engagement was announced to a man thirteen years her senior, the family covered the hole with cardboard and placed a lock on the shutter so that the window could not be opened. Several fights occurred when her family found her staring out the window into her old boyfriend's apartment. Although she initially complained about the match, she eventually changed her mind and became anxious to marry. Later, after her family decided that the older groom was irresponsible and broke off the engagement, she went back to staring out the window at her boyfriend, dreaming of marriage to him. Unfortunately, her boyfriend was only a year older than she and still in the army. Even if their families agreed to the match, he would be in no financial position to marry her for several years. Her family would not entertain a formal proposal from his family until he began to accumulate some "marriage capital."

There were several cases in the community of a daughter's marriage causing so much conflict and tension within a family that a younger daughter was summarily married to the first available suitor at a young age. A young daughter is in a difficult position in such circumstances since she has less experience and authority to oppose parental wishes successfully. These struggles over marriage, particularly if the daughter dislikes the groom, can be extremely exhausting for both parties, and if the disagreement breaks out in public it can tarnish the reputations of both families within the community.

When parents or members of an extended family arrange a marriage, part of their motivation is self-interest. Parents must consider how a marriage will influence their future financial security and emotional needs. The familial ethos not only emphasizes that parents provide for their children but also that the children provide for the parents when they become elderly. In *sha'bi* communities, there are almost no elderly men or women who reside in public or private nursing homes, except the utterly indigent.[7] It is for these reasons, among others, that families are reluctant to allow their daughters and sons to marry foreigners. Even if financial support continues from abroad, they lose important emotional support and security.

Links between mothers and daughters are quite strong in these communities and often continue long after marriage. Even though sons are supposed to support their parents later in life, it was very common that daughters actually cared for them and supported them financially. Even when married, a daughter will maintain very close ties to her family. Daughters-in-law, on the other hand, have to develop and nurture their attachments with their husband's family, which often remain quite formal for many months after the marriage. Additionally, she must balance the allocation of resources between her own family and that of her husband's without creating offense.

Another criterion used in the selection process in arranged marriages is a young person's economic position. People in central Cairo often refer to classes (*Tabaqaat*) when comparing individuals and families. However, the use of this term refers to status as well as conventional notions of class. For example, the daughter of an imam of a very old mosque in a popular quarter attended the girls' college of al-Azhar University and was also a fairly accomplished artist. In a rather unusual arrangement, foreign tutors gave her private painting lessons at the family home, which was attached to the mosque. Local men, noticing these visits and assuming that the visitors were suitors coming to ask her father for "her hand," often followed her to school and promised her expensive apartments, a large dower, and costly jewelry if she would marry them instead. Although the men were the sons of prosperous local merchants, she explained that they would not have dared to approach her father because they understood the class difference between them and knew her father would refuse any offers of marriage. These young men had far more wealth than her father, but came from less-educated families with lower status in the community. As a religious scholar and preacher, it was her father's status, not his financial position, that entitled her to marry someone with a similarly honored position. The local boys became even more confused when they found out that her tutors had not been asking to marry her, prompting suspicions about both the girl and her tutors.

Local wisdom discourages the marriage of people from different classes. As one very successful *xaTba* (marriage broker) in the community explained, the best formula for a successful marriage was when both partners were from the same class, and when the man loved the woman more than she loved him. This belief is reinforced by the Islamic principle of *al-kafa'*, or social equality in marriage, which prescribes that Muslims marry someone equal to them in lineage, financial standing, and profession.[8] At the same time, films, television, songs, and popular literature express the dreams and aspirations of many men and women who marry "above themselves." In a very popular soap opera on television in September 1986 the rage that many in the middle class feel against the nouveaux riches who dare to marry "above" them was expressed very directly. A stereotypically poor, naive peasant had moved to Cairo and found a job selling soft drinks on the street. He lived in the same small pensione as a sincere, fatherly, government employee for the railroad, Baba Aniis. Soon the peasant began earning £E50 per day selling dollars in the black market (this sum would probably represent a third to a half of Baba Aniis' salary). He flaunted his new wealth with grilled meats and similar treats for the other residents of the pensione, one of whom was a well-educated woman searching for her husband, who had mysteriously disappeared and was feared dead. One day the now wealthier peasant suggested to Baba Aniis that he was considering marrying the woman in order to help her out. Baba Aniis turned furiously on the peasant, shouting, "How could you possibly consider marrying such a respected, educated, honorable, well-bred woman [*sitt muHtarima, muta'allima, mitrabiyya, sitt 'uSuul*]? There is no way someone like you could marry someone like her. How dare you even suggest such a fallacy of logic?" The peasant "remembered" his place and, of course, in the end reverted to his humble status. Many of the films or television serials that chronicle these matches end in tragic circumstances and therefore reinforce the popular adage that people should stick to their own kind.[9]

MARRIAGE PROTOCOL, OR THE RULES OF ENGAGEMENT

Once two families and two individuals have agreed to marriage, the complicated, trying process of actually accomplishing that goal ensues. Great tact, negotiating skill, resourcefulness, and patience is necessary since the process is not only protracted but well-defined and highly ritualized. Each party to the marriage must be cognizant of their duties and obligations. If they are not, it reflects poorly on their upbringing and the reputation of their families and can diminish the probability of a successful and fulfilling marriage. The community assumes that an adult is aware of the prerequisites of marriage and seeks to fulfill them in a responsible and mature way. If an affianced man or woman ignores these responsibilities, or acts disrespectfully or immorally, the marriage can and will be called off. (Marriages that fail due to other reasons, particularly economic pressure, will be discussed later in the chapter.)

Among Muslim couples the formal announcement of the engagement is marked by reading the opening verse of the Koran, *'il-fatHa*, together. Long after families have publicly announced the engagement of their children, the moral behavior of the couple and his or her family is constantly evaluated and monitored until the marriage finally occurs. To these ends, the family expects its members to act as private investigators. After one engagement in my community, the eldest son and eldest son-in-law in the family were directed to inquire about the fiancé, but did not approach their task with sufficient enthusiasm. They simply contacted a friend who worked with the fiancé and asked him about the fiancé's reputation and character. As the son said, everyone knew that as a low-level government clerk his salary could not have exceeded £E100 a month, but the least they could do was investigate his moral character and whether or not he was a good man or *'ibn naas*. After the engagement, the nephew of the fiancé began attending a day-care center that the bride's mother administered. One of her employees walked the young boy home every day. In her attempts to acquire more information, the mother of the bride asked this employee to ingratiate herself with the fiancé's mother in order to be invited into the latter's apartment. After having an observer describe the home, of course, she would be in a much better position to evaluate the wealth and standard of living of her prospective son-in-law's family. While in the fiancé's home, as part of her "duties," the employee praised her employer's family and the virtues of the prospective daughter-in-law.

The groom's family had told them at the reading of *'il-fatHa* that he had broken off a previous engagement to a neighbor.[10] The bride's family immediately tried to discover the name of this girl's family and the nature of the problem in order to protect their daughter. When this engagement eventually broke up, the mother accused her son and son-in-law of having shirked their duty to investigate the fiancé's character, maintaining that had they conscientiously and carefully "asked" about this man, they would have discovered his major faults. As things stood, the engagement continued for much longer than necessary, and since it was now broken it could harm the family's reputation within the community. While it is not uncommon to break engagements, there is a great deal of speculation in the community concerning the causes of the ultimate disagreement. When engagements fail, each family blames the other side in order to protect its own pride and reputation in the community.

The reading of *'il-fatHa* is basically a declaration of serious intent to marry, but before that ritual takes place the families have to agree upon the financial arrangements of the marriage and the timetable leading to the final consummation, the *duxla*. Depending on the age of the couple, their financial resources, and the limitations of their employment or education, the two families negotiate—before *'il-fatHa* is uttered—the timing of the formal engagement party (called the *shabka*, although the term really refers to the expensive item of gold jewelry the groom must give to his prospective bride),[11] the official religious ceremony recording the marriage (*katb il-kitaab*, where the marriage contract is signed), and the consummation of the marriage. Fixed timetables are difficult to maintain and are usually left somewhat ambiguous. For example, the young man usually suggests dates for each stage of the engagement that will give him enough time to earn and save the necessary funds to purchase an apartment, furnish it, and provide the dower and the *shabka*. If a young woman is still completing her secondary or university education, her family will usually insist on waiting until her exams are complete or until she finishes her education before the *duxla*. The latter precondition to a marriage can cause serious problems if the young woman (or young man) fails the exams and the marriage must be further delayed.

During these negotiations before *'il-fatHa* is read, the presence of the young girl is superfluous, since her family negotiates on her behalf. She is supposed to act very embarrassed, shy, retiring, and almost frightened of the proceedings. Often a prospective groom has only seen his fiancée for the first time during his family's first visit to her home. She is sent into the most formal sitting room in the apartment to serve Pepsi and cake to the guests, and it is at this time that the couple have their first sanctioned opportunity to see each other. Similarly, the groom usually sits very quietly during these proceedings, allowing his father, mother, or older relatives to negotiate the terms of the marriage with the bride's family.[12] If a woman is widowed she may ask her older brother to attend the engagement ceremony, although she has probably already concluded all important negotiations with the groom's family without the assistance of her male relatives. The presence of an older male member of the family is an indication that her family is strong, unified, and supportive.

Some families combine the signing of the wedding contract with the *duxla*; others sign the marriage contract long before the consummation of the marriage occurs.[13] Signing the marriage contract at the time of the *shabka* signifies a stronger commitment to the marriage than choosing to wait until the *duxla* occurs. Couples who have signed their marriage contracts are allowed more freedom to see each other and spend time together than couples who are merely engaged.[14] Shortly after the engagement ceremony, the groom is allowed to visit the bride in her home, under the watchful eye of members of her family.[15] When he visits his fiancée's home the groom is treated as an honored guest, and the fiancée or her mother will prepare more elaborate meals than are normally served in the home. To reciprocate such hospitality, the groom is expected to bring small gifts to his fiancée and her family, and on important religious and national holidays these gifts are expected to be more substantial.

The prospective groom in one young couple visited his fiancée at her family's home several times a week after he had given her the *shabka*. He would watch television, share meals, and listen to the news and events of her family in order to learn about his new in-laws. On one of these occasions he stayed until two in the morning watching the end of the last movie on television before the station closed down for the night. On his next visit he accompanied his future mother-in-law and fiancée on their visit to another married daughter who lived nearby. After the visit, the mother returned home alone and the young couple followed a few hours later. This prompted a furious reaction from her youngest son as he yelled at his mother for allowing them to be out alone and unchaperoned.

On his next visit to their home another sister asked the groom to drive her home in his taxi, since it was late at night and she lived in a distant neighborhood. The engaged daughter asked her mother if she could accompany them, promising to return home directly after they dropped off the older sister. While the daughter and her fiancé tried to convince the mother to allow them to go, the youngest son accused his older married sister of being selfish, sacrificing the reputation of her younger sister and family for her temporary comfort and convenience. Both sisters laughed at his protectiveness and finally the mother agreed to allow her daughter to accompany them, warning the fiancé to return directly.

In the next few days several violent fights occurred between the two siblings over this issue. The youngest sister claimed that she was certainly able to take care of herself and resented the paternalism of her younger brother, pointing out that her fiancé was a man to be trusted and was not a young, irresponsible boy like her brother (the fiancé was thirty-four, the brother seventeen). The mother claimed that her son had never fought her like this before. The fiancé soon heard about the fights between the two siblings and tried to reassure the youngest son of his good intentions, suggesting that he should trust him as a brother. The youngest son responded that he would never consider him a brother and pointed out that until they actually married, his sister was his family's responsibility.[16] Deaf to all complaints, the brother refused to leave them alone whenever the fiancé visited.

The family's involvement in the negotiation of the marriage in the first place, and in supervising the progression of the engagement, is obvious from the discussion above. Usually the opinions of family members overrides the opinions of the couple. In the words of the eldest married sister, mentioned above, the bride's opinion is not to be trusted since "all she wants to be is an ʿaruusa [a bride] and only sees the new clothes, new furniture, and the new freedom she will have from her mother, sisters, and brothers." Expecting to marry in the near future, and with her fiancé as an ally, the youngest sister tested the limits of her freedom and her growing power by openly provoking the older sister. One day, after she arrived home from school later than usual, the older sister asked her where she had been. The youngest sister responded by saying that she had visited friends. After several taunts and more questions, the youngest sister answered sarcastically that she was ʿandu (at his place). Everyone immediately knew that the masculine pronoun referred to her fiancé and was astonished by her shocking and provocative suggestion that she might have visited her fiancé at home (which she, of course, had not done).[17] A very serious fight erupted as the older sister and mother physically and verbally attacked the young woman. They yelled that she did not deserve to marry and that since she was so impolite and vulgar they would not pay for her wedding procession. Others soon pulled them apart, but the sarcasm and lack of respect for this older sister was not forgotten and led to future arguments.

If a young woman cannot be trusted, then it is up to the family to test and evaluate a man, to make sure that he is worthy of her. Using the same logic, the parents of a young man who is anxious to marry may insist on a long engagement to give them time to evaluate the character of a young bride, rather than permit a hasty marriage and risk a poor marriage. Family elders feel a responsibility to arrange marriages that will enhance the good of the family rather than fulfill individual desires, which explains why the process of arranging a marriage itself is a collective endeavor. While people in the community are not immune to love stories and romanticism, they have pragmatic notions of the impermanence of passion and infatuation and deep commitments to reproduce the family.

Unless a young woman is forced to marry someone she despises, she views marriage as an opportunity to rule her own household and to manage or control its resources. For both partners, marriage can be an attractive proposal. Interestingly, the early stage of marriage allows more independence for young women than for men. As bachelors, young men are allowed an independence that is curtailed upon marriage. The movements of a young husband are often the subject of many disagreements once a couple marries. If the wife believes her husband is too close to his relatives, she may insist on their spending holidays with her relatives, rather than with his.

As fiancés and new husbands, young men are expected to be very polite, almost docile, when interacting with their fiancée's family. Tempers do flare occasionally, but the respect a fiancé demonstrates to his in-laws and wife is extremely important in earning the respect of his in-laws and the general community.[18] For example, one engagement was destroyed by a young man's casual, straightforward response to a question from his future mother-in-law. The young man had no idea that he had offended her, but in her mind it ended his chances of marrying her daughter. He had come to accompany his fiancée and her family to his brother's engagement party (which the bride's family had helped to arrange). He had given his fiancée money to pay for a visit to a hairdresser, and she had borrowed a very fancy and somewhat revealing long dress to wear to the party. Once the young man arrived, the mother found it necessary to tell her daughter she looked like a whore in the dress although she had approved of it earlier. The fiancé did not object to the dress, but the mother had wanted to publicly demonstrate her standards of respectability by condemning her daughter's apparent immodesty.[19]

The mother then asked the young man if she could put several large bags of pasta in his trunk to deliver to another daughter, whom they were to visit the same night. He answered that he did not think it would be possible because his taxi was parked far away from their house due to a neighborhood funeral. The mother did not respond immediately but subsequently complained to another daughter that the fiancé had yelled at her and treated her disrespectfully, like a young child. The groom was oblivious to the implications of his casual remark. While he and his fiancée walked ahead to his taxi, the mother decided not to ride with the young man and took a taxi with a married daughter instead. Upon arrival in the neighborhood she immediately took refuge in her daughter's flat, telling everyone in her family how the fiancé had insulted her, and that as a result she would not honor his family by attending his brother's engagement party. They insisted that she had to pay her respects to his family by attending the party for a short while at least, but she refused until the party was almost over. She was finally persuaded to make an appearance but on the way slipped on the stairs, badly cutting her forehead. Her fall forced the fiancé's family to come to the daughter's house and make sure that she was not severely injured. Despite suffering a serious wound, tactically she had won that round. Other difficulties followed afterwards and eventually the engagement was officially canceled, but the "pasta incident" was constantly cited as an example of this groom's unsuitability.[20]

Public demonstrations of respect are extremely important components of the rules of engagement, and it is common for marriages and other types of celebrations to be delayed for a year after the death of a parent. One young couple's engagement was plagued by the deaths of members of their respective families. They were engaged in 1983 and signed their marriage contract a year later. Then her father died, and the marriage was delayed a full year, out of respect. Since the groom was still saving money to prepare for the marriage, this first delay was not very distressing, although at the time of her father's death they had already been engaged for three years. In April of the same year, his father died. In this instance, the two families decided to postpone the marriage several more months but not another full year, since the couple was eager and ready to marry. It was only a matter of months before disaster struck again when this time the young woman's mother died. The groom insisted that he would only postpone the marriage an additional four months since he already had an apartment and had been paying its fairly sizable monthly rent for the preceding year. Unfortunately, despite his fiancée's desperate arguments with her family, they still refused to permit the marriage, and so the young man canceled the engagement and reluctantly married another woman within six months.

When serious problems arise in an engagement, people are extremely anxious to maintain and safeguard their "respect" in the community. The party that believes it has been slighted will wait until the other side visits to apologize or accept responsibility for their mistake, which proves their guilt. If a groom does not appear for his routine visits to his fiancée, and her family does not believe they have done anything wrong, they will not approach his family in an attempt to discover the reason for his absence. If necessary they will assume the engagement is broken, rather than visit the groom's home, because by doing so they would lose the community's respect by appearing desperate to marry off their daughter. Under these circumstances the members of the extended family may resort to informal, discreet channels to discover how the groom or his family has been offended and what steps, if any, can be taken to repair the rift.

11. The young couple celebrates their marriage with relatives and neighbors after persuading their families to conduct the ceremony during the groom's vacation from his job in Saudi Arabia. Even though the groom had become more religious while living in Saudi Arabia, his bride still insisted on showing her hair (after a costly visit to the coiffeur) and wearing the elaborate wedding dress, accessories, and makeup that is typical among Egyptian women across an economic spectrum.

12. Musicians, family, and friends sing to the couple after they went upstairs to the groom's apartment to pay their respects to his mother, who was too ill to attend the festivities. During the *zaffa*, or wedding procession, local musicians (in this case the boyhood friend of the groom and his cousin) serenade the bride and groom as they walk from the coiffeur, the bride's home, or the groom's home to the marriage celebration. Wealthier families often hire professional musicians for these exciting processions.

While various members of the family conduct the negotiations surrounding a marriage, the bride and groom have a small measure of power to influence the course of their marriage. At times, they may successfully oppose family decisions, though more frequently they will bow to family pressure or communal norms. For example, one young man returned from his job in Saudi Arabia on his month-long vacation during Ramadan. He had been engaged to a relative of a neighbor for three years and had saved enough money finally to marry. His mother had been ill for many years, her condition had recently worsened, and he worried that his mother would die before seeing her only son married. Even though his fiancée would be in the middle of her final high school examinations, and he would have to leave only a week after the *duxla*, he insisted on marrying before returning to Saudi Arabia. Both his parents thought his plan was unfair to his fiancée and worried that the couple would not have enough time together before he left. But he persuaded people that she would join him only a few months later and that he was determined to marry while his mother was still alive. In the end, he persevered, and they were married a week before he flew to the Gulf.

In other instances, young men and women are able gradually to persuade their families to accept their choice of a suitor. Occasionally, women in the community have cleverly sabotaged their engagements to men that their families had arranged for them to marry, but whom they did not desire. Some women, on the other hand, cannot afford to antagonize their families for various reasons and have little recourse but to accept suitors that they dislike and even abhor.

In many ways, an engagement can be likened to a minefield, waiting to be detonated by those who tread clumsily or obliviously. The respect, morality, and propriety of all parties to an engagement are carefully monitored and constantly judged. These qualities are so important to families in this community because in other circumstances a family's position determines its access to informal networks that bring a range of goods and services. Maintaining the trust of others facilitates inclusion in wide-ranging networks. From time to time, disagreements can arise from certain incidents that dishonor one of the parties and thus quickly sabotage the engagement. What constitutes dishonor and disrespect is decided upon by standards of propriety shared within the community. Functionally, these norms offer a common standard to guide delicate and complex negotiations. Ideologically, they promote behavior that reinforces the shared goal of reproducing the family.

SEXUALITY AND THE TRANSGRESSION OF PUBLIC NORMS

To support the position of family in the community, it is necessary to enforce sexual conduct that reproduces the family. The community is deeply involved in regulating and ordering sexual relationships and, as mentioned in previous sections, marriage is considered the proper institutional outlet for sexual activity and emotional fulfillment. However, deviance from the norm, such as premarital, adulterous, or homosexual affairs, may be tolerated if it does not conflict with the goal of creating and maintaining family. These activities, although they do not receive such public attention and publicity, are nevertheless a part of life (and love) in the community.

Throughout this section I cite examples of frank, public discussions about sexual affairs by members of the community. Men and women flirt, joke, and argue with each other about their relationships, and other licit and illicit relationships in the community, in front of family members and friends: men and women, young and old. These public conversations provided the material for this section, rather than any intentional questioning on my part. It is not only that people enjoy gossip, but these public discussions of sexual mores educate younger people and enforce proper behavior among all members of the community.

Since the relationship between men and women is the most basic component of the reproduction of the family, the community adopts a supervisory and almost intrusive role to ensure that gender relations lead, quite directly, to marriage and procreation. Sexual relationships are far more than a private matter in Egypt. Gender relations, the position of the family in Egypt, women's dress, and dating protocol, for example, are extremely contentious public issues. As secular and religious ideologies confront each other at many levels of society and the polity in Egypt today, sexuality and gender relations become subjects through which political activists and organizations articulate their positions.

An example of the ways in which sexual or "private" issues are used to discredit and oppose the state is the well-publicized wave of rapes that occurred in 1985 (to be discussed in the final part of this section). It must be remembered that the government barely tolerates direct opposition, and therefore opposition groups use more indirect methods to attack the government and promote their interests. Islamic activists believe that these type of issues are public matters central to their vision of a state and a society based on religious laws and ethics as defined by religious scholars and jurists. There is a vibrant publishing industry producing manual after manual on proper relations among the sexes, according to various Muslim theologians and activists. These small books are very inexpensive and available at kiosks or from sidewalk vendors. Typical titles in one series on Muslim women, published by an Islamic press, include: "Adornment," "The Mother in the Koran," "Islam and the Direction of the Modern Muslim Woman," "Motherhood and Childhood in Islam," and "A Husband's Rights Toward His Wife and a Wife's Rights Toward Her Husband."[21] Religious opposition to the Egyptian government is quite broad and diverse, ranging from members of Parliament who are known as Islamists to members of Parliament (1987–1990) from the Socialist Labor Party (which entered into an alliance in the 1987 elections with the Muslim Brotherhood) to clandestine groups that promote violent opposition to the state and its tainted bureaucracy.[22]

Although few people in my community participated (as far as I knew) in more organized Islamicist opposition to the government, many people supported the imposition of Islamic law in Egypt and others were involved in religious brotherhoods, study groups at mosques, or benefited from the services of religious associations. Few of them had very radical positions, but many people used religious ethics and prescriptions as a way to condemn the corruption, repression, and ineptitude of the government.

As the Egyptian government defensively wrapped itself in religious symbolism and piety after the 1981 assassination of President Sadat by Islamic activists, more mainstream Islamic activists gained greater influence in defining public issues and placing those issues on the public agenda. They have been so successful in redefining political debate and discourse that leftist secular politicians enter alliances with Islamic groups and cloak their speeches in religious rhetoric and references—the logic being, if you can't beat them, join them and co-opt their rhetoric at least.[23] The final part of this section illustrates how a sudden wave of well-publicized rapes in Egypt became an extremely controversial political issue.

Strong moral and sexual codes limit the open expression of sexual relationships, and it is extremely uncommon to observe public displays of affection by men and women, other than walking arm in arm (engagé) in the street. Although sexual relationships are themselves as discreet and private as very densely populated neighborhoods and crowded housing allows, it is common and appropriate for people to discuss, judge, and try to control intimate conduct between men and women. In contrast, while public displays of affection and public knowledge of licit and illicit sexual affairs is more common in Western nations, authority figures and relatives have very little influence or control over the intimate behavior of others.

In Egypt, because of constant public discourse on sexual propriety and gender relations, people are aware of what is considered acceptable and unacceptable public behavior. The basic rules are clear, and even after a couple marries, people in the community will continue to act as advisers, though others might call them meddlers. Strict standards govern what is thought of as proper dress (for both men and women), polite conversation, physical relationships, and the manner in which a personal relationship is portrayed and discussed in public.

One of the compliments a young woman can receive from members of the community is that she possesses 'il-Hishma, or modesty. Particularly in the increasingly conservative social environment of the 1980s in Egypt, this word describes women who dress modestly and do not flirt or engage in casual conversation with young men who "hang out" in the neighborhood. In sha'bi communities women have traditionally worn the milaaya laff (often shortened to just milaaya), a modest, long black cloak that was conveniently wrapped around a woman when she went outside the home.[24] However, the milaaya is now considered more traditional, and younger, more educated women, in particular, dress in long-sleeved and ankle-length dresses that are identified as Islamic dress or ʾ*iz-zayy il-ʾislaami*. These women are described as *muHaggabaat* (pl.), or women who cover themselves (usually with a scarf over their hair). Very few women in the community veil their faces completely, wear gloves, and allow no skin to show at all. Many variations of Islamic dress are now mass-produced in Egypt and are available in fashionable colors and styles in specialized boutiques that were patronized by women from this *shaʿbi* community.[25]

An indication of the extent of changes in the communal definition of modesty is illustrated by the demise of the bathing suit. In old pictures of families from my community at the beach during the summer, many of the younger women were wearing bathing suits. However, in the past several years bathing suits have been condemned as immodest and lewd by Islamic activists and ideologues, and pictures from summer vacations now show women wading in the water in skirts, scarves, and *gallabiyya*s. Even those who are not *muHaggaba* would not dare to wear bathing suits on public beaches, although some upper- and middle-class and foreign women in more exclusive beach areas do.

While modesty and conformity are valued by the community, women who are strong, determined, and resourceful are also admired. One young woman in the neighborhood from a particularly rough merchant family of rural origins claimed that people were afraid of her because she would not tolerate attacks or slurs from others. When a woman feels compelled to react violently to a man's comments or actions, it is a clear indication that the boundaries of propriety have been transgressed.

Usually, men and women speak to each other sensitively and cautiously in order to avoid confrontations while flirting and communicating sexual innuendoes. Since there are relatively few opportunities to meet members of the opposite sex outside the family environment, young men and women become skilled at conveying their desires and romantic interests without making blatant, explicit statements. These encounters are even more complicated since someone is usually watching or supervising these brief but public meetings (a situation that continues until a couple marries). Even couples who have been engaged for several years are rarely left unchaperoned.

The following characterization of gender relations within an Islamic tradition, while written by a Jordanian Minister of Religious Affairs, reflects a segment of popular sentiment in *shaʿbi* communities in Egypt.

> Islam accepts neither unrestrained mingling of sexes, nor their complete seclusion from each other. It is not permissible for a single man to sit alone with a single woman (who is not closely related to him). The Prophet said "If a man and a woman meet alone, the third to join them is the Devil" (Al Tirmizi). Association for the purpose of prohibited activities like drinking, gambling, dancing, or for sheer self-display and flirtatious conversation is also not allowed. However, Islam places no restriction on socialization of families in a clean atmosphere of mutual respect and observance of the rules of decorum and

modesty. At the same time, association of sexes is permitted to the extent it may be necessary for meeting the requirements of worship, public administration, political participation, trade, education, war, and other genuine needs of the individual or the community. Such association should again conform to prescribed rules of dress and behavior. The Islamic norm is thus the Middle Path. It does not exclude women from the life of the community and gives them full opportunity to make use of their talents and energies. Yet it protects them from slander, disrespect, and temptations, which ruin individual lives and create social evils.[26]

While young people do meet each other more frequently than the above quote suggests, men and women in the community often reiterated the belief that when a man or woman were alone together, the Devil would soon join them. The idea that temptation is beyond the limits of self-control is deeply ingrained in the rules and morality of the community, thus enforcing cautious interaction between genders. While the community is very suspicious of relationships between men and women, very close friendships with members of one's own sex are quite acceptable and pervasive.

Because of the constant interaction between the sexes within the household, however, Egypt is not a highly segregated society. While men fill the sidewalk cafés, streets, shops, and cinemas, women are certainly visible on public transportation, in offices, and in markets. However, they are seldom seen sitting alone in cafés, restaurants, or other public places. This partial segregation in public, however, is not replicated in private. As I argued in the previous chapter, the public realm extends into the household within *sha'bi* communities, although limited numbers have physical access to the household. Within the household and the extended family, there is a very active and open "mingling" of the sexes. In *sha'bi* communities, far more flirting, sexual innuendoes, and physical relationships appear to occur within the household than outside of it. Furthermore, since almost a quarter of marriages in Cairo are between relatives, these intrafamilial relationships often have an explicitly sexual aspect to them. Relatives and close friends spend much time within the home and entertain there as well. A young boy can grow up in almost constant contact with a cousin who lives in the same building or neighborhood, and subsequently marry her. People always tease young teenagers about which cousin they will marry, and it is obvious that attractions develop between relatives. Parents monitor these flirtations carefully, and teenagers know the boundary between flirtation and impropriety.

It is clear from observation and the accounts of young men and women that the involvement of family in their personal lives is extensive. Communal norms govern friendships and relationships with members of the opposite sex, and when the decision is taken to marry, the community celebrates each stage of that long process with the traditional rituals described earlier. The ultimate symbol of a couple's incorporation into the community is the custom of showing members of the community a white handkerchief, stained with the bride's blood, after the marriage is consummated. The *duxla* itself, then, is a public event.

As noted, in *sha'bi* communities the bride is expected to be a virgin on her wedding night. Depending on the origins and traditions of the families of both the bride and the groom, there can either be a *duxla baladi* or a *duxla 'afrangi*.[27] In the *duxla baladi* (or traditional, Egyptian consummation) either an experienced woman, often a midwife or *daaya*, or the groom wraps a white handkerchief around a finger and tries to break the woman's hymen, which is expected to bloody the handkerchief. Although more common in the past, a *duxla baladi* often occurs while the guests are still crowding the bride's home. Under these circumstances the community acknowledges the bride's virginity, congratulates her family, and continues to celebrate the wedding. In a *duxla 'afrangi* (or foreign consummation, because people argue this is a tradition imported from the West) the couple is left alone to consummate the marriage, but they must still produce the same handkerchief, stained by blood, during the traditional morning visit of the couple's parents after the wedding, the *SabaHiyya*. This proof of virginity is kept by the couple throughout their marriage.

The couple usually has little choice in the type of *duxla* for their marriage. The family commonly decides such a matter, although very strenuous opposition may influence the decision. Many couples in Cairo today have what is still referred to as the "foreign type of consummation." Women often express very negative feelings about their *duxla*, particularly in the case of a *duxla baladi*. Although young women have usually discussed the sexual aspect of their marriage with female relatives at great length, the *duxla* is commonly embarrassing, painful, and humiliating. Similar emotions are expressed by men who are sometimes traumatized and rendered impotent by the pressure to consummate the marriage as people knock on the door eagerly awaiting proof of her virginity.

If the woman's blood does not flow freely, then her virginity is suspect. Obviously, this crude method of "proving" virginity is medically unsound. Many popular novels and films depict tragedies that occur if a woman's blood does not flow freely on her wedding night. However, in my year of fieldwork, I did not hear of a woman within this community whose virginity was questioned on her wedding night. It is important to note that constant reminders of the violence and tragedies that befall women who are not virgins serve to reinforce communal norms and traditional gender relations. Egyptian novels, plays, television serials, letters to the editor, and newspaper articles are filled with lurid accounts of women who are murdered, thrown out by their families, or who commit suicide because of illicit sexual affairs, or even the hint of them. If a man is to blame or a man is the partner to an illicit affair, she is the one who will suffer and bear the consequences of his and her behavior. On the other hand, popular novels and the media also discuss well-known procedures women and their families can use, under certain circumstances, to produce a blood-stained handkerchief.[28] Although the ideal of virginity is supposed to be so powerful, families, in certain circumstances, will decide to protect their daughter if she is not a virgin rather than expose her and the family itself to public disapproval. This tolerance coexists with far less tolerant attitudes about virginity in the community which are the cause of violence against women and their lovers.

Once a couple marries it is expected that they will have a child within the space of a year. If they are unsuccessful at producing a child, they will often begin consulting physicians and traditional healers to remedy the problem. Couples without children, whether they wish to be or not, are the focus of increasing concern. Egyptians are typically extremely fond of children and very eager to have children and enjoy them or, as they put it, *yifraHu biihum*. However, the average number of children per family and the total fertility rate has been steadily declining.[29] Women practice birth control more commonly and effectively than in the past, and the percentage of married women in their reproductive years using various birth control methods now reaches 47 percent, according to one study.[30] In my community the most popular form of birth control was oral contraceptives. Contraception was a common topic of conversation among women, and they were not reluctant to continue these discussions when men, women, and children were present. Despite the smaller size of families, having children is still a very important goal for almost every couple and a cause for celebration and pride.

Children are totally incorporated into the community and highly visible, no matter what time of day or night.[31] After the birth of a child, a couple's position in the community is strengthened. Seven days after the birth of a child, families celebrate the new member of the family by holding a *subu'* (from the word *seven*). While they are not as common today as they were only a few decades ago, many couples still invite their families and the neighborhood children to these ceremonies. The child is passed over a flour sifter containing grains of wheat and herbs (symbols of fertility, health, and prosperity). At the same time, the heavy brass pestle commonly used by women for pounding garlic and other staples of the Egyptian diet is struck against the mortar, directly next to the ear of the infant. The guests sing a refrain, commanding the infant to listen to his mother and father throughout his life (socialization begins at a very early age). Some families print their infant's name and date of birth on a five piaster note ($.03 in 1986) and purchase small boxes of candy and popcorn to distribute to relatives and neighborhood children. In a charming scene, neighborhood children welcome the new infant by holding candles in a short procession on the staircase, while they anxiously await the distribution of sweets and desert. If a midwife (*daaya*) has delivered the baby, her participation in this ceremony brings good luck to the child. In some wealthier families, a lamb may be slaughtered in celebration of the birth, though this is a more common occurrence after the birth of a boy, or a first child. Many of these rituals date back to Pharaonic Egypt and are intended to protect the child from the evil eye and

13. During a *subuʿ* (or the ceremony that is held seven days after a child's birth), it is traditional for the guests, particularly children, to light candles and sing in celebration of the birth of a new child as they accompany the child into its new home. Neighborhood children are always anxious to participate in a lively *subuʿ* because sweets and very small denominations of money (typically a five piaster note, on which the family prints the name and birthdate of the child) are distributed. The baby's aunt carries him in the procession, along with the midwife or *daya* (the woman in black) who delivered the baby. It is considered good luck if the *daya* also presides over the *subuʿ*. She is carrying wheat and other herbs that have symbolized health, prosperity, and fertility since the Pharaonic era in Egypt.

other dangers. Most importantly, the relatives and neighbors welcome the new child to the family and community.

The overriding goal of creating and maintaining families in this community exists simultaneously with contradictory beliefs and practices. The presence of this "norm," by definition, implies a diversity of behavior and opinions. Analyses of Egyptian society often ignore alternative and less socially acceptable patterns of behavior and action among more marginal segments of the community. For example, the ideals of virginity and marriage are inculcated into the collective conscience in many ways, but adultery, premarital sexual relations, homosexuality, prostitution, rape, incest, and child abuse all exist concurrently. These issues are raised, not to analyze sexual mores and gender relations in Egypt, but to emphasize the community's diversity. Far more toleration and pluralism exists within these communities than is normally acknowledged and publicly discussed.

For example, while homosexuality is not publicly condoned, people in this community know or know of men who engage in homosexual activities.

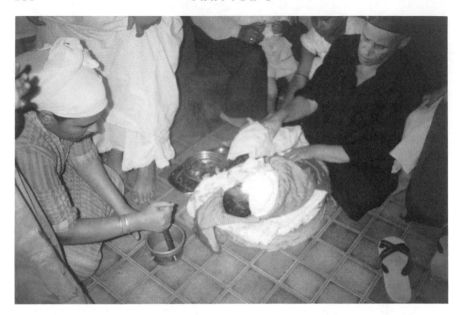

14. Although the baby does not always appreciate it, as the midwife passes the child over a flour sifter containing herbs during the ceremony, people sing a song encouraging the child to obey his or her parents in the future, as a mortar and pestle is struck just next to the baby's head, perhaps to imprint this advice into its consciousness.

Here, the social construction of sexuality is quite important and demonstrates the difficulty of assuming that certain concepts mean the same thing to different people. Being branded a homosexual in Egypt, *bitaaᶜ 'ir-rigaala*, describes only those men who are the "passive" partner, and people harass and condemn men who are identified as homosexuals, in this sense. They use the term *xawal* to refer to homosexuals and use it as an insult against men when they want to challenge their masculinity, much as Americans use the term "faggot." However, men who are "active" when they have sexual relations with men (i.e., they penetrate but are not penetrated) are not considered by Egyptians to be homosexuals but only as having sex with men because it is very difficult to have sex with women before marriage. While there is a small, tightly knit and distinct subculture of gay men in Cairo or Alexandria that views homosexuality in a more Westernized sense (where such roles are not so strictly segregated), they are fairly marginalized from mainstream society and lead relatively closeted lives.

If men in *shaᶜbi* communities occasionally indulge in discreet homosexual liaisons, while they are harassed by some people, others are not offended or concerned, unless the young man refuses to marry and produce children. One eighteen-year-old young man in the neighborhood was met by his uncle at five in the morning, leaving his home with a male friend. When asked where they were going, the young man responded, "To pray at al-Hussein."

The uncle suspected that his nephew was sexually involved with the other man and was not going to dawn prayers. Once before, he had discovered his nephew sleeping with another teenager. Both his uncle and his aunt condemned the nephew as a *xawal* or passive homosexual, yet they did little to prevent his liaisons beyond this verbal harassment.

In the popular media, journalists, religious authorities, and sociologists condemn the increasingly common practice of 'ish-shuzuuz il-ginsi, or sexual deviance. These supposed experts believe homosexuality is one of the more troubling manifestations of perversion. They do not believe that anyone is naturally gay or chooses to become gay, but explain the increase in incidence of homosexuality as a consequence of the high cost of marriage, which has delayed marriage for many young men who, unable to fulfill their "normal" sexual needs through marriage, have turned to homosexuality. (The singulate mean age of first marriages now reaches 28.9 years for men, and 23.4 years for women.)[32] Whatever the reasons, homosexuality is a preference within this community, although probably a minority one.

A similar argument was used to explain a sudden increase in violent sexual assaults, particularly those of rape and child abuse.[33] In the first four months of 1985, a highly publicized wave of rape cases swept Egypt. As journalists described incidents of rape (approximately thirty cases gleaned from published accounts), a public debate on the sexual mores of youth and the healthiness of family life filled the front pages of newspapers,[34] and fear filled the streets.[35] The Ministry of Interior released figures during this period which claimed that only twelve to eighteen rapes occurred annually.[36]

When a woman is raped in Egypt, it is not only the victim that receives attention and empathy. Rape is seen as an attack on the honor of women, the honor of the family, and the honor of Egypt. The connection between sexual violence and the decline in the authority of the state and in religious values, as well as rampant consumerism and political repression, was drawn again and again throughout this public debate. It was not marginalized as a "security" problem and left to the police to deter. It was seen as being symptomatic of wider, sensitive trends in society and the polity.

Some Egyptian psychiatrists and criminologists reject explanations of rape as a result of sexual frustration due to the late age of marriage and identify rape as a violent crime by aggressive, violent personalities and psychopaths. National statistics and character profiles of sexual offenders contradict the hypothesis that the delayed age of marriage has encouraged sexual assaults. Furthermore, according to a survey by the security police, 40 percent of the men who had been arrested for crimes of rape and sexual abuse during the past five years were married. Furthermore, many of the thirty-one rapists who attacked women during the first four months of 1985 were married.[37] Dr. Ahmed Akaasha, a professor of psychiatry at the Faculty of Medicine and Ain Shams University blamed the epidemic of rapes on migration, government policies, and changing values among young people.

In my opinion, these are individual cases that do not form an epidemic and are nothing more than individual personalities who live in an improper domestic environment. You find the disintegration of the family because of divorce or the departure of the head of the household to chase after sustenance for his family in the Gulf.

Sexual energy is found in all of us, but we must rise above it and channel it into the following five elements: religion, science, culture, art, or sport. If we look at these five elements we find that physical sports have almost been abolished from educational institutes as classrooms for morning and afternoon sessions were built in the playing fields. Sports are important because they promote mutual competition and group solidarity (community). Science has become a process of stuffing the minds of students so that they succeed in examinations. It is not, in the real sense, to acquire learning or conduct research. Culture has been transformed to a type of rapturous entertainment and opulence, and films have fallen to the level of only trying to excite people at any price. Television programs are boring but, more than that, have nullified the presence of the author from our lives and covered over libraries in our homes. Religion has become the sole comfort for a large part of our youth but, unfortunately, they take an extreme path because they have not found any of the five elements which reminds them to find balance in their lives.

Thus the decision is basically political and not economic. We should not use the problem of housing or the difficulties of marriage and the formation of a family as an excuse. For Gulf countries do not have a housing problem, but they also have the problem of rape and abduction. Thus we must be concerned about these five elements and a youth must work to absorb his energy and to have a sense of belonging and patriotic conviction to absorb his aggressive energy.[38]

Tawfiiq al-Hakim, one of the eldest and most prominent members of Egypt's literati, condemned the rising rate of violent sexual crime in a newspaper interview, but excused the violence of young men, like many others in Egypt, with the following story:

When I was a public prosecutor . . . we gave a summons to a peasant for washing his clothes in an irrigation canal and he was arrested for violating health codes and brought to the court. The peasant responded to the charge by asking, "Where am I supposed to wash my clothes, judge?" The judge turned to me and said, "Answer that, professor, where is he supposed to wash his clothes?" I responded, "This is not my job to tell him where to wash his clothes. As the prosecuting attorney I execute the law and this man has broken the law and must be punished."

With the same logic I say to you that I am unable to tell young men what they should do, but I demand that the law against the perpetrator of these crimes be enforced and that they hang in Abadiin Square.[39]

In the same article Tawfiiq al-Hakim proposed that Islamic authorities allow temporary marriage (*zawaag il-mutᶜa*) as a solution to the problem of rape in Egypt, although it is only permitted by Shiʾa law.

Naguib Mahfouz, the 1988 winner of the Nobel Prize for literature, explained that in his youth the state had recognized the "normal" sexual needs of men by licensing prostitution. Because men married at a much younger age in the past and were kept extremely busy in the fields, he argued, "deviant" or perverse sexual practices were minimal and limited to extremely small circles associated with the Westernized upper class or foreigners living in Egypt.

Individuals and groups that promoted the application of Islamic law and a more Islamic culture in Egypt used the wave of rapes in arguments to justify not only the imposition of Islamic law but also greater religious education for young people, the return of working women to the household, increased censorship of sexually provocative films, magazines, television, and literature, and the reversal of the Open Door policy, which they blamed for increased Westernization, consumerism, and decadence in Egypt. As *al-Sha'b* commented in its introduction to a full-page article describing the sordid details of several rape cases, "Although we fully realize that it [the incidence of rape] is only a part of the crisis of Egyptian society, we believe that its quick and just treatment presents itself in the application of Islamic Law."[40]

Forces on the left of the political spectrum and their newspapers argued that society had not become too liberal, but that it remained repressed, both politically and psychologically, and thus young men resorted to rape. At the same time, they argued, like Islamic ideologues, that the Open Door policy promoted consumptive habits and a set of inappropriate and dangerous values in young men and women. Dr. Salah Qansua, chief of the Department of Philosophy in the Faculty of Arts at Zagazig University, a provincial capital, explained the relationship between consumptive values and moral decay in society:

> A young man knows that he is unable to marry with ease. This creates a trap which he then falls into and the same thing happens in relation to women. For a natural life or natural hopes lie in marriage, but this has almost become impossible now. Frustration accumulates continuously and the sense of failure continues. Thus sexual behavior does not follow a natural path. And from here the phenomenon is built with repeated deviations. What is happening now is that youth are frustrated and they are affected by the prevailing modes of behavior in society today, which are abduction and flight. These are the successful models now. Anyone, no matter what their differences of opinion are, or what their economic views are, knows that the way of possessing ['il-'imtilaak] in our society is not on a normal level. And from there a girl or a "thing for pleasure" [mut'a] is transformed into an object to be possessed.[41]

Each political viewpoint placed partial blame for these sexual assaults on the influence of foreign sexual mores in Egypt, transmitted primarily, the argument suggested, through illegal pornographic or sexually provocative films, produced either in the West or other Arab capitals. In fact, many

Egyptian families in rural and urban areas now own VCRs, and small, licensed shops that rent and sell video films pervade *sha'bi* neighborhoods. Several of the reports of rape cases during 1985 mentioned that the rapists had viewed pornography shortly before committing rape. In one small village, a report of two rape-murders mentioned that a local coffeehouse showed pornographic films to villagers, who would fight each other over the limited seating in the small establishment. And along similar lines, an officer of the Alexandria traffic police was accused of rape, and one of his accomplices was identified as the owner of a video club. In the context of an accusation of rape, any association with pornographic videos almost automatically implied guilt and, for some people, justified the actions of rapists.

People believe that pornography excites men, but because they do not have a "normal" outlet for their sexual energy, they resort to sexual assault and "deviant" practices. The popularity of pornography, despite its high purchase and rental costs, causes concern among many social commentators, public officials, and individuals in Egypt. The state fears the effect of sexually explicit films enough to heavily censor imported and domestically produced provocative films, to confiscate all video cassettes that they discover in routine customs inspections, and to prosecute individuals who illegally sell and rent pornographic videos. Yet pornography is still easily available through black-market channels.

While most newspapers covered the rape "epidemic," journalists of opposition papers used the phenomenon to attack the government's economic and political policies. As several papers called more vociferously for the imposition of Islamic law as a means of confronting the "moral disintegration" of Egyptian society, the President finally responded. In his annual Labor Day speech on the first of May in 1985, President Mubarak chastised those elements in Egypt who, he claimed, exaggerated the extent of crime and corruption in Egypt.[42] His defense of Egypt's safety and integrity was a warning to journalists to stop printing stories and investigating rape and sexual assaults. Shortly after the President's speech, screaming headlines and exposés on rape and sexual assault disappeared from the front pages. It was impossible to know whether the wave of rapes continued but were not reported, or if they actually declined in number.

While rape and sexual assault are uncommon according to official sources, the community does not deny the occurrence of illicit or extramarital affairs. Behavior that transgresses sexual norms may be tolerated if it is discreet and does not harm members of the community. For example, a middle-aged man described his encounter with a prostitute during a family gathering of several generations of relatives. His wife jumped in, volunteering to explain the story. He had stopped at a traffic light when a young woman with a child asked him where he was going. Out of curiosity, he offered her a ride and she directed him to an apartment building with elaborate security measures, where she rented a room from a married couple for £E5. At this point, it was very clear that she was a prostitute. A bit frightened by the locks on the door, he asked to see her I.D. card to ensure that she was not an undercover policewoman (she was officially a teacher).[43] She explained that she usually charged £E5 to have sex with customers but would forgo that on his account. He suggested that they go to the market to buy some food before proceeding, which provided him with an opportunity to lose the woman in the crowd. The wife of this man explained that he had never intended to have sex with the prostitute but was only curious about how such transactions occurred. Throughout her somewhat bawdy rendition of her husband's caper, the wife surprisingly never condemned her husband's behavior and only claimed that he was *shaaʿi* (mischievous).[44]

Less frequently, people would gossip about the adulterous affairs of their neighbors or relatives. Some of these affairs were the source of great family friction, while others were long-term and tolerated by wives and husbands, perhaps because they had little alternative. Rumors of married men and women having affairs usually had very serious implications, and people would not make accusations lightly. At times, someone would call into question another's fidelity during the heat of an argument, but this served as a dramatic form of slander rather than a serious accusation.

One local Casanova in the neighborhood explained that married men and women indulged in affairs because husbands and wives did not communicate well with each other. He claimed, almost braggingly, that women who confided in him often complained about their husbands, and then they tried to seduce him. He suggested that one of the causes of frustration and conflict between men and women was the very common practice of female circumcision in these communities. Within my community, the women claimed that every woman they knew, with the exception of the daughter of a distant relative, was circumcised. Girls are usually circumcised between the ages of five to twelve while boys are circumcised at birth or between the ages of five and seven.

Female circumcision, or clitoridectomy, is another very sensitive issue that is treated delicately by the state, health care professionals, and women's organizations.[45] Circumcision seems more concentrated among lower social classes and women from rural areas. However, the extent of female circumcision is very difficult to determine since it is not a subject that has been extensively researched in Egypt, due to political and personal sensitivities. Despite its prevalence, debates occur occasionally among women and between women and men over the necessity of the operation. The rationale behind the practice, according to people in my community, is that circumcision enhances cleanliness (the word for circumcision, *ʾiT-Tahaara*, derives from the word for purity) and feminine characteristics (people believe that a clitoris resembles a penis and therefore it is better to reduce its size or excise it), and that it also discourages promiscuity (removing the clitoris reduces sexual feelings among women and will therefore discourage them from sexual activities). Some women suggested that without circumcision a woman's sexual appetite would be too dangerous and disruptive to society. Many people in *sha'bi* communities believe that women have a far greater sexual drive than men, and therefore families, society, and religious laws need to protect the community from the disruptive influence of women. Sabbah argues that this view of woman as "omnisexual" is deeply embedded in the Muslim cultural order. Because many powerful groups in society believe that the sexuality of women should be controlled, individuals and groups who are working to end the practice of female circumcision face many obstacles.[46]

In one discussion that occurred when many members of an extended family were visiting each other, the women in the family argued that circumcision was "Islamic" while one of the husbands claimed that it was a Pharaonic and African tribal custom that the Prophet MuHammad did not impose on the community of believers.[47] Male circumcision was a precept of Islam, but female circumcision a matter of custom or ritual, he argued.[48] One of the married women maintained that circumcision caused frigidity or sexual coldness (*'il-baruuda*). Upon hearing this, a husband turned to his wife, in front of her relatives, and asked her what she would have been like if she had not been circumcised, intimating that she was hardly sexually frigid. Laughter followed, but the exchange between the couple touched upon two of the most critical issues that surround the extremely sensitive political debate over the practice of female circumcision in Egypt: the belief that circumcision performs a social function by controlling the dangerous libidinous appetite of women and that it is a religious duty to circumcise one's daughters.[49]

Circumcision is seen as a rite of passage, which occurs before a girl reaches puberty and prepares a woman to engage in sexual relations when she marries. There are women and men in the community who specialize in the procedure, but they are not trained or licensed by the state.[50] They are paid significant sums (£E50) to circumcise the young daughters in a family, and often cousins will be circumcised on the same day so they can convalesce together. When a young girl has been circumcised, her condition is carefully monitored for a week and she is fed more nutritious, expensive foods to celebrate the ritual and encourage her convalescence. In a tradition that probably dates to pre-Islamic Egypt, the part of her clitoris that was removed is wrapped in a black armband and worn for a week, before it is then thrown into the Nile or any *baHr* (sea) to ensure her fertility.

After a girl is circumcised, people make fairly lewd sexual references to her approaching sexual maturity. The ritual is highly public and is almost treated as a celebration within the family (although they carefully monitor her health). On one such occasion, a middle-class family suggested to the very poor mother of two daughters, who lived in a one-room shack without plumbing, that she have the girls circumcised in their home. The neighboring family took over the care of the two young children, feeding them nutritious meals and caring for their wounds until they convalesced.

Many Egyptians wrongly assume that female circumcision is practiced in most other Muslim countries.[51] Within this community, circumcision is identified as an Islamic prescript that responsible believers must maintain. One religious middle-aged woman who had never married argued that even if the government tried to forbid the practice, people would continue to circumcise their daughters because they believed it was an Islamic practice. This woman pointed out that the government had indirectly tried to eradicate the practice by withdrawing the licenses of trained women who performed circumcisions. During the conversation, she told her colleagues about the much more radical form of female circumcision in the Sudan where they "cut away everything," which she had learned about from a Sudanese neighbor. These women were horrified, particularly when she also told them about the practice of infibulation among Sudanese women.[52] These women seemed to be aware of the major health risks that infibulation would cause, but did not associate the less radical *sunna* type of circumcision in Egypt with medical complications.

The history of the campaign to eradicate circumcision in Africa and other parts of the world was linked for many people with the colonial period of occupation and influence. In the Sudan and less directly in Egypt, colonial authorities and foreign associations viewed female circumcision as proof of the barbarism and lower "civilization" of the colonized populations. Deniz Kandiyoti has suggested that during the confrontation instigated by the West's increasingly successful Christian, European encroachments on the Muslim territories of the Ottoman Empire, " 'The woman question' emerged as a hotly contested ideological terrain where women were used to symbolize the progressive aspirations of a secularist elite or a hankering for cultural authenticity expressed in Islamic terms." Largely unable to resist the West militarily or economically, women and the family became a rallying point of cultural resistance and thus efforts to eradicate female circumcision were seen as bowing to Western dominance.[53]

Since independence, both governments have been reluctant to interfere and directly regulate this practice, in fear of the opposition such a move would cause. When the government sees foreign associations attacking the practice, it is even more reluctant to act, fearing that it will be accused of submitting to foreign and non-Muslim interests. Within the past decade Egyptian and Sudanese health associations and women's groups have begun a campaign to end female circumcision by concentrating on the medical complications that frequently occur at the time of the operation or later as a young woman matures sexually and gives birth. Some of these efforts have been assisted by nongovernmental international organizations such as UNICEF and the World Health Organization, thus minimizing any negative association with Western governments or organizations.

In 1985 a group of Egyptian women from various disciplines established a collective to produce a revised Egyptian version of the Boston Women's

Health Book Collective's *Our Bodies, Ourselves* that would provide accessible, simple, and objective information on a wide range of health and sexuality issues from the perspective of Egyptian women. The collective filled a large gap in the market for this type of information, and after a great deal of effort and discussion the book was published in 1991.[54] Segments of the book also addressed the issue of female circumcision. In an article describing the efforts of the collective, Nadia Farah, its supervisor, explained the sensitivities surrounding the issue of female circumcision:

> In many Western feminist health books that discuss Middle Eastern or Muslim women, the entire issue of women's health is reduced to that of female circumcision. An understandable reaction to this attitude was an aversion by Arab women to discuss the issue at all. After many discussions, the members of the collective agreed to present the issue of circumcision in a way that explained the cultural context allowing the continuation of the practice and that offered objective information on the drawbacks of the practice to women readers.[55]

In their book the authors clearly explain the negative medical, psychological, and sexual consequences of circumcision and refute the claims, on medical grounds, of the role of circumcision in controlling chastity and female sexuality. "We stress that female circumcision does not lead to an increase in chastity and perhaps evidence for that is that circumcision is widespread in parts of Africa where sexual relations between young women and men are allowed before marriage."[56] To counter the assumed connection between circumcision and Islam, they stress that "the clitoris is a creation of God so that man and woman can be equally happy since the sexual experience will be completed easily and both of them will take pleasure and reach a state of orgasm within minutes."[57] This collective, facing the challenge of changing deeply held cultural and sexual norms, concluded that the most effective strategy to change this custom was by making more information available to a wide cross-section of women through the book (including a plan to record the book on audio cassettes for illiterate women), pamphlets, and public-speaking engagements by Egyptian professionals involved in the project.

> We believe that the act of mutilating the sexual organs of women is nothing but one of the methods of subjugation which women in our society must face and which is forced on them and inherited by them over time. It is not possible for us to look at this issue except with a comprehensive view of the problems of women in society and her unfortunate situation in it. We must bear in mind that the physical subjection of women takes many forms in human societies, which maintain their inherited customs and traditions. There is no doubt that it is difficult to change what is harmful in those customs until society changes as a whole and its economic and social structure, education, and culture changes. And, as a result, the unequal relationship between men and women changes to a more equal and healthy relationship. But, it may be possible at the present time for us to focus on the fact that circumcision is a health problem which

causes physical and psychological damages to women, just as it is possible, with medical and scientific facts . . . to demonstrate to women and men alike that circumcision is one of the unfortunate inherited traditions in our society and that it causes health problems for women. We must avoid it so that she can live a more healthy and harmonious life.[58]

The amount of attention that sensitive issues such as virginity, rape, child abuse, or female circumcision receive by various organizations, the media, or the government varies over time, but these issues touch the vital concerns of a broad section of Egyptian society. As the sections above have illustrated, communities exert considerable individual and collective efforts to maintain communal norms of morality and to promote the common goal of reproducing the family. Norms of sexual behavior and gender relations are bound by the rules of the community, and if it believes that government initiatives may threaten those norms the government should expect them to express their sentiments. While the form of this expression and its strength depends, of course, on the particular issue and context, it could be argued that the issues of sexuality and gender relations, right or wrong, are as sensitive to the *sha῾b* as national security is to the state.

THE COST OF MARRIAGE: AN ECONOMIC NIGHTMARE

The struggle to marry off children receives prominence in this chapter because it was the single most concerted financial and social effort that every family with children confronted. It is a common, shared struggle that is deeply influenced by larger phenomena. Reproducing the family and the re-creation of community is a question of survival. Yet this supposedly apolitical social goal rarely figures into the explanation of economic phenomena in Egypt—either from the perspective of how government policies affect the goal of reproducing the family or how the goal of reproducing the family affects government policy. This section will examine both sides of this question.

The families least absorbed by this issue are those with very young children who have not yet had to face this dilemma. Alternatively, young married couples can usually recount the price, quality, and origin of each and every item they brought to the marriage. In many young households, the wife or husband may have younger siblings who are just beginning or older siblings who are deeply involved in the process of marrying. Marriage preoccupies an extensive cross-section of the community.

Many stories, often repeated, concerned the dowries of young girls in the neighborhood, the price and quality of housewares or fabric for a young woman's trousseau, or new housing or apartments that had come on the market. Fortunately, Egyptians constantly discuss the price of goods and services and have an uncanny ability to remember purchases or expenses made years earlier.[59] An inventory of the items purchased, exchanged, or produced for marriage makes it apparent that marriage demands a larger investment of capital than any other single factor in the lives of most men and women in *sha'bi* communities (with the possible exception of capital investment in business or trade among the few wealthy families in this community).

As outlined earlier in the chapter, very straightforward financial negotiations between the family of the bride and groom occur at the earliest stage of arranging a marriage. Both families contribute to the costs of the wedding. However, the groom's side (either the groom himself or with the assistance of his family) must spend approximately twice the amount that the bride's family is expected to contribute (either the bride herself or her family). More specifically, in 1985 the average cost a groom in my community had to bear amounted to £E10,000, while a bride and her family would spend approximately half that amount, or £E5,000.[60] Exceptions, however, are common, particularly if the circumstances are unusual. A poor couple might only be able to purchase two rooms of furniture or even one, or else take a small apartment in a low-rent district far from the center of Cairo, or even have to live with their in-laws in an extra room to minimize expenses. Other couples or their families may enter into unusual arrangements for various reasons. For example, an illiterate young man who had become wealthy due to a productive workshop or shrewd trading deals wished to improve his social status by marrying an educated woman from a prominent local family. In order to make the match more attractive to her parents, he refused to accept any contribution from the bride's family and offered to bear the considerable cost of the marriage alone.

In another case, a father who worked in Libya for many years as a skilled worker became friends with two Libyan brothers. When the brothers visited Egypt, they brought presents to his five daughters from their own father. Upon their return to Libya they informed the girls' father that they wanted to marry his eldest two daughters and live with them in Libya. The father arranged for the two daughters (one only thirteen, the other twenty-eight) to fly to Libya for the wedding with only the clothes they were wearing rather than the usual bride's trousseau. Because the Libyans expected the daughters to remain there and were far wealthier, they agreed to bear all the costs of the two marriages. Although the father found a way around financing his eldest two daughters' marriages, he remained in Libya for seventeen years to save enough money to marry off his remaining three daughters (and to open a small automobile repair workshop that would sustain his family once he returned to Egypt).

Typically, a groom must provide the marital abode (usually an apartment or, for poorer couples, a room in an apartment), major appliances, a dower, and a significant gift of gold jewelry (*shabka*) as well as bear the expense of the final wedding celebration. The bride's family uses the dower to purchase usually two or three matched furniture sets for the new couple's home (part of the woman's dowry, or *gihaaz*). The dower alone, however, is not enough to purchase this furniture, and the bride's family must supplement it with a sum that is usually double the original amount of the dower (people speak of completing or adding to the sum of the dower, *yikammilu-ha*). Within my community, three rooms of furniture were routinely provided for newly-weds. In addition, the bride's family provides kitchen ware, some household items, and the bride's wardrobe.

In order to convey the extent, value, and quantity of the material requirements of a marriage, two case studies will be presented. These young people and their families are representative of others in the area. Each match faced serious difficulties and periodic crises that were typical of many marriages and engagements. Table 2.1 presents the expenses of the young man referred to earlier whose initial engagement was canceled due to a succession of untimely deaths. Table 2.2 details the wedding expenses of the youngest daughter (age nineteen) of a large family with limited financial resources. Although this woman was engaged and her wedding was imminent, problems developed between the groom and her family and the engagement was finally broken, against the young woman's wishes. The tables portray in detail the expenses and specificity of components of *il-gihaaz* (which refers to all the material goods the bride's side must bring to a marriage). Incidental costs of marriage such as gifts to a bride and her family and entertainment are not included in these tables.

The most costly outlay for the groom is an apartment (or set of rooms if he is very poor). In Egypt the demand for affordable housing is greater than the supply of apartments.[61] Although rents are very inexpensive for older housing units due to pre–World War II rent control laws and politically motivated rent reductions during the early Nasserist period,[62] the cost of housing for newlyweds has skyrocketed during the last fifteen years.[63] One in-depth study estimated that couples within the lowest quartile of income distribution in Egypt now spend 30 percent of their income on rent.[64]

A greater expense for couples creating a new household is the price of "key money," which has become the prevailing strategy used by landlords to circumvent strict rent control laws. Landlords and contractors demand that new tenants pay a large sum before occupying an apartment because, once the lease is signed, they have the right to remain there for life, with subsequent rent increases mandated only by the government. *Xiliww rigl*, or key money, is, literally, the cost of removing someone's foot (the previous tenant's) from the apartment. While key money was not uncommon before the mid-1970s, the average sums involved were much lower, particularly for low- or middle-income housing.[65] One estimate suggests that both the incidence and amount of key money has increased at a rate of 30 percent annually, equaling or even exceeding increases in the cost of land and construction.[66] One couple in my community, after three and a half years of an exhausting and frustrating search for an apartment, paid £E2,000 in key money and a rent of £E20 in 1981. Four years later the price of key money

TABLE 2.1
A Groom's Marriage Expenses

Item	Cost (£E)
Dower	1,500
Shabka (jewelry gift at time of engagement)	500
Wedding ring for bride	70
Housing	
Key money for three-room apartment	3,500
Rent (12 × £E50 due to delay in marriage)	600
Furniture	
Entré (informal living room)	1,200
Kitchen cabinets	500
Finishing costs of new apartment (wiring, plumbing)	250
Appliances	
Lamps (chandeliers)	150
Audio cassette player (i.e., "boom box")	150
Washing machine	80
Stove	125
Color television	760
Assorted small appliances	100
Clothing	
New wardrobe for groom, wedding suit	750
Wedding dress and accessories for bride	150
Cost of coiffure for bride	50
Final celebration of wedding (music, rented chairs, lights, refreshments, tent, photos or video)	250
TOTAL	£E10,685

TABLE 2.2
A Bride's Wedding Expenses

Item	Cost (£E)
Furniture (bedroom, dining room, salon)	4,000
Final cost = cost of furniture (6,000) − price of dower (2,000)	
Wardrobe for bride	400
Carpet	150
Cotton mattresses and pillows (hand-stuffed and -sewn)	150
Sheets and linens	130
Kitchenware	470
Wedding ring for groom	70
Engagement party	225
TOTAL	£E5,595

for the same apartment had risen to £E5,500 with a rent of £E45 per month. In 1985 a young couple paid £E5,000 for a three-room apartment in an area of Imbaba that was barely settled, and still under construction. Built on former agricultural land, no paved roads existed in the neighborhood, public transportation did not serve the area, and livestock wandered the streets. Yet this area was attractive to newlyweds and returning migrants who had savings for a new home because of comparatively low prices.

The prohibitive cost of marriage for both the groom and the bride can be reduced in a variety of ways. By moving in with in-laws, newlyweds can greatly reduce housing costs and a lengthy engagement. It is more common that a couple share their living quarters with the groom's parents, but these arrangements depend on the age, financial condition, and health of respective in-laws. In Cairo more than one-third of newly married couples live in complex family households.[67] If a young couple is eligible for subsidized public housing (*masaakin sha'biyya*), their housing costs will be lower than for private-sector housing, although the down payment and monthly rent of even subsidized housing is still prohibitive for some couples.[68]

Many parents plan years in advance for the day when their children will marry. If they own an apartment building, they might be able to add floors or rooms to already existing buildings, or they might be able to build a new apartment building. Parents will keep apartments vacant rather than rent them to outsiders they will not be able to evict when their children need the apartment to marry. Al-Hag SubHy Wihdaan, a member of Parliament and its Standing Committee on Housing, argues that, for this reason and contrary to public opinion, Egypt does not suffer from a housing crisis, but rather that 200,000 apartments lay vacant. In a volatile and highly inflationary housing market, he argues, many families have invested surplus savings in land or real estate in order to ensure that their children can marry at a later date, but the apartments often stand vacant for years.[69] Handoussa argues that housing has been one of the most dynamic sectors of the economy, absorbing over 50 percent of private-sector investments in the decade between 1976 and 1986. Even though an estimated *four million* housing units were built during this time period, as many as 1.79 million completed units remain unused.[70] Several young people in my community were able to marry within a relatively short time either because their parents had set aside an apartment in their building for them or added several floors to an existing building, or else they had invested in land and constructed new housing for their offspring and other relatives.

In order to afford marriages, families engage in long-term financial planning, often for years before their children reach puberty. They reduce their consumption level in order to save for this future investment in the family. From the time of a daughter's birth, the parents, particularly the mother, put aside attractive bargains and gifts that she herself receives over the years, for her daughter. Thus the cost of a trousseau is absorbed by the household's daily budget and, once a daughter is actually engaged, a family can concentrate on meeting other significant costs.[71] An example of this type of planning is detailed in the *gihaaz* of a young woman in Table 2.3. I discovered this cache of goods in a family's storage space by accident one Friday morning. The family was searching for part of the mother's trousseau to sell to a metals dealer, since they no longer used the brass serving trays and cookware. The engaged youngest daughter wanted to see some of her trousseau, which was carefully packaged in boxes and stored under old sheets in the attic. She began opening box after box of kitchen ware, noting what she still needed to purchase. The quantity of goods was staggering (particularly since this family hardly spent any money on food or housewares, and each time a child broke a glass it was treated as a major crisis). Yet upstairs they had a virtual storehouse of kitchen ware. I teased them that they needed a government inspector to come license their store. They were obviously proud of their ability to accumulate this treasure and began to show me each and every item. They also remembered many of the prices of each item and whether they were purchased (P), received as gifts (G), or self-produced (S). The total cost of this trousseau equaled approximately £E1,000, a significant sum in this family whose breadwinner officially earned £E50 per month.

These items had been purchased over a period of five years by the mother and her clever older daughters, who were always looking for bargains. During the exhibition of the trousseau, mother and daughter argued briefly over whether this daughter would receive all of these items when she married in the near future. The mother yelled at her daughter that she was incredibly greedy and certainly did not need twenty-four teacups or thirty coffee cups, for example. The mother thought she might use some of the items for the trousseaus of the next generation—her granddaughters, who were now approaching puberty (the eldest granddaughter was thirteen at the time; the youngest, two and a half). One of the daughter's friends, who visited while the attic was open, claimed that there were certainly enough items stored away to satisfy two or three brides. One of the older sisters, married for more than a decade, jealously argued that the youngest sister was spoiled and that she and her sisters had not been able to marry in such luxury. She argued that each sister should be treated the same. The youngest daughter dismissed such talk and demanded that they begin purchasing the items that were still missing from her trousseau.

Unfortunately, the bride's family can do little to reduce the high cost of furniture. The average cost of a bedroom set that people in this community purchased was approximately £E2,000; a salon, £E1,000; a dining room, £E3,000; and an entrée (informal living room), £E850. Some couples cannot afford such sums and purchase lower-quality, less expensive furniture. However, even those couples with very limited resources will endure great sacrifices to purchase matched furniture sets. Since almost all wood is imported in Egypt, the cost of furniture (sometimes referred to as *xashab*, or wood) is nearly always quite high.[72] In *sha'bi* neighborhoods, when the

TABLE 2.3
A Typical Trousseau

Item	Source
Cups	
18 champagne glasses	P[a]
18 water goblets	P
6 teacups with saucers	P
12 small teacups	P
6 goblets	P
6 inexpensive teacups	P
6 tumblers with pitcher set	G[b]
6 glasses	P
6 small glasses	P
12 inexpensive glasses	P
6 tumblers with pitcher set	G
12 traditional small coffee cups with saucers	G
12 small coffee cups and saucers	P
6 glass Turkish coffee cups and saucers	P
Trays	
12 plastic trays	G
3 plastic Chinese trays (set)	G
1 aluminum tray	P
2 large, glass fruit trays	P
2 plastic-coated wooden trays	G
Cookware	
4 oven trays	P
1 pot (*labbaana*) for heating milk	P
1 frying pan	P
1 aluminum roaster	P
1 oven roaster	P
8-piece aluminum pot set	P
2 aluminum coffee makers	P
Bowls and plates	
6 glass bowls (in shape of apple) and spoons (set)	G
6 plastic bowls	P
12 inexpensive, aluminum bowls	P
1 glass bowl with cover, 6 matching plates	P
6 china bowls with large matching bowl	G
6 glass bowls with matching fruit tray	G
8 inexpensive bowls	P
3 flowered plastic bowls	P
1 large mixing bowl	
6 plastic plates	P
15 inexpensive plates	P
12 plastic plates	P

TABLE 2.3 (*cont.*)

Item	Source
Cutlery	
18 tiny spoons	P
2 large knives	P
1 set of hanging kitchen utensils	P
1 set of cutlery, service for 12	P
1 set of 12 steak knives	P
Incidentals	
1 set of spice jars	G
2 sets of plastic bowls	P
1 sugar bowl	P
9 ashtrays	G
China saltshaker	G
Set of decorative swans with plastic flowers	G
1 glass apple, from China	G
2 porcelain boxes	G
Aluminum bath for infant	P
Three-tiered cake stand	G
1 funnel	P
1 soap dish	P
5 large plastic tubs (laundry, dishes)	P
1 colander	P
Clothing	
12 *gallabiyyas* (housedresses)	G, S[c]
3 pajamas	P
2 sets of a robe, nightgown, underwear	G
1 nightgown and robe set	S
5 robes	P
Underwear (one dozen)	P
4 bras	P
10 slips	P
2 sets of Chinese slippers	G
11 pieces of fabric for dresses, skirts	G, S
Linen	
3 sets of bedsheets (one for the wedding night)	P
2 bedspreads	P
4 single sheets	P
1 set of pillow cases	G
1 elaborate bedspread for the wedding night	P
12 towels	P
6 linen napkins	P
4 sets of handkerchiefs	G
Still to be Purchased	
1 expensive set of china dishes	(£E160)
1 set of everyday plastic dishes	(£E70)

[a] P = Purchased.
[b] G = Received as gift.
[c] S = Self-produced.

furniture arrives from a local workshop or is delivered from Dumyyaat, the provincial capital known for its furniture workshops, people form a lively, noisy procession behind the truck or cart, and women *byzaghraTu*, or ululate (the unmistakable high, shrill cry that signifies a wedding or part of a marriage ritual or other significant event).[73] Since everyone can see the style and wealth of the bride's family, now open to public view, the family usually makes sure everyone knows how much they spent on the furniture, sometimes slightly inflating its value.[74]

According to one young groom from the area, this propensity to show off each and every item in the *gihaaz* inflates the cost of marriage. It is *kalaam in-naas*, or "what people say" that provokes competition and envy in the community between families who try to prove that they provide only the best for their daughters (and sons). An editorial in an Islamic weekly, published by the government's National Democratic Party, addressed this issue when it chided the public for ostentatious living, particularly the increasingly common phenomenon of large wedding receptions (the article claimed that twelve million pounds are lavished on wedding receptions in hotels each year). The paper did not condemn the wealthy but encouraged people to spend their money on the poor since "to be a Muslim is to be charitable."[75] A member of Parliament, who was often asked by people in the community to loan them money to finance a wedding, criticized *shaʿbi* people in her district for their propensity to buy the most expensive sets of furniture as a way of showing off their wealth to "keep up with the Jones's." These comments seem justified when one visits any woman who has been married within the past five years because she will usually insist on showing off every piece of her trousseau and *gihaaz* and volunteer the price and origin of each item without any encouragement.

When a couple finally marries, they are extremely proud of their new home. Their standard of living and material possessions are proof not only of their own sacrifices and resourcefulness but the status and wealth of their families. Since marriage is a collective endeavor, all those who have also contributed to the match's progress are proud when a couple finally occupies their new home. For this reason they brag and display the couple's possessions. A bare household or cheap furnishings reflects poorly on the couple and their families. In one incident, a younger brother was engaged and married to a woman within a few short months, while his older brother's engagement dragged on and was beset by disagreements between the two families. As the latter's fiancée explained, the father of the younger brother's bride was extremely stingy and unconcerned about his daughter. He made very few demands on the groom and contributed even less to his daughter's marriage. In contrast, the older brother was having endless problems with his future in-laws because they were quite specific and demanding in their expectations of him and he never seemed able to satisfy them. When he would complain and wistfully compare his experience to his brother's, they would retort, *'ig-gawaaz mish saahil ʿandina* (marriage does not come easily, or cheaply, within our family). A family would not be protecting its daughter (or son) and doing its duty if it did not place considerable material demands on a young man (or daughter).

Marriage has not always been such a formidable economic obstacle. After the introduction of the Open Door policy in 1974, economic liberalization, deregulation of parts of the economy, foreign investment, and rising wage rates sparked a period of high inflation and greater consumption. Wages for skilled and unskilled workers rose as Gulf countries attracted more Egyptian workers, thus pushing up domestic wage rates. As workers returned to Egypt with labor remittances, rising consumer demand spurred local production of cheap consumer goods as well as encouraging many moderately prosperous merchants to import finished, expensive consumer goods. The range and price of housewares, clothing, and furniture rose tremendously—thereby inflating the costs of getting married.

An analysis of changes in the value of dowers over a 23-year period within one family offers interesting comparisons that confirm national economic trends (Table 2.4).

At the height of the Open Door policy, between 1975 and 1979, the value of a dowry in the family cited in Table 2.4 increased by 25 percent per year in real prices and 58 percent in nominal prices. By the 1980s the dramatic increase in the value of dowers leveled off, with only a 2.9 percent increase per year in real terms. Even though the percentage change in real terms was much lower than in nominal terms, people still think in terms of nominal prices when they calculate their financial needs, and thus these increases were considered very dramatic. Furthermore, wages in the public and private sectors did not rise nearly as quickly as the value of dowers. Part of the reason for this steep increase of dowry costs within this one family can be explained by the educational qualifications of the daughters. The second and third daughters had only finished intermediate school (the equivalent to junior high school in the United States) while the fourth daughter graduated from commercial secondary school, thereby increasing the value of the dower that she expected. The changes in this family are representative of a general trend within the community as more women from this socioeconomic background complete secondary education, particularly commercial education. Within one family, it is not uncommon for some children (male or female) to be literate and even to enter university, while other children may leave school at twelve and remain functionally illiterate.[76]

To a large degree, communal norms determine the value of a dowry and dower, and there is reluctance to increase them since members of the community would themselves bear the burden of inflated dowries. Further study is needed before it can be determined whether changes in the value of dowers and dowries corresponds to inflationary pressures and the cost of living. In a similar fashion, the value of the *shabka* given to the bride as an engagement present is determined by standards set by the community. If a sudden rise in the price of gold occurs, families will usually accept fewer gold bracelets or a less expensive necklace, recognizing the limits of the resources of young men.

TABLE 2.4

The Dowry of a Mother and Her Daughters from One Family in the Sample, 1947–1985

Year	Nominal Prices (£E)[a]	% Change per Year[a]	GDP Deflator[b]	Real Prices (1980) (£E)	% Change per Year[c]
Mother, 1947	50	—	—	—	—
Eldest daughter, 1969	150	—	35.1	427.3	—
Second daughter, 1973	200	8.3	42.0	476.2	2.9
Third daughter, 1975	300	25.0	51.3	584.8	11.4
Fourth daughter, 1979	1,000	58.0	84.9	1,177.8	25.3
Fifth daughter, 1985	2,000	16.6	144.0	1,385.0	2.9

[a] Figure represents percent change per year between each interval.
[b] World Bank and International Finance Corporation, *World Tables: 1988–89*, pp. 234–35.
[c] Figure represents percent change per year between each interval.

Exploiting a groom, or demanding a high dower, occasionally backfires. If a bride receives a large dower, the groom and his family will expect her family to use the money to purchase at least three sets of high-quality, expensive furniture. They know the cost of the furniture from their knowledge of the market, and the value of the furniture is eventually registered in the *'ayma*, or list. An important document, all receipts of items in the *gihaaz* are saved and their prices are registered in this list of goods. The document is signed by the bridegroom and usually remains with the bride's mother for safekeeping. In the event of divorce, the couple and the families consult the *'ayma* to divide the property (the party that purchased a good keeps it in the event of a divorce). Thus when one woman asked for a high dower for her daughter, she agreed to purchase three rooms of furniture, knowing that the groom and his family would expect nothing less for such a high dower. The older married children of this woman argued with her, pointing out that she would be the one to bear the financial burden of finding thousands of pounds needed to purchase three rooms of furniture. Of course, they also realized that their mother's decision would increase their own expected contributions to their sister's marriage. Regardless of the financial burden, the mother maintained that her daughter should receive a large dower and thus committed herself to several years of economic austerity. In this instance, the goal of marrying off her daughter outweighed other less compelling personal and familial needs.

In the late 1940s, couples did not have to wait many years in order to accumulate the items and money needed for marriage. A groom's family supplied most of the provisions, including all the furnishings, which were simple and inexpensive in relation to the standard of living. However, the material side of marriage was not ignored. In the family referred to in Table 2.4, the mother's marriage had been delayed for fifteen days at the last moment. She lived in the same building as her fiancé, and his mother had refused to sign the copy of the *'ayma*, suspecting that her family had inflated the value of certain goods. (When each family signs the *'ayma*, they are publicly accepting the listed value of the goods.) Only after fifteen days of constant pressure from the groom did his mother allow the wedding to take place. The *'ayma* protects the material interests of both the bride and groom. This system is still very pervasive in *sha'bi* communities, particularly these days as the material investment in marriage has soared.[77]

While certain costs of marriage are controlled more by the community than by pure market forces, the impact of the Open Door policy on the cost of marriage can be clearly seen by the skyrocketing cost of furniture. National demand and the international market determines the price of furniture—although communal norms determine how many rooms of furniture a proper family should purchase for their daughter(s). In the early 1970s the family mentioned in Table 2.4 purchased two rooms of furniture each for their second and third daughters; by the late 1970s this increased to three for the fourth daughter. While three rooms of furniture sold for £E700 in 1973, the price had risen to £E5,000 by 1979. Another family that had purchased two rooms of furniture for £E600 in 1975, purchased three rooms of furniture for £E5,000 in 1979. If we estimate that an additional room of furniture in 1975 would have cost £E900 (assuming each set cost £E300), the price of furniture over the course of four years rose 455 percent in nominal terms.[78] Thus, changes in the market, over which the community has much less control, deeply affect the cost of marriage.

There are certain limits to the sacrifices men, women, and their families will make for marriage. In some cases, a family's demands are so excessive, or their expectations for the material well-being of their sons or daughters so unrealistic, that the groom (in most cases) cannot deliver, and the engagement is broken. Prominent members of the community often condemn excessive materialistic burdens on young men or women. Young people complain about the greed and materialistic fantasies of some members of the community, because they are the victims. One young man who witnessed the negotiations relating to his younger sister's betrothal had been working two jobs to save enough money to marry his fiancée and rose at four in the morning each day to begin his first job. Despite his efforts, his future father-in-law was dissatisfied at his progress. He begged his mother not to place excessive demands on his sister's fiancé and to lower her financial expectations. His sister, hoping to enjoy a high standard of living after she married, told him in no uncertain terms to mind his own business.

The cost of a wedding remains the most demanding financial burden in the community.[79] As one young man explained, one cannot judge the wealth of people from visual appearances, since so many young and middle-aged couples save all their money to finance the eventual marriages of their children. They sacrifice their youth and live modestly, carefully investing their savings in land and property (for future housing needs). And while the sums mentioned above may seem excessive, they are typical of *sha'bi* communities, which suggests that communities in Egypt with more resources spend even larger sums to meet the goal of reproducing the family. In a sense, the capacity of people to raise such large amounts, under conditions of scarcity, is evidence of how important this goal is to individuals, families, and the community. The following section describes some of the mechanisms that *sha'bi* communities have created to facilitate this goal.

RAISING THE CAPITAL TO MARRY

The words diligence, ingenuity, discipline, and sacrifice aptly describe the characteristics needed to reproduce the family in Cairo today. Throughout *sha'bi* communities, men and women utilize a variety of strategies to accumulate the capital to marry. They will exploit their own labor power by working two or three jobs and long hours of overtime. Some, primarily young men, travel abroad in search of more lucrative wage rates and increased savings. Since the family also contributes material resources to a marriage, young men and women must protect their power and position within the family, as a means of securing an appropriate proportion of scarce family resources for their marriages.

Individual, familial, and communal resources are devoted to fulfilling the common goal of reproducing the family. This goal can only be met, within this community at this particular time, through elaborate processes and collective institutions that the community supports. Men and women from the extended family as well as neighbors and colleagues contribute their expertise, whatever it may be: knowing an inexpensive jeweler, pursuing a tip about an affordable apartment, arranging a job for a young man, sewing part of the trousseau, cooking the food for a wedding celebration, organizing a savings association, or arranging the match in the first place.

Within *sha'bi* communities the financial, political, or social resources of families vary considerably. Some families were prosperous enough to contribute cash or housing to their children, while other families could only contribute modest sums, after considerable sacrifices, leaving the bulk of the financial responsibility to their children. One rich merchant offered his son a large, modern flat in a new building he had recently constructed, while a young woman's father, who owned a small textile factory, could employ her as a machine operator (by working for her father she escaped the opprobrium of working in a factory shared by many in the community, particularly toward unmarried working women). Another young man's uncle, who had worked for years in Libya and Saudi Arabia, arranged a lucrative, upwardly mobile job for his nephew through his personal contacts.

While there are many examples of couples who receive the unqualified support of their immediate and extended families, there are other couples who must rely on themselves to finance their wedding. Some families simply do not have excess money since they must spend all their income just to support a large family. Other young adults already support infirm, elderly, or retired parents who have no resources except advice and support to contribute to their marriage. In such cases, elderly parents will still try to use their knowledge of the community and their networks to search for an inexpensive apartment or a more lucrative job. An elderly mother may sew most of the trousseau for a son or daughter. On the other hand, couples who marry against the wishes of their families risk losing their financial support, or receive minimal support at best. Some parents may formally agree to the child's choice of a spouse, but then proceed to make excessive financial demands or find fault with every move, so that ultimately the engagement collapses under the pressure.

In general, however, the support that children receive from their families in order to marry is remarkable. Even if a family is not pleased by the choice of spouse, they will usually assist their son or daughter by devoting considerable resources to the marriage, while supporting the rest of the family as well. Relatives typically come to the rescue of a young cousin, sister, niece, or nephew experiencing difficulties in meeting the final costs of a marriage. While some men, as a way of proving their resourcefulness and maturity, insist on financing their marriage expenses without any help from their family, others absorb vast proportions of familial resources without remorse. One young man in the community even went to the extent of hiding some appliances he had purchased for his marriage, in order to receive greater assistance from his family. Each household's circumstances differ, as well as the capabilities and resourcefulness of each couple. Incidental factors can jeopardize any match between two families, but the process of marrying is always costly.

A basic reality, which cannot be emphasized enough, is that at an average cost of £E15,000, marriage is an extremely expensive undertaking within this community. For many months I found it very difficult to understand how people managed to accumulate such sums, particularly in view of their low salaries. Young men typically earned between £E100 and £E150 per month (government employees were at the lower end of that spectrum, skilled workers in private workshops working long hours were at the higher end). With overtime and two or three jobs, that figure could feasibly be raised to £E200 or £E250 per month. Using a monthly income of £E175 per month, it would take a young man four years and nine months to earn £E10,000, assuming he saved completely all his earnings. In the marriage referred to in the previous section, which occurred in 1947, the groom earned £E10 per month and only needed to save his salary for one year to accumulate the cost of his dower, *shabka*, and household furnishings. These days, since the family of the groom usually contributes to his wedding expenses, he does not need to save every penny of his salary for four years and nine months, but there is still a looming gap between income and the capital needed to marry. Young men generally expect to devote five or even ten years of their lives to the process of capital accumulation, before they can marry.[80] They plan their education, career path, and love life around this financial campaign.

Women at a young age generally have lower earnings potentials than men and often take positions as low-ranking government employees, low-paid workers in private stores or organizations, or moderately paid workers in small workshops and factories producing textiles or ready-made clothes. These women usually cannot work long hours because they are also expected to take care of domestic chores, and it would be socially unacceptable for them to work late at night or for hours on end in stores or artisanal workshops. A typical salary for a young woman might approach £E60 per month ($45), while many women earn less, and only a few earn more.[81] It would take a young woman approximately seven years to accumulate wedding expenses of £E5,000 at the above rate. Although most families finance most or all of a bride's wedding expenses, in some situations she must finance her wedding herself, and the ability of these women to reach this goal despite unequal wage scales and job constraints is impressive.

Many women who work in order to finance their wedding quit their jobs just before getting married. Other women, however, intend to continue working after marriage and carefully inform their fiancés before the marriage to negotiate their support. A large number of men in this community believe that it is the man's responsibility to support the household and view a working wife as an indication of the husband's inability to support the household.[82] Several engagements in the community ended when a woman realized her future husband would not allow her to work after marriage. In many cases, it was the woman who would break off the engagement, rather than quit her job. (A profile of working women in this community will be discussed in Chapter 4.)

Men can accelerate the process of capital accumulation for marriage by seeking higher-paid jobs in Gulf countries, Libya, or Europe.[83] They are usually willing to endure poor living conditions and separation from their families in order to marry sooner. Some men who have little education or marketable vocational skills have few options other than to become migrant workers. An unskilled worker abroad can earn much more than an unskilled worker in Egypt (although frequently expectations are disappointed and migrants return to Egypt with only moderate savings). Until the economic recession in the Gulf countries in the late 1980s and the severe disruption in opportunities abroad caused by the Iraqi invasion of Kuwait and the ensuing war, many men who were recently married or engaged had worked abroad in order to finance their wedding expenses. Some of these young men became so dependent on their employment abroad that after marrying they left Egypt again to begin saving money to finance businesses that would support their family once they finally returned to Egypt. In some cases these men returned to their jobs abroad as little as a week after their wedding, and the bride returned to her parent's home to await her husband's return or the birth of a child. After a woman has had several children, she usually stops returning to her parental home when the husband returns abroad.[84] Each additional birth places contradictory pressures on a migrant: to return to Egypt permanently to raise and enjoy his family or to return abroad to earn a salary that can support a larger family.

Often the father of a family with many daughters worked abroad to raise their marriage expenses. The fathers of both families in the community with five daughters and no sons had spent most of their adult lives working abroad. Both of these men did not return to Egypt until they had accumulated enough capital to establish workshops that would support them once they returned. One of the fathers began building a three-floor apartment building in one of the newly settled residential areas surrounding Cairo, to reduce the future costs of his daughter's marriages.

Women, in albeit fewer numbers and generally in more professional capacities, have also exploited lucrative opportunities in the Gulf.[85] But the growing difficulty experienced in securing employment abroad has diminished the financial opportunities for both men and women. If they must depend on the Egyptian economy and limited salaries to finance a marriage, average lengths of engagement will increase and frustration with the political and economic system may be aired more publicly and more aggressively. Egyptian government officials realize the importance of migration to the economy and to political stability, and cooperate with their counterparts in the Gulf to keep these opportunities available.

Young men are so eager to migrate abroad that the financial lure outweighs concerns for personal safety. To illustrate, Egyptian men traveled readily to Iraq during the long war with Iran (1980–1988). Iraq was one of the few countries that did not require Egyptians to have a work contract and an official sponsor before they were granted entrance visas. Thus, Iraq became one of the most popular destinations for Egyptian workers, particularly those who did not have the skills, contacts, or references to obtain contracts elsewhere.[86] An undisclosed number of Egyptians were killed in Iraq during the war, and these men often came from *sha'bi* communities. People in these communities mentioned neighbors or friends who had died there. The extent of the Egyptian government's official role in providing Egyptian workers to the Iraqis was vague and unpublicized, but there were rumored reports that Egyptians were used extensively to supply services for Iraqi troops engaged at the front.

Earning a high salary, or working sixty hours a week, or migrating abroad does not necessarily mean that people will save their money unless there is an efficient savings mechanism and reinforcement from others. Because Egyptians labor so hard to accumulate "marriage capital," they have developed an extremely impressive savings ethic. Almost every wedding in these areas was financed, in part, by a *gam'iyya* or informal savings association. In a savings association, a small number of associates contribute a fixed sum to the leader of an association at a regular interval (while some associations are daily or weekly, particularly among merchants, more commonly they are monthly). The leader collects the money at each interval (the end of the day, week, or month) and gives it immediately to one participant, in a lump sum. The order of the lump sum payment to each member is agreed upon ahead of time. For example, if an association is organized among ten participants, with a monthly contribution of £E50 for a period of ten months, each month one member of the association receives £E500. While some of the costs of marriage were funded directly from salaries or wages, the more imposing costs such as housing, key money, expensive appliances, the dower, and the *shabka* were often saved through a *gam'iyya*.

The groom uses *gam'iyyaat* (pl.) to finance his greatest expenses. He may participate in several associations in order to purchase different items, coordinating the time he receives his lump sum payments with the timetable of the engagement negotiated previously with his bride's family. For example, he may begin saving his salary with one association for his fiancée's dower. If he has a good reputation (i.e., a strong credit rating) and close ties to a leader of an association, she will schedule him to receive the first lump sum collected. As will be discussed further in Chapter 3, women are much more commonly leaders of *gam'iyyaat* than men, although men may organize associations in workplaces or markets where few women participate. Women are commonly the organizers of informal savings associations throughout the world.[87] As he continues to contribute to the first association, the groom may begin to work a second job and use that money to participate in a second long-term association to accumulate the key money for an apartment, knowing that he will not be able to meet this large cost for a year or eighteen months. Saving money in two associations doubles the financial pressure, since he cannot renege on either commitment or everyone else in the association will lose money and his reputation will suffer tremendously. If there is any extra money after meeting these two payments, he may purchase the small appliances, clothes, or gifts that are expected by his bride and her family during an engagement.

Since the costs of marriage are so high, a long engagement allows a couple and their families to participate in several long-term savings associations, each of which finances a particular component of the marriage. One groom demanded a short engagement since he was completely prepared to marry (he had already been engaged to another young woman and had worked abroad for years to finance both his and his sisters' weddings). The mother of the bride, however, resisted his demands because she needed time to "work" her money in several savings associations. Only by careful budgeting, loans, and participating in long-term savings associations could she amass the £E4,000 needed to purchase her daughter's *gihaaz*.

These associations are not profit-making, since no interest is given to participants and the leader of the association does not claim a fee or salary. While many members of the community have bank accounts in public- and private-sector banks, they are under no obligation to make regular deposits. (In addition, since formal interest rates hardly keep pace with inflation, there is little incentive to use the banking system.)[88] However, in a *gam'iyya*, once a person is committed to participating, he or she is forced to make regular payments for the duration of the association. These associations, therefore, enhance a savings ethic in the community. The logic of the *gam'iyya* is similar to that of a "Christmas Club" in the United States, where banks offer customers a structured program that forces saving for a particular end.

The money saved in these associations circulates and is reinvested in the community through purchases of jewelry, housing, furniture, or dowries. While people use these associations to finance many other needs, young couples and their families rely on *gam'iyyaat* to help them raise the capital needed for marriage. *Gam'iyyaat* lie completely outside the formal banking sector and elude government regulation or taxation. While these associations have existed for several decades, if not longer, recently they have filled an important need for credit and savings institutions in this community.[89] Yet informal savings associations, despite their importance to *sha'bi* communities, have remained hidden from national accounts and deserve much greater attention from scholars, particularly economists and historians. Standard analyses of the Egyptian economy rarely make reference to informal savings associations, either as a source of credit or as a vehicle for savings. In the next section the position and role of *gam'iyyaat* in Egypt's national economy will be analyzed (a more detailed discussion of the structure and internal dynamics of savings associations will be presented in the following chapter).

In family after family within this community, the decision was made to invest limited financial resources in engagements and marriage. Despite differences in familial and individual resources, expectations, and marriage protocol, people struggled to marry off their sons and daughters. Through marriage, the family transferred wealth and status to the next generation. En masse, these individual and family decisions influence the political economy of this community and, as shall be discussed in the next section, resonate upward as well.

Conclusions: Marriage, the Economy, and the State

Throughout the world, political preferences and demands evolve from people's most urgent needs and problems. At the same time, these desires and preferences are deeply affected and influenced by larger political, social, and economic phenomena, structures, and ideologies. This chapter has argued that reproducing the family is one of the universal goals of individuals and families within *sha'bi* communities. As the first two sections of this chapter demonstrated, individual and collective behavior reinforces this goal, and the community's actions are devoted to its realization. At some point, when a broad constituency shares a common objective, they expect their government to be sensitive and responsive to it—or to at least acknowledge the issue as part of their calculations when they consider new policies. In this case, the *sha'b* believe that the government should consider the intended and unintended consequences of policy changes on the cost and complexity of getting married. However, the government does not address this need, except in certain indirect ways (to be discussed below).

The government is sensitive to other issues that directly and indirectly impinge upon the cost of marriage, such as government subsidies, inflation, employment policies, migration, or housing and so on. It may expect the public to object to price increases or reductions in government employment but often seems surprised by the severity and spontaneous nature of public opposition. Minor policy changes (or even rumors of such changes) can produce major challenges to the government, as evidenced by the extensive food riots in 1977 and the Security Forces rebellion in 1986. At times, the public's responses to government policies can be better understood by considering the collective need to reproduce the family.[90] For example, government food and commodity subsidies are critically important because they keep daily expenses to a minimum, thereby allowing the *sha'b* to accumulate the savings needed to fund the significant costs of marriage (and other expenses). The daily lives of people revolve around watching prices, finding bargains, using public and private services with the most value for the cost, and so on. Minimal changes in household budgets can upset carefully laid savings strategies and prolong marriages even farther into the future.

Since migration has been such an important outlet for young workers in Egypt, people monitor foreign affairs in order to keep track of new opportunities. A rhetorical conflict between Libya or Saudi Arabia and Egypt is not cause for concern, but when Egyptian migrant laborers are expelled and visas revoked, Egyptians understand the seriousness of the dispute. A sudden decrease in migration opportunities would have direct consequences on many sectors of the Egyptian economy, but most importantly for younger men it would cut off one of the most dependable sources of marriage "capital." Popular attitudes and reactions to the government are certainly not only motivated by the need to reproduce the family, but it is a common and necessary preoccupation among a broad constituency in Egypt.

The government indirectly supports the goal of reproducing the family when it distributes bonuses to dependent children of government pensioners when they marry,[91] when it constructs cooperative and public-sector housing exclusively for newlyweds,[92] and when it offers "social loans" without interest through public-sector banks to engaged couples.[93] Yet these programs benefit only a small fraction of the "engaged" population and are available selectively to those who meet certain requirements. More commonly, government policies designed to meet other goals have unintended consequences on the struggle to marry. For example, the government's reduced commitment to guaranteed employment for graduates in the civil service has increased unemployment among new entrants to the labor force. In *sha'bi* communities, it was common for secondary school and university graduates to wait three to five years before obtaining a low-paying position in the civil service in 1985. More recently, the "queue for government jobs" has lengthened to five years for university graduates and six years for intermediate degree holders. More alarmingly, "the proportion of new entrants to the labor force among the unemployed has exceeded 90 percent since 1979." The more educated a young person is today, the likelier he or she is to be unemployed, since "over 80 percent of the unemployed have at least a high school degree. Among women the proportion climbs to 95 percent." On the other end of the spectrum, according to Ragui Assaad, "the unemployment rate for uneducated individuals is less than 3 percent."[94] Although beginning civil service positions are low-paying, they offer attractive benefits and job security, and therefore some families made their daughters wait to marry young men until they were officially appointed to the civil service, even if they had already accumulated the necessary funds.

The previous two sections of this chapter presented marriage almost as an issue of accumulation or the allocation of scarce resources. Individual, familial, and communal resources were invested in the goal of reproducing the family. Informal financial institutions evolved within the community to facilitate accumulation (and other financial needs). These institutions also influence, in indirect ways, the ability of policymakers to control the economy. While certain government policies may have unintended consequences on the *sha'b*'s capacity to reproduce the family, the *sha'b*'s strategy to reproduce the family has unintended consequences on government capacity and its resource base.

Earlier I noted that a significant share of marriage expenses are accumulated through *gam'iyyaat* on the part of the bride, the groom, and their families. The average cost of a marriage within this community approximated £E15,000. Accumulation on this scale within a low-income community suggests an impressive capacity to save. In fact, the pervasive savings ethic within *sha'bi* communities should render any development economist speechless. Yet this prudent and disciplined behavior is barely mentioned in standard economic analyses. The following exercise (Table 2.5) will make some very crude but surprising estimates of the resources circulating in *gam'iyyaat*. Comparisons will then be made between the assets and services of the informal and formal banking system in Egypt.

In order to estimate the sums circulating in savings associations, the marriage rate, averaged for the previous five years, was used to estimate the number of marriage contracts signed in 1986, based upon preliminary figures of the 1986 Population Census ($.92 \times 50,455,049 = 464,186$ marriage contracts).[95] Because people throughout Egypt from different economic strata use *'ig-gam'iyya* to save for marriage expenses, three different estimates of the cost of marriage were used to arrive at a national total of the funds circulating in informal savings associations.[96]

Because they use standards of *sha'bi* communities as the upper limit, these estimates are conservative. It is safe to assume that marriages of the middle and upper strata of Egyptian society are far more expensive and elaborate

TABLE 2.5

An Estimate of the Assets of Informal Savings Associations throughout Egypt

	Estimated Costs of Marriage for the Year 1986		
	Estimate A: £E15,000	Estimate B: £E7,500	Estimate C: £E4,000
Total sum	£E6,962,790,000	£E3,481,395,000	£E1,856,744,000
Percent of gross domestic savings (£E5.31 billion in 1986)	131%	65%	35%
Percent of gross national savings (£E3.831 billion in 1986)	164%	91%	48%
Percent of GDP (£E38.356 billion in 1986)	18%	9%	4.8%

(housing costs, dowries, and dowers would all be far more expensive). The first estimate (A) uses the figure of £E15,000 (the average total cost of a marriage within *sha'bi* communities: see Tables 2.1 and 2.2). The second figure (B), £E7,500, is half of the previous estimate and recognizes that a significant portion of marriage expenses may not be saved through *gam'iyyaat*. The third figure (C) of £E4,000 purposefully reduces the average cost of marriage, to account for many rural or very poor urban families in Egypt who do not spend as much on marriage as their urban or wealthier counterparts.

The extent of informal savings associations is only crudely estimated in Table 2.5. But even if the assets of *gam'iyyaat* approach the lowest estimate (C), they represent 35 percent of gross domestic savings. Because individuals use savings associations for other specific financial needs, and as a vehicle for routine savings activity, it is safe to assume that the assets of *gam'iyyaat* are really much higher.

While individuals use informal savings associations as a savings vehicle, an economist might argue that this does not represent savings in a technical sense because they merely finance someone else's consumption, as each lump sum payment is immediately disbursed to a member of the association, who then spends it on consumption. For example, a young man who contributes £E100 per month to a *gam'iyya* may be saving for an apartment, but each month the person who receives the lump sum payment uses it for consumption (i.e., gross savings, as opposed to net savings for the economy). Research is needed to understand whether the final payment of a *gam'iyya* is used primarily for consumption or investment.

More importantly, whether economists recognize this activity as savings or investment, *gam'iyyaat* offer communities a source of credit that may not be available through the formal banking system. (Further details of the credit function of savings associations will be discussed in the following chapter.) They provide credit to individuals who may not have the collateral or meet the other preconditions of eligibility that banks require for loans. Furthermore, these associations are popular because they do not charge interest, and their leaders do not make a profit or receive a fee. They embody the principles of Islamic law (which forbids usury) and traditional communal solidarity far more than the formal banking system (with the exception of the new Islamic banks that have sprung up throughout the Middle East). In addition, as mentioned earlier, informal savings associations induce savings in a community which may only be able to set aside very small amounts of cash each day, week, or month.

It can be argued that the creativity of financial institutions such as *gamʿiyyaat* weaken the resource base of the state as private resources are diverted from the banking system and remain within communities. Some people prefer informal associations over banks, specifically to avoid the regulatory power of the state. The state's capacity to extract surplus revenue from its citizens is somewhat complicated by *gamʿiyyaat*. The government has far more regulatory power over individuals who deposit funds in banks, than in *gamʿiyyaat*. They cannot tax funds that are not known to them. As powerful as the state is in Egypt, economic institutions in *shaʿbi* communities may have unintended consequences on the ability of the government to use private and public financial institutions to promote its economic objectives. Finally, the pervasiveness and efficiency of *gamʿiyyaat* suggests that some institutions are able to remain autonomous from government regulation and control, yet meet critical needs for communities. As a whole, these savings associations represent a public service that benefits individuals and their communities, without cost. The explicit trust and cooperation that must necessarily exist between members of an association suggest that elements of the familial ethos, as described in Chapter 1, support the economic dynamism of *shaʿbi* communities as well.

The unintended consequences of micro behavior has had a "macro" effect in the area of housing as well. Like the need for savings, a lack of affordable housing has forced families to either privately finance housing construction or additions, rent expensive apartments and pay exorbitant key money, or use every possible connection with politicians and bureaucrats to obtain subsidized public or cooperative housing. In fact, the construction in residential housing during the decade between 1976 and 1986 has been tremendous, "with the number of housing units built during the boom decade reaching more than 40 percent of the initial stock of housing at the national level in 1976."[97] The demand for housing by newlyweds, rural-to-urban migrants, and prosperous returning migrants has been met, in part, by a surge of informal or unregulated, unlicensed, and illegal housing construction in what was previously agricultural or marginal land surrounding Cairo. One study estimated that over 80 percent of the housing constructed since 1960 has been built without permits,[98] while another estimates the figure at 50 percent.[99] This informal construction is theoretically illegal, but people are rarely prosecuted since the cost of enforcement would be prohibitive and the state indirectly benefits from this private investment in housing. Many of these communities are populated by lower-income groups but not by the poorest strata of society. They must be wealthy enough to afford the costs of constructing an apartment building or paying the average monthly rent of £E44–60 and key money of £E3,000–4,000.[100] For many families, the cost of housing is out of their reach, particularly for those on fixed, low-paying government salaries. Handoussa warns about the ill effects of this situation on Egypt's future. "The most striking anomaly is that a long-held and secure job in the most representative of middle-income occupations does not guarantee being able to afford even modest housing under any possible arrangement: lease, mortgage, purchase, key money, etc. . . . Yet the acquisition of a home is one of the most fundamental of needs and an essential determinant of social stability."[101] The difficulties facing lower-income groups will, no doubt, be more daunting.

In their very informative study, Oldham, El Hadidi, and Tamaa describe one of the newer informal residential areas near Imbaba as a magnet for newlyweds from Cairo and immigrants from the countryside. Because these communities are built on agricultural land or state-owned property without authorization from the government, many are not serviced by government utilities, sewerage, transport grids, or public educational, health, and welfare institutions. Either a community begins the process of negotiating with government authorities to provide these services and resolves issues of property ownership and taxation, or it pays for these services from private entrepreneurs.

Collectively, these communities place greater and greater demands on the state's infrastructure. Eventually, leaders within a community begin the process of articulating those demands by trying to incorporate the community into the state's delivery system through political negotiations.[102] Although it has selectively reasserted its authority in some areas by evicting residents and bulldozing housing, the state has not been able or willing to control this massive growth in informal housing. If the state is unable to control the physical growth of the Greater Metropolitan area and the very visible settlement of large numbers of its population, it may not be able to control the political and economic activities in these new areas either. Businesses and trade are not regulated, taxes are not collected, and the community develops its own mechanisms of law enforcement and arbitration. The growth of illegal settlements and communities, due in part to the seemingly innocuous "social" goal of reproducing the family, presents a political and economic predicament, if not challenge, to the Egyptian state. But apart from the predicament that the state may, or may not, find itself in, the struggle to reproduce the family has strengthened collective political, social, and economic institutions of the *sha'b*.

Networks

THE POLITICAL LIFELINE OF COMMUNITY

I am tempted to believe that what we call necessary
institutions are often no more than institutions to which we
have grown accustomed, and that in matters of social
constitution the field of possibilities is much more extensive
than men living in their various societies are ready to imagine.

—Alexis de Tocqueville, *Recollections*

ONE DAY an elderly woman, 'Umm Taahir, dressed in traditional mourning black (the custom of a widow), entered the local branch of a women's association with her four-year-old grandson. 'Umm Taahir had assumed responsibility for her grandson after the untimely death of her daughter-in-law, while her son provided financial and paternal support.[1] That day, she sought out the administrator of an association that ran several local day-care centers in order to pay her grandson's entrance fees. The young *muHaggaaba* daughter of the administrator was sitting in the office when 'Umm Taahir complimented her on her manners and beauty.[2] She asked this younger woman if she was a girl or a woman, *bint wala sitt?*[3] The younger woman responded, "I have two children and am married." 'Umm Taahir's disappointment was evident, but before she could explain the younger woman quickly responded, "But I have a younger sister who is still at home." "Is she as beautiful and well-mannered as you?" "But, of course," was the reply.

Both of these women immediately understood that marriage was the subject of their conversation and that 'Umm Taahir probably was seeking a match for a particular young man, most likely a relative. She continued, "I want to become related to you ['*anaasib-ik*] since the entire area loves your mother." More than a mere compliment, this candid public comment was a testament to the political power and standing of the administrator's family in the neighborhood. Becoming related to such a woman would offer 'Umm Taahir's family greater access to the power this woman and her family commanded. The source of her power was the web of networks that she had slowly cultivated in the neighborhood. The marriage of 'Umm Taahir's son to a well-connected family would incorporate his family within that network or, at least, parts of it.

The "love" that everyone displayed toward the administrator of the day-care center was not mere sentimentality but part of a strategy to incorporate themselves into her informal networks. The administrator's networks influenced the local distribution of public goods such as education, housing, charity, subsidized food, credit, and community child care services. Her networks also organized the exchange and distribution of information and assistance, at times providing critical material and moral support for individuals and groups. She consciously incorporated both powerful and less powerful members of the local community in her networks, including unemployed, impoverished single mothers, local bureaucrats and merchants, skilled workers, and members of Parliament. While the majority of her networks were geographically centered in her immediate neighborhood, they extended to other areas of Cairo where her relatives, colleagues, and friends lived and worked.

This woman's networks are representative of an important avenue of political participation for the *sha'b*. Networks are the political lifeline of the community, allowing individuals and groups to cooperate with other members of the community to achieve individual and collective goals. Informal networks provide a mechanism for individuals and households to influence the allocation and distribution of public and private goods in their community and in their nation. Informal networks organize, coordinate, and direct individual actions. In short, they aggregate the interests of the *sha'b*.

Networks are a concrete manifestation of extrasystemic political participation not controlled by formal political institutions or the political elite. Neither state institutions nor the political elite dominate informal networks, although the *sha'b* consciously strive to incorporate local state bureaucrats and political elites into their networks to facilitate access to public goods controlled by the state. Informal networks are penetrative, efficient, flexible, and encompass a diverse membership. They fill a political need in the community by representing and furthering the interests of the *sha'b*, which have little access to, or influence over, the formal political system. Formal and informal networks permeate daily life and are a critical, though ambiguous and concealed, arena of micro and macro political processes in Egypt.

Networks are designed not only to obtain more soap or frozen chicken from food cooperatives but to solve intrafamily and intercommunal conflicts and promote morality in the community. Through informal networks, the *sha'b* not only seek access to public goods and services but promote the ideals of the familial ethos, thereby supporting the rules, order, and public and private morality of the community. People understand the ties that join an individual to his or her household, family, school, marketplace, neighborhood, mosque, food cooperative, and even to national institutions such as the army or Parliament. Their political perspective extends to both very personal and more distant institutions. A constant articulation and refinement of right and wrong and propriety pervades daily discourse. This propensity to judge, to voice one's opinions on a particular issue and relate one's experience, is not circumscribed by a Western division between what is public or private. As argued in the previous chapter, the household is neither isolated nor secluded but incorporated into the public life of the community through informal networks.

These avenues of political participation among the *sha'b* have remained obscured from public view and from the attention of political scientists largely because they lack formal, juridical recognition. Informal networks are not licensed or regulated, nor are they the direct beneficiaries of state largess. They are overlooked or tacitly tolerated by the state, unless they become vehicles for opposition and resistance or merely work against the interests of state policy. From this obscurity and autonomy, however, they derive their strength, since public sanction and legitimacy are not a monopoly of the state.

This sense of public sanction and communal support encourages the creation of networks. The familial ethos, which supports cooperation and conflict resolution, encourages people to form networks to pursue shared goals. Common material interests and goals (such as education, earning a livelihood, reproduction of the family, and bureaucratic wrangling) encourage people to work together through networks and, at times, unifies the community. Material interests, however, make up only one component of informal networks, and an ideological current and outlook (which I have referred to as the familial ethos) legitimizes the principles that sustain informal networks. Informal networks have not only a pragmatic dimension but, within the authoritarian context of Egyptian politics, they serve as a collective institution to pursue common objectives, based on a normative commitment of cooperation and mutual reciprocity.

Many scholars reduce informal networks to a purely materialistic base, stripping them of any ideological legitimacy. Graziano argues that clientelistic exchange is based on "extrinsic benefits, that is, individualized or noncollective advantages." Ideology, on the other hand, is "the polar opposite of exchange in the specific sense that exchange subjects the person to an instrumental logic which facilitates the social and political control over him, while ideology gives an individual autonomous ends on which material and immediate rewards have no hold."[4] While social exchange will not undermine the status quo, "ideology, in contrast, has an expressive value and may allow the transformation of the system."[5] The tenacity with which urban residents (and peasants in the countryside) protect their autonomy and communal solidarity may be influenced by specific material issues, but to argue that these concerns lack ideological content or the potential to transform the status quo reflects a condescending view of people's ability to understand their relative position and daily struggle in political and ideological terms. It suggests a false dichotomy between the context in which people live, and their beliefs and political preferences. It is impossible to understand people's material context without understanding the ideology of various power centers in the polity and impossible to understand people's political preferences and beliefs without understanding their material context. A deep sensitivity to material interests as well as new hopes about the nature and practice of politics has most recently led to a resurgence of social movements in many developing nations, and in Europe, among constituencies that have felt excluded from both liberal and authoritarian states. In Mexico, Foweraker argues,

> the goals of popular movements are immediate, pragmatic, and concrete; and they play an analogous role to that of trade unions at an early moment in liberal state welfarism in Western Europe—those movements were successful if they solved the immediate and practical problems of the group or community. In Latin America, this usually requires negotiation of some sort with the state; in Mexico, popular movements must have the ability to get their demands met.[6]

The popular sector is drawn into further organization by the issues they confront in their daily lives and new institutional vehicles they have devised since they are no longer served by traditional trade union movements (often co-opted by the state and concerned more about the interests of workers in the public-sector or large private-sector factories rather than those who are self-employed, unemployed, or engaged in informal economic activity) and populist political parties that only come around to poor neighborhoods during election time. As Mainwaring explains in his discussion of social movements in Brazil in the 1970s and 1980s:

> [Urban] popular movements . . . [are a] subset of social movements. These are poor people's movements that develop in urban areas, but they are also different from the labor movement. Labor struggles involve the sphere of production, *while urban popular movements focus on demands related to the sphere of reproduction.* Urban popular movements attempt to improve urban living conditions, usually through demands on the state for public services including sewers, paved roads, better transportation facilities, better medical facilities, running water, and electricity.[7]

Unlike Graziano's vision of material interests, it is the material dilemma of their lives that urges on the creation of institutions that can further the interests *and* ideals of these excluded communities. Even within the post-materialist era of European politics, Hellman argued that the rise of new social movements in Europe in the 1960s and 1970s extended "the 'political space' available to citizens, bringing into the public realm the concerns of 'everyday life' and of 'the personal.'"[8]

When people develop autonomous collective institutions that operate without formal recognition or license from the state, they develop, at the same time, ideas that legitimate their actions and can be used to persuade others to join and utilize their institutions. Social science research on political networks, on the other hand, has largely revolved around discussions of clientelism and corruption. As Gellner writes, "The kind of patronage which does concern us is a form of power. In part, it intrigues us because we disapprove of it. Why? It offends both our egalitarianism and our universalism.

Patrons and clients are generally unequal. Patronage relations are highly specific. They fail to illustrate the principle that like cases should be treated alike."[9]

Condemnation of personalistic ties in a patron-client relation is contingent upon a belief in a rational, equitable political system where bureaucracies and elected representatives serve the collective needs of the general population. Too often scholars make the mistake of assuming an equality of opportunity, which ignores the experience of underrepresented and marginalized communities that do not experience a great deal of egalitarianism. Some communities and groups in Egypt successfully persuade the state to invest in them and provide services to their inhabitants, and others are left to decay or languish. The state makes little pretense of being egalitarian or fair in its treatment of different groups. Comparative research on party and urban machine politics throughout the world has demonstrated the ability of small segments of the population to seize and maintain power. The party itself functions in a clientelistic manner, providing services and the "spoils of the system" to faithful party supporters, in exchange for their vote and loyal support. "Party-directed patronage is typically directed to 'entire categories, coalitions of interests, groups of employees,' . . . and consists of 'mass favors' granted no longer at the administrative level alone, but also at the legislative level."[10] Machine politics operates in a similar fashion, where politicians succeed in "privatizing" public goods, "that is, by using the immense resources of the state for purposes of private, productive generosity."[11] Yet networks can be a vehicle for those who are not supported by the immense resources of the state, to protect and further their interests in a more subtle, subterranean way, without attracting the notice of the state.

Not merely embodiments of exploitative patron-client relations, informal networks can be more accurately characterized by Lomnitz's notion of "reciprocity networks."[12] In her case study of shantytowns on the outskirts of Mexico City, she found that reciprocity networks guaranteed economic security for recent migrants from the countryside which neither market forces nor the state could do. In Cairo networks provide not only economic but political security.[13] An understanding of networks as both a political resource and a political institution for the *sha'b* moves beyond the negative connotations surrounding clientelism.

Western social scientists typically condemn the inequality of these relationships while minimizing their mutual reciprocity since inequality conveys an idea of dependency. However, in *sha'bi* communities dependency is not a wholly negative relationship since people do not view themselves as individual entities perpetually competing with one another. While competition and self-interest prevail at times, individuals are connected to kin, neighbors, and colleagues in more interdependent relationships than is common in the industrialized West. People who utilize networks to fulfill individual and collective needs, and to influence the distribution of public and private goods and services, engage other people in their efforts. Although far from altruistic, the system allows people who have access to different types of resources to contribute to and prosper within the community, despite vast differences in status, wealth, education, piety, or property. The logic of the system promotes the proliferation of one's networks in an ever-widening web, including, not excluding, more and more people. Personal networks supplement wealth, property, or status as a determinant of economic or political power.[14] Those who may be wealthy, but have not cultivated a complementary system of networks, may be more disadvantaged than an uncritical assessment of their wealth would infer.

The *shaʿb*, understanding their political system, political exclusion, and the limits of state largess, do not depend entirely on the state for their collective welfare, although they continually place demands on those in power to redistribute national wealth and production (through formal and informal means). Informal networks increase the opportunities for individuals to gain a greater share of national resources while maintaining anonymity. Hyden argues that the peasant mode of production in Tanzania produces an "economy of affection" in which familial and other communal ties provide the basis for organized activity.[15] While the conditions and relationship to the state differs between Tanzanian peasants and urban Egyptians, his analysis nevertheless recognizes the political capital people gain if they can distance themselves from state control and maintain a degree of autonomy.

> The interesting thing about the African situation is that despite strenuous efforts both by the colonial powers and the independent governments, peasants in many parts of the continent have retained a considerable measure of autonomy vis-à-vis other social classes. Small has proved its power by remaining economically independent. We are faced with what must appear to most people as a paradox: those with power in Africa are not necessarily those in control of the state but those who remain outside its control.[16]

Because the state controls immense resources, people strive for autonomy to gain some independence of movement, but do not want to cut themselves off from state benefits or isolate themselves. Informal networks strive for both autonomy from and integration with the bureaucracy and political elites, because the objectives of networks are diverse. At times people try to escape the state and, in other circumstances, to exploit it. What they do gain is a modicum of political space, which comes at the cost of extensive organization and intricate webs of association. Building an organizational grid in a society where associational life is tightly controlled, and where the *shaʿb* have little likelihood of upsetting powerful constituencies with far greater resources at their disposal, still allows these communities room to pursue their interests and expand their political space. Again, the dimensions of this space may be narrow and constantly shifting, but the institutional framework of networks remains in place, responding constantly to changing material and political circumstances.

At the same time, there are recognized limitations to political autonomy and expression in Egypt. Individual or collective will and organization can rarely overpower the resources, power, and authority of the centralized, pervasive, bureaucratized Egyptian state. Political demonstrations have been forcibly repressed whenever the population has taken to the streets to oppose increased food costs or other government policies.[17] On the other hand, the government has often been ineffective in controlling or repressing ubiquitous networks that counteract state policies, such as informal commodity distribution networks for food, unregulated and untaxed savings associations, a black market in foreign currency, the unlicensed and unregulated construction of housing, and clandestine religious and political associations that seek political power and, at times, the overthrow of the government.

In order to understand the role of informal networks in *shaʿbi* communities, this chapter examines how networks are used to further common interests in the community. The first section covers four critical components of earning a living: employment, migration, financial institutions, and gifts and networks of exchange. In order to find jobs in Egypt and abroad, obtain credit, and fulfill daily economic needs, the *shaʿb* rely heavily upon informal networks. The second section describes how families use networks to reproduce the family, particularly to find marriage partners. The third section describes the creation of a parallel education system that has evolved during the past decade in Egypt. Teachers and students have devised a costly but successful strategy for students to pass the all-important end-of-year exams. In *shaʿbi* communities, education is a means to upward social and economic mobility, and the community spends significant resources on the education of its children, both formally and informally. The fourth section of the chapter describes how networks are used to obtain publicly subsidized goods and services through local bureaucrats and political elites. As mentioned earlier, the state controls the distribution of goods and services, many of which are in great demand in *shaʿbi* communities (food, housing, clothing, transportation, education, and so on). Because demand outstrips supply and distribution is not equitable, informal networks are an efficient means to obtain scarce goods. This chapter concentrates specifically on the institutional dimension of informal networks as a way to promote shared goals and finally considers certain consequences that the *shaʿb*'s political agenda has on the Egyptian polity and economy.

EARNING A LIVING

In Cairo earning a living is a complex process. An abundance of unskilled and semiskilled workers compete for the limited number of secure positions in the public sector or relatively well-paying jobs in the private sector. Wages for public-sector professionals and clerical workers have not kept pace with inflation, causing many people to seek part-time and full-time employment in the private sector, in fields often unrelated to their training and education.[18] While recent growth in the service sector and migration abroad have increased wage levels for skilled workers and artisans, employment is often erratic and labor is dependent upon middlemen and subcontractors for steady employment.

Whether seamstresses, school teachers, janitors, grocers, clerks, metal-workers, taxi drivers, shop clerks, accountants, or lemon wholesalers, people rely on their personal, familial, and communal repertoire of networks to find employment, ensure job security, earn promotions, and in rare instances, to obtain better positions. In Egypt it is not only individual effort, skills, and capabilities that secure a job but intermediaries and middlemen as well.

Through informal networks individuals and groups create more opportunities to find a job, to obtain credit, or to marry a wealthy or attractive suitor. And because informal networks operate outside the legal, formal system, people may have more access to scarce goods or employment than is apparent from official statistics and accounts. At the same time, however, because some people obtain jobs or laundry soap through informal networks, others are denied them when bureaucrats decide that the civil service cannot absorb any more new entrants or when the supply of soap has run out at a local cooperative. People in *sha'bi* communities plan strategies for earning a livelihood within this context. They might condemn the complex system of formal and informal procedures, or support it, but in order to prosper within this context they must develop strategies to survive and provide for their families. It is from observation of their pragmatic and creative struggles to find employment that I was able to understand the intricacies and importance of networks within the Egyptian polity.

Employment Networks

A young woman in the neighborhood had just sat for her final secondary school exams and doubted that she had passed. Her marriage was scheduled to follow her graduation, which depended on her final exam scores.[19] She had failed the exams the previous year, and her mother would not allow the marriage to take place unless she passed her exams, arguing that her diploma would provide security and the opportunity for public-sector employment. The mother had spent considerable sums on her daughter's private lessons, books, school clothes, and fees and could not face the thought that all her money and effort had gone to waste. The daughter's fiancé had graduated from a vocational high school, and she agreed that she needed a diploma to equal her prospective husband's status. Her commercial diploma would be more prestigious than his vocational school diploma, giving her the edge, which she and her family felt was important.

During the summer, however, she had little to do but worry over her yet-to-be released exam scores. Bored by the prospect of remaining at home under the watchful eye of her brothers, she and her mother agreed that she would work at a local day-care center. She was able to find a summer job only because her mother ran the day-care center and could convince her superiors to hire her daughter. The following account details the daughter's numerous visits to government offices to register as an employee with the private voluntary organization administering the day-care center. During this exhausting process, she realized the importance of informal networks.

First, in order to prepare the papers I had a *fiish w-tashbiih* [a declaration issued at a police station confirming residence in an area and the lack of an arrest record]. Then I went to get a copy of my birth certificate at the civil registry within the police station [*al-'ism*; police and local administrative offices are often housed in the same building]. The employee there said to come back to-morrow. I took the paper and returned the next day. He said to come back tomorrow again. I went the next day and he said my papers could not be pro-cessed because the date of birth was wrong. It was correct, but he was just lying to me, laughing at me. So I went the next day and told him the date was correct. He said to return tomorrow because he was about to leave. He told me to arrive at 1:00 P.M. the next day, which I did, but when I found him he said that he was turning out the lights and leaving and to return the next day. When I returned he told me that he couldn't find my name in the file and to come back the next day to see the person who specializes in birth certificates.

I went the next day and he said that my mother's name was in the dossier but that my name was torn off. By the time the papers had come from the health unit [where births are initially registered] he said that my name was missing, the form thrown away years ago. "There is only your mother's name." "Is that my fault, I asked? It's the fault of those employees, not mine [*mish zambi, ana maali*, it is not my fault, why should I care]. After all this effort and work, you can't find the names?" He said that it wasn't his fault either and that he would prepare other papers that I had to purchase from the post office first. I stayed home for two days, realizing that he wanted money before he would process my papers. But I didn't know how to offer him money. Perhaps he would take the money, perhaps not. If he didn't and was insulted he could make my life difficult and send me to hell [*yiwaddiini f-dahya*].

So, I asked my friend Huda if her father (who was also the father of my brother's fiancée) knew anyone at the police station. She said he did, a police officer named Ustaaz MuHammad. I went to the station the following day, but he wasn't there. Huda's father had tried to find me to go to the station together the next day, but I wasn't home. He told my older sister that I should yell up to him the next morning so that he would come with me.[20] The next morning I called for him and he went with me to the office and introduced me to his friend who told me to get another copy of my birth certificate. After I made a copy of it, I returned and gave it to him. He told me to buy several forms from the post office and to make a copy of my I.D. card and my mother's.[21] He put them with another paper and asked me to get it stamped at the civil registry, which I did.

When I came back he said that only one stamp was missing. I asked if I could take care of it now, he said no, but that I should take the papers home (so they would not get lost or misplaced) and return with them in the morning.

At 8:00 A.M. I returned and he stamped the paper to send it to the Ministry of Health for approval. Then he said that I should come back in twenty-five days. Nearly a month! I asked what I was supposed to do in the interim. He said that the law requires this. I said, is that my fault, those are your laws and your regulations. He said, "It's not in my hands, what do you want me to do?" I had made all that effort, all those visits, and tired myself out [this occurred during the terrible July heat] and all of this was because he wanted money out of me. The paperwork could have taken an hour to finish but they want your money.

This young woman had visited these offices nine times over a period of eleven days. Despite her best efforts to exploit informal networks at the police station and registry, she was unsuccessful and still had to wait for some time before her papers would be processed so that she could receive payment in her new job.[22] She had few expectations of government efficiency or due process but still blamed herself for not mastering the art of informal politics. She admitted her inexperience and admired her older sister's skill in knowing how to deal with (*b-yitSarraf*) bureaucrats and merchants. Her family often asked this older sister to deal with bureaucrats and bargain with merchants on behalf of her extended family because she was very skillful and shrewd.

Relatives are commonly involved in job searches and job placement, not only in offices but in family-owned commercial and manufacturing establishments. In the older areas of Cairo, commercial establishments typically occupy the first floors of residential buildings, and narrow industrial alleyways are set next to heavily populated residential areas. The mix of commercial and residential property use encourages intergenerational labor inputs. Young boys and girls are trained to carry on the craft, skill, or profession of their fathers (and, at times, mothers). During vacations and holidays many children work alongside their fathers to learn the family business. In addition to these children, other children, unrelated to owners, are hired by industrial establishments as apprentices, or *Sabi*.

However, children of some skilled workers, *Hirafiyyiin*, proceed through the public education system, and a sizable proportion enter the less prestigious faculties of universities or technical institutes.[23] Many *Hirafiyyiin*, often illiterate or semiliterate themselves, pressure their children to succeed in school in order to escape the hard lives that they have led and invest in their children's education. They characterize white-collar employment as work where one can wear clean clothes like civil servants or *muwaZZafiin*.[24] At the same time, however, they often teach their children their craft and expose them to the business, to provide a means of livelihood if they fail in school, do not obtain a white-collar job, or economic trends devalue a white-collar profession. Other *Hirafiyyiin*, proud of their craft, do not educate their children or else they allow them to obtain only a rudimentary education before employing them in the family business. Economic indicators confirm the sentiments of both skilled and white-collar workers: the earnings of skilled wage earners have moved much closer to the earnings of salaried workers in public and private enterprises, and certain skilled manual workers are earning higher wages than many clerks and white-collar employees. In particular, employees in government administration and salary earners in public enterprises have seen their real earnings decline sharply since the beginning of the 1980s.[25] These are exactly the largely lower-ranking public-sector positions that many men and, particularly women, from *sha'bi* communities aspired to during the 1960s and that served as the vehicle for their upward mobility and status.

In the past decade many young people have been disappointed by the government's reduced commitment to guaranteed employment for intermediate and higher education graduates, the low pay for public-sector employees, depressed wages in many other sectors of the economy, and the long wait for a government job. Although obtaining higher education still makes one eligible for Egypt's guaranteed employment scheme (although after 1986 this was no longer the case for public enterprises), government agencies now use competitive examinations to fulfill ever-dwindling vacancies, and graduates in my community commonly waited three to five years until they were appointed, if not longer. According to Handoussa's analysis, the situation is even worse. "Since 1984, . . . graduates have had to wait for jobs for periods which have reached five years for those with university degrees, and six years for those with intermediate degrees (from institutes of higher education, the second, largely vocational, tier of the university system)."[26] The increasing scarcity of a government position that, though low paying, offers important social welfare benefits and job security, is a consequence of the government's struggle to increase the productivity of the public sector, to reduce its wage bill (by the late 1980s it constituted 33 percent of all government expenditures, up from 22 percent in the mid-1970s),[27] and to reduce the size of the public sector (government and public-sector employment constituted 59 percent of all wage labor in Egypt in 1984, and 68 percent of all labor in urban areas, though these figures do not include informal-sector employment).[28] Despite these figures, between 1976 and 1986 government employment increased by 3.7 percent per year, accounting for a 53 percent net increase in employment. The most strictly negative trend in the Egyptian labor force has been the increase in unemployment to 12 percent, up from 7.7 percent in 1976 (CAPMAS originally calculated unemployment at 14.7 percent from the preliminary results of the 1986 Census but then revised its estimate downward).[29] It is new entrants to the labor force (76.4 percent of those unemployed), particularly educated young people (between 1976 and 1986 the number of unemployed holders of university and intermediate degrees increased at a rate of 22 percent per year) and women (their unemployment rates reach 24.2 percent as opposed to 10.4 percent for men), who suffer from the highest rates of unemployment.[30] Even though many people still desire a government position, these positions are often completely unrelated to the education and training of the graduate. For example, trained electricians work as office clerks, and English teachers are assigned to teach mathematics or history.

Young men, in particular, who had completed their compulsory military service and were awaiting government appointment, often worked in a relative's workshop in order to accumulate enough money to finance a marriage. During furloughs from military service, they would return to the shops where they had previously worked to earn money in order to augment their low salaries or to support their families. In the same vein, other young men attending university continued to work in the family business during their studies and expected to remain active in the business even after they received a government position. A government position would provide some attractive benefits and status in the community, while their craft would support them.

Two brothers had invested in several pieces of small machinery to produce prayer beads. Their family had supplied the local prayer bead market with their products for several generations. (They lived near one of the most prominent mosques in Cairo, and many shops sold religious items nearby.) Their mother had contributed funds for machinery, an uncle had taught them how to manufacture the prayer beads, and their grandfather had offered them a ground floor apartment in his building to house their small workshop. Both of these young men were students at university and expected to complete their university education and obtain government positions afterwards. In the mornings they would attend classes, and in the afternoon and evenings they would continue their craft. In other instances, young men and women, despite their commitment to higher education and government employment, must honor family obligations to inherit a family business or decide that lucrative commercial family businesses cannot, realistically, be ignored in the face of uncertain economic conditions. These students gave up their plans for government employment entirely.

One young man in the neighborhood, ʿAtif, came from a family, originally from Fayyum Governorate, who sold lemons in the local wholesale produce market. Many of his relatives also had small shops in the same market and retailing networks throughout other parts of the Greater Cairo area. (They also supplied women and children with lemons on credit to sell on sidewalks or in the street.) ʿAtif studied English in the Faculty of Education, an unprestigious department of the university which trains teachers for the public school system. The prospect of working as an underpaid and overworked public school teacher did not excite him, but his low scores on the national secondary school exams prevented him from entering a more interesting and challenging department. Despite his efforts to educate himself and extricate himself from his destiny as a lemon wholesaler, he doubted that he would be able to escape the family business.

His only hope, he explained, was to be lucky enough to find a good job in the Gulf that would allow him to save enough money to marry and to invest in a project in Egypt that could sustain him upon his return. When I asked him what success in the Gulf meant, he said returning to Egypt with £E100,000 (roughly $70,000 in 1985 prices). When I suggested that this might be an unrealistic target, he reduced the minimum figure to £E30,000:

£E15,000 for marriage expenses and £E15,000 for a business investment. He explained that an unusual or inventive project (not working as a government employee or for one's family) demanded money and *naas ma'rifa* (people who can assist you in accomplishing whatever your objective might be) or connections.

As an example, he described a friend's struggle to produce a very inexpensive refrigerator. The public-sector company that manufactures refrigerators in Egypt heard about this young entrepreneur and pressured his investors and manufacturers to withdraw their backing. Because he had not established solid connections and business networks, his venture failed. Although it is fairly common business practice to undercut potential competition from a new producer in the market, 'Atif suggested that one needed to have strong business and commercial networks for any innovation in the market. He claimed that it was also extremely risky for young men to invest in an untried business venture or trade because there was so much pressure on them to save money to invest in their marriage, if they wished to marry before the age of thirty-five. Strong commercial networks were a crucial component of success, and young men did not usually have that essential bankroll of personal acquaintances, even if they had the necessary capital, skills, and creativity to launch a project.

Faatin, a fairly religious young woman studying psychology at al-Azhar University, told the story of a young girlfriend's inability to extricate herself from the family business. This young woman had condemned the behavior of her father, a wealthy lawyer renowned for settling his cases by bribing judges. The daughter swore she would not follow in his footsteps and reprobated him as a hypocrite who grew wealthy from the misery of others while praying and claiming to be a religious man. Yet as soon as she graduated from university, the daughter began working in her father's office. Her means of material support, no less than her emotional and social ties to her family, made it impossible to ignore the family, despite her public denouncements of her father's behavior (which were fairly unusual within this community).

It is very common for young men and women, despite their career and lifestyle expectations, to join the family business, whether it is trading lemons, processing food, selling goods, or teaching. Among the economically active population in my community, 19 percent worked in family enterprises in their primary occupations, and 14 percent earned a secondary source of income from family enterprises. Another 15 percent worked as housewives, a crucial contribution of labor to the family (10 percent were housewives as a secondary occupation).[31] Many others found jobs in private- and even public-sector establishments where relatives were already employed. In some cases, a young man or woman must accept the responsibility of managing a family business, whether they want to or not, because the family relies on its income. Younger siblings and older parents must be supported, compelling the younger generation to join the business and to sacrifice personal aims and dreams. Thus, it is the economic calculus of the family that often determines individual employment strategies.

Since the institution of the Open Door policy in 1974, many young people in these communities have considered fairly lucrative but insecure jobs in tourism, banking, private consulting firms, and joint venture enterprises as a more attractive opportunity than both family and public-sector employment. Even young people with the necessary educational training and language skills usually did not have the contacts needed to find this type of position, although some had been hired by hotels, travel agencies, and foreign companies as drivers, plumbers, domestics, photographers, and secretaries. But during the same time period, many family enterprises prospered, particularly those producing consumer goods for domestic consumption and for tourists who flocked to Egypt after 1977. Thus the younger generation, although perhaps disappointed to end up in family business, was somewhat satiated by its financial rewards.

Within an extended family, decisions are made by individual members to invest in the potential earning power of a member of the family. While some families completely ignore the employment needs of their sons and daughters, leaving them to their own devices, many families expend considerable effort and money to ensure that their sons and daughters can eventually support families of their own. While these campaigns are conducted on behalf of both young men and women, families are more concerned about the ability of men to earn a living since they will be expected to support a family, whether or not their wife earns money.[32] Families are quite involved in securing government positions for daughters and in negotiating and supporting their marriages. Families worry far more about sons who have dropped out of school or who lack a marketable skill.

A family in the neighborhood invested considerable sums in one son over several years in order to "put him on his feet." A brother-in-law had originally found him a position in his company, but the young man decided to seek his fortune in Iraq. The family again lent him money to finance the trip, convinced that he would be able to find a lucrative job in Iraq, like so many other young men in the community. He returned from Iraq with only modest savings, not nearly enough to finance his marriage or invest in a business. In relation to the community's expectations of a migrant worker, he had failed in this venture.

When he returned to Egypt he found a job as a bus driver in a public-sector transportation company, thanks to the intervention of a local politician. Working the early morning shift, he left his house at three in the morning and began driving at five. He would stumble home around four in the afternoon after driving in the busy streets of Cairo. Unfortunately, he could not save enough from his salary to finance his marriage. (He was engaged to a neighbor whose father was growing impatient at his future son-in-law's inability to solve his financial difficulties.) The family decided to buy a Peugeot taxicab through a loan from a car agency. The son could drive the taxi after work or rent out the cab to his friends while he worked. The down payment of £E3,000 for the car (whose total cost was £E11,000) was raised by the son's contribution, the mother's savings from an informal savings association, loans from his older married sisters and their husbands, and a woman in the neighborhood who lent money without interest. Each month the family paid £E230 to the company that held the car loan. The payment greatly exceeded the monthly salary of the son and the mother combined, but the daily income from the taxi was expected to cover the payment.

Unfortunately, the taxi broke down and needed £E200 in repairs. Unable to afford the repairs, the taxi remained out of commission, making it impossible to maintain car payments. In the end, after much family discord, fights, threats of divorce, and violence, the agency repossessed the car; the family lost its down payment of £E3,000—a huge loss for a family with limited resources. The husbands of the older sisters demanded to be repaid, since they could not afford to keep loans of £E650 and £E150 outstanding.[33] At the same time, this young man was under constant pressure from his fiancée and his future father-in-law to buy the appliances and furnishings needed for his wedding apartment. Rather than pay off his brothers-in-law, he used his savings to complete the final touches on his apartment, without telling his family. Despite their conflicting loyalties, his sisters continued to save money on his behalf, using their personal funds and the money that their husbands gave them for supporting their households, to pay off their brother's debt. When his mother and sisters found out about his secret purchases, although they cursed his financial ineptitude and dishonesty, they continued to save money from their limited daily household budgets to alleviate his debts.

In another example, a father and son from a middle-class family fought constantly over the son's decision to work as a tourist guide and papyrus artist rather than to seek a safe, secure job in a bank, which his father could arrange for him. The father worried that his son's future would be dependent upon the fickle tourist trade, even though tour guides in the private sector earned relatively high wages. Hidden behind the issue of secure employment, however, was a conflict about lifestyle. The son refused offers of financial support from his father to maintain his independence, which incensed the father since he expected to support his son until he married and set up an independent household. The father was particularly upset that his son befriended artists and foreigners and stayed out very late at night. He saw his concern for his son as a routine matter of paternal duty. The son, on the other hand, rejected the routine, bureaucratic, secure life that his father hoped he would lead, and their battle raged on.

Even when men and women secure public-sector employment, networks can be instrumental in preserving their jobs and arranging transfers or promotions. It is quite common in this community to be appointed to a government office or school far away from one's home. When this happens, people spend considerable effort to arrange a transfer closer to their homes, thereby avoiding the hours spent traveling from home to office and the cost and aggravation of public transportation (especially for women who are subject to routine sexual harassment). Working in a nearby office also minimizes problems with child care (another primary concern for the majority of working women who have children and work in private and public employment). At times offices are quite sensitive to individual needs and will arrange for working mothers to be appointed to nearby schools or offices, but at other times people spend years trying to work closer to their homes, or at least a relative's home.[34]

Attempts to make a lateral move within the bureaucracy can be extremely difficult. A teacher in an agricultural secondary school commuted an hour and a half each way to Benha, a provincial town outside of Cairo. Unable to support himself on his salary, he worked in a local automobile parts store, but spent most of his time on the train between Cairo and Benha. After years of utilizing informal networks to arrange a transfer, including, according to his father-in-law, *ma'rifa* and *rashwa* (or bribes), the teacher was finally appointed to an office of the Ministry of Agriculture in Cairo.

In other instances, it is quite difficult to move from the public to the private sector because of regulations that require a worker to repay the state for training costs. The government requires conscripts who were trained as bus drivers during their military service to work for public transportation companies for a period of time after their military service is concluded. If a driver wants to leave the bus company before the end of his obligatory civilian service, he must pay £E1,000 to the state, ostensibly as a reimbursement for training costs and a first-class license. According to public school teachers, it is also extremely difficult to leave a public school to work in the private sector without enduring litigation and long, drawn-out bureaucratic procedures. Because of the shortage of teachers and the recent growth of private education in Egypt, the government erects obstacles to maintain its labor pool. At the same time, because university education in Egypt is theoretically free (if one ignores the cost of private lessons), the government does not believe it should subsidize training costs for private schools. Regulations of various occupations impede job mobility, making it even more important to secure a decent position when one first begins government employment.[35]

Within the community, uneducated men and women who cannot obtain public-sector employment rely on informal networks for unskilled employment as domestics, janitors, workers, or occasional laborers. Certain members of the community, who are known to have wide networks of acquaintances, are routinely approached by others in need of jobs. Women whose husbands have recently left for the Gulf, but have not yet sent back money to support the family, use their neighborhood networks to find casual employment. These women are often illiterate or semiliterate, and they would have difficulty finding a job in an office (except as a janitor or *farraasha*) or a store, but may find work as domestics, seamstresses, petty traders in public markets, production workers in small textile sweatshops, or as food preparers.

Men and women always carefully consider the status of potential jobs. Many women who have families and are well-known in the community would never accept employment as domestics since this would necessitate being in someone else's home where one has little control over potential abuses, particularly sexual harassment from the men of the household. When women in these neighborhoods reluctantly accepted domestic work, they kept it secret from their neighbors or masked their work under the guise of nursing or child care. One of the insults that *baladi* women use against one another is the accusation that a woman is a maid.

Among the poorest segment of the community, there is an expectation that those who are *mabSuTiin* or financially comfortable will help the less fortunate to find employment and take care of other pressing needs. Within these neighborhoods there is a wide disparity in income levels, and people in need solicit help from more influential members of the community. While there is a certain reticence to admit need, it is understood that assistance eventually will be returned, even if this occurs years later. This type of network can be exploited in times of need and, though occasional, perseveres throughout decades. It is not unusual for men and women to solicit assistance in a crisis from people with whom they have had little contact for many years. Since these networks include friends, neighbors, colleagues, and local officials, it would be quite typical, for example, for a neighbor to solicit help from her husband's brother-in-law's father, with an understanding that she will return the favor in the future.

In times of crisis, when spouses die unexpectedly, when men migrate abroad but have not yet sent back money, or when sudden expenses arise, informal networks are helpful in securing employment, particularly for women or young adults. After the death of a breadwinner, friends, relatives, and acquaintances immediately devise a means of support for the family (as described in Chapter 1). When one woman's husband died at a very early age, leaving her with six unmarried children to support, a local organization where she had volunteered hired her as a permanent staff person. Men who had provided her husband with wholesale goods to sell from his government office gave her shoes and other items they produced, on credit, so that she could sell them to her wide circle of friends. In another instance, after the death of his father, a young man received assurances from the hospital administrators where the father had worked all his life that they would hold his father's position open for him until he had completed his education and military service. He explained that the job was his right.

If people do not maintain their range of networks, when a crisis occurs they may suddenly face economic or social problems. If, for example, a widow has little familial or communal support, she may be forced to marry the first available suitor that presents himself in order to support herself and her children. Isolating oneself from neighbors and friends can have adverse consequences in difficult times. In one case, a public-sector employee was accused of corruption and prosecuted by the government. Accused unjustly and eventually exonerated, this man decided to leave the government and earn his living in the private sector. However, he had raised his children to follow in his footsteps and become civil servants, and they had not been allowed to socialize with children from their working-class neighborhood. After his traumatic experience with the government, he encouraged them to become *Hirafiyyin*, although they had no training or exposure to the environment of small-scale manufacturing. Because most workers in small-scale manufacturing learn their trade as apprentices from an early age, his children were out of place as twenty-year-old beginners. Though they worked hard, these newcomers were subject to taunts from their coworkers, who laughed at their naïveté and inability to find their way around the neighborhood. Their tribulations as skilled workers were typical of stereotypes and jokes that compare the mentalities of civil servants and skilled workers (e.g., the *muwaZZaf* and the *mi'allim*).

Finding a good job is a particularly important goal in this community, and in Egypt in general, since most people do not change occupations throughout their working lives. Those who train as machinists from the age of eight or ten remain machinists throughout their lives. Those who become civil servants remain employed by the same office throughout their careers (although they may have an additional occupation as a source of secondary income). Those who own a grocery store, or work in the lemon trade, remain there unless they become very prosperous. At the same time, however, job mobility out of skilled public-sector positions to the private sector is increasing, as wages in the private sector continue to rise. Unskilled laborers, in most occupations, who tend to be not very educated, are, however, better paid and receive more benefits as employees in government and public enterprises and thus have little incentive to change occupations.[36]

Whether a mother seeks a decent job for a son or daughter, or a widow quietly investigates employment opportunities although she has not worked outside the home since her marriage, informal networks assist in the search for employment. While other criteria can be equally important in a job search, informal networks provide an additional means to find (and at times maintain) a job. People carefully try to maintain their networks so that they keep informed of the best opportunities for employment, and others carefully gather information and try to incorporate people who might provide the next aspiring young civil servant or worker with a job into their networks.

Migration Networks

Migration abroad has influenced the political economy of Egypt greatly, in terms of both labor and capital resources. It is the subject of great debate and research within policy-making, intellectual, and political circles in Egypt. One conservative estimate in 1985 suggested that 3.5 million Egyptians were working abroad, or 7 percent of the total Egyptian population (the figure includes the families of many workers who accompany them but are not necessarily employed abroad).[37] Another source suggested that, at its height, the regional oil boom created a demand for Egyptian workers which reached 10 percent of the potential labor force.[38] According to an official in the Ministry of Migration, actual worker remittances in 1985 were estimated at $10 billion: $2 billion through legal channels and $8 billion through extrasystemic, illegal channels ("uncaptured" funds enter Egypt at the black-market rate, which in 1985 was £E1.80 to $1 instead of the official £E1.35 rate).[39] In 1985 Egypt's gross domestic product (GDP) equaled approximately £E33 billion.[40] According to such estimates, 1985 remittances from abroad equaled a third of Egypt's GDP. Unfortunately, estimates of the number of workers abroad, their savings, remittances, and the impact of migration on the Egyptian economy remain very crude and vary widely from one source to another.[41]

The ability to travel abroad and save enough money to return to Egypt with a surplus often depends on the support of communal and familial networks, in both Egypt and abroad. For many people, spending more than a year abroad represents a large sacrifice. Isolated from friends and family, foreign workers are vulnerable to unscrupulous labor contractors, employers, and foreign regulations and police forces that often discriminate against foreigners. Yet despite the unknowns, people believe they will have an opportunity to save money far more quickly than would ever be possible in Egypt, considering their education, skills, networks, and the state of the economy.[42] Only this aspect of the complex issue of labor migration will be discussed here.

Many men and women view migration abroad as a unique opportunity to accumulate savings for investment in marriage, land, housing, major household furnishings, business, and commerce. But in order to "strike it rich," men and women first need to discover a way to migrate abroad. Within the community and even within extended families, networks exist and are aggressively cultivated to facilitate obtaining employment abroad. In certain families and workplaces, a system of rotation allows individuals to migrate in an agreed-upon order. One young man, who earned only £E60 per month as a university professor, augmented his salary with private tutoring and translation work. One of the most important unofficial perks of his position, however, was the opportunity to work as a translator for an international agency in New York City. Securing that position depended on passing a very simple exam, and each year one member of the faculty in good standing with his superiors was recommended to sit for the exam.

Another young man had enrolled in a two-year technical institute after his poor performance on secondary school exams. If he studied hard and passed his exams, he would have a second chance to enroll in a university. However, he knew that if he failed the entrance examination, his brother, who worked in a bakery in Saudi Arabia, would find him a position there. Interestingly, his family considered migration a less optimal choice than completing his education, which might lead to a higher-status job in the future. Once he had finished his education and his military service, however, the family still planned for him to work for a few years in Saudi Arabia with his brother to save enough money to marry.

In another case, a self-educated poet and writer who came from a modest background worked as an editor in a public-sector publishing company. An unobservant Muslim, his fellow workers constantly condemned him for not fasting during Ramadan (during the month of Ramadan observant Muslims fast from sunrise to sunset). His colleagues promised that if he changed his secular ways, they would find him a lucrative job in Saudi Arabia, thus assuring that his religious practice would be reinforced by financial gain. He nonetheless resisted such overtures and eventually migrated to the United States.

The connection between religious observance and identity and employment—in Saudi Arabia, in particular—recurs throughout accounts of migrants' experiences. Observant Egyptians revere the holy cities of Mecca and Medina, and to many of them the opportunity to make this pilgrimage or *hajj* (in classical Arabic) is the culmination of a life's dream. It is all the more easy to do if they are working in the country. The entire family is honored when one of its members becomes a *Hagg* (in colloquial Egyptian).[43] When migrants return to Egypt with considerable savings from Saudi Arabia, they proclaim that their good fortune was a consequence of their renewed piety and commitment to Islam. State-sanctioned and regulated observance in Saudi Arabia is enforced further by the Saudi state and the religious police.

For Egyptians who were observant before they went to Saudi Arabia, their prosperity and piety in the community brings them further honor and status. Migrants return and endow local mosques and charitable associations or join with others to support new, service-oriented mosques, which now dominate *sha'bi* and even middle-class quarters of Cairo. These mosques offer medical facilities, both outpatient and inpatient, pharmacies, day-care centers, secular and religious instruction, and charity for the poor. Mosques also organize religious pilgrimages to Saudi Arabia, offer public meeting halls to the community for weddings and funerals, and organize youth programs as well. If people can prosper financially and derive honor by virtue of their piety and support for local charitable organizations, they enhance their status on two fronts.

For example, a young man accompanied his unmarried sister to Saudi Arabia as her guardian.[44] A public school teacher, she was "seconded" to Saudi Arabia to teach Arabic at a local secondary school. He was an unemployed trained electrician who only found a job after a year in Saudi Arabia. Their father supported the migration since he was a deeply religious man and was able to visit his children several times while they were there. The brother profited from his role as his sister's protector since he eventually saved enough money to marry his fiancée. Both he and his sister preferred working in Saudi Arabia not only because it was lucrative but because of its religious atmosphere and lifestyle. The young man hoped that after his marriage his wife would stop working and begin wearing Islamic dress (which she would have no choice about in Saudi Arabia, since women can only appear in public veiled).

The flow of migrants to Saudi Arabia influences the political environment in Egypt. While some of those migrants who return quietly join established mosques or charitable associations, others are offended by what they see as the secular, Western influence in Egypt and a quiescent religious bureaucracy that is controlled and regulated by the state (the Ministry of Religious Affairs). Some migrants, however, are just as critical of the Saudi-sanctioned religious establishment as they are of Egypt's Islamic authorities and join even more radical, populist movements based on the Iranian model of Islamic revolution and government. Many prosperous returning migrants support political parties and politicians in Egypt who call for the imposition of Islamic law through legislative reforms. Secular Egyptians argue that the flow of foreign remittances from Saudi Arabia has funded and strengthened Islamic activism in Egypt and other Middle Eastern countries, even though Saudi Arabia is also now struggling with its own Islamic activists who deny the Saudi government's legitimacy.

Pious migrants who have raised the standard of living of their families and their social and economic status distinguish themselves from those who have prospered under the Open Door policy and spend their money on displays of conspicuous consumption and revelry (stereotypically Westernized behavior). Amin and Awny believe that the numerous complaints of consumerism among migrants found in Egyptian writings is based on very inadequate data and ideological biases. They argue that consumer durables equal only 10 percent of the own-exchange imports of migrants. "But in spite of the lack of any serious evidence to support it, the view that most of the remittances are wasted on luxurious or conspicuous consumption continues to be one of the most frequently expressed opinions in the literature on Egyptian migration."[45] Prosperity and piety are accepted and honored within the community and within Egypt; profligacy, conspicuous consumption, and a fascination with Westernized tastes and affectations are more suspect. The *sha'b* seem to regard the lifestyles and beliefs of wealthy pious individuals as more authentic and indigenous, while they distrust wealthy individuals who are far more secular or Westernized in orientation. However, very few people in this community wasted their money on entertainment and mindless consumption. Great sacrifices were endured by the men and women in my community in order to improve their family's quality of life in very specific and efficient ways: improving one's house; purchasing land for housing, agriculture, or industrial enterprises; financing the costs of one's marriage or one's children's marriage; investing in business enterprises; and purchasing important household appliances and furnishings that relieve the burden of labor on women and provide entertainment for the family.

Another consequence of Egyptian migration abroad is that informal networks designed to facilitate marriages have become internationalized. A family is often anxious to marry a daughter to a man with a steady job in the Gulf, even if that means she will not be allowed to accompany her husband abroad and will remain in her parents home for many years. One woman married a man who worked with her father in Saudi Arabia after he had made enough money to finance the wedding, invest in a poultry farm, and purchase a taxicab in Egypt. After he returned from the Gulf, he managed a public-sector food cooperative, which provided a steady supply of subsidized food to the bride's family. Another man had spent seventeen years in Libya, returning for only one month a year to see his family. In the previous chapter I described the marriage of his two daughters to two Libyan brothers. Every few years his daughters visited Egypt with their children, bearing valuable gifts of jewelry and other items.

The internationalization of informal marriage networks weakens familial involvement and often shortens the long period of engagement. In one particularly tragic situation, a mother approved of her daughter's engagement to an Egyptian acquaintance her son had met while they were both working in Saudi Arabia. The family met her son's friend while he was vacationing in Egypt and proceeded with plans for the wedding. They were a relatively prosperous family (due to the remittances of several sons working abroad), and the prospective groom decided it would be more lucrative to rob them than to marry their daughter. One day the groom came to visit and tied up the mother and her daughter in their apartment, stealing their gold and valuables. He then took the key to another apartment and ransacked that one as well—stealing over £E30,000 worth of valuables.

While migration of family members may disrupt family life and organization, it can also lead to a strengthening of communal networks and the involvement of women in familial decision-making. When their husbands leave, women must place their children in school, send letters to their husbands, receive remittances at the post office, convert foreign exchange into local currency, research the costs of travel, and arrange to receive freight shipments from their husbands.[46] It is very common for women to rely even more heavily on their repertoire of informal networks when their spouses migrate.[47]

In the past decade, migration has been one of the most lucrative employment options for a wide cross-section of the Egyptian population, both urban and rural, professional and blue collar, rich, poor, and middle class. Migration has accelerated upward mobility, particularly for the lower ranks of the social, political, and economic hierarchy in Egypt. As will be discussed in the following chapter, men and women in *sha'bi* communities may earn high wages as skilled craftsmen or traders, but they rarely obtain lucrative white-collar professional positions in the public and private sectors because of their educational and social backgrounds. However, when they obtain a low- or middle-level professional job abroad, they earn much higher salaries than many middle- and upper-class professionals in Egypt.

In *sha'bi* communities in Cairo, men and women are reaping the financial benefits of migration and suffering some of its social and emotional costs.

Despite periods of estrangement from friends and family (which is particularly difficult for family-oriented Egyptians) and poor living and working conditions abroad, many men (and women in smaller numbers) assiduously seek positions abroad and use informal networks to realize their objective. Yet an economy that relies so heavily on migration abroad to employ its citizens, particularly young people, is extremely vulnerable to external shocks, over which it has little control, and it may be subject to serious domestic criticism for its obvious inability to satisfy the employment needs of its population.

Financial Networks

An integral component of an individual's effort to earn a livelihood is his or her access to savings and credit institutions. Among the most important of the informal financial networks, with a great influence on the political economy of Egypt, are informal savings associations, or *gamʿiyyaat*. In the previous chapter *gamʿiyyaat* were discussed as a primary mechanism for accumulating savings for marriage. Individuals save large sums of money in these savings associations not only for marriage but also for purchases of land, housing, machinery, and other investments. Egyptians from all segments of society participate in these associations, but the *shaʿb*, who live with financial insecurity, are particularly drawn to *gamʿiyyaat* because they are a source of interest-free loans in times of financial crisis. Many of these people cannot fulfill a bank's requirement for collateral or a long-standing credit record.[48]

It can be argued that women are really the bankers of Egypt, since women, far more than men, organize and are trusted with the large sums of money collected by *gamʿiyyat*. Men, as the traditional breadwinners of the family, are more familiar with the formal banking system and other financial institutions in the business community. Women in *shaʿbi* communities, who are often not wage earners, carefully save small sums from their household budget and participate in savings associations with close relatives, friends, or colleagues. As women join the labor force in greater numbers, they have been able to save larger sums with not only relatives and neighbors but colleagues. People in *shaʿbi* communities seek out respected women who have a reputation for honesty to organize savings associations. It is said that these women (and occasionally men) run these, or *b-yimsiku l-gamʿiyya*, for altruistic reasons, including a sense of religious ethics (the organizations enhance mutual cooperation and trust and are viewed as more "Islamic" than the formal banking system because they do not charge interest).[49]

The leaders of *gamʿiyyaat* do not receive any fee for their effort, nor do they demand interest. (Due to negative real interest rates in the 1980s, depositing money in banks was not all that lucrative anyway.)[50] They collect each member's monthly payment (associations may be weekly or daily) and then give that money to the person whose turn it is to *yiʾbaD*, or receive payment or get paid. Before the *gamᶜiyya* commences, each member arranges with the leader when he or she will receive their lump sum payment. While members usually have influence over the order of payment, the leader is the final arbitrator, and from this position she derives some power.

Gamᶜiyyaat are very popular because an individual can receive his or her lump sum payment before completing the specified cycle of payments. For example, if someone knows that she must pay for three rooms of furniture for her daughter's upcoming wedding in one month, she can arrange to enter a newly created *gamᶜiyya*, pay her monthly allotment of £E100 the first month, and the following month receive her lump sum payment of £E1,200. For the next ten months she contributes her monthly payments. People prefer savings associations to banks because with a bit of *wasTa*, or influence, with the leader of the association, they can specify when they will receive their lump sum. Almost always, people know the leaders of the *gamᶜiyya* very well before they place their financial trust in them, and it is relatively easy to arrange one's preferred payment schedule. At the same time, a *gamᶜiyya* leader only admits individuals for whom she or he can personally vouch to the association. People are very careful to meet their financial commitments to these associations because the members of the association depend upon them. It is rare to hear of associations that have failed, but it does occur and therefore a small degree of risk is involved.

Even if men and women have no immediate need to save money, they often participate in smaller (in value) associations in order to maintain a good credit rating. One woman participated in four *gamᶜiyyaat*, contributing only one-fifth of a share (£E25) in each monthly *gamᶜiyya*, solely for the reason of maintaining a broad financial network. The practice of saving only shares of a monthly payment is further evidence of the credit function of these associations. Her behavior is similar to financiers who place their assets in several banks or security firms to maintain a presence in the market, spread their risk out, and gain more influence. This security net is very important in times of financial crisis for families with limited savings or liquid assets.

In a crisis, close friends or relative form a new *gamᶜiyya* on behalf of their unfortunate friend, who then receives the first lump sum payment. One of the women in the community who had been organizing *gamᶜiyyaat* for the previous thirty years first organized a savings association at the request of her landlord, who was adding an additional floor to his building for his son's marital apartment. After the *gamᶜiyya* ended, and impressed with her skill, the landlord asked her to start another one, this time to finance his loan payments to a bank. Shortly thereafter, a colleague's money was stolen just before the ʿIid il-'aDHa, one of the most important Muslim holidays, when it is customary for the head of the household to buy new clothes for his children and special foods and sweets for relatives and friends. With other teachers at her school, she organized another *gamᶜiyya* on his behalf and gave him the first payment so that he could at least fulfill his familial obligations. Another colleague did not have enough money to pay for her mother's funeral expenses (funerals are often quite costly). The *gam'iyya* leader quickly organized another association, and the woman was able to give her mother a proper burial. This woman created new associations one after the other—at times to help someone in need or, more commonly, to fulfill the routine savings needs of her friends, relatives, and colleagues. Again, these savings associations are completely informal and under the control of communal rules and arbitration processes.

The very strong savings ethic among the *sha'b* and its impact on the national economy was discussed in the previous chapter. Despite constant savings activity in many families with low incomes, it was very difficult to understand their ability to save considerable sums of money year after year. In one case, a woman participated in three different *gam'iyyaat* with her eldest sister, her oldest friend in the neighborhood, and her most senior colleague at work. She saved a total of £E160 per month on an official salary of £E50 a month, a pension of £E55, and £E70 a month from another temporary source of income, leaving her family £E15 a month for their expenses. Other women routinely saved £E50 per month when they received monthly salaries of the same amount. Their skill and ability to save money is still, frankly, somewhat of a mystery. However, their success is partially due to minimizing daily expenditures and shrewdly shopping for the best quality but least expensive food, clothes, and other daily necessities.

Women and men who run informal savings associations are often the source of occasional small-term loans as well. If approached, they can usually afford to loan money since so much capital is circulating in their associations. Because they know the financial status of many people, they are also a vital source of sensitive economic information in the community. At times wives hide their participation in savings associations from their husbands, fearing that their husbands would decrease the size of the household budget (which is the source of their savings). Other men and women save in the associations of neighbors, instead of families, because they do not want their families to realize the extent of their financial resources. Men may save money with business associates so that their wives and relatives remain ignorant of their worth. And others in the community prefer *gam'iyyaat* to the formal banking system, where their money is vulnerable to financial regulatory agencies and the tax authorities.

In summary, *'il-gam'iyya* offers an alternate source for financing many economic needs within the community; the funds remain in the community and, since they are not reported, they are neither taxed nor subject to seizure and confiscation. This capital is then used to buy land, housing, and household furnishings or to invest in economic enterprises—major productive investments that improve the standard of living of individuals and their families. Without the institution of the *gam'iyya*, people would be far more dependent for credit on the state-controlled banking sector, moneylenders who demand high interest, or on relatives. Like other informal networks, informal savings associations represent an independent and communally sanctioned institution that enhances security, cooperation, and trust among the *sha'b*. As a key financial institution, it performs a vital public service for a constituency with far less access to, and equity in, formal financial institutions.

Other informal financial networks also serve to cushion financial shocks in the community. Businessmen commonly lend money to their associates at a time of need, with varying rates of interest. Although these loans are more of a business proposition than a *gam'iyya*, they are only available to honest and trustworthy businessmen who have also aided others in similar circumstances. For example, one businessman employing eighty-five workers in a machine shop in an outlying industrial area of Cairo impulsively decided to sell his business after some personal problems. Confused, he accepted an offer of £E14,000 for a business worth £E60,000–70,000. The sale was entirely legal and recorded in a binding contract. Very soon after signing the contract, he realized his mistake and unsuccessfully offered to buy back the business for £E25,000, then £E60,000, and finally £E100,000. Word quickly spread through the area of his financial ruin. Within the next few days anyone that had ever borrowed money from him arrived at his house with briefcases filled with cash. Other friends who did not owe him any money, but with whom he had worked, also offered him thousands of dollars in long-term loans. Because, as this businessman explained, his word was "final" and respected, when he was in need his friends came to his aid without even being asked. This type of assistance is available only to members of the business community who support an ethos of cooperation based on the principles of the familial ethos. To benefit from this system, one has to abide by its principles and norms. There is no free-rider option in this system. For these reasons, businessmen and other members of the community carefully cultivate networks with colleagues, who range from apprentices, unskilled and skilled workers, owners of workshops and service establishments to officials of agencies that regulate their trade, tax collectors, and employees of banks and state-sponsored financial cooperatives.

Gifts and Networks of Exchange

A more subtle but significant type of network that men and women use to sustain themselves and their families is a network of exchange and gift-giving. Within *sha'bi* communities tradition, religion, and social convention direct the flow of cash and noncash material exchanges at specific religious and national holidays and rites of passage including birth, marriage, graduation, and death. These exchanges and gifts of food, clothing, cash, labor, and small household furnishings augment the household economy and allow Egyptians to keep routine expenses to an absolute minimum in order to save valuable cash income for major expenses. One particularly well-connected woman in the neighborhood could point to every piece of clothing in her home and recall who had given her each bolt of fabric, blouse, or dress. She boasted that she never purchased clothing, kitchen ware, or other small household items because she had received so many gifts from her family and associates.

Hidden in the storage area or closets of practically every *sha'bi* household with daughters is a wedding trousseau. (See Chapter 2, the section entitled "The Cost of Marriage," for a more detailed discussion.) When daughters are still very young, parents begin accumulating the extensive range of household items that a bride brings to her marital home. In many households a trousseau slowly accumulates in size and value, reaching upwards of £E750–900. When a daughter begins to approach marriage age (approximately sixteen, depending on her education and social class), relatives, friends, and colleagues of the family bring gifts (whatever the occasion) that can be used by the daughter in her trousseau. For example, on Mother's Day, which is celebrated in Egypt, people bring small presents to women who have assisted them during the year. This occasion is an appropriate opportunity to gain favor and demonstrate appreciation to these women, regardless of maternal connection. The tea sets, bolts of cloth, ornamental bowls, or plastic flowers are rarely opened and used, but rather are tucked away in their wrappings to become part of a trousseau or to be recirculated at a later date as a gift to someone else. The value of the gift is carefully noted, for it must be reciprocated at a later point in the form of a favor, service, loan, or gift.

In reality these gifts are considered as debts. When cash is given as a present during an engagement ceremony, a wedding, or on the occasion of a student's graduation, careful records are kept in order to repay it. In a village the system of reciprocity is more direct and public. Each family keeps a ledger to record the community's gifts: from their first child's marriage to the last (a period that can easily stretch through two decades). As guests enter the celebration, they move to a small desk where one member of the family records each gift. At one village wedding the mother of the bride accepted gifts only from people who were repaying her family's gifts; she refused to accept new gifts, since these would incur new debt. While recording wedding gifts in Cairo is less visible, the system operates in much the same way, but it is customary to repay double the amount of the gift one receives (a crude but probably accurate ratio that keeps pace with inflation in Egypt). When people fail to return gifts at the appropriate time, the individual and the family's reputation suffers.

On certain ritual occasions, exchanges of food support networks within the community. People, particularly women, exchange food (prepared and unprepared) on special occasions. After a death, the family mourns together for several days, and relatives, friends, neighbors, and colleagues of the deceased pay formal condolence calls, often bringing gifts of food. On the four successive Fridays after a death, the family brings specific foods to the tomb of the deceased, dispersing some to the poor who circulate within the cemeteries and consuming the rest. Each branch of the family absorbs the expenses of the preparation of *faTiir* (a sweet type of bread that is ritually eaten at the *maytam*, or mourning place) for one of the ritual visits to the family tomb.[51]

Food is also dispersed to the poor during certain religious holidays when families slaughter a lamb. A family must have some means to be able to afford the costs of a lamb, and many families save money throughout the year for this occasion (in 1985 a small lamb sold for approximately £E130 in the market).

The entire lamb is cut up and boiled, and vats of rice are made along with a tomato sauce. Women and children stuff pieces of bread with the rice, sauce, and pieces of meat. These *righif*s (loaves of bread) are not actually distributed indiscriminately to the anonymous poor but are given selectively to one's friends, neighbors, and employees, who are not poor but have assisted the family in one way or another during the past year. Families also distribute them to their poorer neighbors, local beggars, disabled people, and tradesmen or store clerks with whom they interact in the neighborhood. Even in charity, a connection between the giver and recipient is publicly acknowledged, thereby tying the two together. If a recipient of charity has emergency needs in the future, it is expected that he or she might approach the patron again. These relationships are cultivated over many years and reinforce a link, not only between two individuals but among their families.

Networks of exchange and gift-giving provide a cushion to the community during special times, such as weddings, funerals, and religious holidays. However, some rituals are costly, and because rituals are revered and public, people feel particularly inadequate and humiliated if they cannot perform them as expected. For this reason, neighbors, colleagues, and relatives often provide assistance if a family is suffering from financial constraints during these times, even if offering a loan or gift is financially burdensome. Because reciprocity is implicit in these networks, each exchange is seen as part of an older and deeply rooted relationship.

Although exchanges are more important when a family must meet the expenses of public occasions, they are a typical facet of everyday life in *sha'bi* communities. Because informal and formal networks are routinely utilized to accomplish a wide range of mundane and exceptional tasks, people constantly enter into relationships of exchange. Frequent reversals in the direction of exchange maintain the reciprocity of networks and discourages exploitative and manipulative behavior. Roles alternate continually between giver and receiver. One day a woman may receive a loan from a friend and the following week offer food to a bereft widow. For the *sha'b*, the knowledge that they can depend upon a wide range of associates in both good and bad times mitigates fears of slipping back into poverty and financial insecurity.

DEVELOPMENT: EDUCATION NETWORKS

Universal, public education is an integral part of Egypt's development plan and has been since the Free Officers' Revolution in 1952. While the percentage of illiterates in Egypt still remains high, the state provides free primary school education, despite the ever-growing numbers of school age children.[52] Within this particular *sha'bi* community, very few children do not enter school at the required age of six though there are older people who grew up before and just after 1952 who have never attended school. Nationally, "enrollment in primary education rose from 70 per cent to 88 percent between 1976 and 1986 and that in secondary education from 53 per cent to 66 percent."[53] However, leaving school at a very early age, despite the legal obligation to remain until age fifteen, is fairly common in many *sha'bi* communities, particularly those whose local businesses employ children as production workers or apprentices.[54]

The struggle in *sha'bi* communities is to keep children in school, though the dropout rate increases as they grow older. Most parents want their children to remain in school, and they constantly harass them to study and work harder in order to pass their exams. Families value education because they respect knowledge and learned people. They believe that higher education will improve their children's career options, earnings potential, and enhance their social status.

The resources of the public education system in Egypt cannot keep pace with the demand from a population that values education. While every government since 1952 has attempted to extend the reach of the public education system, the state has not, and perhaps cannot, invest sufficient resources for a high-quality education. Since teachers represent such a large share of employment in government services, the government has been extremely reluctant to grant salary increases. The salaries of public school teachers have not increased with the rate of inflation or the rising standard of living. According to a recent study, in 1987 secondary school teachers and kindergarten teachers were the two lowest-paid occupations among both private- and public-sector employees (£E22 and £E15 per week, respectively, although the wages of teachers from informal-sector employment are not included in these calculations).[55] While an analysis of the education system in Egypt is beyond the bounds of this argument, the *sha'b*'s answer to a deteriorating public education system is another example of their use of informal mechanisms to achieve an important objective. In communities throughout Egypt, teachers and other educated members of the community are paid to provide afternoon and evening lessons to augment public instruction. Although teachers are technically forbidden from offering private lessons to their students, these lessons have provided a lucrative secondary source of income. For example, a vice principal of an elementary school in a *sha'bi* community earned £E170 per month but supplemented this income with earnings of

£E1,000 per month from private lessons. A teacher at a commercial girls' high school earned £E55 per month but made £E60 a month from only one of the groups of students he tutored twice a week.

Remuneration for private lessons increases as one progresses through the educational system. In this particular community, parents had begun to insist on private lessons for children in first grade, although these lessons were relatively inexpensive (from £E2 to £E5 per month). At the university level, private lessons are almost more important than formal instruction in huge lecture courses where students have almost no opportunity to interact with professors. For example, one prosperous merchant in the community from an upwardly mobile family paid £E1,500 for private lessons to his nephew's chemistry professor for a one-semester course. The professor received a similar fee from the other three members of the study group, or £E6,000 for only one of the many groups of students that he tutored. The previous year the merchant had paid £E500 to another professor for private lessons for his nephew, and the nephew had passed on the professor's notes from a tutoring session to a student who could not afford the professor's fees. The professor discovered the nephew's gesture and failed both students, though he did not return his £E500 fee to the nephew. Although private lessons are not a new phenomenon in Egypt, during the past decade they have become extremely common. A consequence of positive and negative trends in Egypt, private lessons have become almost a parallel education system for children and adolescents from a wide cross-section of the population (both urban and rural).

Depending upon the particular nature of end-of-year examinations, either a student's teacher from public school or another teacher (or a well-educated neighbor or relative) offer more thorough instruction to a much smaller number of students who meet in one of the student's homes after school.[56] At some grade levels, a classroom teacher's assessment of students constitutes 50 percent of the final grade. In this case, a parent often prefers to employ the classroom teacher as a private tutor to induce the teacher to be lenient with their child. In other years, when final examinations alone determine progression to the next level of education, parents employ a tutor by virtue of his or her success record with end-of-year exams.

The phenomenon of private lessons is more remarkable because students in *sha'bi* communities are not the superachievers of middle- and upper-class families who will enter the most prestigious universities, but are average students from working-class or lower-middle-class backgrounds who will fill the lowest strata of the government bureaucracy or become merchants or skilled workers. Yet their families are prepared to invest a significant proportion of their income on private lessons. For example, a widow spent £E35 per month on private lessons for her two children in secondary school although she earned only £E80 per month. In some families with several school-age children, routine monthly expenditures of £E30–50 for private lessons were not rare. Investing in education represents a financial sacrifice for many people in this community, but it still provides opportunities they value and encourage. However, there are families that cannot provide private lessons for their children, or even afford the incidental costs for school uniforms, notebooks, lunch money, and transportation. Some students complain that their teachers provide hardly any instruction in the classroom, forcing them to pay for private lessons after school if they want to pass their exams. While some private tutors accept reduced fees from poor students, others refuse to begin a lesson without cash payment. Other teachers in the public school system refuse to offer private lessons either because they do not believe in them or because they are not attracted by the remuneration. (Female teachers with families do not usually have the time or the energy to accept private students because of their domestic responsibilities. Unless they are a single parent, female teachers are also supported by their husbands. Male school teachers, on the other hand, cannot support their family from an official salary alone and either offer private lessons or have another job.)

Although parents willingly invest in private lessons for their children, hoping they will master the syllabus, they also exploit informal networks that incorporate teachers, administrators, and educational bureaucrats to ensure their children's success on the all-important primary and secondary school exams. The results of these exams determine which level of secondary school and university (vocational, commercial, academic—public or private) a student will have the right to enter and are considered extremely important.[57] The number of university places available changes from year to year, as do the scores needed to enter certain university programs, and this information receives a great deal of attention and scrutiny in the media.[58] Families pursue several strategies designed to evade or circumvent the official administration and grading of these exams. They offer money and gifts to school officials to look the other way if a child cheats, or they pay officials to alter test scores if a child is in danger of failing.

Despite elaborate and costly plans to take advantage of the examination system, the Ministry of Education strictly regulates the proctoring and grading of exams, building in several safeguards specifically designed to circumvent the intervention of teachers and administrators.[59] Nevertheless, parents try to influence the exam scores, even though they believe that studying and memorizing the syllabi is the surest route to success. In one case, a mother who was worried about her daughter's upcoming exams gave the assistant principal of her local high school a Mother's Day gift worth £E20, and one of her daughter's teachers a gift worth £E10. She then asked a friend of a colleague who worked in the central education authority to change her daughter's failing grade from inside the bureaucracy (for a fee of £E10).[60] Despite these carefully laid plans, the daughter did not pass her exams since she had rarely studied. Even though her mother spent much time and money to help her daughter, in the end she realized that her daughter's laziness (or perhaps her poor education) was really to blame. At the same time, however, the mother condemned all those people who had promised to influence her daughter's exam scores, but who really had no power to do so.

In other situations, however, when a person's means of subsistence is at stake, people will intervene on his or her behalf with little remorse and without any expectation of payment. For example, relatively new government regulations require that every new public-sector employee, whether a janitor, worker, clerk, or manager, be able to sign his or her name to receive a paycheck. Illiterate people seeking public-sector employment are directed to literacy centers located throughout local neighborhoods in Cairo and the provinces to meet this requirement. Periodically, exams are held by these centers, and those who pass receive a certificate of literacy, which permits them to work in a public-sector firm or branch of the bureaucracy.

One day, a literacy exam was held at a local private voluntary association. Only people with a receipt from their local literacy center were allowed to take the exam, although several people from the neighborhood tried unsuccessfully to be admitted. The men and women were asked to copy a short paragraph that was circulated to them on a piece of paper. It was not an oral dictation or a comprehension test, but merely proved that one could copy sentences and form letters and words properly. Some taking the exam were completely illiterate, and others did not know how to hold a pencil. At that point, the employees of the charitable association where the test was held, who had been offered £E2 to assist in the administering of the exam, began to help the people having difficulty to write their paragraph of simple Arabic. When the administrators of the literacy program grew irritated, the employees who had been assisting argued that this exam would put food in their mouths, and that their *riz'* (subsistence) was at stake. They were *masakiin* and *ghalaaba* (poor and miserable) and deserved any help the teachers and the officials could offer them. Although the administrators shared the employees' empathy for illiterates, they had to maintain a public stance of disapproval. Periodically, people who are known to administer or have connections to literacy programs are approached by neighbors in search of literacy certificates. Usually, they do their best to enter these people in programs so that they have a chance at more stable employment and government benefits.

In order to avoid the above dilemma of illiteracy, parents strive to place their children in the best schools available. The reputations of local schools and schools in other areas are often discussed within the community. Families will ask local politicians to intercede on their behalf with the Ministry of Education to place their children in better schools, even if they are farther away.[61] If some schools accept children under the minimum age of six because of low enrollments in a district, parents will travel long distances every morning so that the children will have a slight head start on their peers. Other parents buy fraudulent birth certificates from local officials which list earlier birthdates so that their children can begin school at an earlier age. This practice is common enough that reputable school officials in the city will not accept children with birth certificates from a particular neighborhood that is known for issuing fraudulent birth certificates.

Education is not only important for career opportunities and earning potential, but it also affects the value of dowers (the sum that a groom gives to the family of a bride before marriage). Women with high school diplomas and university degrees can demand a higher dower from their suitors than an illiterate or semiliterate woman since educated women may find jobs and contribute cash to the household economy. More importantly, from the view of both men and women, they can tutor and educate their own children. While education is by no means the only determinant of a dower, there are noticeable differences between the dowers of sisters in the same family with different educational achievements. Perhaps it is best to describe the link between education and marriage as "marriage mobility." The better educated a woman is, the more right she has to demand that a suitor equal her educational achievement and status.[62] While marriages between an educated woman and illiterate man (or vice versa) do occur, the surrounding community questions the wisdom of these matches, even though they might congratulate the parents of the less-educated partner for making such a clever match. One man, who wanted to marry his neighborhood girlfriend, shared a similar background with her, but she had graduated from university, while he was barely literate. They agreed that if they married she would teach him to read and write, and he promised publicly to learn to read and write. He was very proud of his wife and felt that he was lucky to have married such an educated woman.

The public education system in Egypt is clearly overextended, yet education remains a high priority for a majority of the population. Instead of denying universal education to its population, the present system relies on competitive examinations, overcrowded classrooms, frustrated underpaid teachers, and a poorly equipped school system to discourage even a larger age cohort from entering university and postsecondary public institutions. The *sha'b* rely upon a privatized parallel education system and informal networks to claim their fair share of a public good: education.

THE BUREAUCRACY AND THE STATE

Individuals and families with *wasTa* or *ma'rifa* (connections or friendship) among local politicians and state bureaucrats have a better chance to resolve problems and cope with bureaucratic demands. Workers, housewives, and successful merchants alike must constantly interact with various branches of the state, whether the Ministry of Education, Finance (taxation), Social Affairs (social security, pensions, and the regulation of voluntary associations), Labor (employment codes, workplace regulations, and public-sector appointment), Religious Charities (religious associations, supervision of mosques, charitable endowments, and the pilgrimage), Interior (the police), or Defense (the armed forces and conscription), to name just a few.

Bureaucratic processes typically require many trips to various offices around the city and small fees for forms that are generally available at post offices. The *sha'b*, particularly if they are illiterate, rely on more educated and informed neighbors and relatives in their informal networks to direct them to the proper offices and assist them in filling out the necessary forms. Those who have experience in these matters are sought out by others who fear their ignorance will be exploited by uncaring and overworked bureaucrats. Even well-educated, wealthy members of the community can be intimidated or exploited by bureaucrats who send them on endless rounds to process papers. The demand on the bureaucracy is relentless since thousands of Egyptians apply for the same papers and the same service, exhausting the overburdened, limited resources of the state as well as the patience of its employees. Within this context, knowing a low- or high-level employee at a Ministry might translate into better service, fewer required visits to the office, or fewer delays before one's papers are processed.

This section discusses and analyzes informal networks that the *sha'b* utilize in dealing with either bureaucrats or publicly elected representatives whose primary function is to mediate between individuals and the state. The section begins by discussing the networks and strategies the *sha'b* use to purchase publicly subsidized commodities from local branches of state-sector or state-supported food cooperatives. Although 95 percent of the population consumes subsidized food, its distribution is inconsistent, and near riots break out in densely populated residential areas when coveted items such as meat or cooking oil are available at local cooperatives. Food subsidies and price controls in the market are extremely sensitive issues in Egypt and receive a great deal of attention from the government, opposition political parties, the media, academics, and the *sha'b*.

Second, there are some individuals and families who have managed to incorporate important public officials or politicians into their informal networks. Despite limitations that competing bureaucrats or politicians can impose, these networks can provide financial security and benefits for local supporters of politicians and high-level bureaucrats. While not everyone happens to have a powerful protector, because charity, assistance, and political alliances are usually not anonymous political elites are more accessible to the *sha'b* than is sometimes apparent. The *sha'b* do not hesitate to visit politicians and public figures in their offices, homes, and workplaces. (Chapter 5 will discuss in more detail the aggregate consequences of the *sha'b*'s exploitation of informal economic and political networks.)

Third, informal networks are critically important to the *sha'b* because they offer protection from the power of the state and the vagaries of the market. Informal networks provide alternative means for the *sha'b* to withstand the power of the state and create parallel mechanisms that can further their interests in the larger political system. These networks are designed to exploit weaknesses and strengths in the formal political and economic system and thus must be sensitive to the needs of the community and changes in government policy. When community objectives change, networks reemerge in a slightly transformed configuration that adapts to new circumstances, incorporating new constituencies.

Subsidies and Informal Networks

In July 1985, just before the beginning of the ʿIid il-ʾaDHa (a major religious holiday celebrating the conclusion of ceremonies during the *Hajj*, or pilgrimage to Mecca), the government announced on television that meat would be available during the holiday at public- and private-sector food cooperatives. On this holiday, in memory of Abraham's offer to sacrifice his son to God, Muslims slaughter a lamb and distribute a share of its meat to the poor. On occasions such as this, the government makes specific plans to distribute subsidized meat and special foods throughout the country. The government actually imports most of the lambs, ensures that each person with a ration card (almost 95 percent of all Egyptians) will be able to purchase half a lamb at a subsidized price at government food cooperatives, and supervises price controls on lambs purchased from private butchers.[63]

This level of involvement by the government is representative of its role in ensuring that the public has access to relatively inexpensive food. Apart from providing occasional needs, the government wrote in a recent Five Year Plan (1978–1982), one of its primary duties is to "make available to the public both necessary and other foodstuffs, at prices much lower than their actual cost to the government."[64] The *shaʿb* hold the government to this obligation by consuming its legal share of subsidized foodstuffs and using informal means to purchase subsidized goods that have entered the black market. The financial burden of subsidies became significant in the 1970s and early 1980s. The government, fearing destabilizing demonstrations, prefers indirect methods to decrease its subsidy bill, such as reducing entitlements to food and accepting (or perhaps orchestrating) shortages of food in high-demand communities. For example, the government has decreased the weight and quality of wheat used for its *baladi* bread (made out of whole wheat flour) and has marketed the more expensive *shaami* bread of white bleached flour. Khouri-Dagher argues that bread is a symbol of inflation and the cost of living, or a gold standard, so that when the price of bread rises, people expect all other prices to soon follow, in the same proportions.[65] In fact, between 1981–82 and 1986–87 food subsidies declined approximately 50 percent. The subsidy on wheat, in particular, declined by 468 percent, which obviously is the cause of increased bread prices and shortages in the country.[66] One of the ways in which the government succeeded in reducing expenditures and improving its balance-of-payments dilemma was to cut down on explicit consumer subsidies since the mid-1980s (from 13 percent of GDP to 6 percent of GDP).[67] Needless to say, the reduction of subsidies has fallen the hardest on people whose food costs represent the highest share of their annual expenditures. Lower-income groups in Egypt allocate 60 percent of their income to food and beverages whereas higher-income groups allocate 42 percent (which is still quite substantial).[68]

Subsidized food is a scarce commodity in *sha'bi* communities, where market prices are regularly double or triple the price of government-controlled and distributed bulk foods and household products such as soap and cooking oil.[69] Shortages in various commodities, whether produced by speculation, corruption, international market conditions, government ineptitude, or design, become the focus of exposés and screaming headlines in newspapers. In the summer of 1986, for example, three particular crises filled the headlines of newspapers (particularly the pages of opposition newspapers, which publicized these scandals to encourage opposition to the government): a tea shortage, a *kushari* shortage (the famous Egyptian fast food consisting of macaroni, lentils, onions, and spices), and a flour shortage. All three items are even more important to the *sha'b* because they are very inexpensive and essential parts of almost every Egyptian's diet (*kushari* is even referred to in newspaper articles as a *sha'bi* meal). One newspaper reported that the price of *kushari* had risen 500 percent during the previous three years as the government repealed its mandatory price controls. Some owners complained that the price had risen because they could obtain flour for macaroni only from the black market, thus increasing their costs, which they passed on to their clients. The headline asked, "Will a Plate of *Kushari* Turn into a Tourist Dish?" (to be available only at highly inflated prices at five-star hotels?).[70] The headline of an article about the tea crisis was even more interesting: "The *Sha'b* Warn the Government: Stay Away from [Our] Cup of Tea." When a reporter interviewed people around Cairo about their reaction to the price increase in tea, people responded by arguing that it was a national outrage, almost treasonous, since tea, as is well known, is the lifeblood of Egyptians and that the government's plea for people to reduce their consumption of tea was ridiculous.[71] The official government newspaper, *al-Ahram*, quickly published a long interview with the Minister of Food Supply, who is ultimately responsible for food shortages and price increases. He attempted to explain the intricacies of the subsidy system and reported that he was forced to decrease the monthly ration of tea (for all those who are eligible to receive rationed, *tamwiin* goods) by 50 percent because the government did not receive a scheduled shipment of 7,000 tons of tea due to a strike of dockworkers in India. While there are many similar stories on food prices in newspapers throughout the year, what is important to remember is that the government is intricately involved in distributing basic goods and supervising the prices of a wide range of commodities in the market. Ministers in the government are interviewed constantly about these issues, and they promise personal supervision of distribution networks and retribution for those who break the law. The failure of the government to control prices is a frequent complaint, even though many people wish government intervention would decrease so that supplies of certain items might increase. One article, for example, argued that government price regulations no longer mean anything. "They have gone from being something enforceable, to wishful thinking, to nothing but numbers on paper. The prices of fruit and vegetables have risen 300 percent, red meat and poultry 100 percent, fish 150 percent—all this for foods whose prices are government-regulated! Is this greed on the part of some food sellers? Or is this impotence on the part of government price regulation?"[72] In a column entitled "The Consumer Comes First," another newspaper offered the following assistance:

> Dear Consumer,
>
> We are always here to serve you. In order to protect you from the greed and exploitation of traders, *al-Masaa'* presents this column to try to protect you from the hustlers in the black market. Send us your complaints if a trader tries to sell you something for more than the regulated price, or if a taxi driver refuses to let you ride, or if an owner of an apartment tries to demand key money, or advance rent. We will take your phone calls from 6:00 to 8:00 P.M. at the following numbers . . . and our address is . . .[73]

Although the price of subsidized goods is below market value, people must absorb queuing and networking costs to actually receive both legal and illegal goods. Visiting the food cooperatives is practically a daily task in these communities since the supply of commodities is irregular. One must be informed of the availability of commodities, their prices, and the specific documents employees demand to purchase the goods. Some commodities are distributed on a limited basis, others are sold in unlimited quantities until supplies are exhausted. Official procedures are often overlooked for those with connections or cash to bribe the bureaucrats on duty, as long as their supervisors are not watching.

When popular items become available, crowds of neighborhood residents and workers surround the cooperative. In highly populated areas the demand on food cooperatives is much greater than in wealthier, more suburban areas, where one can now find elaborate "supermarket" prefab food cooperatives. Public-sector employees are serviced by small food cooperatives in the office buildings where they work. In *sha'bi* communities a few cooperatives must service a much larger district, whose residents do not have the choice of shopping at other stores unless they are government employees. Even when there are adequate supplies of commodities, lines and disorder are common. The *sha'b* often complain about the government's inability to distribute subsidized goods to those who really need them, and the government itself recognizes this as a problem.

One day, in the heat of July, the cooperative was distributing cooking oil and chickens—two items heavily in demand. About one hundred men and women surrounded the co-op, desperately trying to pay for their items at one small window and get a receipt. They then made their way to another window where they were handed (or thrown) their chickens or cooking oil. Apparently that day there was no limit to the quantity of purchases, but this may have been an unauthorized decision by the co-op's employees. Some women were leaving with cartons of cooking oil, only to return to the crowd once they had deposited their goods in a nearby apartment. These women were 'id-dallalaat (female peddlers), the backbone of the elaborate black-market system, who frequently work in cooperation with employees of food cooperatives. In sha'bi neighborhoods dallalaat distribute food and other commodities (oil, soap, tea) to their clients. Sometimes they borrow ration books, for a price, from local families in order to obtain greater quantities of subsidized commodities. The dallalaat spend long hours in line trying to get food and extorting more supplies from internal sources in the food cooperatives. Occasionally they are prosecuted and jailed.

As the local dallalaat were leaving with cartons of oil, the co-op began to distribute chicken. At this point the crowd surged forward, pressing those in front against the building's metal gates.[74] Elderly women, who wear the traditional black milaaya over their hair, emerged from the crowd with their heads uncovered, their clothes askew. At one point, an employee began swatting the crowd with a large pot lid, but people in the crowd took it away from him. Then the people in the front of the line used the lid to hit those behind them, since they were being pushed up against the metal gates of the building. Soon a fight broke out between two young men, and people struggled to pull them apart. One of them emerged with a cut on his face, screaming that all he wanted was his right to two chickens—was that Haraam, forbidden? One of the more energetic boys from the neighborhood was paid by people on the sidelines, who would not enter the fray, to bring them chicken. He grabbed a high metal hinge that stuck out from the building and literally dove headfirst over the counter where his friends working inside the co-op caught him and filled his sack with chickens.

This chaos and disorder, of course, works to the disadvantage of those who are only trying to get their fair share of the rations, but who do not have the strength or patience to wage virtual war to receive them. Those residents in the neighborhood who have connections with the employees of the co-op, or who can pay inflated prices for goods on the black market, benefit from this system. The chaos and violence of the crowds increase the attractiveness of black-market purchases. People will pay black-market prices for food if they can avoid the humiliation, violence, harassment, and heat stroke from waiting hours in the street for one or two chickens.

Men and women among the sha'b not only rely on each other to find out what items are at the cooperatives, but they stand in line for each other and then redistribute the food they have been able to procure among their own networks. For example, some well-connected individuals may be able to purchase ten chickens from the co-op in a single day, but then they redistribute them at cost to family members or close neighbors. In another instance, a family arrived home with five gunnysacks filled with various types of pasta. One sack was filled with thirty packages of spaghetti, another with twenty-five packages of macaroni, another with twenty packages of vermicelli or *sha'riyya*, which is used to make a popular rice pilaf dish. The pasta was distributed to members of the extended family and colleagues, at cost. The family made no profit from their effort, but expected that the recipients of the food would return the favor when they could.

Those people who are known to be in a strategic position to distribute food to their relatives and neighbors (employees of food cooperatives, *dalla-laat*, or shrewd consumers) are often approached by other members of the community who will pay them higher prices to procure additional quantities of scarce commodities. If someone has arranged a job for a person employed by a food cooperative, it is expected that, in gratitude, he or she will provide a supply of commodities to their family and their informal networks. Even though there is a risk of being prosecuted for corruption or speculation, appointment to a food cooperative is coveted by many. As in any lower-income community, families are constantly concerned about the cost and quality of food. In Egypt, where food is rationed and its prices supervised by the government, informal networks become crucial in fulfilling a basic need in the community.

Politicians, Public Figures, and Networks

Close ties to a powerful, honored, or wealthy member of the community provide men and women with another level of opportunity. Successfully incorporating powerful people into informal networks benefits not only an individual but other individuals in the network as well. The larger community shares knowledge about which person has helped the other, for what reasons, and with what consequence. Some of the details of the exchange might be left vague, but the exchange or favor becomes part of the public record.

When people need the assistance of a public figure or politician, they usually first approach the local contact in the community (there are often many, but only a few who function almost like "ward captains"). After listening to their problem, the local contact will either try to solve it him or herself or will send them on to their "patron." Each time the local leader provides a service to the "patron," it is noted and eventually repaid. In a particular relationship that I was able to observe closely, the ties between the "patron" and the supposed "client" were very close and reciprocal. The "client" received loans from the politician, gifts of food and clothing for her family, publicly subsidized apartments, employment for her and members of her family, assistance with bureaucratic problems, and a great deal of information and knowledge which the "client" then utilized to support her personal and familial networks. Through this relationship, the "client" developed a powerful base within the community, building on her family's already strong ties to the merchant community. At election time, the client returned these services by organizing the election campaign and marshaling local political support in the district. This relationship was extremely well publicized and promoted by both the politician and the local leader. Both publicly proclaimed to each other their loyalty, love, and interdependence. At the same time, however, there are few people in *sha'bi* communities with close ties to elite politicians. It is a relatively rare and privileged person who has been lucky enough to develop such a relationship, and even these figures use their high-placed contacts to increase the reach and value of their informal networks. Those without such access to elites subscribe to those networks that are more vertical (in that they incorporate people up and down the ladders of wealth and power) than horizontal (in that they include people with fairly similar and equal characteristics).

On certain holidays public figures reaffirm their ties to the community by distributing food and clothing to the poor in neighborhoods which have supported them. At one *nadra* (charitable offering during religious holidays), a local member of Parliament visited an ancient mosque to pray and then distributed meat and bread to the poor (which was prepared by her local supporters). She also distributed approximately £E30 to the low-ranking local employees of the mosque, such as cooks, janitors, and guards—apparently from personal funds. Later in the year, the member of Parliament's daughter gave a local supporter a small sum to distribute to neighborhood beggars and disabled people on the occasion of an important religious holiday. Again, this charitable act was not anonymous, but these people were told the identity of their benefactor. When blankets or clothing are to be distributed to the poor in the winter, the benefactor is always identified.

However, the power of public figures and their ability to intervene on behalf of constituents is limited. Repeated requests to assist people cause bureaucrats and those with power to grow suspicious of a politician's motives. And at the same time, a politician may respond to occasional requests from constituents but become aggravated if their assistance is continually sought.[75] It is not that people expect politicians or wealthy members of the community always to resolve their problems, but it is still worthwhile to cultivate the relationship so that one's repertoire of informal networks will be more wide-ranging and include diverse participants.

CONCLUSION

In this chapter I have argued that networks, which pervade all aspects of community life, provide political capital for men and women. Individuals utilize networks to accomplish daily tasks and to build alliances with powerful members of the community, and to organize and strengthen communal norms. Because the community directs and controls these networks, they are sensitive and responsive to their changing needs and to policy changes by the government. When certain networks become obsolete, they die away or are transformed to fulfill new needs of the community. The role of 'id-dallalaat in organizing black-market activities provides one of the most vivid examples of the adaptability of informal networks. Originating in the Mamluk era, these shrewd female businesswomen exploit deficiencies in government distribution systems and follow demand in the market to provide a service to the community (even though some might argue it is a disservice).

Informal networks are described as political because they organize individual consumers and households into a more powerful, collective body. In addition, informal networks increase the community's access to and influence over scarce private and public goods and services. Men and women in *sha'bi* communities who actively cultivate their networks can gain access to powerful politicians, subsidized commodities, savings and credit organizations, and local bureaucrats who may facilitate another range of services. As members of *sha'bi* communities repeat over and over, one must master both the formal and the informal face of any problem. Knowing how to *yitSarraf* (manage) among government bureaucrats and street traders is equally important. Certainly, some problems are best resolved through formal means, and others are left to informal brokers to resolve. Knowing who to approach, at what moment, is a critically important skill that is respected and valued by others in the community.

Many people in *sha'bi* communities are actively involved in the organization, coordination, and strengthening of informal networks. Networks infuse the community with energy and creativity. This vitality, which is overlooked if one concentrates primarily on formal political organizations and visible state-centered political action, suggests that men and women are indeed politically active in their communities and, through geographically disparate networks, in larger areas within Cairo. People use informal networks to gain control over their livelihood, the education system, financial institutions, and publicly distributed subsidized goods. They create a public resource by their organization of these networks, which fulfill shared needs. These capabilities illustrate that informal networks do provide a critical avenue of political participation for men and women among *sha'bi* communities. Individuals organize collective efforts to achieve certain goals—whether that includes marrying off the younger generation, educating the young, financing a loan, or feeding a family. Informal networks articulate and aggregate the interests of their constituents, working to further those interests in legal and illegal, formal and informal, visible and invisible ways. Not every association between three or more people need be an indication of political participation, but if extensive networks coordinate masses of people to achieve particular goals, they clearly serve as a political institution for this particular constituency.

Informality

POLITICS AND ECONOMICS IN TANDEM

THE PREVIOUS two chapters demonstrated that informal and familial networks play a critical political role by furthering the shared interests of *sha'bi* communities. Informal networks facilitated the accumulation of savings within the community, arranged employment for men and women, enhanced educational opportunities for students, arbitrated disputes, and structured the exchange of goods and services, which provided security and support for a community with limited resources. Informal political institutions were communally sanctioned, supported, and legitimated by the principles of the familial ethos. The greater the reach of these networks and the larger their membership, the more useful they became. Networks were designed and manipulated by their members to penetrate all levels of society, the economy, and the state. Although problems of classification and definition obscured this arena of informal networks as a *political* domain, it serves as one of the *sha'b*'s most important avenues of political participation.

In any polity, economic resources enhance the capabilities of institutions and organizations. The case of *sha'bi* communities in Egypt is no different. In a political system where the government discourages and controls political participation, any collective institution that is designed to further specific interests and objectives can only be strengthened by financial support. Institutions without a material base of support have a limited future. If men and women have some financial autonomy, they are in a better position to direct their resources toward ends in which they believe. If they live in societies where the government has a predominant role in directing economic planning and regulating economic activities, and thus the market is intensely politicized, the efforts of other constituencies to influence the market in various ways must be seen in a similarly politicized light. Peattie and Rein argue that political economy "points to the role of social and political institutions in shaping economic outcomes."[1] A great deal of attention has been focused on the ways in which formal Egyptian political and economic institutions and Egyptian policymakers have "shaped economic outcomes" and promoted and/or distorted its economy. Less attention has been focused on the role of *informal* political and social institutions in shaping Egypt's political economy, and it is this question that this chapter will examine through the specific contours of one *sha'bi* community.

Abdel-Fadil defines the informal sector as "economic activities which largely escape recognition, enumeration and regulation by the government."[2] The informal economy, as recent scholarship has clarified, is not only a "specific form of relations of production" but may refer to the status of labor, the conditions of work, and the form of management of some firms.[3] The informal economy, informal networks, savings associations, informal communal goods, and black markets have been devised by men and women as a way to provide for their families, protect their security, and further the collective interests of the community. And examples of informality are everywhere. As De Soto wrote in his study of informality in Lima, Peru, "You only have to open the window or step onto the street" to witness this phenomenon. One encounters the informal sector when tripping over a woman on the sidewalk and thousands like her who sell cheap consumer goods, newspapers, or fast food in Cairo, or when wandering through an alleyway where young boys are crammed into tiny workshops that ignore labor regulations, the tax authorities, and licensing requirements, or when visiting sprawling newly settled residential neighborhoods, which have largely been built illegally on government or agricultural land without regard to building codes or zoning laws. In almost every family in Cairo, children take private, illegal lessons from their school teachers in order to pass competitive national exams that will largely determine their occupational future. In most kitchens in Cairo one finds food purchased from black marketers who illegally and extralegally procure government-subsidized and distributed food and commodities for clients (often neighbors and relatives). Many women in these households organize informal savings associations among their relatives, friends, and colleagues to finance another wedding, another trip to the Gulf, or a family business venture. All these activities are informal in nature and provide much-needed services and resources for *sha'bi* communities.[4]

Since the 1970s, economists and those in the social sciences have debated the substance, influence, and meaning of the informal economy. Hart first introduced the term "informal economy" in a conference on urban employment in Africa in 1971 in order to suggest that perhaps the informal sector was a source of unheralded economic growth in urban settings.[5] He asked, "Does the 'reserve army of urban unemployed and underemployed' really constitute a passive, exploited majority in cities like Accra, or do their informal economic activities possess some autonomous capacity for generating growth in the incomes of the urban (and rural) poor?"[6] Because aspects of the informal economy (wages, hours, production) can be enumerated by careful, detailed fieldwork and then compared or supplemented by national economic statistics, anthropologists and economists have been able to demonstrate the significant value of goods and services produced in the informal sector and the numbers of lower and middle-class urban (and rural) men and women who earn a significant part of their livelihood from the informal sector. Mazumdar argued that the extent of employment in the informal sector in urban settings was very significant, reaching 55 percent in Bombay, just over 50 percent in Jakarta, 69 percent in Belo (Brazil), and 53 percent in

Lima.[7] In a comprehensive study of Peru, De Soto estimated that "48 percent of the economically active population and 61.2 percent of work hours are devoted to informal activities which contribute 38.9 percent of the Gross Domestic Product recorded in national accounts."[8] He suggests that informality concerns more than employment and production and is almost a way of life for the poor in Latin America. Because recent migrants to urban areas were uneducated and unqualified for most employment and had such few resources and opportunities, they devised extralegal means to fulfill basic needs. "If they [the informals] were to live, trade, manufacture, transport, or even consume, the cities' new inhabitants had to do so illegally. Such illegality was not antisocial in intent, like trafficking in drugs, theft, or abduction, but was designed to achieve such essentially legal objectives as building a house, providing a service, or developing a business."[9] Portes concludes that "for Latin America as a whole, roughly 60 percent of the economically active population, or about 80 percent of all workers, can be estimated to be employed outside the formal sector."[10]

Despite the various problems of measurement and definition of informal-sector employment in urban and rural, developing and developed economies, the figures convinced scholars of the vitality and diversity of this sector, though arguments remained about a range of questions.[11] Does the informal economy provide jobs for the poor, migrants, and uneducated workers, or does it depress the already declining wage rates of public-sector and private-sector employees? Does employment in the informal sector offer upward mobility for workers, or is it dangerous, irregular, and exploitative? Does the informal sector provide for its workers even though it remains outside the social welfare net of government pensions, health benefits, and minimum-wage provisions, or does it only serve to decrease the pressure on governments to provide these benefits for citizens? Is the informal sector a positive phenomenon for Third World economies, or is it merely a strategy by domestic and international capitalists to break unions and reverse hard-won workers' rights in economies that are already under pressure to privatize and undergo structural adjustment? Does the informal sector represent the essence of entrepreneurial, free-market capitalism, or is it a retreat from planned, modern development strategies and a return to preindustrial, self-exploitative, artisanal activities that threaten market rationality and the development of capitalism? Does the informal sector (or second economy, as it was labeled in Eastern Europe) offer a strategy to resist the state and its control of the economy, or is it merely a haven for illegal activity, exploitation, local mafias, corruption, and speculation? All these questions raise complicated economic issues and political questions that are very relevant to the case of Egypt. Some of these questions have been addressed in more recent studies of the informal sector in Egypt.[12]

My limited interest here, however, is twofold. First, I argue that informal economic activities are conceptually very similar to informal political activities. Both largely escape recognition, enumeration, and regulation by the government. In Egypt the government has consistently regulated, licensed, and supervised politics, just as much as it tries (but seems to succeed less) in carefully regulating and supervising the economy. Nevertheless, certain excluded, disadvantaged, or "marginal" economic groups depend on the informal economy, despite the degree of state intervention in the economy. In a similar fashion, certain constituencies that are excluded or marginalized from the formal political system depend on informal political activities, despite the desire of the Egyptian elite to control all political participation. Unfortunately, scholars have not addressed the political dimension of the informal sector as forcefully as they have its economic characteristics.

Second, there is a symbiotic relationship between informal economic activities and informal political institutions. Groups that feel their interests are being ignored by the powerful use their financial resources to promote those interests, and the informal sector—in both its political and economic manifestations—provides the means for these struggles. More simply, informal institutions and the informal economy operate in tandem, one supporting the other. As most people would agree, political institutions that are embedded in economic structures are far stronger. Political parties have difficulty flourishing unless someone pays their bills, whether it is private interests, the government, or some combination thereof. Grass-roots organizations have difficulty surviving unless a mass network supports them. In Egypt many regulations sabotage the financial autonomy of opposition parties and independent political views while the government pours its money into the National Democratic Party and other legal political institutions that are used to co-opt and control its citizens. However, because of the extent of the informal economy in Egypt, some of its financial resources are available to support informal political institutions. *Two-thirds* of the men and women in the community I studied were supported by the informal economy in either their primary, secondary, or tertiary economic activity. The informal sector is an integral and significant part of the economic life of this community although, like the informal political arena, it has a relatively hidden, illicit, and underreported character. Furthermore, recent statistics, which can only underestimate the size of this sector due to measurement problems, have suggested that the informal sector accounts for 43 percent of all private nonagricultural employment in Egypt.[13] I am not suggesting an explicit, organized, and institutionalized link between the informal economy and informal networks, since both are very amorphous in shape and quite diverse, but merely that if the *sha'b* control even a proportion of the resources circulating in the informal economy, they are in a better position to support and promote objectives and preferences in which they believe.

The question of visibility surrounds the study of the informal economy as much as it does informal politics. This chapter demonstrates the ill effects of economic analyses that do not go beyond visible activities and conventional methodologies by examining the economic activities of this community in two distinct ways. "The Formal Picture," the first part of the following section, analyzes the economically active population of my community through an occupational, industrial, and sectoral (employment share in the public and private sector) analysis. According to the United Nations, the economically active population "comprises all persons of either sex who furnish the supply of labour for the production of economic goods and services . . . during a specified time-reference period."[14] While a significant share of the 292 men, women, and children in this community were employed by the public sector (30 percent), an even greater share were employed by the private sector (44 percent). In order to measure the extent of self-employment and familial enterprises in the private sector, I added these subcategories to the analysis of the private sector. In order to capture the economic activity of this community more precisely and accurately, I also examined its secondary and tertiary sources of income. Since many sources of secondary and tertiary income are technically illegal, people do not describe them to census enumerators, and therefore national labor statistics severely underestimate secondary and tertiary employment. For example, it is technically illegal for public-sector employees to hold an additional job although the practice is very pervasive. Many self-employed people feared census officials since they did not report secondary income to the tax authorities or underestimated primary income from self-employment. Even though noncash exchanges of goods and services were important to the household economy, women and men rarely reported or recorded them in census data.[15] Zaytoun argues in a study of earnings and the cost of living that it is extremely difficult for Egyptian social scientists to understand the dynamics of the informal sector since national accounts data related to subsidiary occupations and the income received by the self-employed are "completely lacking. In addition, no information is available on earnings in the informal sector."[16] However, by analyzing the community I studied in great depth, much of this information can be presented. The primary source of income in my study refers to each person's official position of employment (which was registered with various government agencies), or the occupation or income-generating activity with which workers in the informal economy described themselves. Secondary sources of income usually refer to part-time jobs, "moonlighting," and semiregular employment or income-generating activities. Tertiary sources of income were rarer but include in-kind exchange and skills of the self-employed which generated income for men and women. Primary sources of income were not always the most lucrative, although they tended to be more consistent and secure than secondary or tertiary sources. Finally, this multi-layered analysis of formal economic activity captures a far more significant role for women in the economy than is typically reported by conventional sources because I was familiar with many common, but somewhat disguised or ignored, income-generating activities of women (because of my knowledge of the households and networks of many women).

"The Informal Picture," the second part of the following section, reexamines employment of the economically active sample using Abdel-Fadil's study of the informal sector in Egypt and his occupationally based methodology of classifying informal economic activities as well as several different criteria. This reexamination of the same data reveals the pervasiveness of the informal sector in this community: informal employment in this one community reached 38 percent of the *active* members of the economically active sample from primary sources of income, 87 percent for secondary sources of income, and 71 percent for tertiary sources of income. (The extent of informal-sector activity among the entire economically active population was slightly lower: 28 percent of the economically active population from a primary economic activity and 40 percent from a secondary economic activity.) Most importantly, 62 percent, or approximately *two-thirds* of the community, was engaged in informal economic activity in either its primary, secondary, or tertiary activity.

The second section, on "Family Enterprises," considers the significance of these endeavors in the formal and informal economic activities within this community. Those enterprises that were owned, operated, and staffed by relatives and self-identified as a family concern were included within this category. In general, family enterprises employ fewer employees than private enterprises and are less capital intensive. A few family enterprises in the community, however, were quite large and diversified and employed workers who were not related to the family in control of the enterprise. While family enterprises are private-sector establishments, they are designed to further familial interests as well as to profit in the market. Familial enterprises are similar to public-sector enterprises in that both are organized to meet market and nonmarket objectives. The government has depended on the public sector to meet its commitment to the employment of vocational and university graduates, to maintain control over certain strategic sectors of the economy, and to fulfill the regime's plans for economic growth and development. Family enterprises are similarly designed to provide employment for family members, to increase and maintain control over the family's financial resources, and to enhance the economic and political status and power of a family in its community. The family's economic position complements its political significance in the community. As a family's economic strength is maintained through its productive activities or its distribution of services, its political role in the community (and perhaps in the larger polity) is enhanced. This section also focuses on the contribution of women to the household economy and family enterprises, and suggests certain explanations for the very high rates of labor force participation among both women and men found in this sample. A methodology of participant/observation, situated in households and workplaces, revealed many economic activities of men and women which were not typically captured by labor force statistics.

The third section, on "Informality Meets the State," examines how businessmen and community members cope with two interdependent systems: formal and informal rules. The Egyptian government engages in binding rule-making in three important areas—labor relations, taxation, and the legal system—yet these are riddled with informal practices. All unions in Egypt are state-licensed, and various ministries regulate labor relations, working conditions, and other aspects of employment policies and production. Only the government legitimately has the right and the mandate to collect taxes in Egypt. And, similarly, only the parliamentary, judicial, and executive branches of the Egyptian state have the right to enact laws and governmental regulations. In *shaʿbi* communities, however, informal rules regulate labor relations; informal procedures riddle both the government's collection of taxes and the ways in which people pay their taxes, and these procedures permeate the legal system as well. Informal activities not only affect employment and production but also the *shaʿb*'s interaction with the state and its various bureaucratic and regulatory agencies.

The final two sections of the chapter consider the implications of informality for the position of the *shaʿb* in the economy and the polity. Due to international trends in the economy and recent Egyptian policies (particularly the Open Door Economic Policy, international migration opportunities, and rising wage rates for some skilled workers), certain sectors of the *shaʿb* have increased their standard of living and experienced upward economic mobility. The upward mobility of the *shaʿb* has adversely affected other segments of the Egyptian population who have watched plumbers, contractors, and merchants of *shaʿbi* neighborhoods move into their buildings and attend their schools. More significantly for elite politics, the wealth circulating in the informal economy does not end up in government coffers but remains within the community. Autonomous financial resources may provide an opportunity for people, who are not controlled or co-opted by the government, to promote their own political and social agenda through the informal sector.

INFORMAL AND FORMAL ECONOMIC ACTIVITY
IN A *SHAʿBI* COMMUNITY

In order to understand the relationship between political and economic life in specific constituencies, it is first necessary to examine their material base and economic organization. Upon investigating one of the most basic issues to the life and character of one *shaʿbi* community (employment), the importance of the informal economy soon becomes clear. The informal economic sector in this community deeply affects employment, production, and the behavior of workers, businessmen, the self-employed, and owners of private enterprises toward regulatory and legal agencies of the state. The data presented below progress from general categories to more detailed distinctions that finally reveal the extent of formal and informal activity. The first part of this section presents the formal picture of employment in the economically active sample population, which includes 292 men, women, and children in the larger community. The sample is divided first into active and inactive employment and then by sector (public and private). The active population includes the employed and the unemployed; the inactive population includes students, pension recipients, retired persons, housewives, and undefined economic activity. Unfortunately, in standard analyses of employment, housewives are considered part of the inactive and nonworking population. This devaluation of their work not only contradicts my understanding of the economic life of this community but ignores the fact that their responsibilities are valued and part of the economic calculus of Egyptian men and women. To include them as "inactive" at least makes them visible until a more sophisticated model of employment can be devised.

The economically active population is divided further within each sector. The public sector is divided by employment in the public sector (both the civil service and public enterprises), the armed forces, and public service. Almost all young men in Egypt must fulfill a period of service in the armed forces, unless they are exempt for various reasons. Women (and men not conscripted in the armed forces) who pursue postsecondary public education must fulfill a year of public service before they will be hired by the government or public-sector enterprises. Since both military service and public service are only temporary (and practically unpaid employment: conscripts receive £E9–15 per month, and public-service workers receive a £E5 bonus at the end of the year), they were distinguished from public-sector employment in the following tables on formal employment. The private sector is divided into private enterprises, family enterprises, and self-employment. Self-employment is defined as "persons who during the reference period performed some work for profit or family gain, in cash or in kind," as opposed to performing work for "wage or salary, in cash or in kind" as in paid employment.[17] Both self-employment and family enterprises will be seen below to provide significant employment and income-generation in this community.

One of the most important motives for classifying formal employment was to examine the extent of secondary and tertiary sources of income in the community. The tables below refer to secondary and tertiary sources of income, rather than employment as such, since many people earned income in cash and kind through the production of goods and the exchange of services, rather than as an employee of a firm or organization. This approach captured a far wider range of economic activities in this community than a conventional notion of formal employment. However, my analysis of secondary and tertiary sources of income in this sample also suffers from imprecision and a lack of data (and thus the tables in this chapter may be somewhat confusing because the size of the group varies due to the consistency of the data). While the primary sources of income for the sample were all known, I did not know the secondary occupations of ninety-three people, or roughly a third of the community. Because I knew some people better than others in the sample and did not visit the homes and workplaces of everyone, I could not specify, with certainty, the secondary activities of these ninety-three people. Just because I was unaware of their varied sources of income, however, did not mean that they did not have any. The ambiguity and inconsistency of the data do not alter the extent of known secondary economic activity among the community. The table on tertiary sources of income (Table 4.3) relies upon an even smaller subset of the economically active population ($N = 16$) which, unfortunately, underestimates the extent of tertiary sources of income. Despite the inconsistency of the data, it still suggests certain patterns of employment and income-generating activities.

The high incidence of secondary and tertiary income in this community encouraged a further investigation of the informal economic activity in the same community. Familiarity with people and visits to their homes and workplaces provided a more detailed account of multiple sources of income than formal interviewing and census schedules generally produce. The section on "The Informal Picture" analyzes informal economic activity of the *active* population of the sample (there was no point in dividing the inactive population into formal and informal activity). A definitional ambiguity of the informal economy and problems of measurement have impeded a precise analysis of the informal economy in Egypt and elsewhere. However, because it takes into consideration characteristics of the Egyptian labor force, the occupationally based classification of informal economic activities that Abdel-Fadil used (which I altered slightly) is adopted here to analyze this *sha'bi* community.[18] The extent of the informal sector in this community will then inform the following discussion of its consequences on the economic and political resources of the *sha'b*.

The Formal Picture

The initial picture of the economically active population of my community presents a fairly typical pattern of employment. A significant portion of the community was employed by the public sector (30 percent) while the largest share of the sample was located in the private sector (44 percent).[19] An almost equal percentage of the sample was employed by private and family enterprises (18 and 19 percent respectively), which was not surprising considering the economic and social bonds between families (as discussed in previous chapters). The unemployment rate of only 1 percent was exceedingly low, compared to the national unemployment rate of 12 percent in the 1986 Population Census.[20] Domestic responsibilities absorbed the labor of 16 percent of the sample, all women (39 percent of all women in the sample).

Table 4.2 reveals a very different pattern of secondary economic activity. Most importantly, 47 percent of the sample was supported by a secondary source of income. Sixty-three percent of public-sector employees found a secondary source of employment (73 percent of all male public-sector employees), which is not surprising considering the financial pressures on households where the major breadwinner has to rely upon public-sector

TABLE 4.1
Total Primary Sources of Income (N = 292)

	N	%
	Active	
Public		
Public sector	66	23
Armed forces	16	5
Public service	6	2
Subtotal:	[88]	[30]
Private		
Private enterprise	52	18
Family enterprise	56	19
Self-employment	17	6
Subtotal:	[125]	[43]
Unemployed	2	1
	Inactive	
Housewife	47	16
Student	22	8
Retired	7	2
Inactive	1	0
Subtotal:	[77]	[26]
TOTAL	292	100

wages that have not kept pace with inflation and the rising cost of living.[21] The only individuals who worked in the public sector as a secondary source of income (four) were either fulfilling mandatory public service before they were appointed to the government or were on maternity leave from a public-sector job.

The private sector provided an almost equal share of primary and secondary sources of income (44 and 45 percent, respectively), and self-employment was more significant in the latter (rising from 6 percent in Table 4.1 to 19 percent in Table 4.2). Family enterprises and self-employment represented 33 percent of all secondary sources of income and 74 percent of private-sector activity.[22] Because self-employment typically relied upon limited capital investment, self-exploitation, and common skills, people in this community could engage in petty trade, produce simple consumer goods (such as custom-tailored clothes or fast-food production), or provide services far more easily than finding a second permanent position in a private-sector enterprise. It was hard enough to find one job in the private sector, and even more difficult to find two, and thus family connections and self-employment were critical ways to earn additional income.

Half the sample with known tertiary employment (sixteen) in Table 4.3 were also public-sector employees (as a primary occupation). These people held three jobs not out of interest but financial need. Again, the most

TABLE 4.2
Total Secondary Sources of Income (*N* = 292)

	N	%
	Active	
Public		
Public sector	2	—
Armed forces	0	—
Public service	2	—
Subtotal:	[4]	[1]
Private		
Private enterprise	34	12
Family enterprise	41	14
Self-employment	55	19
Subtotal:	[130]	[45]
Unemployed	3	1
	Inactive	
Housewife	27	9
Student	4	1
Retired	3	1
Inactive	0	0
Subtotal:	[34]	[11]
No Secondary Source	28	10
Unknown Secondary Source	93	32
TOTAL	292	100

TABLE 4.3
Total Tertiary Sources of Income (*N* = 16)

	Active
Public	
Public sector	1
Armed forces	0
Public service	0
Private	
Private enterprise	0
Family enterprise	3
Self-employment	9
	Inactive
Housewife	0
Student	2
Retired	1
Inactive	0
TOTAL	16

industrious individuals in the sample were primarily self-employed or employed in family enterprises. For example, two relatives participated in the same family enterprise: one owned a grocery store, the other managed it; both were actively involved in the family business, which distributed wholesale honey and clarified butter throughout Cairo (they owned land in Upper Egypt, and relatives managed production there and transported the goods to Cairo); and both were actively involved in another family firm, which imported and exported perishable foodstuffs.

Although only 5 percent of the sample was known to have three income sources (from paying jobs and/or self-employment), these figures underrepresent the widespread production of economic goods—particularly food, clothing, and building stock—for their family, or for gifts and resale. It was common for women in the community to raise chickens, geese, and even sheep for the family's own consumption, or for gifts and resale. In the home where I lived, young chicks would be bought from men who commonly circulate in these areas. For special occasions and religious feasts, geese and sheep were purchased, fattened, and then eaten by the family or given to relatives and the poor. Chicken coops and sheep were visible on many rooftops and in alleyways of older and newer residential areas alike. This type of tertiary activity is significantly underrepresented in the sample because I only became aware of it when I stumbled upon ducks, chickens, sheep, and, in one case, a cow during visits to people's homes and rooftops.[23]

An examination of formal economic activity distinguished by gender in Table 4.4 points out the greater concentration of women among the inactive population (44 percent as opposed to 14 percent for men). This large discrepancy is primarily due to the prevailing definition of housewives as part of the inactive population, which minimizes the value and worth of housework. Thirty-nine percent of women in the sample worked primarily in the household. (For further discussion of the economic contribution of housewives, particularly in the Egyptian context, see the section on "Family Enterprises" below.)

A second gender-based distinction was clear in the high percentage of men employed by family enterprises (27 percent) as opposed to women (8 percent). Family enterprises were largely semi-industrial enterprises or trading and commercial concerns in this community, and it was somewhat uncommon for women to be employed in these types of firms unless they owned them. This difference can also be partially explained by a preference in the community, supported by both men and women, for women to obtain secure appointment in the public sector or a position in a private-sector firm or organization. For educated women the public sector offered job security, government benefits such as generous maternity leave, a low but steady wage, and a relatively short and undemanding workday.

The women who worked in the public sector, as a whole, were the more educated and professional members of the community (such as administra-

TABLE 4.4
Primary Economic Activity by Gender (N = 292: male, 171; female, 121)

	Male	%	Female	%
		Active		
Public				
Public sector	44	26	22	18
Armed forces	16	9	0	0
Public service	0	0	6	5
Subtotal:	[60]	[35]	[28]	[23]
Private				
Private enterprise	30	18	21	17
Family enterprise	46	27	10	8
Self-employment	10	6	7	6
Subtotal:	[87]	[51]	[38]	[31]
Unemployed	0	0	2	2
		Inactive		
Housewife	0	0	47	39
Student	18	11	4	3
Retired	6	4	1	1
Inactive	1	1	1	1
Subtotal:	[25]	[14]	[53]	[44]
TOTAL	171	100	121	100

tors, teachers, clerks, or accountants). Within the community, working for the government brought status for women as opposed to the negative connotations that were sometimes associated with factory, market, or domestic work.[24] In contrast, the men and women who were self-employed as a primary income source were among the least educated members of the community and largely provided services (as barbers, house painters, midwives) or were engaged in legal and illegal petty trade and commodity production (as pudding makers, drug dealers, black-market traders).

Table 4.5 reveals the higher concentration of men who have secondary sources of income than women (61 percent as opposed to 28 percent of the women in the sample, while the figure for both genders in Table 4.2 above was 48 percent). The greater need for men to hold a second job or to have a secondary source of income was due to the rising cost of living and their legal and customary obligation to support their households financially (as explained in Chapter 2). While wages and profits had risen for many men who worked in local workshops producing secondary goods during the past decade, consumption and economic expectations had also increased, forcing men and women to work even harder. As salaries in the public sector atrophied, even well-educated men in the sample who held secure and relatively lucrative public-sector jobs searched for secondary sources of income.

TABLE 4.5
Secondary Economic Activity by Gender (N = 292: male, 171; female, 121)

	Male	%	Female	%
		Active		
Public				
Public sector	0	0	2	2
Armed forces	0	0	0	0
Public service	0	0	2	2
Subtotal:	[0]	[0]	[4]	[4]
Private				
Private enterprise	27	16	7	6
Family enterprise	32	19	9	7
Self-employment	43	25	12	10
Subtotal:	[102]	[60]	[28]	[23]
Unemployed	2	1	1	1
		Inactive		
Housewife	0	0	27	22
Student	3	2	1	1
Retired	1	1	2	2
Inactive	0	0	0	0
Subtotal:	[4]	[2]	[30]	[25]
Unknown	57	33	36	30
None	6	4	22	18
TOTAL	171	100	121	100

As in Table 4.2 above, very few individuals were employed in the public sector as a secondary source of income. Rather, self-employment provided the most significant secondary source of income for both men and women.

While the methodology of the sample could not confirm the secondary economic activity of a large number of men and women (33 percent and 30 percent, respectively), it was possible to confirm that 18 percent of the women but only 4 percent of the men definitely had no secondary source of income. The largest number of women with no secondary occupation were housewives (seventeen), followed by employees of family enterprises (three) and those in the public sector (two, both young unmarried women). Women, in addition to their formal jobs, were almost always responsible for the incessant housework of a typical household in *sha'bi* communities, though elderly in-laws or parents, both male and female, or unmarried older daughters and younger sisters, relieved some of the burden in larger households. It should be noted that all but one of the twenty-seven women listed above who were housewives were also employed or self-employed as a primary source of income (eleven in the public sector, eight in private enterprises, and five as self-employed).

While it was rare for married women to hold two formal jobs, because of the demands of housework, some were able to pursue economic opportunities in their homes or provide home-based services to their relatives, friends, and colleagues (such as being a seamstress, a savings association leader, a female peddler or black marketer). In fact, none of the women who were supported by three economic activities held two formal jobs, although they earned income (in cash and in kind) from their economic activities.

Despite national statistics suggesting very low labor force participation rates for women (as discussed below), almost one-third of those with known tertiary sources of income were women. One woman was a sewing teacher who worked in her home as a seamstress and was also a leader of a savings association. Another woman received a pension from her public-sector position in local schools and earned additional income as a seamstress while organizing four savings associations. Two women were studying for a Master's degree and fulfilling their public service. One earned income from her private (illegal) health clinic while the other was an English teacher in a private foreign language school.

Young men and women, in particular, needed to hold several jobs to finance their marriages (as discussed in Chapter 2), and it was not surprising that half of the sample with known tertiary occupations were under the age of thirty-five. Typical of the men was one young man who worked at a workshop that manufactured aluminum products and as a shoemaker and plumber, depending on labor market conditions and seasonal demand. Another older, more-educated man was a machinist and an electrician as well as a landlord. Men could manage three jobs outside the home because their wives or mothers maintained the home and were responsible for child care. The industriousness and commitment of both men and women to support themselves and their families is demonstrated by the high incidence of secondary and tertiary economic activity in this community.

The particular socioeconomic profile of this community, as well its geographical location in a mixed residential/commercial/manufacturing neighborhood explains part of the ability of these people to find varied sources of income.

In both primary and secondary economic activity, production workers were the most heavily represented occupation (20 percent and 17 percent, respectively). Most of these manual workers were *Hirafiyyiin* or skilled workers and artisans, who provided labor for the many small manufacturing workshops that were tucked away in residential areas or concentrated in industrial alleyways next to residential areas. In both primary and secondary occupations, production workers were overwhelmingly male. The women within this category produced food or beverages for sale in the market, were self-employed seamstresses, or worked as textile workers in small apparel-manufacturing workshops. It was uncommon to find women working with heavy machinery in crowded, dirty industrial workshops.

TABLE 4.6
Distribution by Occupation within the Economically Active Sample:
Primary Economic Activity (N = 292)

	N	%
Professional, technical, and related workers (*male:* 22; *female:* 24)	46	16
Administrative and managerial workers (*male:* 7; *female:* 7)	14	5
Clerical and related workers (*male:* 22; *female:* 14)	36	12
Sales workers (*male:* 30; *female:* 9)	39	13
Service workers (*male:* 4; *female:* 8)	12	4
Agriculture, animal husbandry and forestry workers, fishermen, and hunters (*male:* 1; *female:* 0)	1	0
Production and related workers, transport equipment, operators, and laborers (*male:* 52; *female:* 7)	59	20
New workers seeking employment (*male:* 0; *female:* 1)	1	1
Housewives (*male:* 0; *female:* 47)	47	16
Students (*male:* 18; *female:* 4)	22	8
Army conscripts (*male:* 15; *female:* 0)	15	5
TOTAL	292	100

The next largest share of actively employed men and women were work-ers in professional, technical, and related fields (16 percent primary, 7 per-cent secondary). Many of these were white-collar workers in the government who had successfully completed preparatory and secondary school educa-tion. However, even those who had reached the status of white-collar em-ployment filled the lower echelons of government service and private firms and organizations. For example, the largest share of professional workers in both primary and secondary occupations were teachers. In a girls' commer-cial high school in the neighborhood, many of the teachers lived in the surrounding community and came from families with manufacturing or commercial establishments nearby. These teachers had succeeded in the edu-cational system but received such low salaries that they could only support their families through secondary employment as private tutors or in other nonprofessional capacities. Despite the generally higher educational level of male teachers than female teachers in the sample, which entitled them to higher wages, benefits, and status, six of the nine male teachers supple-

TABLE 4.7

Distribution by Occupation within the Economically Active Sample:
Secondary Economic Activity (*N* = 292)

	N	%
Professional, technical and related workers (*male*: 17; *female*: 4)	21	7
Administrative and managerial workers (*male*: 3; *female*: 1)	4	1
Clerical and related workers (*male*: 1; *female*: 6)	7	2
Salesworkers (*male*: 33; *female*: 7)	40	14
Service workers (*male*: 4; *female*: 8)	12	4
Agriculture, animal husbandry and forestry workers, fishermen, and hunters (*male*: 4; *female*: 0)	4	1
Production and related workers, transport equipment operators, and laborers (*male*: 42; *female*: 8)	50	17
Workers reporting occupations unidentifiable or inadequately described (*male*: 2; *female*: 0)	2	1
Housewives (*male*: 0; *female*: 27)	27	9
Students (*male*: 3; *female*: 0)	3	1
Pension (*male*: 0; *female*: 1)	1	1
No secondary occupation (*male*: 6; *female*: 22)	28	10
Unknown secondary occupation (*male*: 57; *female*: 36)	93	32
TOTAL	292	100

mented their salaries by giving private lessons. These men earned three or
four times their government salary by giving private lessons. Some of the
professionals in the sample, employed as vocational instructors and pre-
school teachers, had not graduated from university or even high school. Of
the seventeen female teachers, none offered private lessons as a secondary
source of income although four were self-employed as seamstresses, and one
was unemployed and actively searching for a second job.

The other common occupation in the sample, in both primary and secondary categories, was sales (13 percent of primary, 14 percent secondary).
Due to the commercial nature of the *sha'bi* community under study, and the
character of central Cairo (where commercial areas are not strictly segregated by the government through zoning laws), many people were employed

as salesclerks in local stores or markets, or were engaged in commerce and trade. Employment in a small shop or establishing a small retail outlet was fairly accessible to many people who needed a supplemental income to support their families.

Table 4.7 lists forty men and women as sales workers in a secondary economic activity. Of those forty, twenty-four were working proprietors of wholesale and retail trading concerns, ranging from large and small grocery stores (eight men), the wholesale trade of foodstuffs (five men and two women), the drug trade (two men), a retail brass shop catering to tourists, a shoe store, a building supply trade, and a small video rental shop, to peddling (two *dallalaat* purchased goods wholesale and then resold them, largely to women associates, in their homes or workplaces). The investment needed to begin some of these concerns was substantial, although others demanded little investment and few overhead costs. The self-employed could establish a secondary economic activity by borrowing money for start-up costs from relatives or saving money in a *gam'iyya*. A densely populated mixed commercial and residential area could easily absorb another small shop to sell cold soda, another stand for *fuul* or *Ta'miyya* (prepared broad beans, a breakfast staple in Egypt), or another seamstress, copying machine operator, or part-time mechanic.

While men clearly outnumbered women in sales, it was not considered improper for a woman to engage in trade, particularly if she was from an old established family that owned a commercial or trading firm where relatives worked together. But like professional women, women were disproportionately represented in the lower-paying and lower ranks of clerical and service workers.

When classified by industry (Table 4.8), the sample is similarly concentrated in manufacturing and trade, although the largest category represented was community, social, and personal services. This concentration can partially be explained by the inclusion of public administration and defense (sixteen people were in the armed forces) in this category and by my familiarity with several private charitable associations in the neighborhood, which provided employment to many people in the sample.

Largely employed by the government or private voluntary organizations (day-care, health, and vocational education), 41 percent of all women in the sample were engaged in providing services to the community. Due to the attraction of public-service employment for women and the propriety of working for a private voluntary organization, it is not surprising that women were overwhelmingly concentrated in service industries.

The industrial profile of secondary economic activity in the community was still heavily concentrated in manufacturing, trade, and services although the percentage of men and women working in community, social, and personal services dropped from 38 percent to 13 percent since some of those women did not have the time or energy for a second position due to their domestic responsibilities. Secondary employment, when classified by

TABLE 4.8
Distribution by Industry within the Economically Active Sample:
Primary Economic Activity (N = 292)

	N	%
Agriculture, hunting, forestry, and fishing (*male:* 1; *female:* 0)	1	0
Manufacturing (*male:* 46; *female:* 9)	55	19
Electricity, gas, and water (*male:* 1; *female:* 0)	1	0
Construction (*male:* 8; *female:* 0)	8	3
Wholesale and retail trade and restaurants and hotels (*male:* 25; *female:* 8)	33	11
Transport, storage, and communications (*male:* 8; *female:* 2)	10	3
Financing, insurance, real estate, and business services (*male:* 3; *female:* 1)	4	1
Community, social, and personal services (*male:* 60; *female:* 50)	110	38
Housewives (*male:* 0; *female:* 47)	47	16
Students (*male:* 18; *female:* 4)	22	8
Inactive (*male:* 0; *female:* 1)	1	1
TOTAL	292	100

industry, was somewhat more diverse than the great concentration of women in services and domestic labor in Table 4.8. Some women worked in productive enterprises and trading concerns as a secondary economic activity.

The formal picture of economic activity suggests a very diligent community characterized by employment in the public and private sector, primarily in manufacturing, trade, and services. The largest percentage of primary employment was concentrated in community, personal, and social services, followed by manufacturing. This industrial profile suggests that the community is dominated by both skilled blue-collar workers and white-collar professionals. Thus the community is financially dependent upon both government employment and private-sector enterprise, the latter being predominantly informal (as we will see in the next section). While it has been noted above that government wages have declined in real terms, the wages of skilled workers in many trades have risen substantially over the past decade. There is a certain tension and envy between these two substrata within *sha'bi* communities, but due to the character of the area and their very recent upward educational mobility, many educated and professional people can still supplement their income by rejoining family concerns to trade lemons, work on a lathing machine, or drive a taxi owned by an uncle in their spare time. It is people who have moved out of these communities into more middle-class residential areas, and who are interested in distancing themselves from their *sha'bi* origins, who are somewhat more vulnerable to financial and political insecurity because they have lost their contacts for secondary employment or else their new status does not allow them to work in occupations that their peers would look down upon. The following analysis demonstrates the extent to which those who still remain in *sha'bi* communities protect themselves from insecurity through informal employment and production.

The Informal Picture

While there has been a recent proliferation of studies on the informal sector, a great deal of interdisciplinary research still needs to be conducted to understand and analyze its nature and consequences. For many reasons, the number of employees, the production and extent of small-scale enterprises, micro enterprises, and informal-sector enterprises are difficult to estimate. The best intentions of economists for precision and uniformity are impeded by the diversity and breadth of informal activities found in particular societies.[25] Crude, inconsistent, and at times contradictory figures abound.[26]

Yet the proportion of informal-sector employment that I found in my community supports various estimates of the significant and growing presence of this sector in the economy and its influence on the direction of the Egyptian economy and, as I will argue below, polity. As mentioned previously, Handoussa has suggested that the informal sector, based on the results of the Employment, Wages, and Hours of Work Survey (EWHW) in 1986, accounted for 43 percent of all private nonagricultural employment in Egypt.[27] However, the definition of the informal sector used here relies only on a size criterion: any establishment employing less than ten workers is labeled informal. This understanding of the informal sector is far too imprecise since many of these establishments pay taxes, follow appropriate legislation for their industry and occupation, and are registered by various authorities.

Research on informality is plagued by debates about definitions, measurement, and enumerator training. The difficulties of relying on national surveys, whose measurement techniques do not capture a great deal of economic activity, challenge the validity of many of these figures.[28] In a recent study of the informal sector which examines the corpus of macro and micro research in Egypt, Rizk presents the range of these estimates: "In 1986, estimates by Birks and Sinclair were 878,000; Abdel-Fadil, 876,000;[29] Charmes, 2,281,000. For 1985, the number rises to about 3 million, according to CAPMAS."[30] Nader Fergany estimates that informal-sector employment, using the same "size per establishment" criterion, has grown from 2,434,000 in 1980 to 2,887,000 in 1985.[31] Rizk criticizes the use of the size of establishments as the definition for the informal sector (as do all the authors of the study) adopted by these researchers and suggests her own criterion of nonregistration.

> The criterion of affiliation proposed in this study is that of the absence of an official administrative registration under any one or more forms such as fiscal, accounting, trade register, social security, etc. In this regard, the distinction between registration 'enacted by a legislative organ' and registration 'without a legislative provision at the origin' is very relevant in the case of Egypt. Given the predominant role played by the State throughout its history and its involvement in all aspects of economic life, it is to be expected that any person engaged in economic activity must have a license of some sort. If this license is considered an official form of administrative registration, then the criterion proposed becomes absurd since any economic unit must be registered one way or another. In line with the ILO, registration of an economic unit must therefore refer to 'a legal instrument enacted by a legislative organ,' e.g., the law on shops and commercial establishments.

Although this criterion may be more appropriate, she too has to revert to the size-of-establishment criterion because the macro data on registration is simply not available and her estimate of informal-sector employment based on 1976 figures (2,416,000) is just as imprecise.[32]

Micro studies, on the other hand, have offered new insights into the organization, management, and size of the informal sector, though their results are not generalizable. A study by CAPMAS in 1985 of urban and rural settings defined the informal sector as "'those non-financial activities which break the laws regulating businesses and labor' and which deliberately sidestep the requirement to keep account books."[33] This study found that families were quite prominent in the management and financing of the informal sector since "in 32 percent of the cases the business was inherited."[34] In another recent study by the National Center for Sociological and Criminological Research (NCSCR) of Maʿruuf quarter in the ʿAbdiin district in downtown Cairo, 35 percent of all economic activities were part of the informal sector. NCSCR defined the informal sector as small units, with limited capital and employees (less than £E10,000 and less than ten employees), whose operators do not keep accounts and only pay a fee in lieu of a tax.[35] In an earlier study of the small-scale private industrial sector in Fayyum and Qalyubia governorates, which surveyed industrial establishments, handicraft, and domestic production in small towns and rural areas in these two provinces, the authors found that 99 percent of the establishments or 94,000 enterprises employed less than ten workers. Some 140,000 men and women in these two provinces alone were employed or self-employed in the artisanal sector. But through a creative and painstaking analysis of various sources of data covering the entire nation, Abdel-Fadil estimated that only 241,498 people comprised the artisanal sector throughout all of Egypt in 1977.[36] It seems highly unlikely that 58 percent of the entire artisanal sector was concentrated in two governorates. Rather the Fayyum and Qalyubia micro study probably captured a much higher percentage of very small-scale domestic and handicraft producers than the Abdel-Fadil study.[37]

My discussion of the informal sector is primarily based on the active population of the economically active sample of my community (introduced above). A distinction between formal- and informal-sector activity was made for only the active population since the inactive population was neither formal nor informal.[38] Due to the limits of my data collection and research objectives, I only briefly mention the internal structure and composition of informal enterprises or the historical evolution of this sector—subjects that deserve far more attention.[39] In the final section of this chapter I will briefly examine some of the consequences of informal activity for the *sha'b* and the nation, and certain policy issues that concern proprietors and workers in the community and the government of Egypt. The informal sector, I will suggest, influences this community's access to, and distribution of, public and private goods and services and has altered class relations and social and economic mobility patterns. However, the sole objective of this section is to understand the general character of the informal sector for this community.

Abdel-Fadil's pioneering study of the informal sector in Egypt used criteria for classification that were a compromise between standard definitions and particular features of the Egyptian economy.[40] To facilitate comparison with other studies, I began my analysis of informal-sector employment with Abdel-Fadil's following criteria:

—the artisanal segment, covering the labour force engaged in small establishments and workshops (one to nine workers), as well as small craftsmen and jobbing and itinerant artisans who usually operated outside establishments;
—the informal services' segment, covering a wide range of occupations relating to domestic and personal services as well as small-scale retailing of a casual nature;
—the "odd-jobbers" segment, comprising all persons not classified by any occupation in official labour and employment statistics.[41]

With these occupational categories as a base, and due to my familiarity with most of the 292 people in this community, I also defined sources of income as informal if this income was unreported to tax officials (such as public-sector employees with two jobs, self-employed people not registered with the proper authorities, or unregistered workers in family enterprises), if the economic activity was illegal (such as drug dealing, black-market sales, or bribery), or if the economic activity was unregulated and thus wages or profits were outside of the formal economy (such as child labor, home production of food products, or secondary products of industrial enterprises such as trading in raw materials).

By reclassifying the economically active sample into formal and informal activities, I found that 38 percent of the active population was engaged in

TABLE 4.9
Economic Activity among the Active Population
of the Economically Active Sample (in percent)

	Primary	Secondary	Tertiary
Informal	38	87	71
Formal	62	13	29

informal economic activity as a primary source of income. Table 4.9 reveals that an even more significant segment of the active population, 87 percent, was engaged in informal-sector economic activity as a secondary source of income. It was approximately six-and-a-half times more likely that a person was employed in a secondary occupation in the informal as opposed to the formal sector. In a detailed analysis of the entire economically active population in this sample ($N = 292$), approximately 62 percent of the sample was engaged in informal-sector activities in at least one of their primary, secondary, or tertiary economic activities.

The following two tables (4.10 and 4.11) demonstrate that most informal-sector activity was concentrated in family enterprises and self-employment within this community. These two segments of the private sector comprised 69 percent of informal-sector activity among primary occupations and 73 percent among secondary occupations. Self-employment constituted almost half of all secondary employment in the informal sector.

The lower share of secondary economic activity in family enterprises in Table 4.11 can be partially explained by workers in family enterprises who seek employment in a strictly private-sector establishment or establish their own businesses, rather than risk offending their family by working for another family firm.

Some of the reasons for the strong role of the informal sector in the political economy of *sha'bi* communities can be understood by its industrial profile. As mentioned earlier, many people in the sample lived in vibrant residential areas sprinkled with commercial and industrial establishments, and many found employment in local manufacturing, trade, and service industries. In an industrial profile of the informal economy, three industrial categories absorbed 87 percent of primary economic activity and 79 percent of secondary activity. Apart from the manufacture of machinery, the character of this sample corresponds to Abdel-Fadil's description of the workshops of the artisanal segment workshops as "heavily oriented toward the production of a wide range of household goods for local markets, including some basic consumer staples—clothes, shoes, food, furniture, metallic products."[42] Even the machinery produced in the community was generally custom-made with very simple tools, which allowed local workshops to purchase it at much lower prices than comparable imported models from abroad.[43] As an example of the skill and creativity of Egyptian artisans, one local producer of metal machinery told me about a man in Shubra, a densely

TABLE 4.10
Informal Economic Activity in the Private Sector,
Primary Occupation (N = 83)

	N	%
Private enterprise	25	30
(*male:* 22; *female:* 3)		
Family enterprise	40	48
(*male:* 30; *female:* 10)		
Self-employed	17	21
(*male:* 10; *female:* 7)		
Retired	1	1
(*male:* 1; *female:* 0)		
TOTAL	83	100

TABLE 4.11
Informal Economic Activity in the Private Sector,
Secondary Occupation (N = 116)

	N	%
Private enterprise	31	27
(*male:* 23; *female:* 8)		
Family enterprise	32	27
(*male:* 22; *female:* 10)		
Self-employed	53	46
(*male:* 41; *female:* 12)		
TOTAL	116	100

populated and slightly more middle-class area of Cairo, who was able to copy a modern envelope-producing machine that a local merchant had purchased for £E70,000 from abroad. The machinist in Shubra sold the machine locally for only £E12,000 and made a sizable profit at the same time.

There were only minor differences between primary and secondary categories in the distribution of informal-sector activity by industry. Manufacturing, trade, and community, social, and personal services remained the most heavily represented industries in secondary occupations (although the manufacturing sector decreased in secondary occupations and the trading sector increased slightly). This pattern can be explained by the common practice among proprietors of artisanal workshops who gained their primary source of income from the production of goods to earn secondary sources of income by investing their profits in the trade of raw materials and other commodities (legal and illegal). Many of these proprietors preferred to "work" surpluses in the market than to save them in the formal banking sector.

In a comparison of the industrial composition of both formal and informal sectors in this sample, manufacturing, trade, and community, social, and personal services were equally dominant in each sector, suggesting that certain activities were common in this community and that people were using the same skills and training to find work in both sectors. An occupational analysis of the informal sector also serves to explain the dominant presence of the informal economic activity within *sha'bi* communities since it basically replicates the industrial profile of the informal sector. Some 92 percent of the men and women in the sample were sales, service, and production workers. In secondary employment, the sum of the three largest categories of workers falls to 77 percent. The higher representation of professional occupations in secondary informal employment is due to the necessity for people who earned their primary source of income as low-level, low-paid professionals to exploit their skills in a professional capacity in a secondary economic activity. While the formal sector employed 89 percent of all professionals in primary economic activity, the informal sector employed 90 percent of all professionals in secondary economic activity. Not only unskilled workers and casual laborers in the community but also its most educated and skilled members must find secondary sources of income to support their families. For example, seven public school teachers earned additional income (probably equal to or greater than their government salaries) as self-employed private tutors. Accountants in public- and private-sector primary employment moonlighted in family enterprises or the private sector as self-employed accountants, and doctors established illegal health clinics while they were also employed by the government.

The predominance of production workers in informal economic activity (80 percent in primary activity and 90 percent in secondary activity) concurs with the concentration of the manufacturing industry in the informal economy, as noted above. In this community, informal manufacturing was obviously very important since the largest single occupation represented in the sample was production workers (fifty-nine workers as a primary economic activity and fifty workers as a secondary activity). In her study of the informal sector, Rizk suggests 85 percent of manufacturing in the private sector is in the informal sector.[44]

From data in Table 4.12 and an understanding of the gender composition of primary and secondary active populations, I constructed ratios that suggest gender preferences for formal and informal economic activity. In primary economic activity the ratio of men in formal-sector employment to informal-sector employment equaled 1.44 to one, while the ratio of women in formal-sector employment to informal-sector employment reached 2.23 to one. Women, it seemed, had stronger opportunities for formal-sector employment. In secondary economic activity, however, there is a striking, similarly high propensity for employment or income-generation opportunities in the informal sector. Men were engaged in the informal sector over the formal sector by 6.14 to one and women 6.77 to one. These indications do not represent choice but the access that men and women in *sha'bi* communities have to certain types of employment and sources of income.

TABLE 4.12

Informal Economic Activity among the
Active Population by Gender (*N*)

Primary Economic Activity	
Male	62
Female	21
Secondary Economic Activity	
Male	88
Female	28
Tertiary Economic Activity	
Male	7
Female	3

TABLE 4.13

Employment Combinations for Those Engaged in the Informal Sector
from the Active Population of the Economically Active Sample

	N
1. Formal primary source of income/ Informal secondary source of income	57
2. Informal primary source of income/ Formal secondary source of income	1
3. Formal primary source of income/ Formal secondary source of income	14
4. Informal primary source of income/ Informal secondary source of income	27

Table 4.13 suggests that both the informal and formal sectors of the economy are crucial to employment among the *shaʿb* and that people survive, and at times prosper, by exploiting opportunities in both sectors. More people kept their feet in both the formal and informal economy to reap the particular benefits, status, and wages of each sector. Table 4.13 demonstrates that the most common arrangement for people in this community was to hold a permanent, legal, registered job in the formal economy and earn additional income in the informal economy.

The bottom line is that the informal sector is not at all marginal to the community or an employment choice of last resort for an unemployable or unskilled population. A majority of this community, 62 percent, depends on the informal sector for economic support. While it is tempting to wonder how communities would fare without a strong informal sector, it has to be understood that this *shaʿbi* community is as dependent on the informal sector as the formal sector and thus it has been, and will continue to be, sensitive and vulnerable to any changes in employment opportunities in either sector—in fact, it will probably be doubly sensitive.

FAMILY ENTERPRISES

Despite their exclusion from formal channels of political participation, *sha'bi* communities have created their own institutions to influence political and economic forces in their community and the nation. Familial and informal networks were found to be particularly influential in organizing these communities and in influencing distribution patterns within them. The entrenchment of those institutions influences the economic affairs of the community as well. Three different types of economic activity—private enterprises, family enterprises, and self-employment—make up the private sector, and it is the particular nature of family enterprises that merits further attention here. In *sha'bi* communities the family met not only social, political, and affective needs but provided employment, income, and wealth for family members. As explained earlier, the category of family enterprise was included to call attention to a particular economic institution in the community whose logic and structure differs from other private enterprises. "Conventional economics tries to describe the distribution of economic resources 'as if' it followed invariant laws; modelling the operation of these laws, economists hope, will make it possible to predict future economic behavior. . . . The primary pattern of distribution is to be understood not as following invariant laws, but as following particular institutional processes."[45]

The significant presence of family enterprises in *sha'bi* communities protects the family from economic insecurity and rapid economic change. The economic logic of family enterprises was not based purely on market principles but on motives to strengthen and enrich the family, as well as individuals within the family.[46] Family enterprises provide opportunities for employment and profit for members of the community that might not prosper in the formal economy (even though some family enterprises, usually the larger and more successful ones, may be part of the formal economy). They utilize unpaid family workers and occasional labor from a family labor pool far more than do other types of firms. They also can provide a more socially acceptable option for employment for female members of the family who, without an uncle or brother in their place of work, might be forbidden to hold a job. The pressures of the market on this lower- to middle-class community are mitigated by family enterprises that are structured to secure the financial interests of the family. On the other hand, competition among families who dominate a particular trade or economic activity can also be ruthless. For example, many branches of a large extended family were concentrated in the wholesale produce trade in this community and, despite their familial bonds, used typical capitalist strategies to gain greater shares of the market from their competitors, who were also their relatives. While conflicts and market pressures plague family enterprises as much as any private- or public-sector firm, a motivation to keep the business in family hands and

TABLE 4.14

Activity in Family Enterprises in the Economically Active Population

	Primary Activity (N)	Secondary Activity (N)
Formal family enterprises	16	19
Informal family enterprises	40	22
TOTAL	56	41

bequeath it to one's progeny is an additional factor in its management principles. Details of the internal workings of family enterprises and the reasons why they continue to persist in Egypt's increasingly capitalist economy merit more detailed attention by historians and social scientists. The limited objectives of this research confirmed that family enterprises ensure that a significant share of local financial resources remain under family control and that wages, profits, and investment remain within the community.

Data from earlier tables are reconstructed in Table 4.14 to highlight the presence of family enterprises. Family enterprises accounted for 19 percent of the economically active sample as a primary economic activity and 14 percent as a secondary one. In the private sector, family enterprises absorbed 45 percent of primary economic activity and 32 percent of all secondary activity (of the private sector). While many people depended on employment from familial sources, the option of working in a family enterprise depended, of course, upon the existence of the enterprise.

Like other firms in the economy, family enterprises were characterized by a labor hierarchy. Positions within family enterprises included the owner or proprietor, manager, partner/worker, worker, and apprentice. It was also common for family members, particularly women, to own shares in family enterprises without directly working in or managing the enterprise. In this case, the family enterprise was often inherited from a deceased husband or father but managed by others.

More than half the workers in family enterprises owned their enterprises, although this percentage decreased in secondary economic activity (Table 4.16). In these tables owners are not categorized as self-employed because they hired other relatives as workers in their firms. It is interesting to note that women were more likely to own family enterprises than to work in them. The fact that as many women as men owned family enterprises as a secondary economic activity confirms, again, the significant economic participation of women in this community and their control of financial resources.

The character of mixed residential, commercial, and industrial space in *sha'bi* neighborhoods occasionally allowed household members (other than the male head of the household) to participate in the family enterprise. Some were unpaid family workers while others received occasional compensation for their labor. Many of the family enterprises in this sample were located within a short distance from the home of the owner. In many *sha'bi* neigh-

TABLE 4.15
Employment Status in Family Enterprises,
Primary Economic Activity (N = 56)

Status	N	%
Owner	30	54
(*male:* 24; *female:* 6)		
Partner/worker	5	9
(*male:* 4; *female:* 1)		
Manager	2	3
(*male:* 2; *female:* 0)		
Worker	18	32
(*male:* 15; *female:* 3)		
Apprentice	1	2
(*male:* 1; *female:* 0)		
TOTAL	56	100

TABLE 4.16
Employment Status in Family Enterprises,
Secondary Economic Activity (N = 41)

Status	N	%
Owner	12	29
(*male:* 6; *female:* 6)		
Partner/worker	7	17
(*male:* 5; *female:* 2)		
Manager	1	2
(*male:* 1; *female:* 0)		
Worker	17	42
(*male:* 12; *female:* 5)		
Apprentice	4	10
(*male:* 4; *female:* 0)		
TOTAL	41	100

borhoods in Cairo, the ground floor of old and new apartment buildings is rented as commercial or manufacturing space (although new regulations forbid noisy or polluting industries to operate in residential areas). In one case the ground floor of the family's apartment building served as the warehouse and distribution point for their wholesale food sales. Their sizable grocery store stood just across the street. When customers flooded the grocery store or orders backed up in the wholesale distribution business, younger men in the family were called upon to lend a hand. Family members often provided services or unpaid labor that directly, or indirectly, contributed to the success of the family enterprise. Family enterprises provided the best source of secondary earnings for young men and women. Yet compensation for workers in family enterprises can also become the source of serious conflicts in families, particularly if the enterprise does not maintain organized accounts. In the family grocery store mentioned above, an elder brother managed various family businesses. When the import-export trading company he had established demanded his attention, he left two of his younger brothers in charge of the grocery store. Although they were only supposed to take £E75 per week from the proceeds of the store for their salary, within several months he realized the grocery store was losing money because they took far more from the till (more than £E1,500 per month). However, he could not do much more than return to the grocery store full-time and keep a closer watch on his brothers, since it was a family enterprise and he could not fire them.

Often children and women are indispensable to a family enterprise. In another business, children were sent to deliver food that women in the family had cooked for workers in nearby workshops. Other women prepared foodstuffs in their homes, which were then peddled on the street or in small kiosks by men. Still other women lent money to their husband's commercial ventures, provided the capital to establish a small business (often from the sale of their gold wedding jewelry), or retained a share in the profits of family enterprises through inheritance, although they were not actively employed by the enterprise. Older members of the family, who may have established the business, were usually consulted for advice. Elderly men, in particular, often maintained an active role in the business until their death or incapacitation.

In Egypt, due to the constant effort needed to purchase subsidized food (as described in Chapter 3), cook, clean, and care for household members, the duties of a housewife are critical to the economic viability of a household. While the household cannot technically be labeled a family enterprise, many of the goods and services produced by women within the household would have to be purchased at market value if not for the unpaid labor of women in the family. While these activities are outside the production boundary generally used to define work by either government planners or statisticians, they provide valuable goods and services for the community, which allow other family members to work for cash in one, two, or even three jobs.[47]

Because of the unpaid domestic labor of women, men are able to work as paid labor. However, the double burden of housework and paid employment places great pressures on women, and several recent studies of female employment in Egypt have noted that a number of women are choosing to quit their jobs (or qualified and educated young women are not pursuing employment options), since government salaries are not lucrative enough to offset the pressures of the "double bind."[48] Approximately twenty-seven women in the economically active sample suffered from this double burden as they juggled their duties as a housewife with primary employment in the labor force (see Table 4.2, above).

When one young married woman in the community complained to her supervisor about a very long commute to work, the supervisor responded by

TABLE 4.17
Labor Force Participation among Women in the
Economically Active Sample (N = 121)

Primary economic activity	56%
Secondary economic activity	27%
Either primary or secondary activity	71%[a]

[a] If we consider both the primary and secondary occupations of women, only thirty-five women were economically inactive (Housewife primary—None secondary; Housewife primary—Unknown secondary; Housewife primary—Retired secondary; Student primary—Housewife secondary). If we exclude the number of women in the sample with an unknown secondary occupation, the percentage of women with a secondary economic activity rises to 39 percent. (Thirty-six women in the sample had an unknown secondary occupation. Many of those women could or could not have had a secondary occupation, but considering them all as inactive artificially lowers the percentage of economically active women.)

saying, "I do one hundred things before coming to work. We all have children and domestic responsibilities, and you must learn to cope." Other young women witnessing the exchange pointed out that a major problem facing all women in Egypt was how to reconcile the demands of being an employee, a wife, and a mother. Some of them admitted that after they married they would become housewives rather than pursue a career in the private or public sector even though they had spent many years preparing for it (at least four years of university and an additional year of a public-service requirement).

For example, two women in the sample earned such low salaries as vocational teachers in a private organization that they were negotiating with their superiors to pay off their remaining contributions to their pension plan before quitting their jobs. These women, who spent approximately two hours each day traveling to their jobs, argued that they could earn an adequate income as self-employed seamstresses and devote more time to their homes and children if they quit their jobs. In the end, neither of them left her job although they continued to complain about their salaries.

Despite the pressures of domestic responsibilities and formal or informal employment, the participation of women in the labor force was much higher in this sample than national rates indicate. Between 1976 and 1982, according to official national statistics (the decennial population census and annual labor force surveys), the overall female labor force participation rate was approximately 6 percent.[49] In 1986 the rate rose to 8.9 percent. The *Egyptian Fertility Survey (1980)*, as part of a World Fertility Survey, estimates that 75.3 percent of "ever-married women" between the ages of fifteen and forty-nine had never worked.[50]

According to the preliminary results of the 1986 Population Census, female participation in overall urban employment was only 16 percent and rural employment was 4 percent.[51] Efforts in the last decade to redesign census questionnaires and standard conceptions of employment and work have improved the precision of figures for the labor force participation of women in Egypt and throughout the world.[52] For example, a joint Methods Test Study by CAPMAS and the ILO canvassed one thousand women in rural Upper Egypt in the early 1980s and intentionally asked far more probing questions about a range of activities that those engaged in the study felt had not been properly recognized or measured. The period of reference was a full year rather than the typical one-week reference period used in national surveys. The methodology they used was far more successful at revealing considerably higher rural female labor force participation rates: activity rates ranged from 12 percent for the paid labor force (persons engaged in wage or salary employment), and 38 percent for the market labor force (persons engaged in activities resulting in monetary transactions of some type), to 85 percent for the standard labor force (which corresponds to internationally accepted recommendations).[53]

The much higher rates of female participation in the labor force in the present sample can be explained by my familiarity with the various economic activities of these women through repeated visits to many of their households, knowledge of their financial affairs, a full year as the reference period, and a much lower minimum work-time criterion (only regular activity was counted, but this did not fulfill an hours per week criterion since I could not calculate that). Many of the women in my sample who were seamstresses, leaders of savings associations, or involved in the black market would not describe their activity as a vocational profession (*mihna*), or as a permanent position (*waZiifa*), or even as regular work (*shughl*), particularly to an unknown government official, such as a census enumerator. To administer the Egyptian Fertility Survey referred to above, census enumerators were instructed to ask women whether they sold things, held jobs, worked on a family farm, or were self-employed.[54] From my experience in Cairo, many women (and perhaps men) who were actually economically active would respond negatively to these questions, despite the fact that their activities fell under the definition of work used in the survey.[55] The higher percentage of economically active women in the present sample is most likely not a reflection of an unrepresentative or particularly industrious community but is rather the result of a methodology that captured primary, secondary, and tertiary economic activities and used a much more generous reference period and work-time criterion. It is important to add here that men in the sample also participated far more extensively in the labor force than national indicators suggest. Some 86 percent of the men in the economically active population participated in primary economic activity, 61 percent in secondary activity, and 98 percent of the men in either primary or secondary activity (i.e., only three men in the sample did not participate in the labor force).

Whether as a housewife or as an owner, partner, manager, worker, or apprentice in a family enterprise, individuals in the community relied on the family for more than social and affective support. Certainly, the household has adapted itself to Egypt's mixed economy, and family enterprises continue to be a source of opportunity, income, and employment for many men and women in *sha'bi* communities.[56] Due to the presence of family enterprises in the community, men and women who did not have the qualifications, skills, or family blessing to work in public- or private-sector enterprises or organizations sometimes had access to employment in family enterprises.

These remarks must be accompanied by caution, since I do not mean to suggest that family enterprises are necessarily productive, lucrative, or happy havens for workers. On the contrary, heads of large families can exploit paid and unpaid family labor perhaps more forcibly than workers protected by government labor legislation of private and public employment. While family enterprises are not exempt from labor legislation, government enforcement of workers' rights is less effective since many enterprises fall within the unregulated, unlicensed informal sector. Since detailed information about the internal structure of the family enterprise, its history, and its influence in the larger economy is beyond the scope of the present volume, I will note only that family enterprises have a significant presence in *sha'bi* communities. Suffice to say that the economic logic and interests of family enterprises reflected another set of interests or claims operating within the community (consider the different set of claims and interests that public-sector employees and management promote as opposed to private-sector workers and businessmen). It is not that family enterprises differ radically from private-sector enterprises or self-employment, but their primary interest in familial, as opposed to individual, prosperity offers certain advantages and disadvantages to the community.

INFORMALITY MEETS THE STATE

> We are caught in the middle of two totally separate systems that do not communicate with each other. One of them is the legal [formal] system. The other one is what we call the traditional system, which is much stronger than the law. That is what really controls us.
>
> —*The manager of a family-owned shoe factory*

Whether seeking public-sector employment, an apprenticeship in an aluminum shop, a telephone for a new office, or permission to export goods, the *sha'b* exploit complicated formal and informal means to accomplish economic objectives. As the experienced businessman noted above, there are two patterns of behavior and norms which regulate the economy. Informal, extralegal norms regulate the extensive informal economy, just as pervasive governmental statutes regulate the formal economy. When people conduct business or file petitions with the government for licenses, they rely upon entangled, and often interdependent, formal and informal rules and procedures. While official papers must be handled by bureaucrats, small and large illegal bribes may facilitate the procedure. And from the other side of the fence, while a government engineer cites one home in a new housing development for building code violations, he knowingly passes by hundreds of others liable to similar fines. While some activities such as private educational lessons or drug dealing lie solely within the informal economy, other services or goods are produced by a combination of inputs—some formal, others informal—making classification and analysis even more complex.

Three particular issues that concern businessmen anywhere, but are particularly relevant to a discussion of informality in Egypt, are discussed in this section: labor relations, the legal system, and taxation. The Egyptian state believes that its rules should regulate each of these three areas. One of the consistent objectives of Egyptian governments, particularly after the 1952 Free Officers' Revolution, has been to regulate labor relations and control trade union activism.[57] Nasser developed corporatist state-controlled unions to contain and placate workers and to meet some of the financial and social concerns of workers, while brutally repressing labor activists who tried to maintain an autonomous base of organization.[58] The Ministry of Labor and other bureaucratic agencies regulate employment, worker safety regulations, and wages throughout public- and private-sector workplaces.

The executive and legislative branches have been responsible for drafting, revising, and enforcing Egyptian law. In Egypt a wide range of laws and executive orders have been devised to regulate many aspects of the economy as well as social and political life. The second part of this section discusses the formal and informal means that businessmen and workers use to stay on the proper side of the law. Since regulations and legislation in Egypt have often changed quickly and substantively within a short period of time, people are particularly wary of the legal system's ambiguity and fickleness. Often, while trying to license a new enterprise or obtain a visa to work abroad, people in this community can be the victims of selective enforcement of ambiguous or contested laws. Thus, it becomes even more important to have informal recourse to important officials or informal means to avoid or escape government provisions. While some of the following accounts are lengthy and based upon a few sources, their rich detail provides examples of activity that was very prevalent in this community.

Finally, the right and ability of the government to extract taxes from its citizens is not only a matter of financial survival but taxation is also used as a policy instrument to further economic and political aims. Despite complicated government regulations and administrative procedures in Egypt, individuals and businessmen use various informal means to pay their taxes and to evade paying their taxes.

Labor Relations: A Case Study in the Shoe Industry

Conditions in the shoe industry have been deeply influenced by labor migration. A high demand for skilled workers in several Arab countries has depleted the ranks of skilled shoemakers in Egypt and raised wage levels. This profession is a fairly common one for men from *sha'bi* communities, and many small shoe factories are located in central Cairo, particularly in the district of Bab al-Sha'riyya. Although private-sector enterprises in Egypt must adhere to provisions enforced by the Ministry of Labor and its administrative Labor Court (regulating the hiring, firing, rights, and wages of workers), at the same time certain industries, particularly smaller enterprises, support a traditional system of labor relations. While businesses pay for social security and health benefits for workers and register workers with the appropriate authorities, they also absorb other costs of informal practices. These enterprises must absorb both the costs of remaining formal (adhering to various government regulations) and the costs of remaining informal (supporting informal procedures and evading or outsmarting government officials).

The manager of a family-owned shoe factory (introduced above) explained the consequences of international migration on wages and the labor hierarchy of his industry:

> The status and wealth of shoemakers has risen quite a bit, particularly in the seventies. At that time, many shoemakers migrated to Iraq, creating a scarcity of skilled shoemakers in Egypt, which pushed up wages. Iraq was known for its shoe industries. Many of my workers have worked there.
>
> Migration to Iraq changed the apprenticeship system for shoemakers in Egypt. Previously there were four types of *Sabi* [apprentices]: *kibiir* [big], *wuS-Taani* [middle], *Sughayyar* [small], and *Sabi mashawiir* [errand boy]. After all the migration to Iraq, the *Sabi* would be trained to become a worker, and the worker would give him more responsibility. With such a shortage, all the *Sabi kabir*s became *'usTa*s [a title more often used for skilled workers, usually seasoned artisans]. Some young men who were only fifteen to seventeen years old became *'usTa*s. Most *Sabi*s left school when they were very young, eight or so, and are therefore illiterate. During this period there were many unskilled workers who ruined the shoemaking industry, which we are still suffering from. Very bad shoes were made, designs that needed skilled workers were canceled and poor quality shoes were produced. The *Sabi wuSTaani* vanished. Only *Sabi Sughayyar* remained but they performed very limited tasks.[59]

With a low supply of skilled workers, wages had risen dramatically within the industry, and there was growing competition between factories to attract and keep skilled workers. In this factory, government regulations were adhered to, more or less, but the cost of labor and conditions of production were also dependent upon traditional business practices, which most likely originated in the medieval guild system, the precursor to contemporary unions.[60] Employers paid salaries that were typically ten times higher than the government-stipulated minimum wage, although their employer contributions to social security were based on the official minimum wage. While the owners of the factory invested time and money in adhering to formal procedures, the cost of informal business practices was quite high, both to workers and employers. While making shoes is a lucrative profession, it is very demanding and based on daily production.

In 1986 the government fixed the minimum wage at approximately £E30 per month, which is periodically modified according to changes in the consumer price index. (About five years ago it was £E15 per month.) As a factory owner I state that my workers receive the minimum wage, but this has no relation to what they really earn. My workers earn between £E200 and £E500 per month, based on prevailing wages for certain skills in the market, not on minimum-wage laws or government regulations. *Sabi*s [apprentices] earn £E100 per month.

Sewers make more than shoemakers—about £E150 a week since it is a skilled profession. They make about £E600 each month without any bonuses. Shoemaking is a secure and financially comfortable profession, but only as long as a man can work. It's a very important point because the day he stops working, he makes no money. I sometimes get beggars in the factory who used to be workers, very good workers, but they only can beg now.

To attract a worker you must give them an advance. This is a legacy of an older system. Usually workers are indebted to their bosses because they also borrow money from them. If you want a worker to begin working for you, he will tell you that he needs money to settle his debts with his former foreman or boss. You give him the advance, which he uses to settle his outstanding debts at his previous workplace. He owes this money to me, but he does not repay it until he leaves the business. Thirteen or fourteen years ago I would pay £E15 to get someone to work for me. Today I pay an advance of £E1,000 to attract a worker.

Workers often try not to pay back the factory. Ten years ago he would bring his tools to the factory and leave them there as a sort of collateral. But legally you cannot hold his tools. Usually I make him sign a piece of paper and a check. Forfeiting a *waSl 'imaana* [I.O.U] is a criminal offense, because the person has betrayed his trust. You are allowed to take him to court if he has signed a *waSl 'imaana* when he began working. It is a more serious offense than forfeiting a check. But often when workers leave the factory you have to run after them because they try to avoid repaying their advance, sometimes they pay half of it. The tools are not really worth anything now, compared to the value of the advance you have paid a worker. Less then ten years ago, the tools were still worth the sum of the advance, which is called a *mu'addam*. You can fire people, but if he goes, he does not have to pay you back his advance. This is part of the traditional system. When some workers want to leave they try to get the factory to fire them first so that they do not have to pay off their debts. Sometimes I resort to the police to collect this debt. I would go to the police station where I knew an officer and ask him to arrest the worker. Although this is not really legal it intimidates the worker and he usually cooperates. But I only resort to this when workers are very nasty.

The worker brings his own apprentices with him and an owner or manager has no authority over them. Anything to do with the apprentice is the worker's business, but sometimes I interfere if the situation is affecting production or relations in the factory. The problem is usually that the worker treats an apprentice badly or has not paid him. I usually encourage workers to employ apprentices, since it increases production, but some workers want to work alone to avoid sharing wages with an apprentice.

These apprentices are not registered with the labor department authorities, who often inspect the factory, unannounced, and record the names of the workers or apprentices they find. If they see an empty chair, they would say that someone must sit there and register another worker. If your relationship is good with the labor department, they do not come; if it is bad, they come more often. These bureaucrats, at times, were coming twice a week. Once they are recorded, I must pay social security for these workers, whether apprentices or workers. During an inspection a labor department employee can ask a worker how long he has worked in my factory. If he says five years, then I must pay five years social security retroactively. If a worker leaves my factory he must sign an official paper, signifying that he has all his tools and has been fairly treated. Then the paper is sent to the Ministry of Social Affairs, and they relieve me of my responsibility to pay for his social security.

Many of the apprentices are underage and the authorities take down their first names only, for example, MuHammad [a first name that probably millions of Egyptian males share]. Then they send me a letter saying you have fifteen days to register MuHammad. An employer is supposed to contribute 22 percent of a worker's salary, which is meant to be of the real wage, but the authorities accept 22 percent of the minimum-wage salary. Although the worker is supposed to pay a contribution of 11 percent, I usually pay his contribution as well or 33 percent of the minimum wage.

Despite elaborate procedures to register his workers, this employer was investing in the retirement pensions of a fictitious or untraceable workforce. How, he asked, can a worker ever expect to receive pension benefits or health insurance if the government only records his first name in official records? From the employer's point of view, which he believed his workers shared, the money he contributed for his worker's social security, pension benefits, and health care benefited the treasury of the government, not his workers, who never received their benefits. He held up his end of the bargain, but the government abrogated its responsibility to workers. Thus, for him, paying benefits for workers loses its legitimacy, and a government that perpetuates this system is seen as grossly inefficient if not morally corrupt.

Social security entitles them to a pension but workers hardly ever receive them. The worker moves around so much and if you work for one boss who does not register you, your coverage lapses. If it is cut at any time, the government will not pay benefits. Even if you do keep it up, it is extremely difficult for workers to get money out of the government and they always complain about the system.

He argued that it was the traditional system of benefits that protected workers, even if it was not perfect. Because workers realized they would never receive their government benefits, they kept group pressure on owners to maintain the traditional system of insurance. The participation of employers in this traditional system was due not to their goodwill but to the necessity of maintaining an extralegal system of worker benefits that was not a facade.

What we do is much better than the government's insurance system. If a worker gets ill or needs money, the *'usTa* of the workshop [manager, foreman, also usually a skilled worker] would still pay him his salary. He does this because of tradition and the fact that his reputation would suffer otherwise. It happens quite often, at times two or three workers are ill. He still sends them money to the worker's home although they do not work. I once did this for eight months for one worker who earned about £E200 per month. He was not an important worker, but if a worker is ill, he is your responsibility. This is a very widespread, normal practice among workshops that do not have "organized accounts" [*da-faatir munaZZama*]. I also give money to workers for weddings, funerals, and on religious occasions. I give apprentices about three to five pounds for *Muulid in-Nabi* [the Prophet MuHammad's birthday, a major holiday in Egypt] and buy every single worker and person in the factory sweets [a traditional holiday gift, which has increasingly risen in cost: in 1986 two kilos of sweets sold for approximately £E15].

An employer is also supposed to give a departing worker a small bonus when he or she leaves. For five years' work they are supposed to receive approximately £E500. The government deducts a small sum from monthly salaries of public-sector workers which they receive in a lump sum payment when they leave or retire. But private-sector employers do not withhold any money from salaries. Although they are supposed to pay a bonus they rarely comply. I never pay a bonus unless someone has worked at the factory all his life. A friend of my father has worked here all his life. When he had a very bad accident recently we still paid him his average monthly wage until he decided he was healthy enough to work. He is almost seventy now. When he wants to work he does; when he wants to leave, he leaves. He actually is salaried. Whenever he retires, my father will probably give him a bonus of £E3,000–4,000.

It is very expensive to support workers and there are many responsibilities. One man rarely worked, at least not efficiently, because he often drank and gambled. But he expected me to pay him as much money as he needed, not even according to his salary or production. I asked him, "What do you think I am your father?" He answered, "No, my God." When a worker needs money, he comes to me, I record it, and then deduct it from his salary, if he made enough money that month to support his family. If I did not provide these services, it would be very difficult to attract and keep my workers.

In addition to their expectation of informal benefits, most workers, despite little formal education, were very knowledgeable about their legal rights and well-versed in both formal and informal means to protect themselves and avoid exploitation.

Workers can complain about factories and bosses at the labor office. About eight or nine years ago the social security people came and asked one worker how long he had been working at my factory. He, wanting to be difficult, said for five years. This guy had a wife whose hobby was to make complaints against the government or employers because she considered herself very well educated. They told me I had to pay back insurance fees of £E400, which is now equivalent to £E10,000. I went to buy a book on labor law and read it. The worker said he had a right to vacation, insurance, and a bonus [mukaaf'a]. But he thought that he would be able to work at the factory during his official vacation time and get paid doubly. I read the laws which said that a worker could not officially work during his vacation at his primary place of employment or anywhere else for that matter. In the end I was able to avoid paying the insurance after bribing several people, but sometimes I do wind up feeling like a criminal.

Some people have taken me to Labor Court, which is a very efficient operation. The day after filing a complaint employees of the court come to the factory to begin the investigation. But they take the side of the worker all the time. In the Labor Court, a worker can get something out of an employer but I can usually get nothing from the worker. To be fair, employees of the Labor Court work on behalf of workers and sometimes the workers receive a considerable settlement. Workers know about the Labor Court, but a worker can develop a bad reputation and may not be able to find work easily if he constantly takes his employers to court, although he may be awarded a couple of hundred pounds or even a thousand.

You attract workers through your other workers but they can also be the source of letting people know that a factory owner has a bad reputation. One factory owner used the police to really harass his workers for not repaying loans and checks and he would put them in prison. For many years he could not get any workers and the factory was virtually shut down.

Throughout *sha'bi* communities, if not all Egyptian society, people develop an acute sensitivity to legal and illegal norms and their rights in various spheres, even though people also understand that many formal rules do not bear up over time. The pursuit of benefits and court cases may not be successful, but because of the ambiguity of certain regulations and their irregular enforcement and supervision, people always try any promising avenue before they give up.

In order to avoid provisions that regulate their working conditions, hours of business, wages of workers, and so on, businessmen must be willing to absorb the costs of informality, as De Soto refers to them.[61] They must be willing to absorb the costs of fines, bribes, the threat of government seizure or padlocking a business or property, and imprisonment. Minimally, businessmen squander significant financial resources and numerous man-hours to adhere to, and avoid, government regulations.

Despite regulations for industrial safety, sanitary working conditions, and limited working hours, prevailing work habits and working conditions are not usually affected by fines, undercover inspection, and government prosecution. Several years ago, working hours were limited by President Sadat, to alleviate traffic congestion in urban areas and supposedly to reduce energy consumption. If manufacturing workshops were found open after seven o'clock in the evening they were fined £E100, and if they were caught a second time by the police, the fine increased to £E500; but that did not stop many workshops.

> Many of my workers are from Cairo, but some come directly from the countryside. I said workers earn a lot of money, but it goes quickly and much of the money is spent on food and drugs. Shoemakers are notorious for taking drugs. The nature of the work is that one has to sit down all the time. There is a joke: "Someone says to the *gazmagi* [shoemaker], 'Take a breather and rest.' He gets up and stands." They work too much and sometimes stay up all night to work, or make up their own hours and work all night. Twelve- and fourteen-hour shifts are very common. So they use drugs, primarily hashish. When opium used to be cheap many shoemakers were addicted to it. There are legal working hours but it does not matter. My factory is open as long as workers are there. There are always workers there when I leave around nine or ten at night. I just close the office of the factory and the last person closes the door.

Since most workers in this factory were not salaried but were paid according to their output (piecework), their use of drugs to stay awake and increase production was a consequence of the structure of their industry and its system of compensation. While workers earned more in this industry due to the high demand for skilled workers, they also suffered from the negative consequences of self-exploitation. As the manager noted earlier, once a shoemaker produced less, he could no longer support himself and had to find another source of income.

Emphasizing customary labor relations and other informal economic practices is not intended to minimize the importance of government policy and regulation. As demonstrated above, employers and employees spend considerable time and money to adhere to government regulations, whether voluntary or involuntary, and they exploit whatever benefits the government offers. While people develop intricate strategies to exploit opportunities, they often complain bitterly when they are restricted by the obligations accompanying the benefits.

For example, a young man used the considerable connections of a member of Parliament to obtain a relatively well-paid though stressful position as a bus driver in a public-sector company. After he was frightened by a near miss with pedestrians, he asked the same politician to intercede on his behalf to pressure his employer to allow him to quit his job without reimbursing the government for his training costs. In order to maintain a supply of bus drivers, the company required all employees to sign an agreement when they were hired that if they left they would reimburse the company for their training costs (the training entitled them to a commercial driver's license, which was valuable in the labor market).[62] In a similar scenario, teachers must stage a long battle in court to leave public education and teach in a private school. Since university education is free in Egypt, and a severe shortage of teachers plagues the school system, the government insists that teachers return their investment by staffing the public education system after it has financed their education.

Despite the government's supposed intent to regulate working conditions, wages, and workers' rights, a wide range of informal practices still prevails. Various industries and sectors of the economy are characterized by particular relationships between employers and employees which have deep historical roots in traditional labor practices. Even in larger manufacturing and service industries, where owners and workers adhere to formal labor regulations, vestiges of informal practices are demanded by workers, in some cases, and owners, in others. General conclusions about the costs and benefits of formal, as opposed to informal, practices cannot be formulated without much broader analyses of various industrial sectors and their history of labor relations. Yet particularly for the *sha'b*, who are engaged primarily in manufacturing, service, and sales occupations in small enterprises (as described in the previous two sections), traditional labor practices remain an important component of their working environment. Under some circumstances, they can benefit from them; in other cases, they are exploited by their employers, who have successfully evaded the bureaucrats from the Ministries of Labor or Social Affairs. In this *sha'bi* community, a mix of informal and formal labor practices usually characterized the workplace since workers (and owners) were quite shrewd in claiming whatever rights they were entitled to in either system.

Negotiating the Legal System: Formal and Otherwise

Within *sha'bi* communities the intricacies of government regulation, informal practices, and social and political networks can overwhelm individuals and institutions. People are not always successful in negotiating the fine lines between pragmatism, necessity, opportunism, and crime. Men and women suffer the consequences of being caught between the vicissitudes of government regulation and the unwritten rules of the informal system. As I have mentioned throughout the previous chapters, the Egyptian state maintains a strong presence in *sha'bi* communities and enforces legislation and legal codes. While the state categorizes certain activities as illegal, its institutions enforce the law selectively. The state, even if it so desired, probably could not afford to enforce its extensive regulations, nor is it interested in discouraging certain unregulated or illegal economic activity (such as the illegal flow of remittances from migrants abroad, private tutoring, the construction of illegal or unlicensed housing, or the production of cheap consumer goods by unlicensed workshops). The legal system and the courts are overburdened and paralyzed by 6,000 laws, 12,000 executive decisions, and 18,000 regulations, all of which are still in force.[63] Because laws regulate so many aspects of the *sha'b*'s daily life, it is difficult *not* to disobey the law.

Although the community may agree on the illegality of certain acts, people may not be condemned or censured by their peers for other activities such as petty corruption, moonlighting, unlicensed construction or renovation, forging official documents, or tax evasion. The social definition of criminal behavior often contrasts to its institutional definition.[64] Whether people in the community support or condemn the legal codes, fines, jail sentences, court cases, civil complaints, and housing codes of the government, they constantly confront the regulatory power of the state and develop an expertise in maneuvering through the judicial system. Others fall through the cracks to face legal ambiguity, selective enforcement, or, at times, the relentless pressure of government prosecution.

Charges of corruption are greeted with particular ambivalence in *sha'bi* communities. Although many people complain incessantly about the government's inefficient distribution of inexpensive, subsidized commodities and point out the inequity of the black market, others often defend employees of cooperatives once they are arrested for corruption.[65] Both the government and customers know the extent of black-market operations, but many people excuse low-paid employees for their involvement in the black market.[66] It is usually expected in large families that employees who have access to scarce goods will use their influence to obtain them. One man who worked for a food cooperative and was an important player in the black market was also expected to provide food to members of his family, but he was caught, suspended, and prosecuted before an administrative court on charges of corruption.

When two employees of a local food cooperative in the community were arrested after a local *fitiwwa* (local strongman, protector)[67] walked off with a carton full of soap while inspectors were present, people who had previously benefited from the black market rushed to the local police station to defend the accused and praise their moral character. In order to protect themselves, employees of food cooperatives must not appear condescending to local people, since many people are aware of their illegal dealings and can inform the police. When employees develop reputations as "fat cats" and sell commodities to outsiders or distribute food in other neighborhoods, local customers are more likely to inform on them.

Businessmen and private individuals who devote their efforts to evading state policy and regulations also try to obtain (legally and illegally) whatever public goods or benefits the state provides. When the state maintains a monopoly or monopsony over the production, distribution, or marketing of goods and raw materials, a businessman's access to those goods may be essential for his business needs. Stories of public employees profiting by selling public goods to middlemen (*simsaar*) in the black market are common in *sha'bi* neighborhoods and are publicized in newspapers when arrests and court cases come before the judicial system. According to grocers in my community, inspectors and supervisors of local food cooperatives are those ones who supply commodities to the black market. They estimate that three-quarters of the supply of publicly subsidized food is smuggled to the black market by government employees. *Simsaar*s eagerly await to distribute it quickly and profitably to private merchants.

One very prosperous grocer with extensive international business dealings (he had tried to buy a diner in the Wall Street area of New York City, arranged many import-export deals around the globe, and was planning to open a food production plant, described below) used his friendship with a smaller grocer to obtain government-distributed commodities for his supermarket. Certain goods, carefully controlled by the government and distributed through its system of food cooperatives, were only available to grocers who distributed rationed food (*tamwiin* goods).[68] However, it was possible for a *tamwiin* grocer to procure extra allotments of soap or oil, if he had the funds (larger than the allotment for the patrons registered at his store). The richer merchant asked the smaller grocer to buy as much soap as he could for his supermarket. The smaller grocer was happy to do this for his wealthy friend, whom he knew would finance the purchase and return the favor later. Despite his involvement in this deal, the smaller merchant would still complain about the thieves in the government who accepted his bribe to buy more soap. The fact that the government was corrupt absolved him of any guilt of wrongdoing since "if they are such thieves we should at least benefit as well."

Adhering to government regulations can be so labor intensive and complex that businessmen either resort to extralegal practices to conduct perfectly legal and productive business transactions or develop and invest in another venture. Even when businessmen have spent time and financial resources cultivating complicated international business deals and attaining government approval to import commodities, they are always in fear of new legislation or a government regulation that would jeopardize the venture (for example, a change in the exchange rate of the Egyptian pound or new customs regulations that might render a former agreement unprofitable). For example, the merchant who owned the supermarket, referred to above had traveled to Europe and arranged an agreement there to import butter to Egypt. Upon returning to Egypt, however, he discovered that the government had just changed the regulations governing imported food, and the deal had to be postponed.

Each load of commodities imported into Egypt needed special permits, for which this businessman had to reapply each time, in person, along with hundreds of other Egyptian businessmen. The *lagnit 'it-tarshiid* (the committee supervising imports) met for only a few hours, twice a month. During appointed hours, every businessman or woman who wanted to import or export food products had to physically appear and present proper documentation. The hall was always packed and anarchy prevailed. In order to obtain legal clearances, merchants needed informal ties with employees in this office to gain their attention and their signatures on clearances.

When regulations overwhelm businessmen and increase their business expenses to the point where they abandon the project, they concentrate on other opportunities subject to less government intervention. Disgusted by these ever-changing regulations and bureaucracy, this particular businessman realized that he could import food products more easily and lucratively if they were used to produce secondary products within Egypt. I was asked to call trade associations for appropriate companies that could cut and package butter when I was on a short visit to the United States, since the government would then allow him to import butter for resale in Egypt. The government would facilitate the importation of the machinery and offer a tax incentive because he would locate the new factory in October 6th city (one of the new satellite cities the government has constructed in sparsely settled areas to relieve population and industrial pressures on the Greater Cairo region). But he was not excited by the information I gave him when I returned from the United States and so initiated another project with a wealthy family from his village of origin to produce cheese from imported milk powder. His prospective business partners were contractors with extensive international networks and projects in Saudi Arabia as well as Egypt.[69] A brother from the family lived in Britain and had already contacted an English firm that sold dairy manufacturing equipment and milk powder. The English company sent a representative to negotiate with them in Egypt, and during a meeting (which I attended), he explained the details of the manufacturing process.

The representative had been briefed by a commercial attaché at the British Embassy before the meeting, and he relayed several of their suggestions to make the project more financially attractive. For example, if the British company described the composition of the milk powder on their invoice as a food product, it would be exempted from taxes because the project would fall under the provision of the Food Security Project (projects that increased domestic food production were encouraged by the government because Egyptian food needs have outpaced domestic production and scarce foreign currency is spent on food imports).[70] While the project would escape taxation (for an initial period at least), the Egyptian partners would be dependent on the English company for shipments of milk powder needed to produce the cheese. Despite the grocers' past experience with the fickleness of import regulations, they did not seem afraid of a dependence on imported milk powder which, if interrupted, would quickly bring their factory to a standstill.

While the grocer who supervised an import-export firm and negotiated with a transnational firm to build a capital-intensive plant was far wealthier than many businessmen in the community, there were other even more prosperous merchant families from these neighborhoods. When this grocer would sit in his supermarket attending to his customers and business associates, he would point to other men walking past the store in relatively modest dress and identify them as millionaires with legal and illegal business interests in Europe, the Arabian Gulf, or Africa. In fact, international business networks in the communities were extensive, reaching the Sudan, Yemen, Saudi Arabia, Nigeria, the United Arab Emirates, Iraq, Kuwait, Libya, France, Germany, Italy, the United Kingdom, the United States, and the Soviet Union. He explained that some of them had made their fortunes in the drug trade and were able to accumulate hundreds of thousands of dollars within only a few hours since their activities were completely outside the formal realm. However, as an honest businessman willing to invest his money in productive enterprises that would benefit the economy, he was stymied at every turn by his own government.

In another area of chronic scarcity in *sha'bi* communities, the government played a similarly inconsistent role in regulating real estate, including private residential buildings, subsidized and cooperative housing, new construction, and renovation (particularly the common practice of adding additional floors to existing apartment buildings). The cost of residential and commercial real estate has skyrocketed throughout Egypt, and prices are extremely high in densely populated areas where there is little physical space left for expansion. A prosperous businessman had recently offered one family £E250,000 for their apartment building in central Cairo, which also housed a small warehouse and office. A very small shop selling old brass to tourists exchanged hands for £E50,000 in key money. An aluminum products shop had been sold for £E100,000 (key money). Even an extremely small kiosk, appropriate only for a single self-employed artisan, exchanged hands for £E12,000 (key money) in 1985. An industrial workshop that barely held six workers (approximately 180 square feet) had been secured for £E1,000 in key money in 1977, but by 1985 its value had risen to £E15,000. According to merchants in the area, a single room in a newly constructed commercial building would rent for £E10,000 in key money. A piece of land in a densely populated residential area quadrupled in price within a three-month period in 1984—from £E100 per meter to £E400. Even land in newly settled informal areas that ring Cairo have been appreciating in value very rapidly. A man who had paid £E300 for key money for a workshop in a newly settled informal area a few years ago explained that its value had risen to £E7,000 by 1985. Land that had been available for £E2 per meter now sold for £E300–500 per meter.

In new and old areas of Cairo, poorly constructed buildings and very old buildings are inspected by government authorities to ensure that they do not collapse. In one neighborhood within my community, government inspectors had warned residents about the impending collapse of a building on a main street in the late 1970s. People could not arrange alternate housing very easily, and because one of the most important religious holidays was approaching, the government agreed to postpone its evacuation order until after the holiday. Unfortunately, the building collapsed during the holiday and brought down three adjacent buildings, killing many people who were trapped inside.

When people are evacuated from housing in danger of collapsing, they are theoretically entitled to emergency public housing. However, the wait for temporary or permanent public housing was usually very long, and many people could not afford prevailing rents or the costs of commuting from outlying areas where new housing was available (many had been paying very inexpensive rents of two to five pounds per month). One man in the community lived in a medieval apartment house until a neighbor flooded a kitchen, which caused extensive structural damage. Although he was entitled to public housing and was pursuing his legal rights, he expected a very long fight between residents and the government before he would actually be relocated. In the meantime he borrowed money from his associates and illegally subletted a public-sector apartment (however, he carefully asked more experienced neighbors how to register his illegal agreement with the former owner of his apartment at the notary office).

Some people in these communities believe that bureaucratic inertia is an intentional strategy by the government to dissuade people from pursuing their claims for housing and other government services. For many years, the government was content to house the homeless (victims of collapsed housing or those evicted from condemned housing) in temporary tents or improvised facilities in courtyards, mosques, and other public spaces. Some people had remained in "temporary" facilities for ten to twenty years, in very poor living conditions, with government approval. As the wear and tear on medieval mosques and apartment buildings worsened and tourism in Egypt increased after the Camp David Accords, the government's interest in preserving medieval historic areas in Cairo grew. However, the concerns of preservationists superseded the needs of the "temporary" residents, and they were thrown out of their former quarters before receiving proper housing.[71]

Wealth usually facilitates access to those in power and the ability to bribe government inspectors in *sha'bi* neighborhoods. In a tight housing market, wealthy businessmen have been known to influence an inspector and engineer's decision to condemn a building, so that he can tear it down and erect an extremely profitable new residential or commercial building. In several cases landlords deliberately weakened buildings in order to force the government to condemn the building. Again, since much of the physical stock in these areas is very old and in disrepair, owners of buildings (who may also reside there) can deliberately destroy a building without being caught or prosecuted by the government.

For example, two families distantly related by marriage lived next to each other in separate buildings. One family owned both buildings but schemed to destroy one in order to rebuild it, unburdening themselves of low-paying tenants in the process. Because the building was in danger of collapsing, the tenants agreed to allow the owner to carefully demolish the upper floor. However, the landlord instructed his workers to destroy the central staircase surreptitiously, leaving the entire building uninhabitable and forcing families to find new accommodations in more expensive housing farther away from their workplaces, relatives, and networks. Despite the ties between the families in both buildings, hard feelings remained years after the incident.

In certain situations, even when the government takes explicit steps to enforce rent-control policies or the condition of physical stock, people often find ways to evade the government, for better and worse. In one of the new, recently settled, and increasingly popular neighborhoods surrounding central Cairo, the government had tried to enforce rent-control laws. The popularity of the area had increased prevailing rents (to say nothing about completely illegal key money payments), and government officials demanded that landlords lower rents in compliance with rent-control legislation. According to residents, landlords instituted lower rents but then charged tenants for services that had previously been included in the rent (such as access to water, electricity, and so on) until the monthly total equaled the previous inflated and illegal rent. In another popular new neighborhood, landlords occasionally bribed housing officials to investigate rents in their buildings, hoping that the committee would raise, not lower, the rent. Occasionally, the scheme backfired when the committee discovered illegal high rents and forced the landlord to reimburse tenants retroactively for having paid inflated rents.

People in this community willingly and shrewdly exploit the formal legal system if they believe it will further their interests, or if they have no alternative. The above cases are not meant to suggest that their experience with the law is always negative. Individuals in the community will use the legal system and the local police to protect their interests and reputation. Earlier, in Chapter 1, I noted that people preferred to resolve differences among themselves, rather than utilize the formal legal system. However, if a conflict becomes too antagonistic or if it is only resolvable through the legal system, people will not hesitate to file complaints against each other, file court suits, or summon the police to arrest business associates, relatives, and colleagues. Property disputes, in particular, can rarely be resolved informally and are handled through the court system in generally lengthy proceedings. Due, in part, to the Islamic inheritance system, which splits an inheritance among many heirs, many businesses, buildings, and plots of land in the area were jointly owned by several people. Thus, if one partner tried to sell a building, to renovate it, or even to rent his or her share to new tenants, the other partners had to be consulted and to give their consent or long entangled disputes and law suits could ensue.

Several lots in my community stood empty or were filled with rubble, and when I asked why these plots remained vacant in such a tight housing market, people explained that they were owned by many partners who could not agree on how to develop the property. Due to their indecision, and after many years of litigation and attempts at mediation, the government was in the process of sequestering the property.

In another property dispute, a large extended family owned a share of a building where a relative resided. A company that also owned part of the building was trying to sell its share, but the family took them to court to prevent the sale. It was not clear to me what effect the sale of half the building would have on the value of the family's share or their ability to remain there (everyone agreed that they could never be evicted from their apartment), but this case had languished in the court system for the past four years.

Many other families in the community were involved in various court cases: civil, criminal, labor, military, personal status, and administrative. People became enmeshed in the system when one man was imprisoned in a military jail for desertion, a worker was forced to pay £E1,000 for failing to fulfill his military service before the age of thirty,[72] a woman filed a case for support against her husband who had divorced her, a mother filed a complaint at a public hospital against her doctor for improperly setting her broken arm, a young woman filed a suit against her employer for dismissing her after an argument, a businessman argued his tax bill before an administrative court, and a widow filed suit against her in-laws for excluding her from her husband's inheritance. Official documents and papers were carefully stored in the safest places in homes. Although many of the people involved were illiterate, it did not seem to prevent them from finding lawyers to represent them or from seeking the intervention and expertise of more knowledgeable people in the community.

It is not an exaggeration to describe Egyptians, and this community, as litigious. Six million court cases are heard by very overburdened judges in Egypt each year (out of a population of approximately forty-nine million, many of whom are too young to file a case). Only 5,400 judges hear five million of those cases, postponing an additional million until the next year. A typical judge issues about eight hundred decisions each month and hears about two hundred cases in each of four three-and-a-half-hour sessions when the court is sitting. The number of judges in Egypt, unfortunately, is much lower than in other nations (Germany and Italy have 16,000 judges and other officials who hear court cases, and England has 20,000).[73] While complaints were often voiced over the length of court cases and costs for lawyers and official papers, people seem to believe they will benefit from participating in the system since they proceed with lengthy cases and invest financial resources in them.

It may appear contradictory to argue that people in this community were litigious and not reluctant to file suits for perceived wrongs, but at the same time relied upon informal, extralegal norms to resolve disputes or conduct business. As was apparent in the case of the shoe factory or the supermarket and import-export family business discussed earlier, the dichotomy between legal and illegal behavior, and licensed and unlicensed commerce, production, or employment, is often unclear. While the *sha'b* and segments of the business community may devise ingenious strategies to circumvent inefficient, costly, or unpopular regulations, it does not necessarily mean that they have overcome the system or secured long-term interests with ease. Their persistence shows, instead, that their interests are not being served by the present system, but they use whatever means they can exploit to maneuver through the judicial system.

The Vexation of Taxation

"Taxes here, in particular, are wrong, wrong, wrong." So went the complaint of a *tamwiin* grocer. Taxation, through which governments create public revenues and finance the provision of public goods and services, is rarely popular in any nation. While people usually support more extensive government services, they reluctantly part with personal wealth. Despite the often negative image of the tax authorities by those whom are taxed, the economically active population in this community eventually interacted with the tax authorities, experiencing the regulatory power of the state. Taxation commonly entails not only a very sensitive encounter with the government, but "the taxation system of a certain country highlights its economic, social, and political system and the state of its economic development," according to the National Bank of Egypt.[74] Since the 1952 revolution, taxation has become even more important as an instrument of policy and a means to supposedly redress inequity in Egypt.

> The role of taxation in the past was confined to the coverage of public expenditure, i.e., the financial purposes were the main concern of the tax to the exclusion of any direct objectives in the economic or social fields. However, in light of the developed and enhanced economic role of the State, coupled with the evolution of economic and financial thought, a concomitant change in the role and function of the tax took place. Consequently, taxes became an instrument of economic and social planning which was increasingly resorted to as a means of directing investment, checking inflation, and redistributing incomes and wealth, as well as other goals that go beyond the traditional function of the tax (i.e., the financial objective normally associated with the alleged tax impartiality).[75]

Rather than analyze whether the government has met its goals, this section will concentrate primarily on the men and women in a particular *sha'bi* community and their experiences with the tax authorities. After hearing several complicated accounts of cases and appeals, I decided the issue of taxation seemed to symbolize the *sha'b*'s interaction with the state (although the complaints were a bit harsher in this realm than in others). People did not see themselves as direct beneficiaries of the tax system, as they did when dealing with civil servants in the educational system, a public utility, or a food cooperative. An overwhelming sense of inefficiency, mistrust, and exploitation surrounds the public perception of taxation in this community, as can be seen in the following examples. While some of the accounts presented may be long, excluding the details would distort the lengthy, Kafkaesque process of paying taxes. Businessmen use both formal and informal means to resolve their tax problems with the authorities. It should be noted that the accounts and explanations of taxation from people in this community were accepted at face value since it was impossible to corroborate them from official sources. The following account should not at all be seen as a history or analysis of taxation in Egypt, but rather an explanation of my informants' experiences and their perceptions of taxation.

The probability of paying taxes in Egypt depends on one's position in the economy—a situation that offends popular notions of justice. Any employee of the state or person who enters into a business relationship with the state (subcontracting, receiving allotments of public-sector raw materials, distributing public-sector goods, and so forth) is far more likely to pay taxes than a self-employed or private-sector businessman or woman. In order to increase tax collection, the government taxes at "the source" as much as possible. For example, income taxes are subtracted from the wages of public-sector employees while private-sector employees and the self-employed are required to file tax returns if their income exceeds a certain amount. Not surprisingly, compliance with tax regulations is much lower in the private than public sector. The private sector accounted for only 28 percent of all direct taxation revenues (taxes on individuals' income, taxes on business incomes, and property taxes) during the period 1974–1979. State-owned enterprises provided the vast majority of direct taxes during this period (72 percent) and also comprised the largest share of business income taxes in the mid-1980s.[76]

The government admits to a massive problem of tax evasion in Egypt and introduced new legislation in the late 1970s and early 1980s to increase compliance and tax revenues.[77] The government estimated publicly that evasion of taxes on commercial and industrial profits and the tax on professions reached 60 percent.[78] In 1980–81 official estimates of tax arrears reached £E356 million and £E230 million for the taxation and customs departments, respectively.[79] The actual incidence of tax evasion and tax arrears is probably much greater.

To ensure a steady flow of public revenue, the government relies primarily on indirect taxes, including excise duties, customs duties, price differentials, consumption duties, royalties, *gihaad* tax, stamp tax, and a consumption tax on domestic products and imported products (the latter two initiated under Law No. 133 in 1981).[80] In general, one can say the burden of paying taxes falls on the *sha'b* since regressive indirect taxes are more of a burden for the poor and middle class than the rich. Taxes are levied even on such important basic commodities in Egypt as flour, tea, sugar, and oil products.[81]

Accounts within this community confirm the prevalence of tax evasion in Egypt, but they also provide explanations for such behavior. According to many people in *sha'bi* communities, tax regulation and collection is idiosyncratic, inefficient, and unfair. While there may be grudging respect for the persistence and expertise of some tax collectors, the demands of the tax authorities overwhelm small businessmen and absorb their attention and limited resources. In a strategy to register new businesses with the proper authorities before they may disappear into the informal economy, the government demands that a businessman first must obtain a license from the local administrative unit (*'il-baladiyya*) and a tax identification card (*biTaa'a Dariibiyya*) before he can legally open a new establishment. At the *maSlaHit iD-Daraayib* (tax department), a businessman fills out a trade register (*sigill tugaari*), which lists his starting capital, including the physical capital of the enterprise, if any. Those businessmen who expect to earn profits in excess of £E1,200 (the figure for 1978) must also file a declaration of personal wealth (*'iqraar zimma maliyya*) stating all personal assets and property (including gold, jewelry, automobiles, bank accounts, and so on). Each five years the tax department reestimates a firm's taxes, and for the next four years a businessman pays a sum based on that first year (*sanit il-'asaas*). These new tax assessments are often the source of much disagreement between the government and its taxpayers.

The government records the tax I.D. number, volume, and value of any exchange of goods and services which involves a private-sector businessman and a public-sector firm or goods produced by public enterprises (including subcontracting) in order to ease its burden of estimating taxes.[82] A grocer who purchases foodstuffs from a public-sector macaroni factory, for example, knows that the sale of goods has been recorded at the tax authority. Because the wholesale cost of the sale was recorded and the government fixes the retail price of the goods at his grocery store, the tax authorities can easily estimate his profits. Grocers complain, however, because the authorities completely ignore their expenses (labor, rent, transport, overhead).

Because many private-sector businesses have little interaction with public-sector industry, the tax authorities have particular difficulty estimating their taxes since many firms do not even keep written financial records (or organized books, *difaatir munaZZama*). Thus the tax authority resorts to other, less direct means of estimating business profits. The following account returns to the experiences of the manager of the shoe factory.

> The tax authorities estimate profits once every five years and they come to look at your place. They are completely free to estimate how much money you make, to take anything they see or hear into account. You do not know when they are coming, they do not even have to show you their identity card. They just come, go straight to the factory, and count the workers. They operate like security men all the time. After they come in, they suggest a meeting in your office. Eventually you realize this guy is the tax official.
>
> Then he questions you. He is free not to believe you. According to your answers and his information, he estimates how much money you make. He could come to the factory and pick up a pair of shoes with their price written on the bottom. Then he would count the workers. Then he would estimate how many shoes a worker could produce in a week and a year and what my costs are. By experience they know the price of the shoes, but they can't be all that experienced because of all the industries under their jurisdiction. Their information is not at all specific. They pay no attention to one's real costs, changes in the cost of raw materials, bonuses that you need to attract workers, slow periods, etc. They come up with huge sums of money that they claim are owed the government. For example, a *makwagi* [someone who irons clothes] I knew was told he must pay £E50,000 in taxes. They do that.
>
> There is a funny game going on between us and them. My report is actually false and they know that. They never look at it and they never accept it. They know I am lying and I am lying. The last time I told them I made £E1,700 profit but that cannot be possible and they know it. For the first £E1,000, you pay 20 percent tax, for the second thousand you pay 30 percent tax. After £E3,000 or £E4,000, you pay 70 percent tax. So, I cannot say I made £E4,000 in profit. You just make up numbers. I say how many shoes I have produced, how much profit on each shoe. Then I take out all expenses like rent, phone, electricity.

Tax collectors routinely operate undercover, and businessmen are suspicious when a stranger enters their workplace or invites himself into their home. One man owned a tailor shop in a *sha'bi* neighborhood. One day a customer inquired about his ability to make a suit after he had looked around the small shop and did not see a particular machine that is used to produce men's suits. The tailor, hoping to gain a new customer, told him that he kept the machine at another workshop (he actually could not afford this machine and rented the use of one at a colleague's more elaborate workshop). Some time later the tailor received a letter from the tax authorities with a tax assessment for two factories. The man could not understand why they insisted that he had two workshops until he realized that his inquisitive customer was really a tax collector.

On another occasion, which I witnessed, several well-dressed men approached a merchant in a small commercial alleyway. Without stating their business they asked to speak with him in private, and the merchant reluctantly invited them to his nearby home. They claimed they were selling insurance, and the merchant politely declined their sales pitch since the Ministry of Social Affairs already insured his workers. After they left, the merchant suspected they were undercover tax collectors. He had recently submitted a very low tax report, and he feared that these inspectors were judging the condition of his home against his report. Unfortunately, the family had just remodeled the apartment and purchased new furniture. In the end, the identity of these men was not confirmed.

In a commercial manufacturing area, the owner of an enterprise that produced chicken-grilling machines was arrested for tax arrears of £E26,000, a sum the owner thought ridiculously high. He was taken to the local police station, arrested, and had to pay £E5,000 before his release on bail. According to several people, his taxes had been estimated in the following manner: The tax officials had visited his workshops (he had two) and estimated that they produced two machines a day and sold them for £E100.[83] They calculated a 44 percent tax rate for industrial profits for £E200 and multiplied the figure by the number of working days per year to reach the tax assessment of £E26,000 (£E88 × 293 days = £E25,784, assuming the workshop closed for a day and a half each week). They made no calculation of his costs, fluctuations in the market, or unsold inventory.

This method of ignoring the cost of labor, raw materials, inoperative machinery, and price fluctuations in the market is very widespread and infuriates private-sector businessmen. For this reason, many businessmen hide machinery from public view and keep their workshops (and, at times, homes) in a disreputable state, in constant fear that undercover tax collectors will use such visible physical improvements and investment in machinery against them in the form of much higher taxes. Some businessmen are prosecuted when the tax authorities examine their declaration of personal wealth and note a substantial increase in wealth, although they have paid very low taxes on their business. In these cases, they are arrested and charged with tax evasion. For example, in a routine reassessment of a businessman's personal wealth declaration, the tax authorities discovered that his assets were worth £E83,000, yet the man had only paid £E100 in taxes for the past four years. He was quickly arrested.

Visual judgments of wealth in workshops and homes in this community can be extremely misleading because most businessmen do not flaunt their wealth since it attracts the interest of the tax authorities. Businessmen with assets over a certain ceiling must also file a declaration of personal wealth and revise it periodically, and thus they prefer to invest excess profits in the informal economy rather than purchase highly visible new machinery, enlarge or renovate workshops, or engage in conspicuous consumption. On the other hand, some businessmen proudly park ostentatious Mercedes or BMWs in front of their homes in narrow alleyways and brag of their recent purchases of beach villas, land, video cameras, and gold to anyone who will listen. Some of these conspicuous consumers do not fear the tax authorities because their businesses are completely illegal and they have already spent small fortunes bribing public officials.

Despite the arbitrary estimation of taxes and undercover visits, the process of paying taxes also involves a fair degree of negotiation and bargaining. While the method of estimating taxes is viewed as idiosyncratic and capricious by businessmen, they routinely file appeals and many are engaged in court cases for years on end.

> I have the right to disagree with their estimate before a committee called *lagnit is-sulaasa*, composed of three people, which is an internal appeals committee [*lagnit Ta'n*] of the tax organization itself [*maSlaHit iD-Daraayib*]. If they do not accept your estimate, you can go to court against them. The burden of proving the government estimate wrong, however, is on you, not them. In the committee it is pure bargaining—the amount you have to pay goes back and forth. 'I can't pay more than this,' 'We can't accept that, why don't you pay this.' Usually you bring an official licensed accountant [*muHaasib qaanuniyya*] with you. Typically you pay him £E150–200 ['*it-ta'b*], at least. In cases involving larger sums they receive a percentage of the settlement and so have a stake in a higher tax estimate.[84]
>
> The wait for the *lagnit is-sulaasa* can be very long. The problem with the tax authorities is that they vanish for years on end and then they come and say you owe all this money. You must file the declaration or pay a £E200 fine. But you cannot pay your taxes until they send you two letters: Forms 18 and 19. The first says you owe this amount of money, but you are still not fined until you officially receive the second letter.[85] Upon receipt of the second letter you are allowed fifteen days to either pay the tax or file an appeal. And you cannot even appeal until you get the second letter and it may take several months or even a year for it to arrive. If you decide to pay while pursuing an appeal the payment will go toward your account. But as a businessman, why should I freeze up my cash like that, if I am not obliged?
>
> Nothing goes smoothly with them. Going through the appeals process can take years even before a court case [an appeal is internal to the tax authority]. Last time there were so many complications because we were exporting shoes to Russia. They estimated that we had made huge profits, when in fact we lost money at the end of the contract. They had based their calculations on the first year and estimated our profits for the next four years, on that basis. They decided that if we were exporting shoes to Russia we must be making a profit, and therefore raised our taxes—that arbitrarily. Initially, many businessmen who exported shoes to Russia made a lot of money. We [Egypt] owed them lots of money and we paid it back in goods. The government would offer loans to factories to expand production in order to export. The National Bank in the early 1970s charged only 2 percent interest on these loans. The dirty thing was that you got paid in Egyptian pounds and they got the hard currency. They determined the contract on the basis of the price of the English pound, according to the time you signed the contract. If the price of the pound rose, the businessman lost money—not the government, which received the hard cur-

rency. All the people who exported commodities to Russia lost money because the price of the pound rose so dramatically. [The trade agreement with the Soviet Union was abrogated in 1976 by President Sadat] They claimed we had made £E7,000 in profits over five years, which is now [1986] equivalent to £E70,000. We had to pay eventually. I tried to go before the appeals committee but it was suspended while the Parliament discussed reforming the system. In the meantime there was no appeals process for many years. If I had not paid they would have sealed the factory. This happens often in our business. Their next step would be to sell the business.

This tax case concerning exports to Russian began twelve years ago. My taxes were reestimated seven years ago and then two years ago. I haven't started paying for the estimate that came two years ago. I did not appeal the second one since it was reasonable. But I will appeal the third one as soon as the second letter arrives. But perhaps it will never arrive and in ten years' time they will come and say I owe them a huge amount of money. I did inquire about when the second letter would be sent, since I wanted to sort it all out, but they said that I just had to wait. A routine wait.

In my community one successful merchant had received an estimate from the tax authorities demanding £E12,000, and he expected to pursue appeals for three or four years. Another grocer was in the process of appealing a levy of £E7,000 for the previous four years. Although he had not opened his business until the very end of the first year, the tax authorities treated each year similarly and estimated his taxes at £E1,700 per year. The government had ignored his low estimate of profits although he claimed the authorities knew the profits of *tamwiin* grocers were very low because of strict pricing regulations. "If the tax should be five, they will say fifty, *Haraam 'aleehum* [shame on them—implies something is forbidden by religious precepts]. Taxes are far too high."

In a more general conversation about the government in Egypt during a taxi ride, the cab driver suddenly pulled a fistful of receipts from his glove compartment. He had recently been informed by the tax authorities that he owed £E4,000 in back taxes for the past several years from his income as a taxi driver. He was paying the sum off slowly in installments of £E50 per month, claiming that the government was taking the food from the mouth of his family. His feelings about the government were anything but positive.

An additional factor creates antipathy among private businessmen. They complain that their businesses are productive and profitable yet they are not entitled to benefits that public-sector enterprises routinely receive, such as cheaper raw materials, protected markets, and stable labor relations. Public-sector and large-scale enterprises have clever accountants and lawyers to reduce their taxes while most private-sector businesses do not even keep organized or written accounts. Pursuing appeals against the tax authorities absorbs a great amount of time, effort, and financial resources. To further their interests, businessmen pay for legal and illegal services. Accountants, lawyers, and official paperwork all demand outlays of cash. In addition, public employees, representing a wide spectrum of the bureaucracy, often demand small and large bribes before they will sign the appropriate papers.

From the other side of the fence, however, the responsibilities of a tax authority employee are overwhelming, and there are many opportunities to accept tempting bribes. According to one tax collector who lived in my community, the government offers high salaries to its tax collectors as well as bonuses (which can be three times the salary), to minimize internal corruption.[86] This man, in his early forties, had been transferred from the customs department to the tax authority after his discharge from the army in 1973.[87] According to his estimate, approximately 95 percent of the staff accepted bribes, but he had been able to walk a straight path (*maashi dughri*) until now and had been made a supervisor of the other employees because of his integrity. Employees are often transferred internally to minimize their exposure to taxpayers and tempting bribes.[88]

Despite the bureaucratic routine of the tax authority, employees have a high degree of personal interaction with the industries and establishments they regulate. For example, the tax collector mentioned above regulated the entertainment industry and was expected to visit the cinemas and theaters in his jurisdiction each day to guarantee that the number of tickets sold corresponded to the number of tax tickets that were torn up as customers entered the cinema. Cinemas had to buy these ticket books from the tax office in another example of taxing at the source. The tax inspector was expected to attend every performance at theaters in his district as well. In a similar manner, regulations require a tax official to sign the contract of live musicians who perform at weddings. He must also visit swimming pools, hotels, restaurants, bars, and places where live music is performed each night to ensure that entertainment taxes are being properly collected.

The tax authority divided all places of entertainment in Cairo into six divisions, and each division was staffed by twelve employees and two inspectors. Thus only eighty-four people regulated a very large and diverse industry. Their task was much more complex due to the high degree of personal surveillance and inspection demanded by the system. Clearly, the tax authority does not trust taxpayers and vice versa; nor does the authority have the administrative resources to fulfill their task.

This tax collector concluded his account and criticism of the tax authority by stating that the present system oppressed average taxpayers and businessmen since wealthy businessmen had clever accountants to reduce their taxes. A small grocer, on the other hand, was unsophisticated and did not have even written accounts of his profits and costs. "The government takes from the small fish and leaves the big businessmen, with their accountants and connections, to prosper."

But the shoe manufacturer, mentioned earlier, believed that most businessmen pay reasonable taxes, after all their machinations. However, the government receives only *half* the sum. An almost equal sum is claimed by public employees, accountants, lawyers, and other intermediaries in the informal economy. Perhaps it can be argued that the informal system, like the supposed objectives of taxation, redistributes wealth to an appropriate segment of the population, which serves progressive goals although massive tax evasion clearly weakens the government's capacity and solvency. Businessmen also deplore the waste of labor they invest in resolving tax problems. As the manager of the shoe factory explained, "My taxes cost me £E7,000 in labor and £E7,000 in cash."[89] Industrial productivity and the Egyptian economy suffer when businessmen use scarce financial resources for lawyers fees, bribes, and settling tax cases. The present system discourages businessmen from investing legal profits and new sources of capital in businesses due to the fear of suffocating regulations and higher taxes.

Even during the Sadat era of the Open Door policy, when newly created joint venture enterprises were offered tax holidays for eight years and some industries located in newly developed satellite cities received a tax holiday of ten years, businessmen still suffered from excessive and, at times, archaic regulations. For example, an established businessman, who wanted to introduce wooden heels, rather than leather, into a new line of shoes, abandoned his plans because he would have to file a completely separate tax return for the new line (wood products fall under a different industrial classification and therefore section of the tax authority, despite the fact that shoes were the final product). While the Egyptian government has sought to attract new sources of foreign and domestic capital to bolster its economy, existing regulations restrict innovation and discourage investment from small-scale capitalists and entrepreneurs who cannot benefit from the bold new financial opportunities.

It seems unlikely that the state will capture increased revenues from this segment of the economy unless it encourages investment, diversification, and even-handed regulatory practices. Yet these practices benefit certain segments of the Egyptian economy, and therefore it would be naive to expect serious reforms from the same government that is responsible for these regulations and policies in the first place. Unfortunately, among the *sha'b*, a common response to government regulation in this realm is evasion, dishonesty, and withdrawal from the formal economy. Paying taxes remains one of the more negative experiences with the state, encouraging cynicism and distrust. A noted Egyptian economist, Galal Amin, suggests a more direct link between the rising social and economic mobility of the *sha'b* and its attitudes toward the government and taxation:

> Complaints about the tax system in Egypt usually refer less to the low level of tax rates than to the high rate of tax evasion. Tax evasion is, in its turn, blamed on the decline in moral standards and the weakening of loyalty to the state. But this very weakening of loyalty may indeed be seen as partly the result of the change in social structure and in the relative social position of tax payers, tax legislators and tax collectors. One may argue that there is a big difference between the attitude to the state of the old class of big landowners and industrial-

ists who constituted the main tax payers in pre-1952 Egypt, and that of the new classes who made their fortune in the 1970s whether from migration, trade, real estate, and speculation or from being connected in one way or another with foreign sources of income. One would indeed expect the former classes to have a stronger sense of loyalty and to feel more indebted to the state—which provided them with the necessary infrastructure, invested on their behalf in irrigation and drainage projects and enforced the law and order necessary for the protection of their interests. In contrast, much of the new income and wealth accumulated in the 1970s may be attributed not to state activities but rather to its inactivity, to the merely passive role of the state in allowing people to migrate, and to its failure to regulate the rate of inflation and the pattern of investment. If readiness to pay one's taxes has any relationship to the sense of indebtedness to the state, the newly rising classes in Egypt would indeed be expected to show a much higher propensity to evade taxation than the older classes of tax payers whose income came from agriculture and industry. . . . It is also quite possible that the attitude toward the payment of taxes of someone whose taxable income is relatively recent, unreliable and irregular and whose newly acquired income has served to raise him to a higher social class, should be very different from the attitude of another whose source of income is long established and more secure, and to whom an increase in income or wealth does not basically change his social standing. While to the latter, the payment of taxes may be like dispensing with some extra fat of the body, to the former it may seem like giving away part of the flesh.[90]

Amin's metaphor accurately captures the feelings of many businessmen and women from this community who often expressed skepticism toward the government and resentment over its tax policies. He vividly captures the underlying antagonism and resentment, which is palpable, even within *sha'bi* communities, between rising and declining social classes. For many businessmen within my community, tax evasion and extralegal investment and production were the norm, yet because of their suspicion of government bureaucrats and regulations, their technically illegal behavior was socially acceptable, certainly rational and usually legitimate in the eyes of the community. Furthermore, investing in the informal economy meant that the community had greater financial resources and, through informal economic networks, more interaction in Egypt's larger political economy. Rather than ending up in government coffers, these resources remained within the community. Certainly, there are both positive and negative consequences of this phenomenon, depending on an individual's position, interest, and opportunities. Even if funds are invested abroad, new factories are built in satellite cities, or houses are constructed in middle-class areas, these economic ventures remained tied to the people and interests of *sha'bi* communities. The implications of a strong, diverse, and extensive informal economy suggest that the financial and political assets of the *sha'b* are growing and changing the distribution of wealth and the formation of social classes in Egypt.

THE *SHAʿB* AND INFORMALITY: WAGES AND WEALTH

The preceding sections have attempted to demonstrate the high incidence of informal economic activity and the coexistence, if not interdependence, of formal and informal business practices in *shaʿbi* communities. It has been argued earlier that a dynamic informal economic sector providing employment and income to many families also offers a stronger economic and political resource base for this community than a "formal picture" of this community would suggest. Estimates of the value of sums circulating in the informal economy, based on several recent studies, suggests that the informal economy is quite large and represents significant economic interests. This section examines wage levels of formal and informal economic activity in the economically active sample, to better understand the *shaʿb*'s financial resources and its relative position vis-à-vis other sectors in Egypt.

The disparity of wages and income among individuals in the economically active sample and a sample from another *shaʿbi* community is evident in Tables 4.17 and 4.18. Wages and earnings for the self-employed, and for workers in the private sector and in family enterprises, were generally higher than wages in the public sector. And within sectors, wages varied greatly between young workers, workshop owners, and older skilled craftsman. While some workers—disproportionately female and public-sector employees—did not earn high wages, ten earned over £E300 per month (the average wage in Table 4.18, excluding the nonmonthly wages, equaled £E260).[91] Few of the individuals listed in Table 4.18 can be considered members of the 'working poor,' despite common assumptions about widespread poverty and marginality in *shaʿbi* communities, particularly among those who work in the informal economy.[92]

The following chart, from a forthcoming study of a 25-year-old densely populated informal housing settlement near central Cairo, depicts the earning differentials between private and public employment.[93] In this community, it was definitely more lucrative for these people to work in the private sector as well. Their generally low levels of literacy and training meant that their best options were generally in private or informal employment. None of the men or women in this particular sample happened to hold secondary jobs, and none worked with a family member or relative (unlike Table 4.18 where many individuals held second jobs or had secondary sources of income). In the complete sample some government employees held second jobs (particularly married conscripts who could not support themselves or their families on their symbolic wages—£E6 per month). The more common solution for employees of small private-sector enterprises in this informal settlement to earn a "secondary income" was to work longer hours, not to hold two jobs. The generally lower wages in Table 4.19 probably reflected the fact that this community, located in a "squatter's settlement," was comprised of rural migrants from outside Cairo and newly married young

TABLE 4.18
Prevailing Wages in the Economically Active Population

Job Description	Age	Sector	Monthly Earnings (1985)
Army conscript	24	State, government	£E 15
Engineer/researcher*	28	State, government	34
Teacher (secondary school)	38	State, government	55
University professor	37	State, government	66
Member of Parliament*	57	State, government	120
Administrator*	34	State, government	(incl. bonuses) 150
Principal (primary school)	48	State, government	170
Medical doctor*	35	State, public service	15
Bus driver	25	State, public sector	175
Vocational teacher* (PVO)	28	Private employee	32
Administrator* (PVO)	58	Private employee	55
Clerk (luxury hotel)	30	Private employee	330
English instructor	37	Private employee	350
Textile worker*	11–16	Private workshop	48
Textile worker*	17	Private workshop	88
Worker (auto repair)	26	Private workshop	110
Worker (aluminum)	25	Private workshop	110
Shoemaker	25	Private workshop	132
Worker (aluminum)	20	Private workshop	132
Worker (aluminum)	28	Private workshop	154
Worker (aluminum)	26	Private workshop	192
Wall plasterer	26	Private workshop	220
Machinist	45	Private workshop	330
Machinist	37	Private workshop	900
Brass maker (apprentice)	14	Family enterprise	44
Shoemaker (apprentice)**	12	Family enterprise	100
Worker (aluminum)	24	Family enterprise	(excl. overtime) 200
Grocer	42	Family enterprise	340
Shoemaker**	40	Family enterprise	400
Shoemaker (sewer)**	35	Family enterprise	600
Paper/box production	25	Family enterprise	700
Owner (aluminum factory)	47	Family enterprise	1,200
Private tutor (primary)	50	Self-employed	(only one group) 28
Private tutor (secondary)	38	Self-employed	(only one group 60
Wall/floor tiler	40	Self-employed	50/day
Private tutor (primary)	48	Self-employed	1,000

* Female
** Not related to owner

couples who may not have had the earnings potential, educational background, and familial and informal opportunities that the older, more established merchant community in central Cairo enjoyed (Table 4.18).

Despite a range of earnings potential, it is clear that few of the individuals in my community and the other sample from a squatter's settlement repre-

TABLE 4.19
Profile of Resident Labor Force, Squatter's Settlement
(Representative Sample 1 in 50)[a]

Job Description	Age	Sector	Monthly Earnings (1984)
Draftee	19	State, government	£E 6
Sweeper	40	State, government	60
Policeman	34	State, government	65
Railway conductor	35	State, government	120
Laborer	52	State, public sector	70
Guard	42	State, public sector	100
Laborer	40	State, public sector	143
Janitor*	32	Private employee	50
Carpet factory worker	14	Private employee	52
Bread salesperson	35	Private employee	60
Laborer	29	Private employee	102
Lathe operator	38	Private employee	130
Mechanic weaver	42	Private employee	130
Gold salesperson	14	Private employee	130
Baker	28	Private employee	156
Tile layer	22	Private employee	182
Notions salesperson*	60	Private employee	200
Plasterer	35	Private employee	234
Electrician	26	Private employee	234
Laborer	35	Private employee	250
Seamstress*	23	Self-employed	31
Laborer	35	Self-employed	94
Painter	18	Self-employed	105
Upholsterer	49	Self-employed	136
Mobile clothing vendor	22	Self-employed	182
Workshop owner (unspecified)	27	Self-employed	260
Aluminum metal works (owner)	34	Self-employed	315
Car paint shop (owner)	34	Self-employed	390
Contractor	36	Self-employed	481

* Female

[a] The data set included 1,550 cash earners from 1,118 households. The workers were sorted alphabetically and a representative subsample was taken by systematically selecting every fiftieth person. In 1984 the approximate foreign exchange value of the Egyptian pound was approximately one U.S. dollar. I have rearranged the individuals in ascending order of wages by sector. See Tekçe, Oldham, and Shorter, *A Place to Live*, chap. 3.

sent the "working poor," who are often assumed to comprise the majority of *sha'bi* neighborhoods. Abdel-Fadil has noted the recent rising economic mobility of important strata within the working class in urban Egypt:

> Some groups belonging traditionally to the informal sector managed reasonably well in recent years to improve their relative share in the earnings' structure

15. This father and daughter relax in their new apartment,
which this young man had purchased in one of the few recently
constructed "skyscrapers" located in a densely populated
neighborhood. Their expensive, gilded wood furniture
(labeled Louis Faruq by Egyptians) is a sign of the new wealth
that has come to many skilled artisans or *Harafiyyiin*.
This particular very industrious young man owns a successful
factory that produces brass tacks used to upholster furniture
(and visible here in his chairs).

within urban Egypt. This particularly applies, with some force, to almost all
types of independent artisans and craftsmen. . . . The same holds true for a large
section of people performing personal services such as cooks and waiters, those
undertaking washing and ironing, and hairdressers. Thus, it is our judgment
that people belonging to these groups no longer qualify, at least for the time
being, as members of the "working poor" section of the urban population.[94]

In Abdel-Fadil's estimation of the "working poor," which employs the same occupational system of classification, the following five occupational groups comprised the working poor: "odd-jobbers," petty traders and retailers, people performing various domestic services to families and individuals, operators of traditional means of transport and porters, and other unclassified informal services. According to his calculations, based upon national census data, the total number of people in this type of employment equaled 380,000 in 1976. He suggested that if "each breadwinner supports three people, on average, then the number of people whose livelihood depends in a major way on the employment status and earnings possibilities of the working poor belonging to the urban informal sector can be put at 1.14 million people."[95]

A calculation of the "working poor" in my economically active sample, using Abdel-Fadil's method of equating a certain occupational status with poverty, identifies only fifteen people (primary economic activity, male: 8; female: 7) and twenty-nine people (secondary economic activity, male: 17; female: 12) as part of the working poor.[96] After I examined the economic circumstances of each of these men and women, I found that very few of them were actually poor and that some were solidly middle and even upper middle class.[97] Among the fifteen men and women employed in the informal sector as a primary economic activity, six were part of the working poor, four were lower middle class, and three were quite well off from solidly middle-class merchant families (one of the three was a successful drug dealer who had prospered in the hashish trade). Among the twenty-nine people employed in the informal sector as a secondary economic activity, seven were poor, eighteen were lower middle class, and four were middle to upper middle class. Accepting my assessment of each individual case (based on my knowledge of each particular economic situation) leaves only 7 percent of the economically active sample in primary informal-sector employment and 6 percent of the sample in secondary informal-sector employment among the working poor. The very low incidence of poverty within this sample reflects the rising economic mobility and wage levels of certain segments of the working class, particularly since the mid-1970s (the time period of Abdel-Fadil's study). A study of the informal sector by CAPMAS in 1985 found that about 75 percent of workers in the informal sector drew a salary above minimum-wage level. Some 30 percent of the sample earned between £E3 and £E5 daily; 20 percent earned between £E5 and £E7 daily; 6.5 percent between £E7 and £E10; and 3 percent drew a daily salary above £E10.[98] As Rizk argues in a study of recent research on the informal sector in Egypt, "Polemics surrounding such concepts as 'wages of the poor', 'survival', 'marginality' and the like tend to distort the more positive picture provided by research in Egypt."[99]

Wages are certainly not the only source of wealth and financial resources in this community due to the high incidence of secondary and tertiary

TABLE 4.20

A Summary of Total "Quantifiable" Black Economy Transactions for the Year 1980 in Egypt (in millions of Egyptian pounds)[a]

Transactions and Activities	Value
A. Black money income accruing to factors of production	
Labor income	
Moonlighting earnings	514.4
Employee theft (seized)	0.2
Business profits accruing to capital	
Amount of tax evasion on business profits	250.0
Gross trading profits from hashish	128.0
B. Institutions' current account (household sector and private companies)	
Speculative profits from real estate	328.8
Evaded customs duties on smuggled goods (Port Said)	109.0
Commissions on real estate dealings	33.0
Brokerage from foreign exchange dealings	14.4
C. Consolidated capital account	
Informal housing construction	260.0
D. Commodities account	
Volume of smuggling of goods out of Port Said	177.5
Volume of transacted "hashish" at wholesale price	254.5
E. *Total volume of "quantifiable" black money transacted in the economy of 1980*	£E2,069.8

[a] The Central Bank's official exchange rate in 1980 was £E0.70 = $1. Thus the funds circulating in the black economy would equal approximately $3 billion (£E2069.8 billion = $2.96 billion). See "Egypt," *Country Profile Reports*, pp. 8–9.

economic activities. In addition, although the methodology employed in this research did capture some additional sources of income, other sources remained unknown since some people did not call attention to their illegal activities or the extent of their wealth (there is also a superstitious reluctance among the *sha'b* to publicize good fortune and tempt fate). In particular, while some people in this community were known drug dealers and black marketers, incidental income from bribes or occasional illegal and legal activities was underestimated in my analysis.

In a fascinating study of the "black" or underground economy in Egypt, Abdel-Fadil and Diab made the following estimate of its assets, all of which remain outside the extractive and regulatory capacity of the state (see Table 4.20 above). They emphasize that these figures underestimate the extent of the underground economy because of their conservative interpretation of available data and the exclusion of many activities that could not be quantified due to a lack of data.[100] In 1980 the official GNP of Egypt was estimated to be £E17.5 billion. According to Abdel-Fadil and Diab's calculations, the quantifiable black economy in Egypt constituted 12 percent of GNP that year. Moreover, they suggest that a more realistic estimate of "the total volume of the black economy transactions in 1980 ranges between 15 percent to 30 percent of the *official* (i.e., *recorded*) GNP in Egypt."[101]

A more recent analysis estimated that the hidden economy had grown in size to approximately $8–10 billion in 1988, representing one-third of reported GNP for that year. As components of the hidden economy this report identified: illegal labor remittances, a larger drug trade ($2–4 billion per year), the growing unrecorded economic activities undertaken by the military, including real estate speculation, importing of goods, food production, smuggling of foods through free zones ($1–2 billion), unreported and unrecorded trade with Israel through the free zones ($65 million, also controlled by the military), unreported and unregulated deposits at Islamic investment companies (estimated at $7 billion), and unlicensed housing speculation, construction, and improvement.[102] Precise estimates of the informal economy remain very difficult to construct. In his conclusion Roy argues that the hidden economy of Egypt in 1988 had risen, at a minimum, to 35 percent of recorded GNP and guessed it was closer to 45–55 percent of GNP.[103] In another study, based on a questionnaire for a stratified sample of five hundred households in Egypt in December 1988, Oweiss defined the informal economy as that "which encompasses all economic activities unknown to established authorities—or unadmitted by them even if known—and all incomes generated thereof but not reported to the government and not included in the country's national income accounts."[104] Calculating Egypt's total savings from a variety of sources, Oweiss argued that Egypt's informal economy reached a minimum of £E50 billion and that if one included the informal economy as part of Egypt's national income, it was in fact double its official size.[105] Since I am not an economist, I have very little expertise in evaluating the accuracy or methodologies of these studies. However, various estimates of the informal economy from national accounts data along with the conclusions of various microstudies, including my own, offer convincing proof that the informal economy comprises an increasingly important and significant component of the Egyptian economy.

The growth of the informal economy in *sha'bi* areas during the past fifteen years was confirmed by individuals in the economically active sample, particularly since the proclamation of the Open Door policy in 1974. One young man, whose father owned an older manufacturing establishment, pointed to eight workshops in one very small alleyway that were all established by successful workers in the past ten years. Before 1974 his father had owned the sole workshop in the alley.

In a detailed survey of manufacturing enterprises in another *sha'bi* neighborhood, and during the same time period, Meyer found that two-thirds of the manufacturing enterprises had been founded since 1980 and about 40 percent had been established between 1984 and 1986.[106] Another worker supported these figures by recounting that one rich, powerful merchant had previously produced most of the aluminum cookware and household items that were now produced in hundreds of smaller workshops in the neighbor-

hood and in other areas of Cairo. Stauth's study of the aluminum-manufac-
tures industry found two hundred aluminum workshops in the district of
Gamaliyya, one of the oldest central areas of Cairo, confirming the account
of the young worker above.[107] The informal sector is clearly a pervasive and
valuable component of *sha'bi* communities.

INFORMALITY: THE ECONOMIC AND POLITICAL
CONSEQUENCES FOR THE NATION

Some economists argue that a pattern of economic entrepreneurship in the
informal sector, while offering opportunities to some segments of the labor
force, lowers the scale of wages and the cost of subsistence for the general
labor force:

> The low levels of employment and limited opportunities in the formal sector
> have forced a sizable section of the adult urban population to find some means
> of livelihood (legal or illegal) outside the formal employment structure. The
> employment problem of the bulk of the urban poor, who are not integrated in
> the formal employment structure, is not that they are unemployed per se, but
> that they are engaged, for short or long hours, in low-productivity jobs at wage
> or income levels far below what is necessary to provide them and their depen-
> dents with a minimum standard of living.[108]

The high (and low) wages of the informal sector, whether among men or
women, are said to be based on self-exploitation. The production of goods
and services in the informal economy, often remunerated in kind not cash,
lowers the cost of subsistence for the working class ("relative to what they
would be in a fully monetized market economy") and thus decreases the
wage levels needed to sustain the working population.[109] In the past, however, lower subsistence costs not only held down the survival threshold of a
petty trader or a skilled worker but also lowered the cost of hiring a domestic,
a guard, or a plumber for a middle-class or upper-middle-class family. As wage
levels for these workers have increased, those higher in the economic hierarchy have had to do without, or hire alternative sources of cheap labor.[110]

One of the distinctive features of the recent economic situation in Egypt,
as demonstrated in Tables 4.18 and 4.19, is that wages in the informal sector
have been generally higher than in the formal sector (this is particularly true
of certain occupations in certain industries). While some typical activities in
the informal sector—such as petty trading and marketing or some lower-
skilled services of the self-employed—may offer far less job security, protection, and benefits, other occupations and activities have been very lucrative.

The assumed lower wage levels of the informal sector are explained as a
structural necessity of many developing countries. Keeping labor costs and
benefits for the informal sector low allows resources to be channeled to
higher wages and expensive benefits for formal-sector employees (particularly benefits to organized labor in state-sponsored corporatist unions). The

formal and informal sectors exist side by side, but the wages, capitalization, and conditions of each sector are dependent upon the other. In Egypt the urban middle class that staffed the bureaucracy—the "new middle class" of the 1960s—had been the beneficiary of the economic franchise while rural agricultural workers, rural migrants to the cities, and the urban working class subsidized the cost of the franchise.[111]

The following analysis by Portes and Walton presents the argument more systematically and generally.

> The class structure of peripheral urban economies can be described in terms of four broad categories:
>
> > 1. Domestic and foreign capital owners, senior executives, and state managers;
> > 2. Salaried professionals and technicians in public and private employment;
> > 3. Clerical and manual wage labor in public enterprises and private industry and services;
> > 4. Casual wage labor, disguised wage labor, and self-employment in petty production and trade.
>
> The first three classes comprise the formal sector. The interests of the first class are, however, structurally opposite to those of the other two. . . . Depending on the specific situation, the relationship between the urban classes is one in which Class 1—the owners—uses Class 4 against the intermediate classes, or one in which Class 1 allows Classes 2 and 3 to exploit Class 4, thereby cheapening their costs of reproduction and reducing upward pressures on wages. In whatever version, the fundamental point is that the informal sector subsidizes part of the costs of formal capitalist enterprises, enabling them to enforce comparatively low wages on their own labor.[112]

Applying Portes and Walton's analysis to Egypt would suggest that Class 1 has used Class 4 to weaken the economic and political power of the intermediate classes and to decrease government expenditure on public salaries and benefits. However, in Egypt class identities are complicated because men and women from *sha'bi* and even middle-class communities may be salaried professionals in the private and public sector and work as an artisan or trader as a second occupation.

However, certain consequences of the Open Door policy and economic liberalization in the past decade would support Portes and Walton's scenario in Egypt. The government invited multinational corporations to attract direct foreign investment and create joint ventures with private and public firms in Egypt. Under Law No. 43 for Arab and Foreign Investment (1974), the government exempted new factories set up by joint venture capital from government labor legislation, which provided certain benefits to workers (job security, minimum wages, representation on management boards, pension and health care benefits, and so forth). At the same time, the public sector has been under the threat of privatization and under attack on many economic and political fronts. Through many indirect and direct policies, the government has attempted to decrease the numbers of employees on the large public payroll, particularly in the civil service.

Whether or not policymakers intentionally sought economic liberalization as a means of weakening the public sector, the unintended consequences of domestic and international forces have created an increasingly dynamic and resourceful working class tied to private interests. The financial resources of this upwardly mobile group (which is only one part of this class), as well as their political ambitions, present a possible challenge to the Egyptian regime, which has traditionally valued tight control of both the polity and the economy.

This chapter began with a discussion of the informal economy and the original concerns motivating this research paradigm. To reiterate, Hart questioned whether "the 'reserve army of urban unemployed and underemployed' really constitute a passive, exploited majority in cities like Accra, or do their informal economic activities possess some autonomous capacity for generating growth in the incomes of the urban (and rural) poor?"[113] He and others were obviously concerned with the informal sector's capacity for generating economic growth and resources for the urban poor. The data presented in the economically active population sample of one *sha'bi* community suggest that a sizable proportion of this population has indeed grown wealthier and experienced upward economic and social mobility.[114]

The political consequences of this mobility for the *sha'b*, and for the nation, can perhaps be understood by substituting the following italicized words into Hart's original question: "Does the 'reserve army of urban unemployed and underemployed' really constitute a passive, exploited majority in cities like *Cairo*, or do their informal economic activities possess some autonomous capacity for increasing *political* power?" The evidence provided above suggests that perhaps the intentions of the elite in Egypt have backfired by facilitating the accumulation of economic resources within *sha'bi* communities, which are now in a stronger position to channel their resources into organized collective political activity.

The most typical, alarmist warnings about this empowered political community in Egypt discuss the support among the *sha'b* for various Islamic organizations and activists. For example, an analysis of the hidden economy concerned with the U.S.-Egyptian alliance warns:

> The pro-Nasserists and the Islamic fundamentalists are also well aware of the long-term political stakes involved in the economic changes that have occurred thus far and will continue to occur in the future. As described, these interests— particularly the fundamentalists—have quickly learned how to tap into the hidden economy to generate the resources needed to sustain their political efforts. Indeed, this is also true of the military."[115]

The growth of a wider range of political interests in Egypt, which are supported by a larger segment of the population, presents a tacit challenge to any regime that values control.

With the decreasing strength of the political center, it is not clear that anyone is 'in charge' and this, increasingly, is the complaint one hears about the Mubarak regime. The hidden economy, the purest form of free-market enterprise that Egypt has, is, politically, neutral. It is an arena in which anyone, of whatever political persuasion, can operate. It is also composed of markets in which a well-organized political group can 'corner' activities and thus be able to exert strong influence over future political directions.[116]

However, if one is concerned with greater diversity, pluralism, and opportunities for a citizenry to influence national and local decision-making, rather than political stability, one should not worry about the National Democratic Party losing control to popular organizations. Amin points out that writers on both the right and left of the political spectrum have, for different reasons, been reluctant to recognize the improved standing of the lower classes and the related decline in the economic and social standing of the middle and professional classes.[117] While his optimistic analysis of this phenomenon in Egypt may be premature, he raises certain psychological and cultural issues that also surround these class tensions but have not been so candidly discussed by others.

> While there is much to lament in the impact of rapid social mobility on Egypt's economic and social life it is possible to see some important reasons for optimism with regard to its ultimate impact on the future economic development of Egypt. So many of the psychological ills that have often been the subject of complaint in the past and which seemed to constitute difficult obstacles in the way toward economic development may very well have been merely the psychological traits of the upper classes which are now in decline. In contrast, the newly rising classes seem to possess exactly the opposite psychological traits which could prove highly valuable for the future economic reconstruction of Egypt. These rising classes seem to possess a degree of vitality, energy and perseverance which the traditionally upper classes seem to have lacked. They are far more ambitious, less sentimental and often ruthless. In spite of their apparently strong adherence to tradition they are really far less fatalistic in outlook and much more confident in what they can achieve through their own efforts. They would spare nothing for the economic advancement of their children while, for the same reason, they may be much more willing to practice birth control than the traditionally poor or the old upper classes. They are much more conscious of the value of time, have more respect for manual labor and much greater admiration for modern technology. Though much of their new wealth and social advancement has been built on breaking the law, their success in maintaining their new social position may depend on greater discipline and stricter observance of rules. While their rapid advance may have largely been due to a period of 'growth without development,' they may well prove to be the builders of a new era of genuine economic progress.[118]

The informal economy was examined in this chapter not as an end in itself, but to demonstrate the links between informal political and economic activity within this community. While I have suggested earlier that informal networks furthered the economic and political objectives of the community, the wealth and rising social and economic mobility of the *sha'b* may provide the financial resources for avenues of political participation in the future. The informal economy is not an autonomous sphere of Egyptian society but a creation of it. It has its roots in the particular characteristics of Egypt's political and social structure, its mixed economy, and its international alliances. It is a reaction to the planned and unplanned policies of the government and various economic interests in Egypt. While this chapter has concentrated on the economic manifestations of informality, I can only emphasize again that this phenomenon must be seen in the context of the structural constraints and political history of the nation. The state in Egypt still owns a considerable amount of property in Egypt, it employs huge numbers of the population, and it is responsible for a significant proportion of industrial production, services, and even trade. The political interests of the regime, varied and contradictory though they may be, must support its economic position. Thus, the growth of the informal economy, with quite different characteristics and interests, erodes the state's economic dominance and control of the larger political economy of the nation.

Though Hart raised the question of the informal economy vis-à-vis employment and growth in developing countries, scholars and dissidents in Eastern Europe generated a similar debate about the "second economy" over the past few decades and its role, more recently, in the demise of socialist economies. Scholars were not only describing an empirical phenomenon of hidden economic transactions, illegal trade, and smuggling but were also arguing that a second economy itself was a means of resistance to the state. Hankiss argues that the second economy has the following characteristics: (1) it is the sum total of the economic activities outside the state sector; it is only loosely integrated into it; (2) it is not planned and organized by the state; (3) it is only partially affected by the formal systems of regulation that govern and control the first economy; (4) it is not linked to the dominant form of ownership, that is, to state ownership; (5) it is not linked to the dominant form of management, that is, to large enterprises; it is centered in small-scale cooperative enterprises, mainly family enterprises; (6) less affected by hierarchical structures of the country, [it] lies outside investment policy of the state, complementary and auxiliary character to the national economy; (7) it is an 'invisible" or less visible economy producing incomes that cannot be, or are only partially, registered by the tax office; (8) On the continuum from political-ideological acceptance (legitimacy) to rejection (illegitimacy, lack of legitimacy) it lies closer to the latter pole; its political and ideological assessment by the authorities is precarious and ambivalent.[119]

The second economy was only one component of the second society, which included a second public, a second culture, a second social consciousness, and a second sphere of sociopolitical interactions. It was an interrelated sphere of alternative interests, organized along different principles.

Where the first society is characterized by vertical organization, downward flow of power, state ownership, centralization, political dominance, saturation with the official ideology, diffuseness, visibility, and legitimacy the second society is characterized, mainly, by the absence of these characteristics, and sporadically, by the timid emergence of some opposite characteristics. And the hypothetical alternative society would be characterized by the fully developed opposite characteristics: by horizontal organization, upward flow of power, predominance of non-state ownership, autonomy of social and economic actors, differentiation cum integration, etc.[120]

Václav Havel used the term "parallel *polis*" to describe a similar world of alternative structures in Czechoslovakia, particularly the second culture of *samizdat*, illegal dissident literature that served to pressure the "posttotalitarian" system of real socialism.[121] The existence of the second economy became an ideological threat to socialist regimes whose legitimacy was based on their ownership of the means of production, their claims to social and class egalitarianism, and their pursuit of the collective good. When the second economy grew, the official economy faltered, inequality and corruption increased, and repression did not seem to work. Even elites no longer believed in the legitimacy of the government. Havel argued that these parallel structures exposed the weakness of the state and upset the power structure. He asked, in musing about the future of his country, "Are not these informal, non-bureaucratic, dynamic and open communities that comprise the 'parallel *polis*' a kind of rudimentary prefiguration, a symbolic model of those more meaningful 'post-democratic' political structures that might become the foundation of a better society?"[122]

I raise the example of Eastern Europe here, even though the economies of Egypt and Hungary or Czechoslovakia only bear passing resemblance, to return to my argument about the relationship between informal political institutions and economic phenomena. The characteristics of Hankiss's second society ("horizontal organization, upward flow of power, predominance of non-state ownership, autonomy of social and economic actors, differentiation cum integration") are to be found both in the informal economy in Egypt and within informal networks.[123] Too much of the debate about the informal economy in Egypt, however, has centered around economic issues and has failed to recognize the political dimensions of informality and the potential impact of a range of symbiotic parallel institutions on the larger polity. While the implications of this alternative sphere remain to unfold in the future, informal institutions are deeply embedded in and pervade *sha'bi* communities. Within the context of political exclusion and state intervention in the economy, these amorphous but deeply rooted institutions provide resources for the *sha'b* and serve to promote their interests in the larger polity.

Politics as Distribution

AT THE OUTSET of this work, I suggested that analyses of political participation must be located in the daily politics of ordinary men and women and take into account the institutional mechanisms that specific communities develop to fulfill their objectives. I have argued that the *sha'b* use informal economic and political networks for a variety of important needs. Regardless of the vitality and pervasiveness of informal political institutions or informal economic activities, however, the state maintains control over the distribution and allocation of many goods and services essential to the *sha'b*.

The struggle over the distribution of public goods is moderated by a constant problem in Egypt: scarcity. The government has increasing difficulties bearing the costs of redistributive policies, while the *sha'b* and Egyptians from all segments of the population insist on the need for subsidies to maintain their standard of living.[1] In 1984–85 total subsidies represented 18 percent of current public outlays and 38 percent of the gross budget deficit; food subsidies alone represented 70 percent of all direct subsidies in 1981–82 and 1982–83. In the previous chapters I have described the scenes outside food cooperatives and the elaborate strategies that people in this community carry out to gain a greater share of government goods and services. In general, subsidies and the provision of government services remain two of the most politically and economically sensitive issues in Egypt. The price of meat or tea, the availability and quality of macaroni or soap, or new requirements for obtaining ration books are issues of national concern that merit extensive coverage in the street, the media, and Parliament—as much as the formation of a new cabinet, a radical change in Egyptian foreign policy, or legislative reforms.

After the previous chapter's discussion of the economic position and resourcefulness of one *sha'bi* community, their heavy demand for slightly less expensive goods and services may seem surprising. While some families in the community were poor, many more were lower- to lower-middle class. They were able to invest thousands of pounds in a wedding trousseau, gold jewelry, or a taxicab, but might be prepared to join violent street demonstrations against the government if it raised the price of bread from five to ten piasters.

Throughout this work, it may seem that people have been depicted as overly concerned with material issues, with prices and the value of goods and services. Part of their anxiety can be explained by their precarious economic position, part can be explained by the rapidly changing economy in Egypt; but their reactions are also shaped by the state's strategy to win popular support through the provision of goods and services. People have developed a type of financial consciousness to judge and evaluate economic policy changes. By maintaining a keen awareness of what they are getting from the government, they protect their interests. Since there are few legal avenues of opposition open to them, small changes in government-controlled prices or reductions in services can ignite direct, illegal opposition to the state.

The notion of a "social contract" is implicit in the government's relationship to its citizens. Official plans and legislation, emanating from various leaders and ministries in Egypt, embody the principles of this contract. For example:

> The Egyptian Five-Year Plan (1978–1982) summarized the Government's existing duties toward the people as being: (1) to guarantee unconditional employment and earnings to all; (2) to provide social welfare through housing, health, education, and other services; (3) to protect the consumer from the increase in the cost of living; (4) to administer all public utilities and most units of national production; and (5) to make available to the public both necessary and luxury foodstuffs, and films, at prices much lower than their actual cost to the Government.[2]

The *sha'b* understand their position in the social contract, and they perform it all too well. Remaining faithful to their role as consumers costs the government dearly. In 1979 direct consumer subsidies and payments to cover public-sector deficits amounted to nearly 13 percent of GDP, and the cost of subsidies in the 1980s had risen even higher (though it began to decline by the mid-1980s).[3] In a 1989 Labor Day speech, President Mubarak chastised Egyptians for an "incessant rise in consumerism."[4] The evils of consumerism are constantly cited by politicians, officials, and political commentators as one of the major obstacles to Egyptian economic development. Yet to blame Egyptians for exploiting the state, when they understand that the state excludes them from any influential role in formal politics, seems unfair. To be political, and remain out of danger, is to consume. To be political, and be in danger, is to participate seriously in formal politics. In essence, the state has reduced formal politics to the issue of distribution, and participation to the realm of consumption. The government maintains its commitment to providing certain basic goods and services to the *sha'b*, in return for political acquiescence. Citizens participate by consuming, and the government maintains its legitimacy through distribution.

My emphasis on political exclusion and mass consumption does not mean to ignore or minimize the importance of the limited pluralist experiments in Egypt, the growth of an opposition media and independent interest groups, or the fact that many people have dedicated their lives to activist politics. But the *sha'b* continue to engage bureaucrats, official organizations, and elite politicians in order to gain services and assistance since they are still very skeptical of their influence with the more formal, and dangerous, avenues of participation.

This chapter investigates two levels of this type of interaction between the *sha'b* and the state. Private voluntary organizations (PVOs) serve as one point of distribution for the government as well as a means of control. They are somewhat more autonomous than state institutions since they are directed by community leaders and financially supported more by private than public revenues. While PVOs must be registered by the Ministry of Social Affairs (MSA), and their programs and administration are supervised closely, they allow community leaders to offer services that are needed by the community. At the same time, they offer politicians, religious groups, or other interests a base of support in the community, which is not as threatening to the government as a "political" organization. While many PVOs are completely apolitical charitable organizations, they frequently have complex relationships with powerful figures and institutions in the community or the nation.

Elite politicians and officials serve as another point of distribution within *sha'bi* communities. Politicians provide many services to their constituents, in return for local support at election time. Through politicians, various government agencies channel resources to individuals and organizations. A base of support in the community, through PVOs, networks, or individuals, allows politicians to keep informed about potential problems, which they strive to contain before any conflict erupts in the community. As we will see in my community, the *sha'b* judge politicians or officials by their capacity to help people, and to provide services or intervene on their behalf with the bureaucracy, far more than by their ideological positions or party affiliations.

Finally, reducing political participation to consumption seems to have had a more negative effect on the political process itself in Egypt than on the *sha'b*. They have developed alternative means to achieve certain goals, yet the government is constrained and entangled by its distributive role. For domestic stability, it must maintain its end of the bargain and maintain its distributive role or citizens will have little reason to maintain their part of the bargain. If the international economy experiences a recession, tax revenues fall off, or economic growth slows, the government is forced to continue its dependence on foreign aid, loans, tourism, and insecure labor remittances from abroad. Such dependency only makes the economy more vulnerable to external shocks and to internal unrest, which may scare off tourists, international capital, and foreign aid. Since the mid-1980s the government has been decreasing its public subsidies and services and privatizing more of the economy, yet it has largely left in place a political system that has become even more repressive and polarized. As the saying goes, the government increasingly finds itself between a rock and a hard place.

Private Voluntary Organizations:
A Mediated Distribution Point

The purpose of this section is not to analyze the important and varied history of PVOs in Egypt, but to suggest that the PVO is as an important distribution point of public goods, which are produced by the joint contribution of the community and the state. For its part, the government views PVOs as a vehicle to distribute basic goods and services at the communal level. By closely supervising and/or financing a PVO, the government maintains tighter control over organizational life in the community and can promote activities which further its priorities. At the same time, the government can benefit from a PVO's relationship with local community figures who have a wider set of networks within the community and a sensitivity toward popular needs and complaints. It directs resources to organizations that can mollify problems in communities, whether a challenge evolves out of pent-up frustrations among young people, or a lack of day-care centers or apartments. Since PVOs can also function as a base of support for politicians, political parties, or religious associations, the government's relationship to them can be delicate and politicized. Delving slightly into the internal administration and programs of any PVO in a *sha'bi* community reveals a set of complex and interdependent alliances among a variety of private and public organizations and public and community figures.

These organizations are not usually established by the government, but evolve out of the efforts and contributions of local figures and organizations. While some PVOs receive limited government subsidies to finance their activities, the government assumes far less responsibility for the daily administration of the organization, which is typically managed by a private board of directors. PVOs, particularly organizations dedicated to serving an undefined constituency (as opposed to professional, labor, religious, or regional organizations that serve a specific membership), are often founded by prominent members of the community. According to one analysis of the funding sources of PVOs in Cairo, by a foreign funding agency, private cash donations are the "single largest source of PVO income."[5] These private donations are an essential source of revenue for many PVOs since governmental support is inconsistent and oversubscribed. For example, in fiscal year 1982, 61 percent of all community-oriented PVOs in Cairo received *no* government subsidies.[6] Despite the supervisory, regulatory, and financial role of the state, many organizations maintain some independence through their local supporters and private financial sources.

The evidence for this section is largely drawn from the daily experiences of men and women in my community. Many of the people I knew worked for one particular private voluntary organization in the community. Thus I became quite familiar with its daily services, administration, and some of its problems. By spending many hours sitting with workers in this organization, I eventually met various officials and workers in the government or other organizations who had some relationship to "our" organization. My account of this PVO's activities and its relationship to the community is limited by what I witnessed, asked questions about, and overheard during the normal course of events during almost daily visits.

This particular PVO offered a variety of services to the community including day-care services (from forty-day-old babies to five-year-old children), vocational training, a birth control program, charity to the poor, and literacy classes. A seemingly routine dispute, which grew into an embarrassing incident, demonstrates some of the political undercurrents surrounding the organization.[7] One of the five children of two state employees had developed symptoms of chicken pox, and the day-care center's doctor, who inspected the children regularly, sent the child home for a two-week period. After a few days, the mother returned to the day-care center to beg them to readmit him, since his symptoms had disappeared. She had already been forced to miss several days of work, and her superiors were beginning to complain. The administrators responded that other children would be at risk by his presence, and they chastised her for questioning the doctor. They also implied that she should be more concerned for her son, and that if the job conflicted with his care, she should quit it.

After the fairly rude and condescending attitude she encountered at the center, the mother returned the next day with her husband. An argument soon broke out, and before long the very proper, middle-aged secretary and the woman were fighting each other. The police were called, and both women were taken to jail and held for a few hours in a holding cell until their release. The following day, as the PVO buzzed with rumors about the incident, the staff was instructed by administrators not to gossip or speak to the officials from the prosecutor's office who had come to investigate it. Within a few days the father of the boy returned, complaining that they would not let his older children remain in another day-care center of the PVO. He asked the administrator of this day-care center to sign a letter stating that she had officially refused his children admittance. She refused to sign it or to accept the letter and, although sympathetic, suggested he place his children in another nearby facility.

The father then traveled to the home of the member of Parliament (MP) from his district, who lived in a wealthier neighborhood, since he was also the chair of the board of the PVO. The MP chided him, saying that he should have never let the situation escalate to the point of a public brawl and should have confided in him much earlier so that they could have resolved the problem without involving the authorities. It was a simple affair that had been blown out of proportion.

The staff of the PVO began to wonder why this family had so tenaciously and aggressively pursued this incident. Soon they developed a theory that the father of the child was a supporter of another politician who had lost the previous election to the head of this PVO. Involving the police and the prosecutor's office in the conflict damaged the reputation of the organization and its founder. Since the MP himself represented an opposition political party, he worried that the government would manipulate the court case to embarrass or discredit him or perhaps even force the closure of the PVO. While the father's alleged political loyalty to another party may have explained part of his motivation, his wife had been treated rather dismissively and condescendingly by the organization's employees. The real facts never came out, since the case was dropped and the incident soon forgotten.

Because of the local MP's involvement in this organization, it served as one of his unofficial district offices. Very frequently, members of the community would visit the PVO to arrange meetings with the MP. The PVO's staff, trained in bureaucratic maneuvering through years of experience with the MP, were also sought out for their experience in solving bureaucratic problems and local disputes. However, the services the PVO provided to the community were equally important and as valued as the access to the MP, which the PVO facilitated.

The day-care centers fulfilled an important need in the community, especially as more and more women within *sha'bi* communities have joined the labor force (the day-care center was open from 8:00 A.M. to 3:00 P.M., and some working mothers would leave their children with the cooks and janitors of the centers, who arrived at 6:30 A.M.). Other mothers, particularly those with large families and small apartments who did not work outside the home, felt that the center offered better facilities for their children than their cramped apartments or the dangerous and busy streets. Still other mothers believed the day-care center would help acclimate their children to the school system and minimize adjustment problems in primary school. Some parents hoped their children would gain a head start in their education by attending day care at an early age.[8] Besides the initial membership fee in the PVO, parents paid £E1.5 per month for each child and were also required to purchase a school uniform (which a different program within the organization produced at low cost). The fees were among the lowest in the area and much less expensive than private day-care centers.

At election time, the MP could point to the organization he had founded as evidence of his concern for the welfare of his constituents, particularly women, children, and the family. People appreciated the services of the PVO, and the MP seemed to be known to many people in the community and generally well-regarded for his efforts. He used his status and power to intercede at higher levels of the bureaucracy to procure additional support for the PVO from the Egyptian government and international agencies. The PVO had received grants in cash and kind from various foreign organizations and governments for many years, due to the reputation and connections of this politician and other supporters of the PVO from outside the immediate community.

The furniture, toys, and vocational training equipment the organization received were carefully guarded and protected by the administrative staff. In fact, most of toys received from U.S. agencies remained unused because the teachers were afraid they would be blamed if the toys were damaged by the children.[9] In addition, there were certainly not enough toys for the 240 children in two classrooms who were supervised by only four teachers (the legal student/teacher ratio was thirty-five to one).

Despite the persistent efforts of local community leaders and the intentions of the government, issues of scarcity plagued PVOs in *sha'bi* neighborhoods, and the demand for popular services routinely outstripped the supply. In this day-care center, for example, rather than turn people away, the administrators accepted more children, overcrowding classes even more. Extremely low salaries prevailed, thereby discouraging the staff's commitment to the PVO. Most employees in PVOs were paid the minimum wage (approximately £E30 per month in 1986), and blue-collar workers routinely earned less. Vocational instructors in this organization earned £E31 per month while an instructor with fifteen years' seniority earned £E49. Some of the staff traveled from relatively distant neighborhoods, spending an hour on the commute and at least 75 piasters per day in travel costs (100 piasters equal one Egyptian pound). An administrator who supervised two day-care centers, a literacy program, vocational training, and a staff of young women fulfilling their public service obligations earned only £E59 per month. These salaries were even lower than the lowest-paid ranks of the civil service. Thus most of the instructors did not feel compelled to invest great energy or initiative in the organization or their responsibilities.

The issue of low salaries plagued the development of the organization and its provision of services to the community. For example, when a member of its board of the directors discovered a potential funding source, she submitted a very general funding request on the PVO's behalf. After receiving the grant application, the local administrator of a Canadian funding agency visited the PVO to decide if the project met the agency's priorities for vocational self-help projects. Concerned as well with community involvement in the project, she asked the teachers what they thought of the proposal. They had never seen the proposal nor been involved in the project's design, which asked for funds to purchase sewing machines and other equipment for a vocational training program. When an interested response was not quite forthcoming from the staff, the Canadian administrator tried to explain the project further and told them that her agency would purchase several sewing machines and knitting machines for the PVO, and these could then be rented to local residents for a modest fee. Local women could make their own clothes or sell their products in the neighborhood to earn cash.

The employees were not at all enthusiastic about this new project for several reasons. First, they feared that heavy use of the machines would damage them and that the staff would be responsible for the damage and repair costs.[10] Second, they realized that such a program would create much more work for them since many more people would use the center's facilities and the program would need greater supervision. The funding agency's concept of a self-supporting, self-help program did not include a provision for higher salaries. Despite the initial willingness of the Canadian agency to fund the project, the staff's muted response to her suggestions made her suspicious of their commitment to such a project. She was right, since they would not support a program that would only increase their responsibilities, without compensating them more.

At the annual membership meeting (required by the rules of the MSA), the attending members of the cooperative (who were all its employees) aired their complaints about low salaries and low holiday bonuses to the chair of the board and the most senior administrator. Since these complaints were expected, and voiced almost daily, they quickly changed the subject to the fees charged for day care. The debate revolved around whether higher fees should be instituted to finance soft drinks for the children twice a week and the composition of school lunches. Higher fees were objected to by the staff, who argued that some members of the community could not afford them. The chair of the PVO, who was also the MP, used the meeting to complain that the staff was becoming lazy, sleeping most of the day at their desks, and that fewer people were using the center because of the condescending attitude of members of the staff when people came to inquire about its activities. The staff of the organization were somewhat scornful of the criticism, pointing out that if the chair wanted them to work harder and to develop a better "attitude" then he should pay them decent salaries.

While the administrator of the day-care centers acted imperiously at times with her staff (even though they earned similar salaries and came from very similar socioeconomic backgrounds), the organization itself was carefully supervised and inspected by bureaucrats from the MSA (the literacy classes were supervised more loosely by the Ministry of Education). The MSA would notify the center of changes in regulations or policies, which the PVO would have to implement, however trivial. Although the MSA contributed only £E1,500 out of a yearly operating budget of £E14,000, it regulated many aspects of the center's program—from such matters as its operating hours to the price of the sweaters and dresses produced in the vocational training program and sold at a semiannual fair organized by the Ministry (the MSA often sold the products of many of the projects it funded). An inspector (*mufattisha*) from the MSA visited the center to inspect all the clothes produced by the center that were to be sold at the MSA fair and debated with the staff about appropriate prices. She told them that the Minister of Social Affairs herself wanted to see samples of their production and an estimate of the amount of clothes they would send to the fair. The inspector explained that President Mubarak would visit the fair and thus the Minister was particularly involved in its preparation. Whether or not the Minister of Social Affairs personally inspected their samples was impossible to know, but the extent of this type of personal and close supervision was surprising. The inspector may have used the Minister and the President's involvement merely to spur on the employees of the PVO, but she seemed genuinely concerned over the fair's success.

Certain programs at the center fulfilled the MSA's priorities, rather than the community's. For example, university graduates were assigned to PVOs through the Ministry to fulfill their public service obligation. The MSA generally used these young people (largely women since most men are conscripted into the armed forces to fulfill their public service obligation) to staff literacy and other programs in PVOs. However, for unknown reasons, one year the MSA changed the responsibilities of the young women from leading literacy classes at "our" PVO to mastering sewing skills, not to train other women but merely so that these university graduates would know how to sew.[11] At the conclusion of a short training program, the women would have to pass an examination proving their skills. For the remainder of their service they would be expected to produce items to sell at an annual fair sponsored by the MSA. The young women felt this program contradicted the supposed goal of service to the community. The staff at the center were expected by the Ministry to teach the young women to sew, but they objected to this arrangement since they were not to be paid more for their effort. Before, the center had merely provided space for literacy classes, which the public service girls staffed. The matter was eventually resolved between the Ministry and the center, and the young women were forced to learn to sew.

The involvement of various government agencies and other private organizations in PVOs is not rare. In order to increase its services and popularity in a community, a PVO, sometimes in collaboration with a government agency, will purposely tie various programs to each other. For example, one national family-planning organization administered very inexpensive health clinics for mothers and children who had joined their family-planning program. At its pharmacy women were able to purchase inexpensive medicine and powdered milk for their infants. The center also offered day-care facilities for its patients and an experimental program designed to educate women about the medical complications from female circumcision. Each service of the organization attracted women for different reasons. Once involved in one program, the organization benefited from a larger target population for some of its other programs. A similar strategy was used by the PVO described earlier to encourage women who sent their children to the day-care center to visit the birth control clinic that the organization had established. The staff of the day-care center publicized the program and encouraged the mothers to enroll. As an incentive, the secretary of the day-care center received a one-pound bonus for every new mother who registered at the birth control clinic.

PVOs affiliated with Muslim and Christian organizations offer a variety of popular services in densely populated neighborhoods to maintain a highly visible and prominent presence.[12] Recently, well-funded Islamic associations, situated within large mosque complexes, have provided many *sha'bi* and even middle-class communities with health care clinics (staffed by well-trained doctors who are paid for their services by the mosque association, not by clients), pharmacies, private tutoring for school children, youth groups, sports programs, halls for public occasions such as weddings and funerals, and vocational programs.[13] Some of the financial resources for these programs are collected through a *lagnit iz-zakaah*, a committee established by mosque leaders to distribute *iz-zakaah*, the Islamic alms tax, the payment of which to the poor is one of the five religious obligations for all Muslims. On certain occasions these committees distribute shoes, clothes, fabric, food, and money, including emergency financial assistance to the poor.[14] Many of these Islamic PVOs are well funded and rival the services and capacities of state institutions and older PVOs.

Within my community several students benefited from private tutoring organized by local mosque associations. In times of crisis, religious organizations also provided emergency aid to families. For example, when one young teenager lost his legs in a train accident, the local branch of an Islamic bank contributed several hundred pounds for the cost of his medical care. The *lagnit iz-zakaah* of the bank issued a check for £E300 in the name of Wafaa' w-'amal, the national organization for disabled children in Egypt which was treating the young man.[15] Another woman in the community was employed by a mosque association to teach sewing skills to local women in a vocational training program.

Because these organizations act as points of distribution for public goods and services, they often serve wide constituencies and are therefore used by some interests as a base of support, loyalty, and recruitment. Since these densely populated communities are in great need of many social welfare services, organizations sponsor PVOs to demonstrate their concern for a community's welfare. For example, a group of medical doctors who had been politically active during their university careers joined together to establish a hospital in a newly settled, densely populated *sha'bi* neighborhood, which had few health services. The doctors invested part of their savings from lucrative jobs in Saudi Arabia and Kuwait to finance the construction and equipment of the four-story hospital.[16] One of the founders of the hospital had unsuccessfully run for Parliament several times, as the local representative of a leftist opposition party. Hoping to increase his popularity and broaden his constituency, the hospital provided proof of his commitment to social welfare goals and the neighborhood. At the same time, the hospital offered many doctors an opportunity to contribute their time and training to a poor community in a facility that they also managed. Many of these doctors were affiliated with prominent hospitals and also maintained private practices. Thus, as the former young radicals aged, the hospital provided a means to maintain their political commitment when few of them as established doctors could afford to maintain an active, time-consuming, and potentially dangerous role in opposition politics.

Recently, as opposition to the government has emanated from religious groups (both Muslim and Christian), the government has supervised the activities of religious PVOs more carefully than other types of organizations. However, most PVOs, whether religious or secular, can only operate in the present political and economic environment through support from the community and the patronage and acquiescence of political elites.[17] The high degree of government control and supervision of any organized association, whether it provides completely innocuous health care or operates as a front for recruiting supporters for clandestine opposition political groups, necessitates that the leaders of the PVO maintain amicable relations with various bureaucracies and political leaders. Even if a group has the financial resources to establish an organization that provides needed services, it must still first obtain various government clearances. Thus, it is not surprising that the history of even a very modest PVO in a *sha'bi* neighborhood is extremely complex and involves elaborate networks of vertical and horizontal linkages.

The political and bureaucratic challenges of administering PVOs can also overcome people with extremely high connections and financial resources, even if their goals are seemingly nonconfrontational and straightforward. Some of the PVOs in my community were supported financially and administratively (through membership on the board of directors) by prominent and wealthy individuals. Some of these people originally resided in the community, and others joined the board for a variety of motives (social welfare concerns, an interest in maintaining the community's culture and historical character, and so on). It was not unusual for some of these upper-class men and women to be very active in many charitable organizations throughout Egypt.[18]

At a gathering at a PVO located in a *sha'bi* community, an upper-class Egyptian woman involved in many associations told of her frustrating efforts to increase popular interest in preserving public gardens and land in Cairo. As a member of another organization whose members were primarily elite women, she had suggested that they hold an upcoming fund-raising event in a beautiful public garden and arrange activities for the whole family. They were able to rent the garden from the government for one day at a cost of only £E70. This woman hoped to raise the environmental consciousness of her fellow members so that they would sponsor a campaign to protect public gardens (the issue was topical because of several recent scandals over the plans of construction firms to destroy old gardens and replace them with skyscrapers). Once people arrived at the fund-raiser, they were struck by the garden's beauty, and the organization was able to raise £E5,000 in one day from the guests for a preservation committee for the garden. Some people who attended, however, remarked that the public should be kept out of such places since they would only destroy them.

After the event, she and others in the organization wrote very solicitous and nonconfrontational letters to various public officials, asking how they could best help the government to maintain its gardens. Unfortunately, after winning the financial support of her association, and cultivating important relationships with relevant bureaucrats, the woman learned that responsibility for the public gardens had been transferred to another Ministry. As she told her sympathetic friends at the PVO in the *sha'bi* neighborhood (who often faced these types of bureaucratic nightmares when they tried to help local residents obtain their rights to a pension, housing, or social security), she felt that their previous efforts were wasted and that they would have to begin again with an entirely new set of bureaucrats.

Within *sha'bi* communities, PVOs represent another point of distribution for government goods and services as well as for private resources contributed by the community. These associations serve their communities with a wide range of programs that benefit men, women, and children. They complement the government's commitment to ensuring social welfare. Yet at the same time, their roles in *sha'bi* communities are more complex. Although their activities are closely supervised by various government agencies, they can provide a base of support for other groups within the community, whether religious, social, cultural, or political.[19] From the government's point of view, it is easier to maintain control over PVOs, and allow the community limited autonomy, than to assume the costs of services and programs offered by thousands of PVOs staffed by volunteers and professionals.[20] The poorly paid staff of these organizations must cope with daily bureaucratic headaches and juggle usually very limited resources and inadequate physical facilities to provide services that are appreciated by a demanding public. Like their management of the household, and their shrewd strategies to fulfill individual and collective goals, the *sha'b* and concerned men and women from other social classes apply their resourcefulness to serve the community, despite sometimes oppressive government supervision and intervention.

ELITE POLITICS, THE STATE, AND THE *SHA'B*

There are two parts to my job: service to the people and legislation.
Only the party with authority can serve the people, and thus opposition
parties in Egypt have little popular support, no roots to the people.
If I ask for something from the bureaucracy, my demands
will be met and theirs [the opposition's] will not.
—*A Member of Parliament*

Every night except Friday, a four-term member of Parliament from the government-sponsored National Democratic Party received constituents and visitors in his branch office from eight in the evening until the early hours of the next morning. A stream of visitors would wait for hours to see this man, who had been born in the *sha'bi* district that he now represented, even though he currently resided in a wealthier part of Cairo. His family had prospered in past decades, but he still maintained extensive business interests in the district. Sons from his two marriages went in and out of his waiting room, greeting and joking with constituents. Some of the visitors that night had moved away from the district but had returned to seek this MP's assistance because they had closer ties with him than with their own MP.

Accompanying a resident of the district on a visit to this man gave me an opportunity to ask the MP several questions about his position and to observe his interaction with constituents. My friend had first visited the MP when she heard that he had access to discretionary funds disbursed through the President's Organization (funds controlled by the President which finance his administration). Due to an accident, she needed to purchase an expensive prosthesis for her son. As a recent widow she had limited financial resources, and the MP was able to arrange a £E600 grant for her son's medical needs. (As noted earlier, an Islamic bank had also contributed to his medical expenses.) The MP asked her to return in a few months and to keep in touch with him because, he assured her, he could provide other services for a disabled person, including transportation (a modified minibike) and an apartment. Later, when she needed a job, she visited him again and he arranged a position for her in a day-care center in his district. His assistance was somewhat surprising since this woman had extremely close connections to another MP; but because her MP was from an opposition party, she had visited him to obtain services that he, as a supporter of the government's party, was in a better position to obtain.

During this particular meeting, however, the MP explained to me that, although he had only known her for a few months, it was not unusual for him to provide these services, at least in Egypt, which was a close-knit society (*murtabiTa bi-ba'Daha*). Connections between people mattered, and he cared about helping his constituents. Although he explained that he also concentrated on his legislative duties and his committee work in Parliament (with the assistance of several experts), he devoted long hours to serving people in his district office and hearing, investigating, and solving their problems. When I asked him about his colleagues, he explained that some of them were not concerned about constituents and did not receive them more than once a month.

Later, the woman visiting him mentioned that he was responsible for providing public housing to many people in a recently settled public housing project. Most of these people were *bita'tu* (loyal to him) because he had provided them with housing. At election time, these people would return the service by voting for him. She noted that only a member of the government-sponsored National Democratic Party had the resources to provide housing and other services to so many people. The MP had frankly stated the same opinion earlier, when he suggested that opposition parties really had no chance in Egypt because they did not control the provision of services and thus could not compete with the government. He pointed to the lack of demonstrations as evidence of their weakness, since if people in Egypt were truly upset, he argued, they would not hesitate to take to the streets. He failed, however, to consider government repression as a possible obstacle to such activity.

Opposition candidates to Parliament confirmed his analysis. A candidate for the Wafd Party (an opposition party with deep historical roots to the nationalist movement in Egypt which was revitalized in the 1970s) from a prominent family campaigned in a lower- to middle-class area in Cairo and she noted that constituents only saw politicians before an election occurred. After the election the party did nothing to serve the people. Her opposition party had not even opened a branch office in her district after the party had lost the election. Thus, she was not surprised that opposition parties had such difficulties attracting voters.

In a similar vein, a merchant from another district in central Cairo ridiculed the service record of a local MP, who appeared in the district before election time to distribute cash (rumored to approach £E15,000 in the 1984 elections) to his supporters after delivering a speech.[21] During his term of office, he rarely visited the district or helped his constituents. Before his parliamentary career, the MP had been a poor carpenter with a workshop in the district. According to this merchant, after becoming an MP the man began importing wood to Egypt, which became very lucrative, particularly during the construction boom in the 1970s. Due to the connections he had cultivated as a member of Parliament, the MP profited even more by evading payment on customs duties and his taxes. A younger skilled worker in the community also argued that politicians only visited the district when an election neared. At his older sister's wedding, just before an election, all the local candidates appeared, uninvited, because they knew her father was a prominent merchant. The wedding offered them an efficient opportunity to meet most of the prominent members of the business community, who actually had been invited.

A politician can earn the favor of political elites and important bureaucrats if he or she distributes resources effectively and ensures the stability and loyalty of an electoral district. If MPs in favor with the government can effectively channel resources to their constituents, they may eventually gain access to more resources. The MP I talked with in his district office believed that he had become more influential in national politics because he continued to press the government to serve his constituents and they realized he could channel government resources efficiently to those in need. In turn, he ensured that his district, where some open challenges to the government had occurred, would be politically quiescent. The following account provides evidence that his constituents understood the bargain and came to him before violence and disputes in the district erupted publicly.

A young man working in a workshop in this MP's district learned of a potentially explosive situation and visited the MP to warn him about it. Apparently, a sixteen-year-old Muslim woman was rumored to be romantically involved with a Christian worker in a neighborhood where Islamic political groups were very active. This neighborhood contained a larger population of Christians than was typical because, in addition to the tradition of Egyptian Copts residing in the area, it had once been a fashionable district populated by many foreign but long-resident Christian merchants and businessmen (Armenians, Greeks, Italians, and so forth). While premarital relationships between a couple of the same religion often provoked neighborhood fights if discovered, a relationship between a Muslim woman and a Christian man was even more sensitive. The typical resolution to this type of problem—marriage—was not possible between a Muslim woman and a Christian man under Egyptian law, unless she converted. (A Muslim man can marry a Christian or Jewish woman, but a Christian or Jewish man cannot marry a Muslim woman, according to Islamic law.) Worried that Islamic activists would discover the affair and use it as an excuse to cause trouble and harass Christians in the area, the young man realized the MP would appreciate being informed of the situation before anyone was injured.[22]

After hearing about the problem, the MP immediately offered to furnish a large government-subsidized apartment and give it to the young man who had warned him about the problem if he would agree to marry the woman in question (as a member of the housing committee in Parliament, he had control over the distribution of apartments in public housing projects). He would also pay for their wedding expenses and arrange everything within a month. At the same time, he would arrange for the woman's boyfriend to be drafted and stationed in a succession of remote provinces. The young man was surprised at the MP's solution to the problem but graciously declined, explaining that had no intention of marrying anyone in the near future. Fortunately, the crisis was averted when the young lover disappeared from the neighborhood and the affair was not further publicized.

According to this MP, he instructed members of the community to notify him of any problems in his district, whether they involved residents without water, an emergency need for housing, or a family quarrel that threatened to lead to violence. His involvement in several local private associations enhanced his "intelligence networks" about problems in the district. If people were in such desperate situations that they were embarrassed to seek his help and come to his office, he would visit them in their homes. In order to serve constituents as well as ensure that stability reigns, politicians typically rely on their informal networks as well as formal ties to PVOs, the business community, local bureaucrats, and state offices. In effect, informal networks serve as channels of distribution for goods and services in return for political control. Thus day-care centers, health clinics, food cooperatives, and schools can provide information about the community for politicians, as much as they provide access to public goods and services for consumers in *sha°bi* neighborhoods.[23]

A prominent member of the community, whose family had lived in the district for generations, served as a quasi–ward captain for another member of Parliament. Her position as an administrator at a PVO the MP had founded in the district provided a convenient setting for serving the MP and constituents simultaneously. When she discovered people with serious financial or bureaucratic problems, she would accompany the constituent to visit the MP and whatever government offices were required to resolve the problem. If a house had collapsed and the residents were entitled to public housing, or an elderly man or woman was destitute and entitled to a pension but was not receiving one, this dynamic duo of the MP and the administrator would tramp the halls of many offices to support a constituent's rights.

However, there were limits to what even MPs could accomplish in the face of bureaucratic obstacles. As the MP from the government-sponsored party noted earlier, opposition members of Parliament have far more difficulty obtaining services for constituents than members of the National Democratic Party. When a respected MP of the opposition party would try to secure public housing for people who were simply and clearly entitled to it, her efforts would fail in the face of bureaucratic inertia. However, because the MP had very deep roots to the district, fought hard to secure public services to constituents despite her political handicap, and worked diligently to attract private and international resources for PVOs, she had been reelected in every election but one since the mid-1960s (despite many changes in electoral law, the party system, and political representation).

In general, the generosity and services provided by elected officials tend to win the loyalty of the *sha'b* far more than their party or ideological positions, which are somewhat irrelevant since political parties have little autonomy from the government. For example, a resident of my community explained the metamorphosis of one man from an *'arbagi* (a driver of an animal-powered cart) to wealthy merchant and long-standing member of Parliament. According to popular mythology, he had begun his life as a poor driver of a donkey cart, collecting scrap iron from house to house. By chance, foreigners gave him an old box that was filled with silver candelabras. Later, when many Jews were fleeing the area after the Suez War in 1956, a family inadvertently left him another box filled with gold. Because he believed his good luck was a blessing from God, he used the unexpected wealth to build the neighborhood a hospital dedicated to serving the poor. The hospital remains one of the largest serving the area.

Whether the story is true or not is beside the point: his constituents repeated it to explain his honorable path to wealth and power, and his commitment to return the good fortune to his constituents. Other residents in the community complained about politicians who never received their constituents or helped them in any way, despite the obvious advantages the politician gained from his or her position. Some people did not know the title or position of local politicians and administrators, but judged them for their service record to the community. A retired military officer who had been elected to Parliament was particularly condemned for ignoring constituents and for his patronizing and cold attitude toward them.

A service record is not only one of the criteria for judging local politicians, but nationally elected officials as well. For example, when the Ministry of Antiquities hosted a reception in a historic site in Cairo which President Mubarak was supposed to attend, the employees of the Ministry were extremely cynical. They explained that they did not care about the visit of the President or the Minister, but they expected a decent meal to be served and would also receive a small bonus if they attended. Some of them had rented jackets for the occasion from the local cleaners (whose customers did not know that their clothes were being rented out for several hours). After the reception, they complained to their friends that they had only been served a slice of cake. All the preparations, which had made their superiors at the Ministry sweat, were for no productive purpose but merely to impress political elites. They joked that justice was served because every time their Minister hosted an important reception and the President or other VIPs were invited, all the local sewers overflowed. It was not unusual for employees to receive bonuses for their participation in public gatherings. At another occasion, when the Ministry of Social Affairs wanted a large audience for an event, people were enticed to attend by the promise of a financial incentive.[24]

The reduction of formal politics to the realm of distribution is intentionally or unintentionally encouraged by the President, the Prime Minister, and other elected and appointed government officials. The President himself announces the bonuses state employees receive on holidays, new benefits for pensions, educational programs, and the prices or supply of subsidized commodities. Government officials and official newspapers announce the size of yearly pay raises for the civil service and public sector. On the occasion of Labor Day, government officials announce new benefits for workers; on Children's Day, they announce public investment in new child care facilities, or projects to increase public libraries; and on International Women's Day, they announce new health services for pregnant mothers and glorify the participation of women in the labor force.

In *sha῾bi* neighborhoods, people constantly complain about the meager holiday bonuses (*῾iidiyya*) and pay raises (*῾ilaawa*) they receive from the government. Since the President announces these bonuses and implicitly claims responsibility for them, he is seen as the culprit or benefactor, depending on the size of the bonus. Since the public sector is such a large employer in Egypt (approximately 3.5 million employees), the size of public-sector raises reasonably becomes a topic of national attention and analysis. One year an employee of a food cooperative complained bitterly that he had only received a monthly pay raise of £E2, another employee had received £E3, and a third £E1.50.

The provision of services and bonuses from as high up as the office of the President allows him to exhort Egyptians to make sacrifices for their government as well. In 1985 and 1986 the government announced the "Love for Egypt" (*Hubb Masr*) campaign to raise private funds from its citizens to pay off Egypt's huge foreign debt. One evening, seated typically around the television set after a large Friday meal, the host explained to me that this particular soccer match on television, between the two most popular teams in Egypt ('il-'ahli and 'iz-zamaalek), was a benefit for the *Hubb Masr* campaign. First he explained it was a duty for anyone who loved his country to contribute. He mentioned that the players donated their time, singers entertained the audience during the breaks, and door prizes donated by businessmen were distributed at the match to publicize Egypt's predicament.

Within five minutes, however, his tone changed and he explained that most of the people yelling *yaHya MaSr* (long live Egypt!) were the biggest thieves in the country since they were the ones who had lined their pockets from foreign aid and joint venture projects. Whenever a new project was initiated, thousands went into the pockets of these dealmakers, who now dutifully attended this symbolic public event. Corruption, he believed, was one of the greatest faults of Egyptians and the government. He asked his son to bring a five-kilo jar of clarified butter to show me the slogan "gift of the people of the United States" written on its side. Despite the fact that he believed the United States had given this butter to the Egyptian people, it was sold to poor and middle-class people for £E6, while the criminals ('*il-Haramiyya*) took millions.

Then he admitted that his family (he and another merchant brother) had "voluntarily" contributed £E1,500 (a very large sum considering his economic position) to the campaign. A committee had been jointly established by the Ministry of Supply and local businessmen to collect contributions in his neighborhood. It was understood that merchants who conducted business with the state would make a "voluntary" contribution. If they did not, my host suggested that the Ministry would use its administrative power to create bureaucratic problems the next time a merchant needed an official permit, signature, or delivery from the Ministry. While the argument to contribute to the campaign had originally been posed in terms of patriotism, as the discussion progressed this businessman perceived his participation as a matter of coercion.

Public-sector employees had also been approached to contribute "voluntarily" to the campaign, but employees found the government had deducted their contribution directly from their paychecks without permission. One very low-paid researcher at a university found £E4 deducted from her paycheck of £E34, and another university professor was missing £E6 from a £E66 monthly paycheck. While the deductions were not large, these well-educated employees felt that the government's action was completely unjustified because they already received such low salaries.

Attacks on the integrity of the government and government officials were voiced repeatedly throughout this community. As many of the previous examples have portrayed, even people who had accepted bribes for an official service or offered a bribe to an official complained about the evils of corruption (although in the same breath they usually excused their own actions). As one educated and wealthy employee of a PVO in a *sha'bi* community admitted, anyone with any connection to the government who said they did not take from the government was a liar. Yet he justified this behavior by noting the pervasiveness of corruption in the system and extremely low government salaries. Since the government had decreased its commitment to the welfare of public-sector employees, they would extract as much as they could from the government.

A public-sector employee who was approaching retirement explained that the type of corruption that prevailed during the Sadat and Mubarak eras differed from the corruption of the Nasser era. Due to the Open Door policy, he argued, consumption had increased, and no one was happy any longer with what they had. During the previous regime goods and services were very cheap, and there was not rampant corruption like there had been recently. Rather, Abdel Nasser knew how to *yimsik il-balad* (or control the country), and his government closely supervised all levels of public-sector employees and civil servants. While corruption may have existed at very high levels of the regime, people in low and middle-level positions would not dare to participate, fearing that the pervasive intelligence apparatus of the state would catch them. They had far fewer opportunities to enrich themselves at state expense. Once, however, more private individuals vied with each other to obtain government clearances to develop new enterprises and new markets, public employees were in a stronger position to extract fees to facilitate paperwork. Since the state still regulated many economic activities, and regulations changed so frequently, procuring the assistance and favor of government employees became more and more indispensable to conduct business in the country. As government officials watched their salaries and prestige decline, many civil servants openly solicited and demanded bribes to perform routine duties.

Many people who were dissatisfied and frustrated with complicated government regulations, inefficiency, or corruption caustically condemned the regime and the formal political process. One young man had made several unsuccessful attempts to obtain $1,500 from the Central Bank, which his sister's husband (who lived in Nigeria) had recently sent to him to support his children after his sister had died suddenly. The bank insisted that the Nigerian brother-in-law must be personally present before the funds could be handed over to the brother's family in Egypt, which obviously was completely impractical since the brother-in-law was in Nigeria. He used this experience as a typical example of how the government acts as the worst criminal in Egypt since it does nothing for people but steal money from them. Because many people had had similar negative experiences with various arms of the state bureaucracy and realized they had very little influence on (or representation in) the government, they often adopted this cynical, bitter attitude.

But dissatisfaction and cynicism rarely erupted into overt organized challenges to the state, although confrontations had occurred in the past, and people suggested they would occur in the future. People in this community made explicit connections between popular dissatisfaction with government policies and demonstrations and violence against the state. For example, after the prices of some food commodities were increased by the government in July 1986, the wife of a worker at a food cooperative explained that people were angry and that the increases would only be rescinded if people demonstrated in the streets. People in the community certainly remembered the food riots that erupted in 1977, which almost toppled President Sadat from power. Troops had opened fire on people, and one man in the community, who was only a young teenager at the time, had been seriously wounded. A taxi driver, during a long list of unsolicited complaints against the government, referred to an Egyptian proverb as an explanation of politics in Egypt. He explained that although people will tolerate a terrible situation in silence for some time, it only takes one spark to light an explosion, and then people will react without thought or concern for anyone or anything. Any catalyst might serve to unleash pent-up resentment and frustration.

This conversation took place several months after members of the *'il-'amn il-markazi*, a branch of the internal security forces within the Ministry of Interior, staged a rebellion in February 1986 that quickly spread throughout Cairo and other parts of Egypt. These men, the taxi driver argued, had patiently borne three years of military service, far away from their families and farms, for the ridiculously low salary of £E6 per month (members of the Central Security Forces are largely illiterate peasants who are fulfilling their national service but cannot meet the entrance requirements to more select divisions of the armed forces). When they heard a rumor that the authorities were contemplating extending their service another year, they mutinied, firing on their superiors and burning luxury hotels next to their barracks just north of the pyramids in Giza. Other units throughout Egypt joined the rebellion and attacked military and police installations in Cairo, destroying state and private property in their path. This type of unpremeditated violent attack against the government should be expected more and more in Egypt, the taxi driver believed, because the government mistreats its employees and citizens for years on end and foolishly expects them to remain docile.

The government responded to the Central Security Forces' rebellion by declaring a general curfew throughout Cairo.[25] At 11:00 A.M., after most people were already at work, the radio announced the curfew would begin at 1:00 P.M. Huge traffic jams occurred as everyone tried to get home at the same time. Some people rode on top of buses to catch rides, while others simply walked many miles to reach home before the curfew began. While there were reports of violence by the security forces, the rebellion had begun on the very outskirts of Cairo and had not yet reached central Cairo. However, as merchants, workshop owners, hospitals, and schools were closing down and the streets filled up with people trying to reach their homes, helicopters began circling overhead and we could hear gunfire in our neighborhood.

In an area just north of central Cairo, a struggle between the security forces and the military raged for almost four hours, according to a woman who lived just next to a security force garrison. Isolated outbursts of gunfire could be heard throughout the area, and citizens directed or blocked traffic, depending upon the direction of the gunfire. By 3:30 that afternoon, tanks and military personnel in battle-gear rolled down the now-deserted street. As they appeared, people explained that the army would take over and put down the rebellion. The reaction of people in my community to the rebellion revealed their views on the military and government. They considered the security forces, which were used to control riots and to guard official buildings, as little more than ignorant troops that would do whatever someone ordered them to do, including attacking unarmed protesters. As we watched the troops and tanks pass by from the roof of a building, several men speculated that civilians would never join the rebellion of the Central Security

Forces over the army since the army was far more popular (although some civilians, particularly Islamicists, did join the revolt and used the opportunity to attack nightclubs on the road to the pyramids). Because the Central Security Forces and the police are part of the Ministry of Interior, rather than the Ministry of Defense, people on the streets also understood that the rebellion indicated serious rifts within the elite and a challenge to the highest level of power and authority. But they also speculated that the military would prevail since they believed it was more powerful than either the Ministry of Interior or the government.[26]

Uncertain whether people would join in the rebellion spontaneously or that organized political groups might exploit the situation for their own purposes, the government imposed a general curfew from 26 February until 9 March 1985. Accompanied by solemn martial music, state television ran footage of the destruction of luxury hotels, places of entertainment, cars, buses, and other property near the Pyramid Plateau in Giza, where the revolt had originated (this destruction was caused both by the Central Security Forces and by civilians who had seized the opportunity to vent anger against the government and the tourist industry). As people gathered around their television sets to watch the news, they condemned the violence and destruction of private property. Condemnation of the rebellion was encouraged by popular personages on television, who vilified the Central Security Forces and thanked God that the army had come to citizens' aid. In this era of economic problems and a huge foreign debt, they asked how anyone concerned with Egypt's future could justify such violence and destruction of public and private property. They praised the air of cooperation and calm that existed between citizens and the army. At the same time, there seemed to be some empathy among the *sha'b* for the soldiers of the security forces because they were exploited by the government and lived under such oppressive conditions.

While news reports minimized the significance and organization of the rebellion, as people returned to work once the curfew was lifted they repeated stories of rebellious troops opening fire on people, destroying public property, and seizing government installations and public thoroughfares. One man had sent a worker in his pickup truck to make a delivery in Rod al-Farag, a *sha'bi* neighborhood in the north of Cairo, and security forces smashed his windshield, using their weapons of riot control against any cars and trucks they met during their rampage.[27] A bus driver heard from his colleagues that security forces had stopped several buses (owned by public companies), ordered all passengers off the buses, and proceeded to smash windows with their billy clubs before setting them on fire.

An older woman returned to work distraught because she had just learned that her ex-husband's son, who was recently engaged to be married, had been killed by the security forces when a group of local people pelted them with stones and they opened fire, supposedly killing forty people. She was particularly upset since she had only learned of his death after his burial, and she had not made the proper condolence calls. Other people had been traveling throughout Egypt during the disturbances and were forced to seek refuge with strangers when the security forces took over several roads and refused to let traffic pass, destroying cars and trucks in the process. A relative of a local family had been traveling by taxi from Upper Egypt to Cairo, and his driver graciously offered his passengers his hospitality when they were stopped in Giza by the rebellion (luckily he lived nearby). After the curfew had been lifted, the passenger's mother-in-law sent a duck, a goose, and pigeons with the next relative traveling to Cairo for the driver's family.

As the curfew continued, many people accustomed to constant activity grew restless, and despite the unexpected quiet and silence of the streets, they were anxious to return to their jobs, shopping, and visiting friends and relatives. People used the extra time to accomplish domestic tasks that they had been too busy for before the curfew, but men and women soon had little to keep them busy. People seemed perplexed more by their quiet neighborhoods and the lack of activity than they did with the outcome of the rebellion and the position of the government. When the curfew was finally lifted and President Mubarak made a major two-hour speech to the nation, it was quickly apparent that the speech would neither address the cause of the rebellion nor suggest any significant policy changes. After a few minutes, people ignored the President and caught up on the news and activities of their colleagues.

Greater confidence in the military rather than the government was expressed by several members of the community in routine discussions, and they made a distinction between the two. One workshop owner believed that the *Dabt w-rabT* (discipline) of the military had exerted a positive contribution to the nation's political history. He added that young people did not understand the enormous changes that had occurred in Egypt since the 1952 Free Officers' Revolution. For example, his younger brother-in-law always compared Egypt's financial predicament to much wealthier European countries or Persian Gulf countries that had wasted enormous financial resources on foolish entertainment and pleasures abroad. Now the young man was determined to seek his fortune and his future outside Egypt since he was frustrated by its problems and lack of opportunities. Yet the older man argued that it was short-sighted to compare Egypt with Europe and to forget all the achievements of the past three decades. The younger man was in the midst of completing his military service and had little respect for his superiors. In fact, he was so disgusted by the opportunism of officers and their exploitation of enlisted men and conscripts that he had served many extra months of guard duty because he could not keep his views to himself.

Despite the relative decline of the power and prestige of the armed forces since the 1960s, a military career still presents some young men in *sha'bi* communities a chance for upward mobility. The military recruited new volunteers through special military high schools. These schools offered a high school diploma but supplemented academic courses with military and vocational training. The incentives to enroll, publicized throughout Egypt through television advertisements, included free housing, board, clothes, and a monthly stipend.

One young noncommissioned officer from the community had spent the past seven years in the army, beginning as a student in a military secondary school. According to one of his best friends, this young man had been more interested in young women than studying for his secondary school entrance examinations and received a very low score. Embarrassed and disappointed, he decided to enter military school, which accepted students with lower scores for its joint program. The young man was obliged to serve in the armed forces for seven years after finishing his secondary education.

Nearing the end of his required service, the young man was stationed in an army motor vehicle repair unit, near his parents' home in central Cairo. The army had trained him in automotive repair, and every three or six months he attended new training courses to learn about recently purchased equipment and new technologies.[28] Although he believed that the young mechanics who were drafted into the army were more experienced than mechanics trained by the army, he had learned enough from them to establish a small unlicensed brake repair shop with a partner. He had planned to return to the workshop after he left the army, but after a dispute with his partner the business failed.

He now earned £E125 per month as a noncommissioned officer. As a student in the military academy, the young man had received £E45 per month. At his present rank, every three months he received a bonus equal to his monthly salary, and he had access to army cooperative stores stocked with imported clothes, inexpensive furniture, and high-quality food products. In addition, he was entitled to borrow up to one-third of his yearly income through military financial institutions (the army paid the interest on the loan). He also had the opportunity to purchase a modern, comfortable apartment for £E15,000 through relatively low monthly installments of £E42. Through the military he could purchase a private car by installment and join a variety of well-equipped social clubs. According to this young man, when a noncommissioned officer (NCO) leaves the military he receives a bonus of his yearly salary and a pass entitling him to free transportation in Egypt and abroad; and with his diploma from an intelligence training course, he can easily find employment in a tourist company as a security agent. In addition, if this NCO were to be hired by a public-sector automotive concern, he would retain his seniority from his years in the armed forces and would be paid accordingly.

Despite the generous benefits available to someone who failed his entrance exams to secondary school, he was planning to leave the army when his enlistment expired. He complained about the manners and mentality that the army fostered, including cheating, petty thievery, and pervasive frustration.[29] Because many officers and NCOs were bored and stationed in remote areas, they relieved their frustration by harassing enlisted men and conscripts. However, if his superiors decided that his position was too important, they could require him to remain in the army for an additional two years while they trained a replacement. During this time the army would review his career and if they wanted him to reenlist would entice him by offering him more stimulating responsibilities and higher pay or promotion.

Although he disliked certain aspects of the military, he believed that its administration was just a bit less organized and efficient than foreign joint venture companies in Egypt. He argued that the current Minister of Defense, Field Marshal Abd al-Halim Abu Ghazala (or "Baba" Ghazala, as his troops referred to him), had improved the quality of the armed forces and the living and working conditions of his troops by sharing the resources the Americans had invested in the Egyptian military with his troops. In contrast to his feelings for Abu Ghazala, the young man spoke derisively about the military's second in command, who had an extremely tough and demanding reputation. This general was infamous for his surprise inspections of military installations and his terrifying treatment of troops he found unprepared and undisciplined. He had just tried to institute a new regulation forbidding recruits from leaving the training camp during the period of basic training. Although basic training lasted only six weeks, the NCO thought the regulation was particularly harsh and unnecessary, since Egyptians were so attached to their families.

While the army had provided education and training for this young man, he still objected to predominate modes of behavior in the armed forces. It is not uncommon for people, both among the *sha'b* and professionals and intellectuals, to blame the armed forces and their "army mentality" for economic failures in Egypt and for abetting an authoritarian political process. As one former conscript explained the predicament, officers are spoiled, stubborn, enamored of authority, and expect to be obeyed. When officers participated in the political process, those attributes quickly led them to dislike political debate, pluralism, and popular participation. Thus, the "army mentality" further reduced the opportunities for free elections and popular rule in Egypt.

As one highly educated older woman who volunteered at a PVO in the community explained, she and others in her generation had welcomed the 1952 revolution because it meant the end of the power of the feudalists, who had exploited peasants and workers. She had marched in nationalist demonstrations and joined literacy campaigns in support of the revolution. But after the revolution, the officers refused to return to their barracks, as they had promised. Within a short time they were placed in positions of power and authority throughout the nation, and the legacy of the "military mentality" had remained part of the political landscape. Even though the regime had been able to limit political challenges from below, it had not been able to provide for or win the confidence and support of the Egyptian people because of this "military mentality." As she and many others in *sha'bi* communities explained, the government was more interested in maintaining rule than alleviating the economic, political, and social problems in Egypt.

Moreover, limiting the *sha'b*'s avenues of political participation increases the pressure on the government to maintain its part of the social contract and encourages the *sha'b* to maintain its part of the bargain to consume public goods and services. Though the *sha'b* perfect their role as consumers, they understand that the government prevents them from acting as citizens due to its exclusionary policies. The bargain, while temporarily ensuring political stability, weakens the nation, and thus the nation as a whole loses. As noted in the previous chapter, significant financial resources circulate within *sha'bi* communities and are successfully protected from the extractive power of the state. Informal networks and the informal economy assist the *sha'b* and other segments of the Egyptian rural and urban population in obtaining a greater share of public goods and services. The labor, creativity, and productivity of the *sha'b* are dedicated to furthering certain shared communal goals, while the nation as a whole suffers from their lack of investment and participation in formal, legal collective institutions. The *sha'b* suffer as well from investing their time and resources in endless maneuvering in both the formal and informal sectors. Unless political elites are willing to change the terms of the bargain and opt for inclusion rather than exclusion, the *sha'b* will continue to exploit the government and consume scarce, valuable resources in their typically creative way. In an era of economic recession in the Middle East and in Egypt, the government will have a harder time meeting the costs of this bargain, and if it is not willing to change the terms of the bargain and allow more political activity and expression in Egypt, both formal and informal, the *sha'b* are unlikely to remain quiescent.

I BEGAN THIS STUDY with a problem of definition concerning politics and political participation. Constituencies under authoritarian rule are not only excluded from formal political participation in Egypt but are ignored by reigning typologies of political participation. The political activities they engage in and the changes they foster have been overlooked since their particular strategies for achieving their objectives differ from the typical political institutions that political scientists, steeped in a context of liberal, Western, and pluralist politics, have *counted* as political. Yet my investigation of one *sha'bi* community in Cairo suggests that excluded communities can develop creative and effective strategies to accomplish shared goals, despite the intentions and policies of political elites and the constraints that their security apparatus places on political participation and freedoms of expression and association. While elite policies have, and will continue to have, a great impact on popular classes, the demands and institutions of popular classes have their own set of intended and unintended consequences on elite policy-making and macro politics in Egypt.

Among the *sha'b* in Cairo, familial and informal networks are a concrete manifestation of extrasystemic political participation. The *sha'b* fashion informal networks in order to fulfill a wide range of individual and collective needs. The critical needs and the problems that confront and, at times, overwhelm lower-income communities must be the starting point of our analyses. By recognizing certain issues that are vitally important to the survival and prosperity of these communities, we can then examine the institutions and strategies they use to resolve them. While elites have their own political agendas and political preferences, the *sha'b* also construct alternative priorities and preferences which arise from the material, social, and political context of their lives. For a variety of reasons, the analyses of politics in many nations are unfortunately far more sensitive to elite and middle-class concerns than to the politics of popular classes.

The boundaries of this particular community are not localized, isolated, or insular because the *sha'b* intentionally incorporate more powerful, resourceful, and skilled individuals and institutions into their networks to strengthen them. Networks connect individuals and households with communal and national institutions, thus transcending the supposedly strict boundary between public and private spheres. Informal networks are effective precisely because they are designed to function within a formal system pervaded by informal structures and processes. Although the membership and configuration of each network varies, there is a common reflex in these communities to establish networks to solve problems, arbitrate disputes, and fulfill specific objectives; thus, networks are very responsive to changing internal and external forces. Informal networks routinize and standardize the efforts of the community to achieve collective goals, thus enriching collective life and strengthening its institutional resources. These networks are institutionalized not in the sense that they mimic the formal and legal organizations regulated by the state, but because their organization, durability, and flexibility provides political resources and political capital to their membership. Unlike involvement in formal politics, these avenues of political participation do not endanger men and women since they are designed to be subtle, cautious, and often invisible. They are constructed within the constraints of an authoritarian political system that historically has relied upon indirect and direct methods of political repression and co-optation to maintain its power. Despite these constraints, informal networks can be mobilized to fulfill a variety of material, social, and political aims. Under unusual conditions they can also upset and even reverse the best-laid plans and intentions of government elites.

According to Joel Migdal, creating and controlling the "rules of the game" and forcing others to play by them is one of the most common political struggles. "The major struggles in many societies, especially those with fairly new states, are struggles over who has the right and ability to make the countless rules that guide people's behavior."[1] He argues that what distinguishes the state from other organizations in society is that state officials seek predominance. "That is, they aim for the state to make the binding rules guiding people's behavior or, at the very least, to authorize particular other organizations to make those rules in certain realms."[2] More importantly, through its legislative, regulatory, economic, and judicial institutions, the state attempts to enforce its rules. I have attempted to demonstrate how the rules of the state are resisted through the organization of communities, their norms, their judicial, economic, moral, and cultural preferences. The ability of the state to monopolize power and authority in Egypt remains highly contested, and informal networks keep alive alternative visions of politics and alternative strategies to achieve shared goals, despite the constraints the state's political and economic structures place on these communities. I do not mean to discount or minimize the extent of these constraints or other very powerful interests in Egypt, but rather to suggest that informal networks provide an organizational grid for the *sha'b* which facilitates their political participation. Just as lawyers, engineers, the managerial bourgeoisie, importers, or labor unions are organized in Egypt, the *sha'b* are also organized, and their interests and political preferences shape micro- and macro political dynamics. Since informal networks reach beyond the physical boundaries of specific neighborhoods and the particular status and class character of the *sha'b* through a wide range of informal occupational, educational, business, kinship, and religious associations, their beliefs and organizational capabilities infuse and penetrate different constituencies in Egyptian society as well.

As described in Chapter 1, the principles of the familial ethos order and regulate behavior, opinions, and actions within *sha'bi* communities. This ethos of cooperation, arbitration, and association with trusted individuals is situated within the realities of everyday life among the *sha'b*, yet it also shapes the reactions of the *sha'b* to government policies as well as the state's claim to authority and legitimacy. As I have argued earlier, Sheldon Wolin underscores the political consequences of the endeavor of "theoretical founding" or "the constitutive activity of laying down basic and general principals, which, when legitimated, become the presuppositions of practices, the ethos of practitioners."[3] These general principles then work to supplant or destroy rival theoretical claims, or what Migdal calls the "rules of the game" and what Gramsci called the ideological hegemony of the state. Because the *sha'b* not only retain and promote their rules of the game but use their resources and institutions to support those rules, they are increasingly seen as legitimate among a growing constituency throughout many densely populated neighborhoods in Cairo. In particular, I described earlier how the sums circulating in the informal economy provide critical financial resources for furthering the *sha'b*'s individual and collective interests. Because the interests and institutions of the *sha'b* are supported and promoted with financial resources that lay beyond the reach of the tax authorities or the regulation of government bureaucracies, the *sha'b* clearly have a better chance to further their agenda.

The politics of the *sha'b* and other excluded constituencies must be taken seriously for two reasons: first, to understand the political life and preferences of the majority of Caireans and, second, in order to construct any dynamic and comprehensive analysis of national politics. To understand state-society relations in Egypt more comprehensively, a study of *sha'bi* politics must be combined with an understanding of elite politics, the bureaucracy, Islamic activists, classes, interest groups, and the military, among other forces. These major actors in Egypt compete for power, legitimacy, and resources, and this study attempts to persuade others that the *sha'b* are also a major political actor in Egypt, even if not the most *visible* one. In order to understand the nature and dynamics of political life in Egypt, various constituencies and institutions (both legal and illegal, formal and informal) must be analyzed, particularly in a political environment of repression and authoritarianism which drives certain types of power struggles and political competition underground.

While my particular focus on the politics of the *sha'b* cannot answer questions about the resolution of contemporary political and social conflicts in Egypt, I would argue that the *sha'b*, as a very significant constituency in Cairo (and other major cities in Egypt), will be a crucial component of the ways in which future conflicts are resolved. More specifically, the organizational grid of informal networks and institutions within this community will play a role in these conflicts. The political infrastructure of this community is both an integral component of daily life among the *sha'b* and a dynamic factor in macro politics. Understanding the politics of this community will not answer questions about what might happen to the stability of the Egyptian government, the strength of Islamic activists, or the direction and health of the Egyptian economy, but it does suggest that this community will be engaged in these conflicts and party to them.

Predictions about contemporary conflicts varies considerably, depending on whose interests in Egypt one considers. If an attachment to the familial ethos and a pervasive organizational grid among the *sha'b* means that many men and women will support Islamic political activists and their campaign against the state, secularists and the current political elite in Egypt will see their power diminish. If the state dismantles public-sector companies, state employees in both blue- and white-collar positions will suffer and organized labor will either become more radical or emasculated. If the informal economy continues to thrive and channel resources to the collective institutions of the *sha'b*, the fiscal strength of the Egyptian state will suffer, though economic growth may increase. In addition, the ability of the government to control political life and repress the political preferences of most Egyptians may decline if other interests have stronger economic resources to pursue their agendas.

Very simply, by incorporating the politics and institutions of excluded constituencies into our analyses, we can portray a more representative and realistic image of politics in developing and developed nations. As Chazan argues, politics is not coterminus with the state, and political elites and organized interest groups do not have a monopoly or even a monopsony on political leadership or political legitimacy.[4] Competing notions of good government and appropriate policies emanate from various constituencies. When, for intended or unintended reasons, formerly excluded constituencies gain control of significant economic resources, political elites may have to take notice. The *sha'b* in Egypt may be in a position to claim a greater share of political power due to their organizational resources, upward economic mobility, and the enhanced social and educational status of significant portions of this constituency. Whatever the configuration of elite politics and macro political and economic policies in the coming years, the *sha'b*'s control of informal political institutions and informal economic activities will promote and protect their interests throughout the Egyptian political system.

• N O T E S •

INTRODUCTION

1. James C. Scott, *Domination and the Arts of Resistance*, p. 199.
2. Sidney Verba and Norman Nie, *Participation in America*, p. 2.
3. Samuel Huntington and Joan Nelson, *No Easy Choice*.
4. Joan Nelson, "Political Participation," in *Understanding Political Development*, ed. Weiner, Huntington, and Almond, p. 104.
5. Richard Newbold Adams, "The Structure of Participation: A Commentary," in *Political Participation in Latin America*, vol. 2, *Politics and the Poor*, ed. Seligson and Booth, p. 13.
6. This study is indebted to the rich tradition and scholarship of anthropological studies on women, family, and communities in urban Egypt. My questions and the initial direction of this study emerged out of the important work of Nawal al-Messiri Nadim, "Family Relationships in a 'Harah' in Cairo," in *Arab Society*, ed. Hopkins and Ibrahim, pp. 212–22; Sawsan al-Messiri, "The Changing Role of the Futuwa," in *Patrons and Clients in the Mediterranean Societies*, ed. Gellner and Waterbury, and her *Ibn al-Balad: A Concept of Egyptian Identity*; Unni Wikan, *Life Among the Poor in Cairo*, trans. Ann Henning, and her "Living Conditions Among Cairo's Poor," *Middle East Journal* 39 (Winter 1985): 7–26; Andrea B. Rugh, *The Family in Contemporary Egypt*; and Nayra Atiya, *Khul-Khaal: Five Egyptian Women Tell Their Stories*.
7. For more recent anthropological, historical, and sociological studies of women in Egypt see Homa Hoodfar, "Survival Strategies in Low-income Households in Cairo," *Journal of South Asian and Middle Eastern Studies* 13 (Summer 1990): 22–41, and her "Household Budgeting and Financial Management," in *A Home Divided*, ed. Dwyer and Bruce; Lila Abu-Lughod, *Veiled Sentiments*; Judith E. Tucker, *Women in Nineteenth-Century Egypt*; Kathryn Kamphoefner, "Voices from the Bottom: Women of Cairo View Literacy"; Evelyn A. Early, *Baladi Women of Cairo*; Helen Watson, *Women in the City of the Dead*; and Mona Abaza, "Feminist Debates and 'Traditional Feminism.' "

For more attention to the political life of women and the role of gender in Egyptian politics see Arlene MacLeod, *Accommodating Protest*; Cynthia Nelson, "Public and Private Politics," *American Ethnologist* 1 (1974): 555–64; Ann Mosely Lesch and Earl L. Sullivan, "Women in Egypt," *UFSI Reports* 22 (1986); Mervat Hatem, "The Enduring Alliance of Nationalism and Patriarchy," *Feminist Studies* 21 (Spring 1986): 19–43, and her "Egypt's Middle Class in Crisis," *Middle East Journal* 43 (Summer 1988): 407–22.

Several studies of elite women and women's organizations have recently been published and add important new details and analysis of their role in Egyptian politics. See Earl L. Sullivan, *Women in Egyptian Political Life*; Huda Shaarawi, *Harem Years*, trans. and ed. Margot Badran; Kathleen Howard-Merriam, "Egypt's Other Political Elite," *Western Political Quarterly* 34 (March 1981): 174–87; and Cynthia Nelson, "Biography and Women's History," in *Women in Middle Eastern History*, ed. Keddie and Baron.

8. See Carole Pateman, "The Civic Culture," in *The Civic Culture Revisited*, ed. Almond and Verba, pp. 57–102.

9. Chapter 1 will argue that Weiner's conceptualization of politics and of political participation is built upon a Western, classical understanding of the public/private dichotomy, which placed women and slaves in the sphere of "unfreedom" or the household (*oikos*), where both production and reproduction was centered. Only free, male citizens of erudition and property could participate in the public world of politics (*polis*). According to Carole Pateman, liberal theorists reaffirmed the normative and patriarchal implications of this construction of the public realm when they argued that women, like children, were "naturally" subordinate to men and were not free individuals or citizens. See Jean Bethke Elshtain, *Public Man, Private Woman*, and Carole Pateman, "Feminist Critiques of the Public/Private Dichotomy," in *Public and Private in Social Life*, ed. Benn and Gaus, pp. 281–303.

10. Myron Weiner, "Political Participation," in *Crises and Sequences in Political Development*, by Leonard Binder et al., p. 164 (emphasis added).

11. For some reason, intentionality does not seem to be such a problem for elite politics. The pressures that mold policymakers are far more complicated than their intentions, and the import of actions or consequences are not constrained, when judged by commentators or history, on the strict link of causality to what someone thought or hoped to achieve.

12. James C. Scott, *Weapons of the Weak*, pp. 295–96.

13. Charles Taylor, "Interpretation and the Sciences of Man," in *Understanding and Social Inquiry*, ed. Dallmayr and McCarthy, p. 125.

14. See Adam Przeworski, "Marxism and Rational Choice," *Politics and Society* 14 (1985): 379–409.

15. Przeworski, "Marxism and Rational Choice," p. 393.

16. See Robert H. Bates, "Macropolitical Economy in the Field of Development," in *Perspectives on Positive Political Economy*, ed. Alt and Shepsle, pp. 44–45.

17. Timothy Mitchell, "The Limits of the State," *American Political Science Review* 85 (March 1991): 90.

18. Scott defines the public transcript as "the self-portrait of dominant elites as they would have themselves seen" (Scott, *Domination and the Arts of Resistance*, p. 18). This discourse is lopsided, designed to be impressive, to affirm and naturalize the power of dominant elites, to conceal or euphemize the dirty linen of their rule—while they must make an ideological case that they rule, to some degree, on behalf of their subjects.

19. Kathryn S. March and Rachelle L. Taqqu, *Women's Informal Associations in Developing Countries*, p. 5.

20. See Joseph Gusfield's critique about the "linear image of social movements." Linear, because it "directs attention to a discrete association of people whose activity is perceived as using means to gain an end. . . . The focus of attention on empirical events is on how they advance or deter the achievement of goals consciously stated in organizational programs." Gusfield proposes that "a more fluid perspective toward the meaning of a movement emphasizes the quickening of change and the social sharing of new meanings in a variety of areas and places. It is less confined to the boundaries of organizations and more alive to the larger contexts of change at the same time as it is open to awareness of how the movement has consequences and impacts among nonpartisans and nonmembers as well as participants and devotees. Rather than success or failure of a movement, it is more likely to lead to questions

about consequences: What happened?" Joseph R. Gusfield, "Social Movements and Social Change," *Research in Social Movements, Conflict and Change* 4 (1981): 319, 323.

21. See S. al-Messiri, *Ibn al-Balad*.

22. Arthur Goldschmidt, Jr., *Modern Egypt*, p. 5.

23. Joel Gordon, *Nasser's Blessed Movement*, p. 197.

24. Gordon, *Nasser's Blessed Movement*, p. 197.

25. Chapter 1 briefly discusses formal political participation in Egypt and the record of popular exclusion. For sources on political participation in Egypt see John Waterbury, *The Egypt of Nasser and Sadat*, esp. Part 4; Robert Springborg, *Family, Power and Politics in Egypt* and *Mubarak's Egypt*, and his "Patterns of Association in the Egyptian Political Elite," in *Political Elites in the Middle East*, ed. Lenczowski, pp. 83–107; Robert Bianchi, *Unruly Corporatism*; Mahmoud Hussein, *Class Conflict in Egypt, 1945–1970*, trans. Michel and Susanne Chirman et al.; Raymond William Baker, *Egypt's Uncertain Revolution Under Nasser and Sadat* and his *Sadat and After*; Manfred Halpern, *The Politics of Social Change in the Middle East and North Africa*; Fouad Ajami, *The Arab Predicament*; Leonard Binder, *In a Moment of Enthusiasm*; Marc N. Cooper, *The Transformation of Egypt*; Raymond A. Hinnebusch, Jr., *Egyptian Politics Under Sadat*; Nazih N. M. Ayubi, *Bureaucracy and Politics in Contemporary Egypt*; Saad Ibrahim Gumaa, *Youth and Political Participation*; Hamied Ansari, *Egypt: The Stalled Society*; R. Hrair Dekmejian, *Egypt Under Nasir*; and P. J. Vatikiotis, *Nasser and His Generation*.

26. Gordon, *Nasser's Blessed Movement*, p. 197.

27. In order to offset the remaining power of Nasserists within the bureaucracy and elsewhere, President Sadat decided to create three "platforms," a rightist, centrist, and leftist one, to participate in parliamentary elections in the fall of 1976. Shortly thereafter these state-created institutions became legal political parties. The Arab Socialist Union was not officially scrapped until 1978. Waterbury, *The Egypt of Nasser and Sadat*, pp. 355–59.

The centrist platform became the National Democratic Party, the Tagammu' the leftist party, and the Ahrar the rightist party. Later in 1978 Sadat created a new loyal opposition, the Socialist Labor Party, with roots to the nationalist Islamist group Misr al-Fatat (Young Egypt), which was popular among nationalist youth in the 1930s and 1940s and grew into the Socialist Party. The new party had no organized support from labor. Sadat denied the Muslim Brothers the right to form a political party but did allow its publishing ventures to reopen and promoted Islamic student groups at universities to offset the strong leftist, Nasserist student groups. Sadat also allowed the Wafd, the nationalist party of the prerevolutionary period, to reestablish itself as the New Wafd Party. See Erika Post, "Egypt's Elections," *MERIP* 147 (July–August 1987): 18–19.

28. Daniel H. Levine, "Religion, the Poor, and Politics in Latin America Today," in *Religion and Political Conflict in Latin America*, ed. Levine, p. 6.

29. Levine, "Religion, the Poor, and Politics in Latin America Today," p. 6.

30. Philip Oxhorn, "The Popular-Sector Response to an Authoritarian Regime," *Latin American Perspectives* 18 (Winter 1991): 67–68 (emphasis added).

31. See Guillermo O'Donnell, "Tensions in the Bureaucratic-Authoritarian State," in *The New Authoritarianism in Latin America*, ed. Collier, p. 289.

32. Charles S. Maier, "Introduction," in *Changing Boundaries of the Political*, ed. Maier, p. 12.

33. Gusfield, "Social Movements and Social Change," p. 336.

34. See, for example, Nadim, "Family Relationships in a 'Harah' in Cairo," pp. 212–22; Rugh, *The Family in Contemporary Egypt*; and Hoodfar, "Household Budgeting and Financial Management," pp. 120–42.

35. Until fairly recently, public contestation was a colloquial art form where audiences and crowds would gather to hear people trading ritualized insults and to judge the individual performance on its spontaneity, its puns and rhymes. Found in many other cultures and languages as well, this form of interactive, ritualized insult is called *'affiyya* (*qaffiyya* in classical Arabic), and until the popularity of radio and television in the twentieth century in Egypt it was a much appreciated popular tradition that allowed men to vent some of their frustrations while gaining prestige for their wit and command of the language. Today the tradition only lives on in the performances of well-known comedians who skirmish with a counterpart, trading puns, insults, and double entendres. Personal communication with Professor Carol Bardenstein, Dartmouth College.

36. See, for example, the work of Judith E. Tucker, *Women in Nineteenth-Century Egypt*; Joel Beinen and Zachary Lockman, *Workers on the Nile*; Nathan J. Brown, *Peasant Politics in Modern Egypt*; Carl F. Petry, "Class Solidarity versus Gender Gain," in *Women in Middle Eastern History*, ed. Keddie and Baron, pp. 122–42.

37. Clifford Geertz, *Local Knowledge*, p. 156.

38. Geertz, *Local Knowledge*, p. 156.

39. For more detailed information on a demographic profile of Cairo, see Frederic Shorter, "Cairo's Leap Forward," *Cairo Papers in Social Science* 12 (Spring 1989): 5.

40. The demand for housing is so great in central Cairo that some of the original barriers to expanding these neighborhoods (such as cemeteries, public lands largely reserved for military purposes, the desert, and land-use zoning codes) have recently been overcome. The *Qaraafa*, the northern, eastern, and southern cemeteries (Bab al-Nasr, Qayt Bay, and al-Xaliifa, respectively), some of which predate the medieval period, are now heavily populated by people living both in tombs and in buildings they have carefully constructed around the tombs. Manshiet Nasser, another new community, was founded on empty quarry land that was state property. Muqattem Hills, which until the 1978 Camp David Accords was the strategically important and off-limits eastern heights above Cairo, has been transformed into a largely upper-middle-class residential area. At the same time, it is home to the Zabaleen, a largely Christian community that has a monopoly on refuse collection and recycling in Cairo. (Their religion is a factor because one of their main activities includes raising pigs fed on garbage scraps for local markets. Muslims do not eat pork or encourage its production.)

Bulaq al-Dakrur in Giza Governorate (just behind Cairo University) grew through largely informal private housing construction on former agricultural land. In the 1960s the Egyptian government began building public-sector housing in a largely agricultural area, al-Zaawiya al-Hamraa', in northern Cairo, just north of al-Sharaabiya. Shortly thereafter, informal-sector construction mushroomed there as well. Because the area is not too far from central Cairo, families compete for the limited supply of public-sector housing and save carefully to rent a relatively expensive apartment in a new privately constructed building. Yet, this neighborhood is one of the bleakest landscapes in Cairo as few roads, amenities, or services interrupt tract after tract of apartment buildings. Public housing suffers from all the unfortunate aspects of contemporary, inexpensive "modern" architecture where identical cubicle-like buildings rise out of the dusty roads and lack any influence from indigenous architecture. In 1982, in response to the growth of these newly settled residential areas, the Ministry of Interior elevated the status of al-Zaawiya al-Hamraa' and Manshiet Nasser from being quarters in other districts and made them into their own districts, splitting them in turn into various quarters or *shiyaaxa*. See Central Agency for Population Mobilisation and Statistics, *1986 Population Census* 1:1–3.

For further information on some of these new areas see Shorter, "Cairo's Leap Forward," pp. 35–39; Linda Oldham, Haguer El Hadidi, and Hussein Tamaa, "Informal Communities in Cairo," *Cairo Papers in Social Science* 10 (Winter 1987); Ragui Assaad and Leyla Neyzi, "Locating the Informal Sector in History" (Paper presented at the Social Science Research Council's Workshop on the Informal Sector of the Economy in the Middle East, Munich, 28–31 July 1986); Belgin Tekçe, Linda Oldham, and Frederic Shorter, *A Place to Live*; and Huda Zurayk and Frederic Shorter, "The Social Composition of Households in Arab Cities and Settlements," *Regional Papers* (Cairo: Population Council, 1988).

41. The historical and administrative development of Cairo as well as other Middle Eastern cities accounts for the particular distinctiveness of certain urban quarters.

42. Nadim, "Family Relationships in a 'Harah' in Cairo," p. 213.

43. Janet L. Abu-Lughod, *Cairo: 1001 Years of the City Victorious*, pp. 24–25.

44. Abu-Lughod, *Cairo: 1001 Years of the City Victorious*, p. 24.

45. Ibid., pp. 188–93.

46. The soundness of housing and construction procedures has been a constant problem in many areas of Cairo, and it is not a new problem, particularly since high population densities and commercial needs encourage speculators to construct buildings quickly and there is not enough government supervision to ensure proper construction methods and zoning requirements. Even in the 1960s, residents of Bab al-Sha'riyya listed the poor conditions of housing as one of their worst problems, and the authors of a study explained that 30 percent of the families surveyed had recently moved because they feared that their previous residence would collapse. Hassan al-Sa'aaty, *A Sociological Survey of the District of Bab al-Shaʿriyya*, pp. 21–22, 41. See Nawal Mahmoud Hassan, "Beyond Western Paradigms of Development," in *Development, Change and Gender in Cairo*, ed. Singerman and Hoodfar.

47. Heba Handoussa, "Crisis and Challenge: Prospects for the 1990s," in *Employment and Structural Adjustment*, ed. Handoussa and Potter, pp. 16–17.

48. Eleven in this group of 350 were under the age of fifteen. These children were included in my "sample" either because they worked (seven of the eleven) or were otherwise central to an important event or problem in the community. However, most of the children of the men and women in the sample were not included. The thirty-two children of the members of the family I lived with were nevertheless a major source of knowledge, distraction, and affection during my fieldwork.

49. The plurality of men in the sample can be partially explained by my interest in the political economy of the community, which developed later through introductions made by several men to local businessmen, merchants, and manufacturers. Through one intermediary, referred to below, I met thirty-three local workers, workshop owners, and people who serviced the commercial areas. Only two of those were working women, and I met very few of their relatives, since they were interviewed at their workplace. Earlier during my year of fieldwork I had visited most people in

their homes, or the homes of others, and therefore met relatives and neighbors of both genders.

50. Some of the concerns of Cairene young men did not differ enormously from their rural counterparts because, as one young man explained, television and films have spread the dreams, aspirations, and demands of urban youths to rural areas.

51. The only people in the sample that I did not meet personally were three local politicians, one long-deceased head of a family, and eight members of an army platoon. However, others provided sufficient detailed information about these people to include them in the sample.

52. These figures include five boys and one girl under the age of fifteen, who worked as apprentices in local industries (the girl was unemployed but seeking employment as a seamstress in local establishments). In Egypt the Central Agency for Public Mobilisation and Statistics (CAPMAS) includes persons twelve to sixty-four years of age in its surveys of Egypt's economically active population. International Labour Office (ILO), *Statistical Sources and Methods*, vol. 3, *Economically Active Population*, p. 49.

Three criteria were used to exclude fifty-eight people in the larger sample (twenty-six men and thirty-two women) from the economically active sample: first, those individuals who were students and had no economic activity (nine men and eighteen women); second, those individuals whose occupational and employment status were unknown to me (seven men and three women); and finally, those individuals from a village in the delta which I had visited and were important to the larger sample but did not include in the economically active sample (since the analysis had a focus on Cairo).

53. ILO, *Economically Active Population*, p. 183 (appendix).

54. Ibid.

55. The walled city was residentially segregated by religion, occupation, and nationality. For more details on the historical development of Cairo see Janet Abu-Lughod, *Cairo: 1001 Years of the City Victorious*, pp. 17–18, 60.

56. See Nikki R. Keddie, "Problems in the Study of Middle Eastern Women," *International Journal of Middle Eastern Studies* 10 (1979): 238–39.

57. Gabriel A. Almond and Sidney Verba, eds., *The Civic Culture*, pp. 16–18.

CHAPTER ONE

1. This almost exclusively female profession has persevered despite rapid social, political, and economic changes in Egypt. In the late nineteenth and early twentieth centuries they circulated among wealthy households, generally servicing many of the needs of women by selling fabric, jewelry, and bulk commodities. Middle- to upper-class women relied on these women for information from other households since they had little freedom of movement or mobility and less access to markets. Often these women were instrumental in arranging marriages and political alliances among the elite. For a description of the economic role of 'id-dallalaat in nineteenth-century Egypt see Tucker, *Women in Nineteenth-Century Egypt*, pp. 82–84. For more recent activities of 'id-dallalaat see Evelyn Aleene Early's research on another sha'bi neighborhood, Bulaq Abu 'Ala, "Getting It Together," in *Arab Women*, ed. Tucker, pp. 96–98; and S. al-Messiri, *Ibn al-Balad*, pp. 63–64.

2. In July 1986, in an effort to reduce its subsidy bill and direct subsidies to the more disadvantaged in Egypt, the government introduced a two-tiered pricing system

for certain subsidized commodities. Greater quantities of certain goods that previously had only been available at public food cooperatives through a ration-book system would now be available at higher prices in greater quantities at special stores throughout Egypt. Interestingly, 'id-dallalaat still charged less for the same items on the black market than the government's prices at the new special stores.

3. As Khouri-Dagher points out, people depend on 'id-dallalaat for goods they cannot obtain, but also condemn 'id-dallalaat for exploiting the government and, in some ways, the community. For a comprehensive study of the issue of subsidized food in Egypt see Nadia Khouri-Dagher, "Food and Energy in Cairo," and "The Answers of Civil Society to a Defaulting State."

4. In August 1986 the director of the Ministry of Food Supply's investigation bureau began a crackdown on black marketers in Cairo and announced the arrest over a two-day period of 173 people, including thirty-nine dallalaat and balTagiyya (pl.), local male thugs or bullies often involved in the black market. "Australian Sheep . . . Ordered and Butchered . . . and Leaving. The Minister of Food Supply Passes the Test of the 'Iid al-ADHa [Greater Bairam]," al-Masaa', August 12, 1986, p. 1.

5. Dale F. Eickelman, The Middle East: An Anthropological Approach, p. 105.

6. C. Wood, "Equilibrium and Historical-Structural Perspectives on Migration," International Migration 16 (1982): 339. In a recent study of another, more recently settled sha'bi community, Homa Hoodfar critiques Wood's privileging of monetary income in his explanation of the household. She argues that four different elements comprise the full income of a household, particularly in developing nations: "First, it is cash income raised through wage labor, profit and remittances. Second, the use-value consumption by subsistence activities such as household, production of food stuffs, repairs, construction, sewing, etc. Third, the extent to which a household draws on public services such as free schooling, medicine, or utilizing subsidized goods. Fourth, is rent and other transfers such as gift exchange. These categories embody in themselves the outcome of other activities such as networking and information gathering." Hoodfar, "Survival Strategies in Low-income Neighbourhoods of Cairo, Egypt," pp. 39–40.

7. Zurayk and Shorter, "The Social Composition of Households," p. 23.

8. I do not mean to suggest that the family functions exclusively as a political institution. The political, social, moral, and economic aspects of familial structures are interdependent and important to this community as well. Economic aspects of familial structures will be discussed in Chapter 4, and the moral influence of the family will be addressed in the following chapter.

9. Clifford Geertz, The Interpretation of Cultures, p. 126.

10. Naomi Chazan, "Patterns of State-Society Incorporation and Disengagement in Africa," in The Precarious Balance, ed. Chazan and Rothchild, p. 123.

11. Sheldon S. Wolin, "Max Weber: Legitimation, Method and the Politics of Theory," Political Theory 3 (August 1981): 402–403.

12. In the Middle East women have traditionally gained power and authority through their position in the family or as brokers of information and marriage. See, for example, Cynthia Nelson, "Public and Private Politics," pp. 555–64, and her "Women and Power in Nomadic Societies in the Middle East," in The Desert and the Sown, ed. Nelson, pp. 43–60. See also Soraya Altorki, Women in Saudi Arabia.

13. Elshtain, Public Man, Private Woman, pp. 1–16.

14. Elshtain, Public Man, Private Woman, p. 12.

15. Ibid.

16. Amal Rassam, "Toward a Theoretical Framework for the Study of Women in the Arab World," in UNESCO, *Social Science Research and Women in the Arab World*, p. 17.

17. Maier, "Introduction," in *Changing Boundaries of the Political*, p. 2.

18. James A. Bill and Carl Leiden, *Politics in the Middle East*, p. 90.

19. Bill and Leiden, *Politics in the Middle East*, p. 27.

20. Ibid., p. 130.

21. Bill and Leiden, *Politics in the Middle East*, p. 28, emphasis added.

22. Ibid., p. 149.

23. Bill and Leiden, *Politics in the Middle East*, p. 98.

24. Ibid., p. 157.

25. For an excellent critical review of liberal and Marxist analyses of the role of the household in economic development see Nancy Folbre, "Cleaning House: New Perspectives on Households and Economic Development," *Journal of Development Economics* 22 (1986): 5–40.

26. Rassam, "Toward a Theoretical Framework," pp. 122–38.

27. It was very common for physical fights to erupt in households between husband and wife, siblings of various ages, children and parents, and extended family members. While the propensity to resort to violence varied from household to household, supposed authority figures were no more immune to attack than others. Contestants in these battles would perhaps be publicly chided by others for fighting a man, an elder, or a woman (depending on the gender mix), but reality differed from usual generalizations about the patriarchal family. Wives fought husbands, daughters fought mothers, sisters fought brothers, and daughters fought fathers.

28. Nancy Folbre, "The Black Four of Hearts," in *A Home Divided*, ed. Dwyer and Bruce, p. 248.

29. Amartya Sen, "Gender and Cooperative Conflicts," in *Persistent Inequalities*, ed. Tinker.

30. See, for example, Nadim, "Family Relationships in a 'Harah' in Cairo," pp. 212–222; Rugh, *The Family in Contemporary Egypt*; and Hoodfar, "Household Budgeting and Financial Management," pp. 120–42.

31. Samir Khalaf, *Lebanon's Predicament*, p. 14.

32. Barakat calls the family the "basic unit of social organization in traditional and contemporary Arab society." Halim Barakat, "The Arab Family and the Challenge of Social Transformation," in *Women and the Family in the Middle East*, ed. Fernea, p. 27.

33. Elizabeth Warnock Fernea, "The Family," in *Women and the Family in the Middle East*, ed. Fernea, p. 25.

34. See Suad Joseph, "Working-Class Women's Networks in a Sectarian State," *American Ethnologist* 10 (February 1983): 1–22.

35. Rosemary Sayigh, "Roles and Functions of Arab Women: A Reappraisal," *Arab Studies Quarterly* 3 (Autumn 1981): 267.

36. See Rosemary Sayigh, *Palestinians: From Peasants to Revolutionaries*, and her "Encounters with Palestinian Women Under Occupation," in *Women and the Family in the Middle East*, ed. Fernea, pp. 191–208. For a similar view of family as a resource in industrialized nations see Margaret Stacy and Marion Price, *Women, Power and Politics*, p. 37.

37. Suad Joseph, "Family as Security and Bondage," in *Arab Society*, ed. Hopkins and Ibrahim, p. 248.

38. The empirical evidence of the importance of the family in Egypt was over-whelming, but it remains for other scholars, using a more historical methodology, to explain how the family has maintained its strength and position despite the structural and ideological changes in Egypt since the Free Officers Revolution in 1952. For a discussion of the influence of economic change on the structure of the Egyptian fam-ily in the nineteenth century see Tucker, *Women in Nineteenth-Century Egypt*.

39. This familial protection is expressed even more specifically by the word *Hardaana*, which describes a woman who has returned to her parent's home. Cus-tomarily, the wife cannot return to her marital abode until the husband comes to get her.

40. In Egypt the right of women to divorce is based on specific limited conditions including the lack of financial support, severe or chronic [physical and mental] de-fects, a contagious disease, desertion (including imprisonment), and maltreatment or cruelty (*'iDDarr*), which must be proved before a judge. The criteria of "harm" are specified by six subclauses. A woman may divorce her husband if he: "(1) habitually assaults her or makes her life miserable by cruelty of conduct even if such conduct does not amount to physical ill treatment; (2) associates with women of evil repute or leads an infamous life; (3) attempts to force her to lead an immoral life; (4) dis-poses of her property or prevents her exercising her legal rights over it; (5) obstructs her in the observance of her religious profession or practice; (6) has more wives than one and does not treat her with equality in accordance with the injunctions of the Quran (Section 2.viii)" (see John L. Esposito, *Women in Muslim Family Law*, pp. 77–80). The last criterion of *'iDDarr* was only included in Egyptian Personal Status Law after the 1979 revisions. After the 1979 revisions were declared unconstitu-tional in 1985, the new law made it more difficult for a woman to obtain a divorce if her husband married another woman. For a thorough discussion of the debate and history of the Personal Status Law see Nancy Young Reynolds, "Discourses of Social Change: An Analysis of the 1985 Personal Status Law Debate in Egypt"; Nadia Hijab, *Womanpower: The Arab Debate on Women at Work*; and Hoda Fahmi, "Di-vorcer en Egypte."

41. Many households in this community owned VCRs, purchased to entertain adults and children, since theaters were often far away and crowded with young men who make it uncomfortable for women and families to attend. It was not uncommon for young and middle-aged couples (husband and wife) in these communities to watch illegal, black-market pornographic films. From the questions of men and women in the community about the pervasiveness of certain sexual practices in the West, it was obvious that many of these films were hard-core pornography.

42. When an unknown man comes to pay a visit, it is proper that his visit be announced before entering the family's building. Usually the visitor (women also do this occasionally if they are not close friends or relatives) will yell the name of the father, eldest son, or the mother's traditional name (mother of her eldest son or daughter, if she has no son).

43. As in many societies, the costs and social expectations of a second marriage may be lower since either party may already have an apartment and/or other house-hold items.

44. Central Agency for Planning, Mobilisation, and Statistics, *Statistics on Mar-riage and Divorce (1979)*, Ref. 71–12512/81, p. 7.

45. While cases of violence against women who are not virgins when they marry are publicized in Egypt, the cases in which women are not victimized rarely receive publicity. Some couples who have had premarital sex may work together to falsify

proof of the woman's virginity on her wedding night. In other cases the family of the woman and even the family of the bridegroom may conceal the bride's lack of virginity from the public to protect the bride and her family's reputation. Older women, often mothers, help their daughters in many of these situations. But this tolerance is not highlighted in the media, which supports the status quo and the ideal that a bride must be a virgin. (Unfortunately, people's perceptions of virginity differ from a medical definition, and if a bride does not bleed after the marriage is consummated her virginity is doubted.)

46. In general, it is far more common that married women are widowed than the reverse since typically older men marry younger women. In prerevolutionary Egypt, a twenty-year age difference between bride and groom was common. Today in *sha'bi* communities, large age differences are seen in a more negative light, although an age gap of ten or even fifteen years between the groom and the bride is not uncommon (the inability of men to finance their marriage at an early age is more responsible for this age gap than the practice of older men marrying very young girls of thirteen, fourteen, or fifteen). Egyptian law forbids marriage under the age of sixteen.

47. In this community some apartments were owned by more than one family, and although unrelated they shared the same living area and some expenses such as utility costs. Even in cramped living conditions certain rooms or areas of rooms were clearly demarcated as the right of each family. It is rather unusual for a single young man to be a copartner (*shariik*) with a family, but in this particular case the young man's parents had both died and the fact that this woman only had sons and not daughters avoided a more complicated situation.

48. In Lebanon a family's reputation is so important that the heads of family associations issue public statements condemning the arrest or crime of anyone who shares the family name. Khalaf, *Lebanon's Predicament*, p. 169.

49. Zurayk and Shorter, "The Social Composition of Households," p. 30.

50. When the above-mentioned widow's father died in the 1950s, she received an inheritance of £E200, a large sum of money at that time. She purchased a few necessary household items and invested the remainder of the inheritance in her future financial security by purchasing eight gold bracelets worth £E160 (the value of which had increased to £E2,500 by 1986). This is a very typical pattern among women. An investment in gold jewelry is a visible sign of wealth and can always be sold during financial emergencies. Women do not always wear their gold, for safety's sake, but will hide it carefully at home or entrust it to a safe-deposit box. Despite financial difficulties when her husband died and as she raised seven children, she was never forced to sell her gold. Everyone in the community knew she owned these gold bracelets because she often wore them, and they served as collateral for many loans during difficult periods. The people who lent her money knew that if she was unable to repay the loan, she would sell her bracelets rather than lose the trust of the community. Many other women in the community, however, had found it necessary to sell their gold in a financial emergency, or for expenses such as marriage, housing, or an airplane ticket for a migrating son or husband. However, immediately after selling their jewelry, they would begin saving money to replace the items.

51. According to Law No. 100 (1985) revising Egypt's Personal Status Law, a mother has custody of a son until the age of ten and a daughter until the age of twelve. A judge can extend custody of a male child until the age of fifteen and a daughter until she marries, if the mother is fit and capable of supporting the child. The 1979 revisions of the law, which were declared unconstitutional in 1985, had similar provisions for custody. Although the mother may retain custody of a child,

until the proscribed ages, the father is still responsible for all expenses unless custody is extended by a judge and the mother or legal guardian then assumes financial responsibility (Law No. 100/1985 revision). Previous reforms of the Personal Status Law in 1920 and 1929 gave a mother custody of a male child until the age of nine and a female child until the age of eleven. See Reynolds, "Discourses of Social Change," and Iman M. Diaa el Din Bibars, "Women's Political Interest Groups in Egypt," Master's thesis, Department of Political Science, American University in Cairo, 1987.

52. Günter Meyer, "Socioeconomic Structure and Development of Small-Scale Manufacturing," p. 4.

53. Ibid.

54. Although the husband must still support his children in the case of a divorce when his wife has custody, a woman must usually augment the typically meager sum through her own resources.

55. Zurayk and Shorter, "The Social Composition of Households," p. 31.

56. One of the most contentious reforms of the 1979 Personal Status Law required the husband to notify his wife of his marriage to another woman. If the wife decided that the second marriage would cause her mental or material harm, she could petition the court for divorce, without losing her right to alimony and child support.

57. Eickelman, *The Middle East*, p. 109.

58. Khouri-Dagher, "The Answers of Civil Society to a Defaulting State," pp. 20–21.

59. Homa Hoodfar, "The Political Economy of Low-income Households in Contemporary Cairo," p. 1.

60. A large tent is erected by families in honor of both men and women. However, it is more common to erect a tent on the death of a man.

61. Dolls in Egypt are generically called *'aruusa*, or bride. From an early age girls are surrounded by the symbolism of marriage and socialized to conform to prevailing norms.

62. JoAnn Martin, "The Women's Touch: Patterns in Mexican Women's Political Participation," as quoted in Laura Nader, "The Subordination of Women in Comparative Perspective," *Urban Anthropology, and Studies of Cultural Systems and World Economic Development* 15 (Fall–Winter 1986), p. 389.

63. Wolin, "Max Weber," p. 402.

CHAPTER TWO

1. Illegitimate births in this community were rare. However, years ago a newborn baby had been abandoned and left in a vacant lot in the neighborhood. After unsuccessful attempts by the authorities to discover its mother, a local childless couple who lived nearby adopted the baby.

2. As has been noted, in *sha'bi* communities women value jewelry as a financial safety net. They buy or receive gold as a gift and can resell gold jewelry without a financial loss since its value is based almost entirely on the weight, not the design. Women from lower-income communities buy certain standard styles of jewelry whose resale value will not decline (though if the international price of gold falls, the value of the jewelry will decline). Thus jewelry represents savings, which in the event of a financial emergency can be exchanged for cash. While women hate to sell their jewelry, they will do so during a family emergency or to finance sudden investment opportunities.

3. In the first line of a 1985 Egyptian popular song, "Shababiik," MuHammad Munir commemorates love affairs in densely populated neighborhoods when he sings, "Windows, windows, all the world has windows." Since many apartments in Cairo have large French windows and balconies, city residents—particularly young men and women in love or in pursuit of a neighbor—spend much time staring out of their windows or balconies. Indeed, some buildings are so close to each other that a whisper from one balcony can be heard on another. Many matches in central Cairo are made because two young people can communicate from the safety of their balconies when they are not allowed to go out together. And many people refer to their own marriages as "shababiik affairs."

4. In a study of Muslim couples in Beirut, Khlat and Halabi suggest that these couples married earlier because the family arranged the marriages well in advance. M. Khlat and S. Halabi, "Modernization and Consanguineous Marriages in Beirut." *Journal of Biosocial Science* 18 (1986): 489–95, cited in Zurayk and Shorter, "The Social Composition of Households," p. 46. A study of a lower-income Cairo neighborhood found that 55 percent of the marriages were between relatives—45 percent on the paternal side and 10 percent on the maternal side (Rugh, *The Family in Contemporary Egypt*, p. 144).

5. Ibrahim al-'Ashmaawy, "Egyptian Youth," *al-Sha'b*, 19 August 1986, p. 9.

6. Ibid.

7. In more middle- and upper-class communities it is becoming slightly more acceptable to provide care for elderly parents in nursing homes. According to one account, a residential care facility for the elderly, sponsored by an Islamic benevolent society, had to resort to television advertising to fill its beds, since the demand for its services was so low.

8. Although people in this community did not specifically mention *al-kafa'* when evaluating appropriate mates, they believed in the same criteria. For an explanation of the Islamic concept, see Esposito, *Women in Muslim Family Law*, p. 128. Ibn Hanifa's six criteria for measuring *al-kafa'* include: Islam, affiliation, status (slave or free), fortune, profession, and *'at-tadayyun* (conformity of conduct to religious precepts). Fatna A. Sabbah, *Woman in the Muslim Unconscious*, p. 35.

9. For an examination of the ways in which Egyptian soap operas comment upon the issues surrounding marriage, upward mobility, and recent economic changes in Egypt, see Lila Abu-Lughod, "The Journey of Mr. Abu 'Ela al-Bishry, Islam and Public Culture," *Middle East Report* 180 (January–February 1993): 25–30.

10. Shortly after reading *'il-fatHa*, each side of the family should inform the other of past engagements of its son or daughter in order to avoid misunderstandings in the future. To publicly air one's dirty laundry minimizes the possibility of idle gossip ruining the marriage later. Once *'il-fatHa* has been recited, women in a family ululate (*byzaghraTu*) so that the entire neighborhood understands that a son or daughter has been formally engaged and that all former suitors must now keep their distance.

11. The *shabka* refers both to the engagement ceremony and the actual gift of jewelry (among *sha'bi* communities, usually two to four expensive 21-carat gold bracelets) given by the groom to the bride. At the same time, it is also customary for the groom to purchase two wedding rings (simple wedding bands). After the engagement ceremony the young couple wears the rings on their right hand; once they are married they switch them to their left hand.

12. One mother took advantage of her son's visit to the bathroom to negotiate particularly sensitive issues.

13. Due to the growing trend of lengthy engagements, the 1986 Population Census included for the first time, as a category of marital status, people who had signed a marriage contract but not consummated the marriage.

14. These various ceremonies function as both nouns and verbs in Egyptian colloquial. For example, people will ask a woman, *Shabakit, wala daxalit?* (Are you [f.] engaged or did you consummate the marriage?). Passive participles that describe an engaged woman include *mashbuuka* and *maxTuuba* (from *yixtub*, to be engaged).

15. One man visited the family of a young woman several times before a formal engagement, which demonstrated that he had "no personality." Local commentators explained, "Who ever heard of an *'ariis* [groom] who visited a young woman's home without even giving her a *shabka*?"

16. This young man had a very negative but common view of his own gender. When I asked him why it was so difficult to trust his sister's fiancé, he replied that men are like devils and will get away with whatever they can. As far as he was concerned, women had to protect themselves from men. No one should be surprised by their bad behavior because it was only natural for them to be impolite, since they were men. In their own home, however, they were polite and respected any guests, male or female.

17. People automatically assume that sexual relations would occur during a woman's unchaperoned visit to a man's home or an empty apartment.

18. Public demonstrations of respect and propriety are more important than one's actions. A young man refused to allow a picture to be taken of him putting his arm around his fiancée at their engagement party, saying that it was *Haraam*, or forbidden. In her home, however, in full view of everyone present, he often put his arm around her or held her hand.

19. After formal engagements the groom attempts to assert control over his fiancée, if she lets him. One young university-educated woman stopped seeing a potential suitor when he began telling her what to wear and not to wear, and how to act. As she explained, "If he is trying to control my actions now, what will he be like once we marry?"

20. If the bride or her family cancels the engagement, they are obliged to return the *shabka* and wedding band to the groom. If, however, the groom breaks the engagement, the bride is allowed to keep the *shabka* (although this is considered to be in somewhat bad taste and greedy, or *ghilis*).

21. For an analysis of this phenomenon see Barbara F. Stowasser, "Women's Issues in Modern Islamic Thought," in *Arab Women*, ed. Tucker, pp. 3–28.

22. While all religious parties were banned in the 1984 and 1987 parliamentary elections, the Muslim Brotherhood was able to forge alliances with various political parties. In 1984 the Muslim Brothers allied with the New Wafd Party to gain a role, but the Wafd outmaneuvered the Islamists and maintained control of the party. In the 1987 elections individuals were allowed to run for election, and prominent Islamists entered Parliament in this manner. (See Post, "Egypt's Elections," pp. 17–19.) In the 1990 parliamentary elections, however, all opposition parties, with the exception of the leftist party al-Tugamu, boycotted the election in protest over unfair government interference. Thus the presence of Islamists in Parliament who were aligned to political parties declined.

23. See Bertus Hendriks, "Egypt's New Political Map," *MERIP* 147 (July–August, 1987): 23–30.

24. The *milaaya* is not a veil but is a large piece of loosely structured black fabric

draped loosely around the head. It is held up by wrapping the cloth under the arms and holding it close to the body. Often women (particularly younger women) drape the *milaaya* only over their clothes and leave their heads uncovered. Older women also wear a scarf to cover their heads while outside the home.

25. See Fadwa El Guindi, "Veiling Infitah with Muslim Ethic," *Social Problems* 28 (April 1981): 465–85.

26. Abdul Aziz Khayat, "Association of Sexes in Islam," pp. 10–11.

27. The *duxla baladi* is more common among Egyptians from rural origins, although many people in the cities still marry in this fashion. It is also preferred by a family if there is some ambiguity about the honor of their daughter. For example, in one family in the community a daughter was engaged to be married when her father died very unexpectedly. In the months after his death, but before the wedding, the groom would occasionally sleep over at his fiancée's home because he was in the army and his family lived in the countryside. When people began to question this arrangement, and to suspect premarital relations between the couple, the bride's mother decided it would quell all suspicions if she insisted on a *duxla baladi*.

28. For example, a woman may have slept with her fiancée but unexpectedly married another man. In this case the woman and her family (usually her mother) will collaborate with the woman who performs the *duxla baladi* to use a fingernail or other sharp implement to draw blood. Other women secretly have a physician suture the outer labia in order to make sexual penetration simulate virginity. This is a lucrative and not uncommon medical procedure that is more popular among middle- and upper-middle-class Egyptian women than women from lower-income and more traditional backgrounds.

29. The total fertility rate (TFR) measures how many births women have as they pass through their reproductive years. From a high of 6.27 in 1959–60, the TFR declined to 4.22 in 1975–76. However, because of declining infant mortality rates, particularly after 1970, the age cohort of women in their childbearing years has remained large and therefore crude birth rates have not declined as significantly as the TFR. See Frederic Shorter, "The Creation of 'Manshiet Nasser,'" pp. 9–15.

30. Hussein A. A. Sayed and Shadia S. Attia, "Some Demographic and Family Planning Characteristics," cited by Shorter, "The Creation of 'Manshiet Nasser,'" pp. 13–14.

31. Children accompany their parents and relatives everywhere in Egypt. In nightclubs that cater to wealthy Egyptians and foreigners from the Gulf countries, children accompany their parents and remain there until the nightclubs close at four or five in the morning. In lower-income communities, children are not put to bed early and stay awake as long as visitors remain, and often long after they leave. When families go on vacation or on a short trip, or visit relatives, the children come along as well. The institution of the baby-sitter, so common in the United States, is unknown in this community, although neighbors and relatives look after children when their mothers or caretakers must run an errand.

32. Zurayk and Shorter, "The Social Composition of Households," p. 15.

33. The published accounts of rapes during early 1985 revealed that an alarming percentage of the victims of rape were children (22 percent were under the age of ten and 48 percent under the age of sixteen). Some young girls of five, six, and even four had been raped. However, analysts did not concentrate on the young ages of many of the victims. Although there were no accounts of rape in the community I studied, several incidents of child abuse and molestation did occur. In one case, a distant relative of one family visited their home when the parents were away and began

molesting the two very young girls. Fortunately, their mother arrived in time to stop the teenage young man, who fell to his knees and begged her not to tell his family about what had happened because he knew that they would be incensed and beat him severely. She actually never told his relatives or her husband because this young man was her relative and it was therefore her family who was ultimately responsible for his actions. Instead, the mother beat the older daughter (approximately ten years old) for not protecting her younger sister and for allowing the young man into the house when her parents were not home.

34. The material for this section is drawn from an unpublished paper that analyzed public reaction to this wave of rapes in the Egyptian media. See Diane Singerman, "The Recent Phenomenon of Rape in Egypt."

35. During this period, rapes were widely discussed in households as a means of educating and supervising the behavior of members of the community. Mothers warned their daughters about the dangers of unchaperoned dates, and fathers forbade their daughters to leave their homes unless absolutely necessary.

36. Between 1980 and 1985 the Ministry of Interior reported 746 crimes of abduction, rape, and sexual abuse, involving 635 people. This category includes arrests for crimes ranging from sexual harassment in public transportation and public lewdness to sexual assault and rape. "A State of Anxiety in the Egyptian Home," *al-Ahram*, 23 February 1985, p. 3.

37. Ibid.

38. "A State of Anxiety," p. 29.

39. "Rape: Under the Magnifying Glass of the Greatest Sages in Egypt," *Akhar Saaʿa* (February 1985): 28.

40. "Crimes of Rape Break Out in the Egyptian Countryside," *al-Shaʿb*, 12 March 1985, p. 7.

41. "The *Wafd* Stalks the Human Wolves in the Provinces of Egypt," *al-Wafd*, 14 February 1985, p. 7.

42. "Mubarak's Labor Day Speech," *al-Ahram*, 2 May 1985, p. 1.

43. The occupation of all adults is printed on their I.D. card, which can cause endless bureaucratic difficulties when people change occupations or careers.

44. This discussion was part of a longer discussion of the differences between Western and Egyptian sexual mores. It began with a question about whether people really have sex publicly in Hyde Park in London, as Egyptians have heard. When I tried to respond by explaining the range of sexual activity in the West, the members of this large family countered that even in Egypt all sorts of sexual activities occur. One of the men present, a taxicab driver, described overhearing Egyptian women proposition Arab men as they rode together in his taxi by chance. Their primary motive, he argued, was financial, which then launched this second discussion about prostitution.

45. While some experts in Egypt believe that female circumcision is legal, or that the law is neutral regarding the practice, Anne Cloudsley writes that circumcision has been illegal in Egypt for some time, and that in 1967 the *sunna* (or traditional) type of circumcision (removal of the prepuce [hood] of the clitoris) was also prohibited by the government—although she mentions that it is still widely practiced (Cloudsley, *Women of Omdurman*, p. 110). Lightfoot-Klein does not argue that circumcision is illegal in Egypt but only that "a resolution by the Minister of Health recommended that partial clitoridectomy performed by doctors take place of the more extreme procedures performed by the *daya*s midwives. Another resolution in 1978 forbade *daya*s to perform the operations." Nevertheless, midwives continue to perform these

operations, and the practice has continued unabated. Hanny Lightfoot-Klein, *Prisoners of Ritual*, pp. 43–44.

46. See Nawal el-Saadawi, *The Hidden Face of Eve*, and Sabbah, *Woman in the Muslim Unconscious*, pp. 25–56.

47. According to research by Dr. MuHammad Bedawi, female circumcision is thought to predate Islam in Egypt since the procedure was described in hieroglyphics and painted on the walls of period tombs. People commonly associate female circumcision with Islam because many people arrange for circumcisions at kiosks that are often attached to a popular mosque and decorated with religious iconography. If complications develop, people at the mosque will often defend the *muTahiraati* (one who performs a circumcision) who has botched the circumcision. Some *muTahiraati* have followed their ancestors in the trade for generations. One young man had obtained a B.A. in agricultural engineering but then returned to his family's traditional, more lucrative trade of circumcision of boys and girls, which had been maintained for the past two hundred years. Comments presented during a seminar by Dr. Bedawi, Lecturer, Department of Psychiatry, al-Azhar University, Cairo, July 19, 1984. See also John G. Kennedy's monograph, "Circumcision and Excision in Egyptian Nubia," *Man* 2 (June 1970), which confirms that male and female circumcision was recorded as a common ritual in Pharaonic Egypt.

48. However, the question of whether female circumcision is a religious tradition, a cultural practice, or a symbol of honor and embellishment is debated by religious scholars and jurists, and ambiguous references to the practice are said to date back to the birth of Islam. Cloudsley, *Women of Omdurman*, pp. 101–103.

49. "The Nubians argue that the only way to blunt the inherent sexual wildness of girls and to preserve their chastity is through this means, though there is not medical evidence that any diminishing effect on desire is actually produced" (ibid., p. 181). Many Caireans in *shaʿbi* communities echoed this sentiment.

50. Many *muTahiraati* hold licenses as barbers, and they use many of the same instruments for both professions. Midwives also perform circumcisions, although some of these women are licensed by the government and supervised by Maternal and Child health care centers. As one midwife said, "Circumcision is not a ritual anymore, it is now a simple clinical operation that we perform with all necessary precautions." Dagmar Simon, "Dayas in Urban Health Care," p. 57.

51. According to Lightfoot-Klein's research, female circumcision predominates in approximately 40 percent of the African continent. "It is known to exist to a far lesser degree in other parts of the Third World, in the Gulf States, in Yemen, among some Islamic peoples in Indonesia and Malaysia, and in Sri Lanka." Lightfoot-Klein argues, however, that in 80 percent of the Islamic world today, female circumcision is unknown. In a 1982 study Hosken estimated that 80 million women were circumcised annually worldwide. In East Africa a smaller number of Animists, African Coptic Christians, and a small sect of Ethiopian Jews (the Fallashas) also practice female circumcision. Lightfoot-Klein, *Prisoners of Ritual*, pp. ix, 41–42. See also F. P. Hosken, "Women and Health: Female Circumcision." *WIN News* 4 (1982).

52. In the Sudan infibulation was declared illegal in 1945, under the Anglo-Egyptian Condominium government, but the government never prosecuted practitioners and the practice continued unabated. Infibulation consists of "the removal of all the external genitalia, the whole of the clitoris and the entire labia minora. The fleshy parts of the labia majora are then pared down, leaving enough skin on their lateral aspects for them to be sewn together, or to heal together by virtue of being in apposition. In this way the vulva is closed, obliterating the vaginal opening except for a

small posterior meatus left to allow the passage of urine and menstrual flow" (Cloudsley, *Women of Omdurman*, pp. 127, 110). In 1974 the Sudanese government passed new legislation forbidding radical, Pharaonic circumcisions but excision of the clitoris was still permissible. For a comprehensive study of female circumcision in the Sudan see Asma el Dareer, *Woman, Why Do You Weep?* and Cloudsley, *Women of Omdurman*, esp. Appendix 1, pp. 174–76.

53. Deniz Kandiyoti, "Introduction, " in *Women, Islam and the State*, ed. Kandiyoti, pp. 3, 7.

54. See Nadia Farah, *The Life of a Woman and Her Health* (Cairo: Sinai Publishers, 1991).

55. Nadia Farah, "The Egyptian Women's Health Book Collective: Our Bodies, Ourselves," *Middle East Report* 173 (November–December 1991): 16–17.

56. Farah, *The Life of a Woman and Her Health*, p. 71.

57. Ibid.

58. Ibid., p. 273.

59. The memory and concern among Egyptians for the price of goods provides a rich opportunity for researchers to construct consumer price indexes and compare the cost of living, through interviews and oral history. Painstaking though it may be, this approach to economic analysis would complement national economic data.

60. The official exchange rate for the Egyptian pound remained at £E.83 = $1 until 1986. Economist Intelligence Unit (EIU), "Egypt," *Country Profile Reports* (1986–87): 8–9. The same analysts estimated that the black-market value of the Egyptian pound in 1985 equaled $1.43. EIU, "Egypt," *Country Profile Reports* 4 (1988): Appendix.

61. A Ministry of Housing report estimated a need for 1,400,000 new housing units in Greater Cairo alone, between 1981 and the year 2000. On average the government constructed 11,000 public-sector units per year throughout Egypt between 1960–1970. Between 1961–62 and 1975 the largest number of housing units built by both the private and public sector was 42,443. See John Waterbury, "Patterns of Urban Growth and Income Distribution in Egypt," in *The Political Economy of Income Distribution in Egypt*, ed. Abdel-Khalak and Tignor, pp. 335–37.

At the same time, however, an MIT/TAP report claims that there is not a housing shortage due to the construction of informal housing units. "While official statistics show only 550,000 urban units built [between 1960–1975], the net change in the stock is four times that or 2 million!" "Public Policy and the Economics of Housing," *The Housing and Construction Industry in Egypt*, p. 7.

62. For a comprehensive discussion of the history of rent control and the housing policies of the Nasser and Sadat regime see Milad M. Hanna, "Real Estate Rights in Urban Egypt," in *Property, Social Structure and Law in the Modern Middle East*, ed. Mayer, pp. 189–211.

63. During the initial years of the Open Door policy initiated by President Sadat, the price of land increased ten to fifteen times within three or four years. Foreign and joint venture companies entered the construction sector, oversupplying the growing demand for luxury apartments, while driving up the price of land, construction labor, and rents. Hanna, "Real Estate Rights in Urban Egypt," p. 199.

64. Abt Associates, Dames and Moore, and the General Organization for Housing, Building Planning and Research, "Informal Housing in Egypt," p. xix.

65. The cost of key money for a particular apartment, commercial space, or building is calculated, according to Hanna, as the difference in rents between a fixed rent and the rent of a unit that is newly leased, over a three-year period. For example,

if an old flat rents for £E4 per month and a similar apartment is rented for £E20 per month, the key money would equal £E576 [(20–4) × 36 = 576]. However, in my community sums paid by residents for key money were much greater than this formula suggests. See Hanna, "Real Estate Rights in Urban Egypt," pp. 207–208.

66. Abt Associates et al., "Informal Housing in Egypt," p. 167.

67. By the time a couple produces children and needs more space, they usually move into an independent household. Zurayk and Shorter, "The Social Composition of Households," p. 73.

68. The rising cost of subsidized public housing has received the attention of legislators in the Egyptian Parliament. Ulfat Kamel, a member of Parliament from il-Gamaliyya district in Cairo, asked her colleagues in a meeting of the housing committee in Parliament, "How can we take a £E1,000 down payment from citizens for subsidized housing and then ask him to pay £E50 rent per month? How will a recent university graduate find this money, when we know how little he is paid?" New civil service employees receive a monthly salary of only £E40–60. "A Responsible Parliamentarian Criticizes the State Plan to Build Subsidized Public Housing. A Wafd Representative Asks How Will University Graduates Find a Subsidized Apartment?" *al-Wafd*, 25 June 1989.

69. Author interview with al-Hag SubHy Wihdaan, Cairo, July 14, 1988. In a study of a new informal housing area, Sofia Mohsen found that the residents built new homes and bought land when they had unanticipated wealth, in cash. Because this stratum of society usually has less access to formal credit and does not trust the banking system, it preferred to invest its cash in construction or renovation. Abt Associates et al., "Informal Housing in Egypt," p. 238.

70. Handoussa, "Crisis and Challenge," p. 18.

71. To reduce cash outlays for a trousseau, women also sew many of the clothes a bride brings to a new household. However, locally produced ready-made clothes and imported clothes are increasingly popular and increase the cost of a trousseau.

72. The cost of marriage for men can be increased by an agreement between two families that a groom not provide a dower but purchase the required furniture instead. Since the cost of the *gihaaz* almost always exceeds the amount of the dower, this arrangement places more financial pressure on the groom. In one situation where the couple and their families had agreed on this arrangement, the groom did not have to spend a considerable sum on key money or rent for an apartment since his mother had been able to keep a publicly subsidized apartment vacant for several years. In another case, the couple were cousins and the family of the groom was more prosperous than the bride's family. Perhaps because the two families were related, the groom's side agreed to bear an unusually high proportion of the expenses.

73. The popularity of these sets of furniture is demonstrated by production levels in Dumyyaat, the capital of this industry. In 1988, 16,353 workshops employing 49,059 workers and 17,000 apprentices produced 30,000 rooms of furniture a month, or 360,000 sets of furniture a year. This industry consumes 60 percent of all wood imported to Egypt annually, which means that the rest of the country also satisfied a significant amount of the demand for furniture. The most recent national figures (1978) for the number of marriage contracts issued that year is only slightly more than the number of rooms of furniture produced in Dumyyaat: 375,656 marriage contracts as opposed to 360,000 sets of furniture. Thus, one could argue that an extremely wide cross-section of the population is purchasing at least one and perhaps even two sets of furniture for marriage. See "Rescuing Dumyyaat Industries

from Extinction," *al-Ahraam al-IqtiSadi*, 13 June 1988, p. 33, and Central Agency for Planning, Mobilisation, and Statistics (CAPMAS), *Statistics on Marriage and Divorce (1979)*, p. 8.

74. In Egyptian villages one of the rituals preceding the consummation of the marriage is the traditional procession through the village of all the bride's trousseau piled into donkey carts and taken from her parental home to her new home. This provides an extremely public but important opportunity to display wealth and status, without offending communal norms.

75. Kariman Aly Fuda, "Islam Rejects the Phenomenon of Extravagant Weddings," *Al-Liwaa' al-Islami*, 7 August 1986, pp. 1, 21.

76. For a more in-depth analysis of literacy in Egypt, particularly among lower-income women, see Kamphoefner, "Voices from the Bottom," 1989.

77. Another important protection for a woman is the Islamic practice of specifying a percentage (*'il-mu'axxar*) of the dower that will be paid to her in the event of a divorce or if she is widowed. In the postwar period the price of the *mu'axxar* was far closer to the amount of the dower than it is today. In one family's history the amount of the *mu'axxar* equaled the dower in 1947, decreased to two-thirds of the dower in 1969 (£E100 with a dower of 150), and was only half the dower in 1986. The trend seems to have lowered the cost of divorce for men.

78. In this case we have to assume the difference in price is not accountable to taste or the quality of the furniture since the same family made both purchases. The prices for three rooms of furniture in real prices (1980) are the following: £E1,666 (1973), £E1,755 (1975), and £E3450 (1979). Again, in real terms the largest increase in prices occurred between 1975 and 1979. Calculations of real prices were based on figures found in World Bank and International Finance Corporation. *World Tables, 1988–89*, pp. 234–35.

79. Even in wealthier Arab countries such as Saudi Arabia, Oman, and the United Arab Emirates, the government and religious authorities have made public appeals and designed policies to reduce the massive costs of marriage. In Saudi Arabia average dowries equaled 100,000 rials ($27,000 in 1986) while a government employee earned only 6,000 rials a month. An ad hoc committee was set up by the government to investigate the establishment of special funds to supplement the costs of marriage for men without massive resources. In Kuwait and Oman the high cost of marriage has led many men to marry foreign women, whose dowries and demands are usually lower than women from their own country. In Kuwait the government considered imposing duties on foreign brides brought into the country. Even Egyptians who are working in Kuwait and who marry Egyptian women also residing in Kuwait suffer from the high cost of marriage there. One young man, originally from a lower-middle-class area of Cairo, purchased a £E5,500 *shabka* for his Egyptian fiancée (who resided with her family in Kuwait), almost quadruple the price he would have paid if he had married in Egypt. In the Emirates the government discussed giving men who married local brides a grant to supplement their costs, while Oman passed legislation stripping Omani men of their citizenship if they did not first obtain government approval before marrying a foreign-born bride. "Saudis Suffer High Cost of Marriage," *Los Angeles Times*, 21 September 1986.

80. In provincial cities and rural areas, the demands of marriage may be slightly lower since many rural couples move into a room in the paternal home. Some of the furnishings of these homes are produced locally and are therefore less expensive (such as reed mats, carpets, or simple furniture). However, the opportunities to earn

and the ability to accumulate excess savings may be more difficult in provincial or rural areas, where salaries are lower and the economy is less differentiated. One young man from Qena estimated that he needed only £E3,000 to marry since the cost of furnishings were relatively inexpensive, although another young man from Minya thought he would need ten years to accumulate approximately £E5,000 for his marriage. He expected that his salary from teaching in a local primary school, combined with his job in the afternoons at a juice bar, would still not suffice.

81. In 1983–84 women who worked as low-level clerks and secretaries earned approximately £E45 per month, which at that time equaled $50 (at the official, not black-market, rate). MacLeod, *Accommodating Protest*, p. 58.

82. See Hatem, "Egypt's Middle Class in Crisis," pp. 407–22.

83. Amin and Awny roughly estimate that "the foreign earnings of Egyptian migrants may be six to ten times their domestic earnings before migration." Galal A. Amin and Elizabeth Awny, "International Migration of Egyptian Labour," p. 130.

84. Sometimes the consequences of a husband's long absence from Egypt can be tragic. One young man married a woman from his neighborhood and social background and migrated to Saudi Arabia by himself after his wife became pregnant. He prospered there, and when he finally returned with significant savings he decided to leave his first wife and marry a better-educated woman from a more prominent background. Before he abandoned his first wife, however, he beat her so severely that she became deaf.

85. In 1975 more than one half of all Egyptian teachers working in Kuwait, Qatar, and Saudi Arabia and half of all recorded Egyptians working in Jordan (mainly professionals) were women, according to J. Birks and C. Sinclair, "Aspects of International Migration in the Arab Near East." According to another source, 7,817 Egyptian women were working in Saudi Arabia in 1979; a minority worked as domestic servants, and a majority were employed as professionals or white-collar workers (S. E. Ibrahim, *The New Arab Social Order*, p. 92, as cited by Amin and Awny, "International Migration of Egyptian Labour," p. 187). Another source estimates that 23,200 female teachers (30 percent of the total number of teachers) were seconded to Arab and African countries in 1978–79 (Saneya A. W. Saleh, "The Changing Political and Social Status of Women in Egypt," p. 14).

86. One source estimated that 223,000 Egyptians had migrated to Iraq in 1980 (J. Birks and C. Sinclair, "The Socio-Economic Determinants of Intra-Regional Migration," p. 18, as cited in Amin and Awny, "International Migration of Egyptian Labour," p. 16). However, the Egyptian Ministry of Foreign Affairs, which Amin and Awny consider more reliable, estimates that "Saudi Arabia and Iraq alone accounted for as much as 71 percent of all Egyptians living in the ten major Arab labor-importing countries in 1982" and that "everybody agrees . . . that Iraq is now [1984] the major recipient of Egyptian migrant workers." The Foreign Ministry's estimate appears in a paper presented by M. M. Shafiq, "Egyptian External Migration," pp. 1–2, as cited in Amin and Awny, "International Migration of Egyptian Labour," pp. 24–27.

87. See March and Taqqu, *Women's Informal Associations in Developing Countries*, pp. 60–66.

88. "Since January 1976 the interest rate structure has been increased and the withholding tax eliminated; the current effective interest rate on savings deposits has consequently increased to about 8 percent a year. Even this is hardly an attractive

yield in view of a current rate of inflation of perhaps 15 to 20 percent a year and the returns that are available from holding nonfinancial assets." Khalid Ikram, *Egypt: Economic Management in a Period of Transition*, p. 60.

89. Nadim has emphasized the importance of informal savings associations in *sha'bi* communities, particularly among women, and suggests they are "prevalent on all levels of the Cairene culture, if not Egypt as a whole." Nadim, "Family Relationships in a 'Harah' in Cairo," p. 221.

90. It should be noted that one of the most contentious provisions of the 1979 reforms of the Personal Status Laws allowed a wife to remain in the marital apartment, as long as she retained custody of her children. An apartment is one of the most expensive costs of a marriage, which the groom bears. Previously, in the event of a divorce, he would retain ownership and residence in the apartment (its value was recorded in the *'ayma*). While the 1979 reforms were attacked for their supposedly un-Islamic provisions, selfish economic concerns also motivated a considerable share of male opposition. The provision only applied to rented apartments, not residences owned by the husband. See Reynolds, "Discourses of Social Change," p. 32.

91. When a dependent child of a widow who receives a government pension marries, the government grants a bonus (*mukaaf'a*) of £E100, after receiving a copy of the marriage contract. All female offspring, regardless of age, are considered dependents until they marry.

92. To kill two birds with one stone, the government has constructed moderately priced housing for newlyweds, which can only be purchased with foreign currency. These units are specifically designed to attract the remittances of Egyptians working abroad and the savings of returning migrants. In one newly constructed public housing project on the outskirts of Heliopolis, an almost elegant building stood out from among the other very shabby-looking but new apartment buildings. One of the residents explained that a two-bedroom apartment in this building could be purchased by newlyweds for $12,000. Because the complex lay in a remote, recently settled residential area on the outskirts of Heliopolis, and the newlywed apartments were very expensive, almost all of them remained vacant. In the early 1970s, according to people in the community, it had been much easier for newlyweds to obtain an inexpensive public-sector apartment (*masaakin sha'biyya*) after presenting a marriage contract to the appropriate authorities.

93. In a newspaper advertisement in the largest daily newspaper in Egypt, the Nasser Social Bank advertised its policy of offering "social loans" for young couples in need of cash for their marriage. These loans were also available for families with unexpected costs due to illness, death, and other disasters.

94. Ragui Assaad, "The Employment Crisis in Egypt," pp. 5–8.

95. The marriage rates were averaged from figures in CAPMAS, "Marriage and Divorce Statistics," *1986 Population Census* 1:8. The figure for Egypt's 1986 population is available in CAPMAS, *Preliminary Results of the Population, Housing and Establishment Census of 1986*, p. 2.

96. See World Bank and International Finance Corporation. *World Tables, 1988–89*, pp. 234–35.

97. Handoussa, "Crisis and Challenge," p. 3 (emphasis added).

98. Abt Associates et al., "Informal Housing in Egypt," as cited in Oldham, El Hadidi, and Tamaa, "Informal Communities in Cairo," p. xvii.

99. Ikram, *Egypt: Economic Management in a Period of Transition*, p. 152.

100. These are average costs in Mounira Gadid and Bashteel in 1985 and corrob-

orate the costs of key money for members of my community who settled in similar areas in Imbaba or Bulaq al-Dakrur. Oldham, El Hadidi, and Tamaa, "Informal Communities in Cairo," p. 53.

101. Handoussa, "Crisis and Challenge," p. 18.

102. Several businessmen, whose workshops were located in a relatively new informal settlement, explained that although commercial and residential buildings were privately owned, they had been built on public property. Once a community was populated by thousands of residents and workers, the government realized there was no point in classifying the area as state property. In order to levy taxes (among other things), government officials had to enter into delicate negotiations with community leaders to devise a plan to sell residents and businessmen the land underneath their buildings.

CHAPTER THREE

1. In the case of a mother's untimely death, it is common for the father's family to assume responsibility for the child. For further details see Chapter 1 under "The Familial Ethos" (the section on "Bonds of Discord").

2. *MuHaggaaba* (a veiled woman) identifies a wide assortment of modest dress signifying piety and religious observance in Cairo. Most women who are *muHaggaaba* conceal their hair in a scarf and wear long-sleeved blouses with floor-length skirts. Some women only wear a scarf and modest but Westernized dress, while others completely veil their face and hands. In popular quarters of Cairo, women have traditionally covered their dress and head with a single piece of black fabric, a *milaaya* to protect their modesty as well as their clothes from the dusty environment.

3. A girl, *bint*, in local parlance, refers to all unmarried girls and women who are assumed to be virgins. A woman, *sitt*, refers specifically to married women.

4. Luigi Graziano, *A Conceptual Framework for the Study of Clientelism*, pp. 44–45.

5. Ibid.

6. Joe Foweraker, "Popular Movements and Political Change in Mexico," in *Popular Movements and Political Change in Mexico*, ed. Foweraker and Craig, pp. 3–22, p. 6

7. Scott Mainwaring, "Urban Popular Movements, Identity, and Democratization in Brazil," *Comparative Political Studies* 20 (July 1987): 133 (emphasis added).

8. Judith Adler Hellman, "The Study of New Social Movements in Latin America and the Question of Autonomy," *LASA Forum* 21 (Summer 1990): 7.

9. Ernest Gellner, "Patrons and Clients," in *Patrons and Clients in Mediterranean Societies*, ed. Gellner and Waterbury, p. 1.

10. Graziano, *A Conceptual Framework for the Study of Clientelism*, p. 11.

11. Ibid., p. 28.

12. Larissa Adler Lomnitz, *Networks and Marginality*, trans. Cinna Lomnitz, p. 209.

13. Within the Middle East, research on Palestinian refugee communities and shantytown communities in Lebanon have also pointed to the critical role that networks play in providing economic and political security. Anthropologists have frequently suggested that tribal and kinship solidarities provide a cultural explanation for the maintenance of these ties. Although I do not mean to suggest that kin and communal solidarities are not strengthened by Egyptian or Arab culture, it is just as

important to reaffirm that *sha'bi* communities rely on these familial and communal ties as a response to government repression and exclusion. See Sayigh, "Roles and Functions of Arab Women,"and *Palestinians: From Peasants to Revolutionaries,* and "Encounters with Palestinian Women Under Occupation"; and Joseph, "Family as Security and Bondage."

14. In Morocco people accept and even encourage indebtedness, monetary or otherwise, to increase the interdependency of the community and decrease the risk of communal discord. People involved in a network with unsettled claims will hesitate to harm one another for fear of forfeiting their claims. See John Waterbury, *Commander of the Faithful.*

15. Goran Hyden, *Beyond Ujamaa in Tanzania,* p. 18.

16. Hyden, *Beyond Ujamaa in Tanzania,* p. 32. This paradox has been receiving increased attention by comparativists throughout the developing world. See Joel S. Migdal, *Strong Societies and Weak States.*

17. The most recent serious threat to the state from food riots occurred in January 1977 after government officials, under pressure from the International Monetary Fund, made an announcement in the People's Assembly of price increases in subsidies. However, due to the government's strong control of legal opposition channels, opposition has often taken the form of spontaneous violence, whether from student-sparked riots in 1972 or from workers erupting over wages and working conditions in 1976.

18. "Real wages in the government sector have been falling steadily since 1981. In 1984 they were 11 percent lower than their 1974 level, and have probably fallen further since. The situation of white-collar workers in the public sector is virtually identical. Public-sector blue-collar workers have fared a bit better but their real wages in the formal private sector have increased, albeit very slowly in the case of white-collar workers." Assaad, "The Employment Crisis in Egypt," p. 11. For more detailed discussion of wage levels in formal- and informal-sector employment, see Chapter 4.

19. *'Is-saanawiyya l-'amma* is a nationally administered exam taken by all students in their final year of secondary school. Entrance to university and technical institutes depends on the results of this exam. The Ministry of Education determines minimal entrance requirements for each faculty, thus perpetuating an academic and occupational hierarchy. Lower scores admit secondary school graduates to technical institutes or business faculties and higher scores admit them to prestigious faculties at universities such as medicine or engineering. High school students cram for these exams throughout the entire school year, and parents spend considerable sums on private tutors (see following section). Throughout Egypt the tension in families mounts preceding the exam period and ends when results are posted outside secondary schools. Examination results, posted outside schools, elicit traumatic and dramatic responses from students, ranging from suicide to ecstasy.

20. In these neighborhoods it is very common practice to yell up to people's apartments from the street in order to announce that one has arrived or to ask questions, pass on some information, and so on. Young men, in particular, yell up to their friends when they come to meet them, rather than intrude on the household. When a woman or man calls to the wife or mother in a household, if she has any children etiquette demands that they call her "mother of her eldest son" ('Umm MuHammad, for example) rather than use her first name, which is too personal and less respectful for casual acquaintances to use (if she has no sons, the name of her eldest daughter

is used). Few houses have well-sealed windows and most have at least one balcony, and thus one can hear and be heard from the street.

21. National identification cards, 'il-biTaa'a, are carried by all adult Egyptians. After marriage a woman is registered under her husband's I.D. card, but if she is widowed or divorced she receives her own card. Authorities ask to see them during the course of many bureaucratic procedures.

22. As a solution to this long wait she began her job anyway, working without compensation until the papers were processed.

23. The term *Hirafiyyiin* derives from the word *Hirfa* or craft, trade, or occupation. In precapitalist Cairo the term related primarily to skilled workers who knew a craft, such as metalworkers, brassmakers, ropemakers, glassblowers, and so on. In more recent times it includes service workers such as plumbers, wall finishers, furniture makers, and skilled workers, not unlike the term "blue-collar" worker. When a *Hirafi* masters his craft, he becomes either the *kumanda* (shop steward) or an *'usTa*, a skilled master who also supervises the training of apprentices. Typically, when a man (with sufficient capital) earns the rank of *'usTa*, he opens his own small workshop and employs others (including apprentices) since his reputation is acknowledged by the business community. A workshop owner is often called *mi'allim* (one who possesses knowledge).

24. *MuwaZZafiin* translates as "employees," but it specifically means government employees. Other white-collar employees who work in the private sector or are self-employed would be referred to differently, most likely by a professional identification.

25. Mohaya A. Zaytoun, "Earnings and the Cost of Living," in *Employment and Structural Adjustment*, ed. Handoussa and Potter, p. 251.

26. Handoussa, "Crisis and Challenge," p. 7.

27. Ibid.

28. Zaytoun, "Earnings and the Cost of Living," p. 220.

29. Handoussa, "Crisis and Challenge," p. 6.

30. Ibid., pp. 7–8.

31. For a more detailed analysis of the occupational structure of the community and the role of family enterprises in the economy, see Chapter 4.

32. Customarily and legally the husband is responsible for supporting the family (see Chapters 1 and 2). As more women seek employment in the labor force and contribute to the household economy, families have begun to depend on two wage earners (see Chapter 4 for a more specific discussion of female employment). On the question of female participation in the labor force see Barbara Ibrahim, "Family Strategies," *International Journal of the Family* 11 (1981); and MacLeod, *Accommodating Protest*.

33. Their impatience with this young man was due, in part, to competing demands for their financial resources. One of the men was under pressure from his own brother to loan him money, but if he lent his brother money rather than his wife's family, she would give him a very hard time. The influence of wives over their husband's resources is not as passive as appearances may suggest.

34. The urban sprawl of Cairo has compounded the difficulty of transportation and commuting distances, particularly for lower-income families. With the collapse of antiquated residential housing in the central districts of Cairo and little government investment in improving the existing housing stock, more and more lower-income and middle-class housing lies outside central Cairo in areas such as Imbaba, Bulaq al-Dakrur, al-Zaawiya al-Hamraa', Dar is-Salaam, and Madinat Nasser.

35. The state and private companies also maintain control over employees by making them personally liable for damages incurred while conducting official business. For example, when the same young man mentioned above damaged his bus while trying to avoid hitting pedestrians, his employer deducted £E301 from his salary, in installments, to pay for the repair costs. The sum was considerably more than his monthly salary. The driver was incensed and argued that the condition of the bus was obviously more important to the government than people's lives. In a similar situation, an employee of a public agricultural bank was extremely cautious in approving loans since if a borrower defaulted, the bank employee would be held personally liable for the loan. The bank might even accuse the employee of corruption and assume that his personal connections with the borrower had been the motive for his initial approval of the loan.

36. See Zaytoun, "Earnings and the Cost of Living," pp. 235, 241–46.

37. Ann Mosely Lesch, "Egyptian Labor Migration," *UFSI Reports* 38 (1985): 2. See also Lesch, "The Impact of Labor Migration on Urban and Rural Egypt," *UFSI Reports* 39 (1985).

38. Handoussa, "Crisis and Challenge," p. 5.

39. Lesch, "The Impact of Labor Migration," p. 8. The World Bank estimates a much lower figure of $3.5 billion in worker remittances in 1985, although this source probably underestimates the extent of illegal transfers of remittances to Egypt. *World Tables*, p. 237.

40. *World Tables*, p. 235.

41. One source, confirmed by Egyptians working abroad, estimates that they save approximately half their income (56 percent). In 1981 the estimated figure of total savings of Egyptians working abroad reached £E3.1 billion. See National Specialized Councils, *The Economics of Savings of Egyptians Working Abroad*, p. 81, cited in Amin and Awny, "International Migration of Egyptian Labour," pp. 61–62.

42. Lesch reports that an electrician earned £E25 in Egypt and the equivalent of £E500 a month in Saudi Arabia (and sent home a minimum of £E300 per month); in 1977 a public school teacher earned £E40–47 in Egypt and £E250 in Kuwait; skilled laborers who earned approximately £E30–35 a month in Egypt would earn £E146 in Libya and £E123–132 in Saudi Arabia and the Gulf. Lesch, "The Impact of Labour Migration," pp. 1–4.

43. Many people join mosque associations whose primary purpose is to save money to afford the pilgrimage. Savings clubs for this purpose are also available in public- and private-sector companies. During the last month of the Islamic calendar (*Zu l-Higga*), special terminals are used to absorb the masses of Egyptian pilgrims. When people leave for the pilgrimage, family and neighbors decorate the car or taxi that will take them to the airport with white flags and religious sayings. Visiting revered pilgrimage sites in Saudi Arabia at other times of the year is referred to as the *ʿumra*, or "minor" pilgrimage, and people also participate in savings associations to afford this trip. In addition, it is common for family members to contribute what they can to send an elderly member of the family on the pilgrimage, to fulfill a lifelong dream (and religious obligation) before they die.

44. A female cannot travel alone to Saudi Arabia without an escort, *muraafiʾ*, or a close male relative (either a husband or blood relative such as a brother or uncle).

45. Amin and Awny, "International Migration of Egyptian Labour," pp. 91–92.

46. Women are often involved in planning a spouse's or son's journey abroad and willingly agree to sell their gold jewelry and household furnishings to finance the initial costs of migration. Women can also be the main impetus for a husband's plans

to migrate. One woman gave her husband an ultimatum: either migrate abroad to support the family or divorce her. In Cairo the husband had been earning his living as a hashish dealer, and his wife felt his lifestyle and the danger of arrest was jeopardizing her family. He acceded to her ultimatum and left shortly thereafter for a foreign country, the name of which she was not able to recall.

47. In a study of the impact of migration on households in a lower-income neighborhood, Hoodfar and Khafagy found that couples before migration were more likely to share equally in decision-making, since they had few financial resources and each decision affected the survival of the family. However, once a husband migrated abroad and returned with significant savings, he was more likely to make unilateral decisions. His control of financial resources had increased, and he felt more latitude to monopolize decision-making. Homa Hoodfar and Fatma Khafagy, Seminar on Women and Migration (the Population Council, Cairo, 23 January 1986).

48. As mentioned earlier, some families borrow money from banks and insurance companies, but due to irregular sources of income they cannot maintain a schedule of payment. Then they must borrow more money, informally, to avoid default.

49. Men are more likely to organize *gamꞌiyyaat* among fellow businessmen, along occupational solidarities in manufacturing or commercial areas. In the commercial tourist area of Cairo, Khan al-Khaliili, two young men who managed a small brass and antique shop participated in a *gamꞌiyya* where the participants contributed £E30 *per day*, over a period of ten months. The decision among businessmen to put their money in a savings association rather than a bank also stems from a desire to bypass the government's ability to tax and estimate their net worth—a task made easier if assets are sitting in a bank.

50. See Handoussa, "Crisis and Challenge," p. 13.

51. The popular tradition of visiting the tombs and bringing *faTiir* is said to be an ancient Pharaonic custom. The practice of visiting tombs, celebrating the birthdays of saints and prophets, and honoring the dead with feasts is condemned by some Muslims within this community, and within Egypt and the Muslim world in general, as being contrary to orthodox Islamic traditions. However, the practice of tomb visits in many *shaꞌbi* communities is still common, perhaps because many of these areas lie in close proximity to the largest and oldest Muslim cemeteries of Cairo.

52. According to the most recent census, 49 percent of the total population over ten years of age is illiterate, 24 percent can read and write, 22 percent have qualifications less than a university degree, and 4 percent have obtained university degrees and above (postgraduate degrees). The discrepancy between the educational qualifications of men and women is largest in figures for Egypt as a whole: 38 percent of men are illiterate in comparison to 62 percent of women (30 percent of men can read and write, 18 percent of women). However, in Cairo the educational gap between men and women narrows: 23 percent of men and 39 percent of women are illiterate; 28 percent of men and 22 percent of women can read and write; 35 percent of men and 31 percent of women have less than university qualifications; and 13 percent of men and 7 percent of women have obtained at least a university degree. In Cairo Governorate, 31 percent of the population is illiterate, 25 percent can read and write, 33 percent have less than a university degree, and 10 percent have obtained at least a university degree. The most interesting and relevant statistic is the fairly equal percentage of Caireans who have obtained less than a university degree (35 percent of men and 31 percent of women). Many of the young people in this particular *shaꞌbi* community had finished secondary school and entered two-year vocational training

institutes (secretarial, electrical and air-conditioning repair, commercial studies, and so forth). Central Agency for Planning, Mobilisation, and Statistics, *Preliminary Results of the . . . Census of 1986*, pp. 52–55.

53. Handoussa, "Crisis and Challenge," p. 3.

54. Technically, it is illegal for children under the age of twelve to work (except in the agricultural sector), although common labor practices routinely employ under-age children. Based on enrollment figures for preparatory schools in Egypt in 1982–83, Abdalla suggests that about 50 percent of the children between twelve and fifteen were not attending school and were most probably working instead. Ahmed Abdalla, "Child Labour in Egypt," in *Combating Child Labour*, ed. Bequele and Boyden, p. 31. See Chapter 4 for further discussion of child labor and apprenticeship in central Cairo.

55. Zaytoun, "Earnings and the Cost of Living," p. 237.

56. Some extremely busy tutors in *shaʿbi* neighborhoods rent a single room to hold their lessons. More commonly, tutors make house calls.

57. All universities, with the exception of the American University in Cairo, are public institutions. While many middle- and upper-class Egyptians have sent their children to private elementary, intermediate, and secondary schools if they could afford to, private schools, particularly schools that specialize in foreign languages, are becoming more popular among lower-middle-class and *shaʿbi* communities. In addition to private language schools, schools designed for the resident foreign community, and religiously affiliated schools, there are private secondary schools (*xaaS*), which are identical to public secondary schools (*miiri*) but accept students with lower examination scores than a public school. Students who do not meet the entrance requirements of a public school can enter these schools for a relatively low fee (£E50 in 1985). In particular, students who are entitled to enter a public vocational or commercial high school, but who did not receive a high enough score to enter a public academic high school, will often choose to attend a private academic high school rather than be forced into attending a vocational high school, thus foreclosing the possibility of entering a prestigious university faculty (such as medicine or engineering).

58. One article complained that students who attended foreign secondary schools, particularly in Arab countries, and foreign language secondary schools in Egypt, and who took their equivalent secondary school examinations (such as the British GCE), were allowed to attend Egyptian universities, even though their exams were not as rigorous. One enterprising Egyptian student, after twice failing his ʾIs-saanawiyya l-ʿamma examinations in Egypt, attended a year of school in Kuwait and took the Kuwaiti secondary school exams and was finally admitted to an Egyptian university. See Subhy Shabaana, "Arranging Exceptions at the Student Placement Office," *al-Shaʿb* (12 August 1986), p. 9.

59. One clerk at a girls' intermediate school, when asked about cheating on exams, explained that all proctors in an exam were required by the Ministry of Education to sign a written form stating that they had no relatives taking the examination.

60. Even though people paid this man, hoping that he could do what he promised, they realized that he only had access to the test results before they were publicly posted outside the school. He would find out if a student had passed his or her exams before the family could and would visit them to deliver the good news, acting as if he had something to do with the score.

61. After one young man received high scores on his exams for the last year of intermediate school, his parents attempted to enter him in a very good high school in another, more upper-class residential area. The administrators of the school, which had a national reputation, explained that they could accept only students from the local school district. As the family was leaving, however, an administrator suggested to the father that a charitable contribution of £E1,000 to the school might persuade the administration to admit his son. As the father was not a wealthy man, he could not afford this "charitable donation" and instead used his connections with a member of Parliament to place his son in the school.

62. A more serious consequence of the relationship between diplomas, marriage, and status occurred in the neighborhood when a young woman was wrongly told that she had failed her secondary school exams. She had been engaged to a well-educated man and was devastated by the news, fearing that he expected to marry an educated woman and would call off the wedding. Before she found out that she had not failed the exams, she tried to kill herself, luckily unsuccessfully.

63. See "Australian Sheep . . . Ordered and Butchered . . . and Leaving," p. 1.

64. Khalid Ikram, "Meeting the Social Contract in Egypt," *Finance and Development* 18 (September 1981): 30–33, cited in Khouri-Dagher, "Food and Energy in Cairo," p. 9.

65. Khouri-Dagher, "The Answers of Civil Society to a Defaulting State," p. 12.

66. Zaytoun, "Earnings and the Cost of Living," p. 248.

67. Handoussa, "Crisis and Challenge," p. 11.

68. Zaytoun, "Earnings and the Cost of Living," p. 248.

69. For a comprehensive analysis of food subsidies in Egypt see Harold Alderman and Joachim von Braun, "The Effects of the Egyptian Food Ration and Subsidy System on Income Distribution and Consumption," International Food Policy Research Institute Research Report no. 45 (July 1984); and Myrette Ahmed el-Sokkari, "Basic Needs, Inflation and the Poor of Egypt, 1970–1980," *Cairo Papers in the Social Sciences* 7 (June 1984).

70. See MuHammad Abu Liwaayah, "Will a Plate of *Kushari* Turn into a Tourist Dish?" *al-Shaᶜb*, 12 August 1986, p. 3; and Ghali MuHammad, "*Shaᶜbi* Macaroni: Why Has It Disappeared from the Market," *al-Musawar*, 18 August 1986, pp. 52–53.

71. "The *Shaᶜb* Warn the Government: Stay Away from [Our] Cup of Tea," *al-Shaᶜb*, 19 August 1986, p. 3.

72. "Government Price Regulation: What's Wrong with It and So What?" ᶜ*Axbar il-Yoom*, 27 July 1986, p. 5.

73. "The Consumer Comes First," *al-Masaaʾ*, 12 August 1986, p. 6.

74. Technically, there are supposed to be gender-specific lines to wait for goods because of crowds and common disputes. However, that courtesy was not observed in this neighborhood. The majority of those waiting for food are usually women or older children who are given the task of marketing as part of their domestic responsibilities. However, in certain families where women hardly leave their homes the male members of the family are responsible for marketing. Since families can only receive their allotments of subsidized food at specific neighborhood cooperatives and *tamwiin* (public supply) grocers where their I.D. cards are registered, housewives and children who spend more time in the neighborhood usually endure the long lines.

75. A mechanic from a rural area tried to import a truck into the country. When

he went to pick up his truck the customs officials told him that he owed fees of several thousand pounds, which he could not afford. As he argued with the officials, more than two hundred trucks purchased by a large import firm rolled off the docks. He noticed these trucks were not taxed. This man serviced the car of a cabinet minister, and his friends told him to appeal to the minister for help. He told the minister about his problem and mentioned that he had seen 220 trucks belonging to a well-known company escape any duty. The minister, worried that he would publicize the large firm's "arrangement," quickly signed a letter waiving all customs fees for him. Unfortunately, when the mechanic returned to claim his truck, the authorities demanded that he pay £E7,000 for storage fees, for the time that had elapsed in the interim. Unable to beat the system, the mechanic eventually was forced to pay a substantial sum to liberate his truck.

CHAPTER FOUR

1. Lisa Peattie and Martin Rein, *Women's Claims*, p. 4.

2. Mahmoud Abdel-Fadil, *The Political Economy of Nasserism*, p. 15.

3. Manuel Castells and Alejandro Portes, "World Underneath," in *The Informal Economy*, ed. Portes, Castells, and Benton, pp. 12–13.

4. For other studies of the informal sector in Egypt see Peter von Sivers, "Life Within the Informal Sectors," in *Mass Culture, Popular Culture, and Social Life in the Middle East*, ed. Stauth and Zubaida; Meyer, "Socioeconomic Structure and Development of Small-Scale Manufacturing"; and Georg Stauth, "Gamaliyya: Informal Economy and Social Life in a Popular Quarter of Cairo," *Cairo Papers in Social Science* 14 (Winter 1991): 78–103.

5. See Keith Hart, "Informal Income Opportunities and Urban Employment in Ghana," *Journal of Modern African Studies* 11 (1973): 61–89.

6. Hart, "Informal Income Opportunities," p. 61.

7. As listed in Dipak Mazumdar, "The Urban Informal Sector," p. 10.

8. Hernando de Soto, *The Other Path*, trans. Abbott, p. 12.

9. De Soto, *The Other Path*, pp. 11–12.

10. Alejandro Portes, "Latin American Class Structures: Their Composition and Change During the Last Decades," *Latin American Research Review* 20 (1985): 21–22.

11. The strength of the informal sector is not limited to the Third World, and a growing literature has investigated the range of similar activities in industrialized nations as well. See, for example, Stuart Henry, ed., *Can I Have It in Cash?* and various contributions on the informal sector in First and Second World nations in *The Informal Economy*, ed. Portes, Castells, and Benton.

12. Since I completed my fieldwork, Egyptian and foreign scholars have devoted far more attention to the informal sector, and several studies have contributed significantly to many of the questions raised here. See, in particular, Nicholas S. Hopkins, ed., "The Informal Sector in Egypt," *Cairo Papers in Social Science* 14 (Winter 1991); Helmi R. Tadros, Mohamed Feteeha, and Allen Hibbard, "Squatter Markets in Cairo," *Cairo Papers in Social Science* 13 (Spring 1990); Soad Kamel Rizk, "The Structure and Operation of the Informal Sector in Egypt," in *Employment and Structural Adjustment*, ed. Handoussa and Potter, pp. 167–88; Mahmoud Abdel-Fadil, "Labor in the Unorganized Sector," *al-Ahram al-Iqtisadi* 1086 (6 November 1989):

18–21; Alia al-Mahdi and Amira Mashhur, "The Informal Sector in Egypt"; and Central Agency for Planning, Mobilisation, and Statistics (CAPMAS), "A Study on the Labor Market in Egypt."

13. Handoussa, "Crisis and Challenge," p. 17.

14. In my study the reference period was a full year from September 1985 to August 1986. While I understand that the time period is far more limited in national surveys (often only a week), due to the nature of my methodology I needed to consider the bits and pieces of information I had collected over a far longer period in order to understand the sources of income for individuals. International Labour Office (ILO), *Statistical Sources and Methods*, vol. 3, *Economically Active Population*, p. 183 (appendix).

15. See Homa Hoodfar, "Survival Strategies in Low-income Neighbourhoods of Cairo, Egypt."

16. Zaytoun, "Earnings and the Cost of Living," p. 220.

17. ILO, *Economically Active Population*, pp. 183–84.

18. Categories in the tables in this chapter were calculated according to the International Standard Classification of Occupations and the International Standard Industrial Classification of all Economic Activities. ILO, *Year Book of Labour Statistics (1987)*, pp. 1015–1016 and 1009–1010, respectively.

19. Government and public-sector employment constituted 59 percent of all wage labor in Egypt in 1984, and 68 percent of all wage labor in urban areas (though these figures do not capture much informal-sector activity as wage labor employment). Zaytoun, "Earnings and the Cost of Living," p. 220.

20. Handoussa, "Crisis and Challenge," p. 6.

21. The number of individuals with primary employment in the public sector equals seventy-two. If one excludes those with an unknown secondary occupation (twenty-three), the percentage of public-sector employees with a secondary occupation rises to 73 percent.

22. If only the people with a known secondary activity are considered, the share of employment in family enterprises and those who are self-employed equals 48 percent (where $N = 199$).

23. In the early 1960s President Nasser was considering a new law prohibiting raising animals for home consumption in all urban areas as a way to improve the health and environment of urban residents. Apparently, the Ministry of Interior warned him that there was vehement opposition to the rumored law, and Nasser decided against instituting the provision. Nasser had faced feudalists, foreign capitalists, and the British, but the poultry and sheep lobby forced him to back down. Personal communication with John Waterbury, Princeton University.

24. For a more complete examination of working women in Egypt see MacLeod, *Accommodating Protest*; Hoodfar, "Survival Strategies"; and Barbara Ibrahim, "Family Strategies."

25. Abdel-Fadil, *The Political Economy of Nasserism*, pp. 19–20.

26. For further discussion of these ambiguities see Rizk, "The Structure and Operation of the Informal Sector in Egypt," and Mostafa Kharoufi, "The Informal Dimension of Urban Activity in Egypt," *Cairo Papers in Social Science* 14 (Winter 1991): 8–20.

27. Handoussa, "Crisis and Challenge," p. 17.

28. See also Kharoufi, "The Informal Dimension of Urban Activity in Egypt," for a comprehensive review of macro and micro studies of the informal sector in Egypt

and the methodological and definitional issues that researchers have been trying to overcome.

29. In order to arrive at his estimates, Abdel-Fadil designated certain occupations and branches of economic activity, enumerated in national data collected by various ministries, to comprise informal-sector employment. For a detailed accounting of these figures, refer to Abdel-Fadil, "Informal Sector Employment in Egypt."

30. Rizk, "The Structure and Operation of the Informal Sector in Egypt," p. 171.

31. Nader Fergany, "A Characterisation of the Employment Problem in Egypt," in *Employment and Structural Adjustment*, ed. Handoussa and Potter, p. 36, as cited in Rizk, "The Structure and Operation of the Informal Sector in Egypt," p. 173.

32. Rizk, "The Structure and Operation of the Informal Sector in Egypt," p. 171.

33. CAPMAS, "A Study on the Labor Market in Egypt," as cited in Kharoufi, "The Informal Dimension of Urban Activity in Egypt," p. 12.

34. Kharoufi, "The Informal Dimension of Urban Activity in Egypt," p. 13.

35. Al-Mahdi and Mashhur, "The Informal Sector in Egypt," as cited in Kharoufi, "The Informal Dimension of Urban Activity in Egypt," p. 13.

36. See Mahmoud Abdel-Fadil, "Informal-Sector Employment in Egypt," p. 12.

37. See Mahmoud Badr et al., "Small-Scale Enterprises in Egypt."

38. Figures for the informal sector differ slightly from Tables 4.1 and 4.2 above due to the inclusion of retired people and income recipients within the active population. Although these two groups technically were inactive, it was possible to distinguish a formal or informal income source. This particularity of the informal-sector analysis should not skew the results since the number of individuals involved was very small (five for primary activity, three for secondary activity, and one for tertiary activity). The inactive population usually includes students, pension recipients, retired persons, housewives, and undefined economic activity.

39. For greater insight to the particular evolution of the informal sector in urban Egypt and its relationship to the guild system see Assaad and Neyzi, "Locating the Informal Sector in History."

40. Although I partially used this approach to define informal-sector activities, it should be noted that many small workshops (one to nine workers) are not necessarily informal but are licensed, pay taxes, and are properly registered with the Ministries of Labor and Social Affairs. However, because I could distinguish which workplaces employed under nine workers but did not know the legal history of these workplaces, I fell back upon this less precise method of classification.

41. Abdel-Fadil, "Informal-Sector Employment in Egypt," p. 4.

42. Ibid., p. 6.

43. A friend of mine, who happened to be a tool and die maker from the United States, visited a machinist's workshop in my community with me and was very impressed by the workers' ability to produce automated and nonautomated machinery with very simple tools. While struck by their ingenuity and resourcefulness, he was not impressed with the poor safety and working conditions in the shop, where serious industrial accidents were not unusual. As explained, in the United States labor is very expensive and machinery very precise. In American shops a worker is expected to know how to produce high volume without difficulty, whereas in Egypt many workers were expected to produce several different objects, with a high input of labor and low volume. Egyptian machinists explained that they used round-the-clock shifts of workers and several workers and apprentices on each machine to increase volume.

44. Rizk, "The Structure and Operation of the Informal Sector in Egypt," p. 171.

45. Peattie and Rein, *Women's Claims*, p. vi.

46. The role of family enterprises in other Middle Eastern countries is also considerable. In Tunisia most enterprises with one to four workers consisted of family members, those employing five to nine workers included apprentices, and those employing more than ten included regular employees. Some 49 percent of the nonagricultural labor force in 1975 and 43.4 percent in 1980 was engaged in informal-sector activity in Tunisia. Jacque Charmes, "Méthodologie et resultats des enquêtes sur le secteur non structuré en Tunisie," in *Etudes sur l'emploi aux Antilles et en Tunisie*, ed. Charmes, Domenach, and Geuganant, pp. 7, 13–22, as cited in von Sivers, "Life Within the Informal Sectors," pp. 245, 252.

47. Huda Zurayk, "Women's Economic Participation," in *Population Factors in Development Planning in the Middle East*, ed. Shorter and Zurayk, p. 43.

48. See, in particular, Arlene Elowe MacLeod, "Hegemonic Relations and Gender Resistance," *Signs* 17 (Spring 1992): 533–57.

49. Richard Anker and Martha Anker, "Measuring the Female Labour Force in Egypt," *International Labour Review* 128 (1989): 512.

50. CAPMAS, *Egyptian Fertility Survey 1980*, vol. 2, *Fertility and Family Planning*, p. 9.

51. The rate of female participation in the public sector is somewhat higher at 22 percent (30 percent of local government, 23 percent in government service authorities, and 11 percent in public enterprises). The overall rate of labor force participation in Egypt is only 28.4 percent. Heba Handoussa, "The Burden of Public Service Employment and Remuneration," pp. 49–50, 79.

52. For a comprehensive analysis of definitional, methodological, and administrative questions surrounding female participation in the labor force, within the Middle East, see Zurayk, "Women's Economic Participation," pp. 3–58. A CAPMAS pilot study to improve data collection of female labor force participation captured a much greater participation rate by redesigning questions and training enumerators, particularly female enumerators, to direct questions specifically to women in the household. Traditionally, the male head of the household had responded to questions for his wife and other female members of the household, thus intentionally or unintentionally minimizing their labor force participation. These changes have since been adopted by CAPMAS in its annual labor force sample survey, and it has measured higher participation rates. Similar projects in Latin America, funded by the Ford Foundation in cooperation with national statistical authorities, have produced a doubling of the labor force participation rate of women in Latin America. Personal communication with John Gerhart, the Ford Foundation, New York City.

53. Anker and Anker, "Measuring the Female Labour Force in Egypt," p. 517.

54. CAPMAS, *Egyptian Fertility Survey (1980)*, vol. 1, *Survey Design*, pp. 92–93.

55. The definition of work used in the World Fertility Survey was: "Occupation apart from ordinary household duties, whether paid in cash or in kind or unpaid, whether own-account or family member or for someone else, whether done at home or away from home." CAPMAS, *Egyptian Fertility Survey (1980)*, vol. 2, *Fertility and Family Planning*, p. 10.

56. In the economically active sample, one of the more interesting examples of the ability of family enterprises to prosper in a mixed economy was a family enterprise that produced ready-made clothing. It had subcontracted with a large public-sector textile firm to produce a certain number of pajamas and robes, which were then

distributed in public-sector stores (the public-sector textile company provided the raw materials—in this case, fabric).

57. For a history of the labor movement in Egypt, see Beinen and Lockman, *Workers on the Nile*, and Ellis Goldberg, *Tinker, Tailor, and Textile Worker*.

58. The intervention of the post-1952 regimes in the labor movement is explained in Marsha Pripstein Posusney, "Irrational Workers," *World Politics* 46 (October 1993): 83–120; and in Robert Bianchi, *Unruly Corporatism*, and his "The Corporatization of the Egyptian Labor Movement," *Middle East Journal* 40 (Summer 1986): 429–44.

59. During a visit in one home in the area, a young boy of twelve or thirteen explained to me that in Egypt children worked when they were young but then could not find work when they grew older. After young men finally finished their education, he argued, they completed their military service and waited years to be appointed to a government position. A survey of relatively poor families in a *sha'bi* community found that children contributed income in 98 of the 268 households. Nawal Mahmoud Hassan, "Report on Survey of Families in Gamaliyya"; see also her "Social Aspects of Urban Housing in Cairo," *MIRMAR* (1985): 59–61.

60. For discussion of traditional guilds in Egypt see Gabriel Baer, *Egyptian Guilds in Modern Times*; André Raymond, *Artisans et Commerçants au Caire au XVIIIe Siécle*; and Beinen and Lockman, *Workers on the Nile*, pp. 32–35.

61. In his research on the informal economy in Peru, De Soto argued: "We gradually discovered that informality is not the best of all possible worlds, that it involves tremendous costs, that people try to offset these costs in all kinds of novel but inadequate ways, that lawbreaking is not, on balance, desirable, and that the apparent chaos, waste of resources, invasions, and everyday courage are the informals' desperate and enterprising attempts to build an alternative system to the one that has denied them its protection." De Soto, *The Other Path*, p. 152.

62. This young man also complained about the company's policy of deducting wages from bus drivers' salaries if riders had filed complaints about their driving. Apparently, it was not uncommon for riders to come to the company and file complaints against the ticket collector or bus driver. Lawyers for the company would make an investigation and if their judgment worked against an employee, five to fifteen days' worth of wages would be deducted from their paychecks.

63. "Justice May Be Lost Due to the Slowness of the Judiciary: Law and the Judiciary," *al-Axbaar*, 19 December 1985, p. 3. In Peru, De Soto argues that a similar paralysis of the legal system has been caused by special interests who have used executive orders and legislation to gain public resources and special benefits. Approximately 98 percent of all Peruvian law originated in the executive branch, not through the legislature. See De Soto, *The Other Path*, pp. 196–97.

64. Castells and Portes distinguish between formal, informal, and criminal economic activity in their analysis of the informal economy, while noting the variability of definitions between the populace and institutional actors. Castells and Portes, "World Underneath," p. 15.

65. Even as people complain about the black market, Khouri-Dagher argues that people also admit responsibility for encouraging it. "To view oneself as a victim does not prevent from seeing oneself as an actor in these dysfunctionings." Khouri-Dagher, "The Answers of Civil Society to a Defaulting State," p. 16.

66. There are limits to the government's tolerance for beating the system. One older woman in the neighborhood had spent six months in jail for stealing electricity.

She, like many other people, had tapped into a government utility line, but had then sold the electricity to her neighbors and was jailed for her entrepreneurial ingenuity, rather than being merely fined. Local newspapers are filled with story after story of arrests of black marketers and corrupt officials, no doubt to deter the public from illegal activities.

67. "'*Al-futuwwa* . . . " literally means youth, but implies gallantry and chivalry." Even after the creation of a police force in the nineteenth century, local men (and women) protected specific neighborhoods from enemies and mediated disputes within the quarter. *Futuwwaat* (classical Arabic) also served political and defense purposes, mobilizing people within their neighborhoods for patrons and rulers, when necessary. As the most immediate authority in many neighborhoods, at times their reputations degenerated if they exploited the *sha'b* or used too much force to accomplish their aims. Al-Messiri, *Ibn al-Balad*, pp. 4, 62–71; see also al-Messiri, "The Changing Role of the Futuwa." For a discussion of the Syrian equivalent of a *futuuwa* see Philip S. Khoury, "Abu Ali al-Kilawi: A Damascus Qabaday," in *Struggle and Survival in the Modern Middle East*, ed. Burke, pp. 179–90.

But even in contemporary Cairo, tough local young men (and even older men) who often operate on both sides of the law still have a very honorable and respected reputation in local communities. They come to the aid of weaker people in the neighborhood during fights and protect the reputation of the alleyways and streets from outsiders. On the other hand, the families of some legendary *fitiwwaat* (colloquial Egyptian) have degenerated into common criminals. The son of one famous *fitiwwa* from a rough *sha'bi* neighborhood spent seventeen of his thirty-four years in jail for various crimes. When I met the family, the mother wore a scarf hiding the marks that he had left on her neck after trying to strangle her the day before in an argument. I was warned never to visit this family alone because of his temper. As we left the building, inhabited by several families in very difficult circumstances, he pointed out a woman and her entourage who walked by and explained that she was a famous and powerful brothel owner whose place of business was just down the alleyway.

68. "Rationed goods are distributed through private grocers, registered at the Ministry of Supply, who receive at the beginning of every month the rationed commodities to be given to the households that are attached to them. In effect, the ration card, in addition to the holder's name, also indicates the name of the grocer who is to distribute the monthly ration. In other words, each family can take its monthly ration from only one specified grocery, known as a *tamwiin* shop. The grocer is expected to hold a family's ration a whole month and is allowed to sell it if nobody has come to collect it during that month." Khouri-Dagher, "Food and Energy in Cairo," p. 15.

69. This family also owned an apartment building in Mecca that another brother supervised where their father, in semiretirement, often resided. They insisted that the grocer's father stay with them on his next pilgrimage to Mecca. The ties between the two families were strengthened by their common origins, commercial partnership, and religious devotion.

70. For a critical review of recent trends in food production and distribution in Egypt, and the role of domestic and international interests in this question, see Timothy Mitchell, "America's Egypt," *Middle East Report* 169 (March–April 1991): 18–34.

71. It was only through the persistent efforts of local political figures and a private organization that the government constructed another temporary housing site in

a distant area that was barely inhabited and not incorporated into the government's transportation, education, or health services. For an analysis of the living conditions and predicament of residents of "temporary" housing see Hassan, "Report on Survey of Families in Gamaliyya."

72. According to one man who had been fined for evading military service, the judge recommends the amount of a fine according to one's occupation and appearance—a progressive system. "If you dress well, the fine is usually £E1,000 and the *ghalaaba* [paupers] are only fined £E150." This man, a machinist employed in his brother's workshop, was represented by a lawyer and was fined £E700. His lawyer received £E300. Because he was self-employed, he had not needed to submit his military discharge papers before securing a job.

73. "Justice May Be Lost Due to the Slowness of the Judiciary," p. 3.

74. National Bank of Egypt, "The Taxation System in Egypt," *Economic Bulletin* 37 (1984): 9.

75. Ibid.

76. "Egyptian Income Tax Modernization Project: The Transfer from a Schedular Tax System to a Global Income Tax," p. 11, and Handoussa, "Crisis and Challenge," p. 11. The infusion of profits from public-sector companies, most importantly the petroleum sector, has increased tax revenues recently. Waterbury, *The Egypt of Nasser and Sadat*, p. 225.

77. In 1981, in order to increase tax compliance, the government instructed public employees that no benefits were to be provided to citizens without first submitting a tax I.D. number, thus forcing any citizen who wanted a phone, electrical, or water facilities to obtain a tax I.D. card. "Egyptian Income Tax Modernization Project: Hard to Tax Groups," pp. 3–4.

78. "A Declaration Made by the Deputy Chairman of the Central Auditing Agency," *al-Ahram Journal*, 3 August 1984, as cited in National Bank of Egypt, "The Taxation System in Egypt," p. 16.

79. National Bank of Egypt, "The Taxation System in Egypt," p. 19.

80. Ibid., p. 38. The *gihaad* tax (the word for Islamic religious war in classical Arabic is *jihad*) is levied on certain consumer goods and imported goods and provides revenue for the Egyptian armed forces.

81. CAPMAS, "Family Budget Research by Sample in Egypt," as cited in National Bank of Egypt, "The Taxation System in Egypt," p. 18.

82. Enterprises are organized by the type of raw materials used in the business. For example, all tanners, leathermakers, slaughterhouses, and shoemakers are regulated by the "animal wealth" section of the tax authority. All workshops that produce aluminum products are regulated by the same department.

83. One businessman explained that tax experts knew the cost of his machinery because it was produced by military factories and sold at a public exhibition. Tax authorities usually know the cost of locally produced and imported machinery since the prices of domestically produced goods are often fixed by the government, and the price of imported goods is recorded by the customs department. Businessmen explained that tax experts are familiar with the industries they tax and circulate in the market to keep abreast of prices of machinery and finished goods. Thus when a businessman estimates his taxes, the tax official has a rough idea of whether he is lying or not.

84. The manager explains further: "If an accountant saves you £E5,000, then you would easily have to pay him £E1,000. With no contract, you agree to pay them half

in the beginning and half in the end. They are legitimate but they are a bunch of thieves. They take advantage of you, your panic, and they take your money gradually. My accountant did not accept less than £E25 two years ago for writing out an official form that took less than five minutes to fill in. It did not even need a stamp or any official papers. Then he wanted £E50 to deliver an account of a mistake in the tax authorities calculations that I had found. I said it was too much money and we agreed upon £E30. The next time I went myself to the tax authorities, and it did not take more than a few hours to file the papers. They take advantage of uneducated and lazy businessmen."

85. Fines were based on 8 percent of estimated taxes and recently were increased to 14 percent.

86. According to an employee of the tax authority, routine bonuses have increased the salary of tax collectors. However, since 1986 the members of a department or section shared the bonus as a team. Thus, workers resist efforts to hire more employees since they would have to share the bonus with them. Bonuses are also determined by the workload so that, for example, employees who are responsible for one hundred stores may agree to regulate twenty more in order to receive a bigger bonus. However, since they frequently can barely keep up with their former case load, they may estimate taxes even more capriciously, thus creating more cases that are contested and appealed.

87. Originally he had been appointed to the customs authority at the airport, but his father convinced him to seek a transfer when he argued that his son would be surrounded by so much corruption that, despite his honorable intentions, he would soon become a thief like the rest of the employees. The young man followed his father's instructions but soon found himself in more trouble. Initially, he was a zealous but naive young man and was assigned to regulate charities. Each charitable organization was allowed to hold two fund-raising parties each year, but profits over 35 percent after expenses were taxed. He made the mistake of asking Wafaa' w-'amal—a health care organization for children that Jihan Sadat (the President's wife at the time) had founded and supported—to pay taxes on its contributions from the party. Shortly thereafter, he was transferred to the provinces for a few years before he was allowed to return to Cairo. His mistake, he admitted, was in believing that the big are like the small and should be taxed similarly. He suggested that, since Egypt was in the initial stages of democracy, it could still not prosecute public officials for corruption.

88. In some cases, bribing an official can backfire. One businessman bribed an employee of the tax department to destroy a file, but this man was transferred and, years later, the file resurfaced and the taxpayer was subject to even greater fines since it was fairly obvious that he had bribed the former employee.

89. Researchers in Peru found that "remaining formal costs a small industrial firm 347.7 percent of its after-tax profits and 11.3 percent of its production costs. In other words, were it not for the costs of remaining formal, the firm's profits and therefore its savings and potential investment capital would be more than quadrupled. . . . [Some] 21.7 percent of the costs of remaining formal are tax-related, 72.7 percent are other legal costs, and the remaining 5.6 percent are public utility costs." In a survey of legally established companies, researchers found that "approximately 40 percent of all their administrative employees' total working hours [were devoted] to complying with bureaucratic procedures." De Soto, *The Other Path*, p. 148.

90. Galal A. Amin, "Migration, Inflation and Social Mobility," in *Egypt Under Mubarak*, ed. Tripp and Owen, pp. 114–15.

91. In a 1979 survey of people from another *sha'bi* community, 61 percent of the households earned less than £E30 per month. This sample was composed of the poorest stratum of the community, who were forced to live in makeshift temporary housing arranged by the Arab Socialist Union, for various reasons. Hassan, "Report on Survey of Families in Gamaliyya," pp. 7–8.

92. However, because I did not collect comprehensive information on wages in this sample, the data only suggest a crude picture of wage differentials within the community, rather than presenting a representative and precise sample. Table 4.18 includes the wages of people (in at least one of their economic activities) who volunteered this information over the course of a full year.

93. See Tekçe, Oldham, and Shorter, *A Place to Live*, chap. 3, for further details.

94. Abdel-Fadil, "Informal-Sector Employment in Egypt," p. 28.

95. Ibid.

96. It should be noted that most censuses do not record secondary sources of income and employment and therefore probably overestimate the population of the working poor.

97. These classifications are based on observation and knowledge of each individual's lifestyle, income, and property. Because specific information on income, property, and wages was not uniformly collected for this sample, I did not attempt a more general survey of the sample's class composition.

98. See CAPMAS, "A Study on the Labor Market in Egypt," pp. 73–74, as cited in Rizk, "The Structure and Operation of the Informal Sector in Egypt."

99. Rizk, "The Structure and Operation of the Informal Sector in Egypt," p. 174.

100. Abdel-Fadil and Jihan Diab, "The Black Economy and National Accounts in LDCs," pp. 32–34.

101. Abdel-Fadil and Diab, "The Black Economy," p. 34 (authors' emphasis).

102. Delwin A. Roy, "The Hidden Economy in Egypt," *Middle East Studies* 28 (October 1992): 689–711.

103. Roy, "The Hidden Economy in Egypt," p. 707.

104. Ibrahim M. Oweiss, "Egypt's Informal Economy," p. 3.

105. Oweiss, "Egypt's Informal Economy," p. 9.

106. Meyer, "Socioeconomic Structure and Development of Small-Scale Manufacturing," p. 2.

107. The data for Stauth's study was collected between October 1981 to November 1984. Stauth, "Gamaliyya," p. 83.

108. Abdel-Fadil, "Informal-Sector Employment in Egypt," p. 1.

109. Alejandro Portes and John Walton, *Labor, Class, and the International System*, p. 91.

110. Many upper-class families have increasingly hired Filipino and other Asian women as maids, cooks, and nannies. Some of these maids are English-speaking and can also tutor their children.

111. "It is . . . not surprising that rural-urban migration in Egypt has been as massive as in Tunisia. By being officially locked into the cultivation of extensive crops and thereby being made to pay for industrialization, the countryside was unable to provide either enough work or sufficient pay to its growing population. The mini-farmers and landless laborers were no dupes; when they saw the capital disap-

pear from their villages they determined to follow it and migrated to the cities" (Von Sivers, "Life Within the Informal Sectors," p. 249). John Waterbury argues that Nasser and Sadat imported capital into Egypt to finance development after exhausting domestic efforts to finance import-substitute industrialization. Both rulers had been unwilling to force massive and unpopular structural changes necessary to finance industrialization domestically. See Waterbury, *The Egypt of Nasser and Sadat.*

112. Portes and Walton, *Labor, Class, and the International System*, pp. 103–104.

113. Hart, "Informal Income Opportunities," p. 61.

114. Galal Amin does not see rising economic mobility of the lower classes as a result only of the Open Door policy, but of rapid inflation since the early 1970s, the increased demand for vocational and higher education, and international migration. "All of these factors worked together during the last three decades to bring about a rate of social mobility which is probably greater than anything Egypt ever experienced in its modern history, pushing up the social ladder large numbers of the population who traditionally belonged to the lowest levels of society and allowing them to compete successfully with sections of the middle class who found their social status rapidly declining. . . . The resulting change in social structure explains much more of the current economic, social and intellectual scene than is usually recognized." Amin, "Migration, Inflation and Social Mobility," p. 8.

115. Roy, "The Hidden Economy in Egypt," p. 711.

116. Ibid.

117. Amin, "Migration, Inflation and Social Mobility," p. 5.

118. Ibid., p. 15.

119. Elemér Hankiss, "The 'Second Society,'" *Social Research* 55 (1988): 18.

120. Hankiss, "The 'Second Society,'" p. 36.

121. Václav Havel, "The Power of the Powerless," in Václav Havel et al., *The Power of the Powerless*, ed. Keane, pp. 23–96. See also Timothy Garton-Ash, *The Magic Lantern.*

122. Havel, "The Power of the Powerless," p. 95.

123. Hankiss, "The 'Second Society,'" p. 36.

CHAPTER FIVE

1. El Issawy, "Subsidization of Food Products in Egypt" (Cairo: Food-Energy Nexus Programme, United Nations University, 1985), as cited in Khouri-Dagher, "The Answers of Civil Society to a Defaulting State," p. 4. Khouri-Dagher points out that Egypt, which used to produce its own food needs, now imports 60 percent of its food requirements ("Food and Energy in Cairo," p. 21). See also Alderman and Von Braun, "The Effects of the Egyptian Food Ration and Subsidy System on Income Distribution and Consumption."

2. Khalid Ikram, "Meeting the Social Contract in Egypt," p. 30.

3. Ibid., p. 33.

4. "Two Dangerous Phenomena Threaten Egypt: Population Growth and the Incessant Accent of Consumerism," *al-Ahram*, 2 May 1989, p. 1.

5. Membership fees are a far less important source of revenue than cash donations. Religiously affiliated PVOs offering religious instruction or spearheading a building drive of a mosque or church, in addition to providing other community services, "generally receive more private donations than secular PVOs without these

religious activities." "Private Voluntary Organizations in Cairo Governorate: A Profile," p. 46.

6. Ibid., p. 69.

7. At major religious holidays, when it is customary to distribute charity to the poor (food, money, or clothes), the treasurer of the organization would give the administrator £E100 to distribute in small amounts to neighborhood beggars, families in need, and disabled residents. In most neighborhoods there are several people who live in the streets, supported by residents and businessmen, who do not actively beg but receive small amounts of food or cash from local residents.

8. Although teachers did lead the children in songs and simple nursery rhymes, the educational program as such was actually very minimal; the children spent most of their time playing with other children at long tables or playing outside in the bare courtyard of an elementary school or just dozing off.

9. After one child had damaged new furniture, a janitor informed the administrator of the day-care center. She told the teachers to announce to the children that their parents would be responsible for any damage they caused.

10. An imported knitting machine already used in the vocational training program had needed repairs for many months, but its local distributor claimed that its warranty had lapsed and the administrator refused to allocate funds needed for its repair. Because very few grants provided for the maintenance costs of machinery, the PVO was reluctant to commit itself to purchase more imported machinery.

11. Apparently, the MSA had recently become more interested in projects and training programs that produced goods to be sold in the community or at fairs sponsored by the Ministry. In a nearby area another PVO, with a large office devoted primarily to sociological and historical research, was pressured by the MSA (which regulated its activities) to open a vocational training program. The Ministry offered a loan of £E10,000 to purchase four sewing machines and fund the program. The loan would be repaid from the proceeds of production (10 percent annually). The leader of the PVO resisted the pressure, arguing that the objectives of the organization was not to make money but to preserve and promote the heritage of the neighborhood in Islamic Cairo. Perhaps this new sentiment in the MSA was influenced by the funding priorities of the United States Agency for International Development (USAID), which encouraged self-help projects and private-sector development. During this period USAID was contributing millions of dollars in aid to PVOs in Egypt as part of the Neighborhood Urban Services Project.

12. Dennis J. Sullivan, "Islamic Society vs. Secular State: Political and Economic Development in Egypt" (Paper presented at the annual meeting of the American Political Science Association, Atlanta, 31 August–3 September 1989).

13. Students of education in universities can fulfill their requirement of practical teaching experience by tutoring groups of children in programs sponsored by a mosque. For neighborhood children these services provide free lessons that are crucial for a student's progress. Students who attend these study groups usually appreciate the efforts of the mosque and tend to be more observant than their peers.

14. These committees are funded by private donations channeled through the mosque. For example, the Nasser Social Bank contributes the interest on clients' accounts, who so designate, to a general fund that is then distributed to specific committees throughout Cairo. The *lagnit ʿiz-zakaah* funded by the Nasser Social Bank, according to a woman who worked for a local committee's vocational pro-

gram, were directly supervised by the bank rather than the Ministry of Social Affairs or the Ministry of Religious Charities.

15. The teenager's school also contributed £E200 to the family for the cost of an expensive new prosthesis.

16. It is common practice in Egypt for doctors to seek positions in Gulf countries and use their earnings to finance a private clinic in Egypt.

17. As a means of maintaining control over organizational activity, many completely private voluntary organizations were absorbed by the government before 1960. While government provision of social services may have been strengthened, communal participation declined. More recently, in several neighborhoods where international development agencies have invested significant resources in infrastructural upgrading projects, some development workers have noted that community organizations have been weakened by their dependence on external financing. For example, one PVO built a nursery worth approximately £E48,000 from donations by the community. Once USAID became deeply involved in an upgrading project in the area, the board of the PVO would approach USAID for financial support as new needs arose, rather than depend on private contributions, which had been very generous in the past despite the community's low standard of living. (The preceding is a summary of comments by Sawsan al-Messiri at the Population Council, Cairo, December 1985.) For an analysis of recent trends and of organizational activity in Egypt, see Robert Bianchi, *Unruly Corporatism*.

18. A study of organizations affiliated with the Cairo Regional Council for Social Agencies found that 76 percent of the members and 83 percent of the board members of the organizations were women. Soha Abdel Kader, "A Report on the Status of Egyptian Women, 1900–1973" (Cairo: Social Research Center, American University in Cairo, September 1973), p. 15.

19. All PVOs must register with the Ministry of Social Affairs, and by-laws must be approved by the MSA. The MSA ensures strict control of PVO matters in a variety of ways. "Attending private meetings of unregistered organizations is a criminal offense. Private fund-raising activities are strictly regulated, both in order to limit organizational autonomy and to provide a source of income for employees of the ministry [who receive a percentage of donations they solicit for a yearly fund drive]." Robert Springborg, *Mubarak's Egypt*, p. 171. See also Sami Zubaida, "Islam, the State and Democracy: Contrasting Conceptions of Society in Egypt," *Middle East Report* 179 (November–December 1991): 2–15.

20. My sister just had a baby named Cleo Sofie Post! Welcome to the world, kid. There is life out there. August 15, 1989.

21. It is common and traditional practice to distribute cash to political supporters. See Springborg, *Mubarak's Egypt*.

22. A similar relationship between a couple in a nearby neighborhood several years earlier had provoked extensive sectarian strife, riots, and damage to property, which only the heavy presence of the security forces finally quelled. The young man explained that interfaith relationships and conversions are a common source of violence in certain neighborhoods and parts of Egypt. He also maintained that the government was responsible for instigating confrontations at times. He had heard from his associates that in Assiut, a province with a high percentage of Copts, the government offered apartments as incentives to Christians who would convert to Islam. Later, however, another person argued that this was nothing new and that both

Christians and Muslims used similar incentives of education, employment, housing, and marriage to encourage conversion.

23. The ability of the government to control an area is more complicated if few formal associations and official leaders exist. In some newly settled areas, for example, which had originally been settled by close associations of kin or people from a common rural background, local leaders guard their power and protect the community's autonomy. As newer people arrived in the area due to the low cost of housing or its proximity to central Cairo, these local informal leaders began the sensitive process of negotiating with the government for public services such as water, utilities, roads, transportation, schools, health care, food cooperatives, etc. While land disputes had been settled by an authority of a council of elders in the past, after long negotiations with the council of elders the government began the process of selling land to community residents and resolving land disputes. In one of these areas, older residents had typically bought and sold land to newcomers for very low prices but registered the sale by stipulating that he or she had bought a building on government land (*fulaan 'ishtara mabna min 'arD milk 'il-Hukuuma*). Thus, once the government surveyed the area and resolved claims to land, residents could purchase their land from the government by long-term installments. According to a local businessman, this particular community, while originally settled by Upper Egyptians in low-status occupations, was now populated by doctors, lawyers, and military officers. Lots of land had risen from between £E10 and £E20 in 1976 to reach £E1,600 (to construct a building of forty square meters) in 1986. Many businessmen had also located profitable (but polluting) manufacturing workshops there, and thus the area contained much wealth. At the same time, some of the businessmen were attracted by its reputation as a neighborhood where the government was not really in control, and where one's relationship to the council of elders mattered more than connections to local bureaucrats.

24. In a similar vein, at the end of their public service obligation, the young women who staffed a literacy program at one PVO were invited to a "graduation" ceremony where they received certificates of appreciation and £E5 from the MSA. During one of these ceremonies, on a stiflingly hot day in August, a man from the Muslim Youth Society opened the meeting by reciting the opening verse of the Koran. The audience (those finishing their public service, some officials of the PVOs, and others) had been attracted to the event by the promise of an appearance by the Minister of Social Affairs. However, officials of the MSA explained that she had been called away for an emergency and would not be attending. After very formal words of welcome, a young woman described the benefits of public service and her fulfilling experiences during the past year. Suppressed but audible laughter could be heard from her colleagues in the balcony, who apparently viewed their service far more cynically. After the graduates had received their certificates, officials of the PVOs who had supervised them during the past year were also awarded certificates of appreciation and received applause from the audience. Some of these PVO leaders seemed well known by the audience, which also included members of Parliament and both Coptic and Muslim clerics. Another speaker explained that 25,000 graduates of universities and higher institutes (generally technical institutes or the equivalent of junior colleges) were enrolled in public service programs throughout Egypt. Cairo alone absorbed one-third of all public service "volunteers."

25. I was in the community during the rebellion and curfew, and this account is

drawn from people's reactions and experiences, rather than public information about the rebellion. For a more detailed analysis of the intra-elite struggles that were set off by the rebellion, see Springborg, *Mubarak's Egypt*.

26. Springborg explains the rebellion as Minister of Interior Ahmed Rushdi's Waterloo. President Mubarak had attempted to use the Ministry of Interior as a counterbalance to the power of the military and its well-connected and popular Minister of Defense, Abu Ghazala. "When the CSF [Central Security Forces] rose in revolt, only to be crushed by the army, it destroyed the illusion that the Ministry of Interior could guarantee public security, underlining the reality that the real protector of the regime was the military. This of course further elevated Abu Ghazala, raising the President's indebtedness to him." Springborg, *Mubarak's Egypt*, p. 102.

27. Damages to this man's pickup truck reached £E350. After the rebellion the government announced that special committees had been set up to compensate the *sha'b* for any damages inflicted by the security forces. When I asked whether he would submit a claim to these committees, he sneered and said that he doubted the government would reimburse him for the full cost of the damage.

28. Several civilians were employed by the military at his unit to maintain older Russian equipment which new recruits no longer knew how to repair. These men, who had been soldiers during the 1960s and 1970s when the Soviet Union was the primary supplier to the Egyptian armed forces, were retained as civilian employees.

29. For example, a conscript in the military estimated that most of his colleagues had been given 100–150 days of guard duty and minor punishment by their officers for trivial infractions of one kind or another. He had already spent sixty-six days in jail and had ninety remaining days to serve. Although his unit was supposed to receive an additional £E7 for being stationed in a remote province, the officers knew how to manipulate paperwork to steal these few extra pounds from their conscripts. In addition, the NCO feared the more authoritarian aspect of the military. His friend told him that a rifle had been stolen at the unit where he was stationed, and all the conscripts on duty that night were imprisoned by the military for a year while the enlisted men and the officer on duty were imprisoned for six months, with their salaries suspended. The military, after the assassination of Sadat, had increased surveillance of its own troops and feared that the missing rifle had been stolen by one of the conscripts and would be used by Islamic activists to challenge the state. These incidents create a climate of paranoia among young officers, who are very insecure and fear that their careers can be ruined overnight by the disappearance of one rifle. The NCO's friend had been interviewed by his unit's security personnel and registered as someone interested in religion and politics. He worried that officers from the central military security agency would visit his unit soon and imprison him as they had been doing with any conscript with known sympathy for Islamic activists.

CONCLUSION

1. Joel S. Migdal, "Strong States, Weak States," in *Understanding Political Development*, ed. Weiner, Huntington, and Almond, p. 397.

2. Migdal, "Strong States, Weak States," p. 396.

3. Wolin, "Max Weber: Legitimation, Method and the Politics of Theory," p. 402.

4. Naomi Chazan, "Patterns of State-Society Incorporation and Disengagement in Africa," p. 123.

• B I B L I O G R A P H Y •

ARABIC SOURCES

Abu Liwaayah, Muhammad. "Will a Plate of *Kushari* Turn into a Tourist Dish?" *Al-Sha'b*, 12 August 1986, p. 3.

Al-'Ashmaawy, Ibrahim. "Egyptian Youth: Between Tourist Marriages and Foreign Marriages." *Al-Sha'b*, 19 August 1986, p. 9.

"Australian Sheep . . . Ordered and Butchered . . . and Leaving. The Minister of Food Supply Passes the Test of the 'Iid al-ADHa [Greater Bairam]." *Al-Masaa'*, 12 August 1986, p. 1.

Central Agency for Planning, Mobilisation, and Statistics (CAPMAS). *1986 Population Census: Results of the Sample; Population Characteristics and Housing Conditions*, vol. 1, part 1. Cairo: CAPMAS, 1989.

———. *Statistics on Marriage and Divorce (1979)*. Cairo: CAPMAS, 1981.

———. "A Study on the Labor Market in Egypt: The Unorganized Sector." Cairo: CAPMAS, June 1985.

"The Consumer Comes First." *Al-Masaa'*, 12 August 1986, p. 6.

"Crimes of Rape Break Out in the Egyptian Countryside: The Victim Is a Ten-Year-Old and the Criminal Is Her Cousin." *Al-Sha'b*, 12 March 1985, p. 7.

"A Declaration Made by the Deputy Chairman of the Central Auditing Agency." *Al-Ahram Journal* 3 (August 1984).

Farah, Nadia. *The Life of a Woman and Her Health*. Cairo: Sinai Publishers, 1991.

Fuda, Kariman Aly. "Islam Rejects the Phenomenon of Extravagant Weddings: Twelve Million Pounds Are Spent on Weddings in Hotels Each Year." *Al-Liwaa' al-Islami*, 7 August 1986, pp. 1, 21.

"Government Price Regulation: What's Wrong with It and So What?" *'Axbar il-Yoom*, 27 July 1986, p. 5.

Gumaa, Saad Ibrahim. *Youth and Political Participation*. Cairo: Dar al-Thaqafa lil-Nashra wal-Tawziya, 1984.

"Justice May Be Lost Due to the Slowness of the Judiciary: Law and the Judiciary." *Al-Axbaar*, 19 December 1985.

Al-Mahdi, Alia, and Amira Mashhur. "The Informal Sector in Egypt." Cairo: National Center for Sociological and Criminological Research, 1989.

"Mubarak's Labor Day Speech." *Al-Ahram*, 2 May 1985, p. 1.

Muhammad, Ghali. "*Sha'bi* Macaroni: Why Has It Disappeared from the Market." *Al-Musawar*, 18 August 1986, pp. 52–53.

"Rape: Under the Magnifying Glass of the Greatest Sages in Egypt." *Akhar Saa'a*, February 1985, p. 28.

"Rescuing Dumiyyaat Industries from Extinction." *Al-Ahram al-IqtiSaadi*, 13 June 1988, p. 33.

"A Responsible Parliamentarian Criticizes the State Plan to Build Subsidized Public Housing. A Wafd Representative Asks How Will University Graduates Find a Subsidized Apartment?" *Al-Wafd*, 25 June 1989.

Al-Sa'aaty, Hassan. *A Sociological Survey of the District of Bab al-Sha'riyya*. Cairo: 'Ain Shams University Press, 1961.

"The *Sha'b* Warn the Government: Stay Away from [Our] Cup of Tea." *Al-Sha'b*, 19 August 1986, p. 3.

Shabaana, Subhy. "Arranging Exceptions at the Student Placement Office." *Al-Sha'b*, 12 August 1986, p. 9.

"A State of Anxiety in the Egyptian Home: Secrets of Crimes of Rape and Sexual Abuse in 746 Crimes in the Last Five Years." *Al-Ahram*, 23 February 1985, p. 3.

"Two Dangerous Phenomena Threaten Egypt: Population Growth and the Incessant Accent of Consumerism." *Al-Ahram*, 2 May 1989, p. 1.

"The *Wafd* Stalks the Human Wolves in the Provinces of Egypt." *Al-Wafd*, 14 February 1985, p. 7.

ENGLISH AND FRENCH SOURCES

Abaza, Mona. "Feminist Debates and 'Traditional Feminism' of the Fellaha in Rural Egypt." Working Paper no. 93, Sociology of Development Research Centre, University of Bielefeld, 1987.

Abdalla, Ahmed. "Child Labour in Egypt: Leather Tanning in Cairo." In *Combating Child Labour*, ed. Assefa Bequele and Jo Boyden, pp. 31–47. Geneva: International Labour Office, 1988.

Abdel-Fadil, Mahmoud. *Development, Income Distribution and Social Change in Rural Egypt, 1952–1970: A Study in the Political Economy of Agrarian Transition*. Cambridge: Cambridge University Press, 1975.

———. "Informal-Sector Employment in Egypt." Series on Employment Opportunities and Equity in Egypt, no. 1. Geneva: International Labour Office, 1980.

———. "Labor in the Unorganized Sector." *Al-Ahram al-Iqtisadi* 1086 (6 November 1989): 8–21.

———. *The Political Economy of Nasserism: A Study in Employment and Income Distribution Politics in Urban Egypt, 1952–72*. Cambridge: Cambridge University Press, 1980.

Abdel-Fadil, Mahmoud, and Jihan Diab. "The Black Economy and National Accounts in LDCs: The Case of Egypt" (unpublished paper). American University in Cairo, August 1983.

Abdel Kader, Soha. "A Report on the Status of Egyptian Women, 1900–1973." Cairo: Social Research Center, American University in Cairo, September 1973.

———. "A Survey of Trends in Social Science Research on Women in the Arab Region, 1960–1980." In Abdel Kader, *Social Science Research and Women in the Arab World*, pp. 139–75. London: Frances Pinter (publisher for UNESCO), 1984.

Abt Associates, Dames and Moore, and the General Organization for Housing, Building Planning and Research. "Informal Housing in Egypt." Report to the U.S. Agency for International Development (Cairo, January 1981).

Abu-Lughod, Janet L. *Cairo: 1001 Years of the City Victorious*. Princeton: Princeton University Press, 1971.

Abu-Lughod, Lila. "The Journey of Mr. Abu 'Ela al-Bishry, Islam and Public Culture: The Politics of Egyptian Television Serials." *Middle East Report* 180 (January–February 1993): 25–30.

———. *Veiled Sentiments: Honor and Poetry in a Bedouin Society*. Berkeley: University of California Press, 1986.

Adams, Richard Newbold. "The Structure of Participation: A Commentary." In *Po-*

litical Participation in Latin America, vol. 2, *Politics and the Poor*, ed. Seligson and Booth, pp. 9–17. New York: Holmes and Meier, 1979.

Ajami, Fouad. *The Arab Predicament: Arab Political Thought and Practice Since 1967*. New York: Cambridge University Press, 1981.

Alderman, Harold, and Joachim von Braun. "The Effects of the Egyptian Food Ration and Subsidy System on Income Distribution and Consumption." International Food Policy Research Institute Research Report no. 45 (July 1984).

Almond, Gabriel A., and Sidney Verba, eds. *The Civic Culture: Political Attitudes and Democracy in Five Nations*. Princeton: Princeton University Press, 1963.

————, eds. *The Civic Culture Revisited*. Boston: Little, Brown, 1980.

Altorki, Soraya. *Women in Saudi Arabia: Ideology and Behavior Among the Elite*. New York: Columbia University Press, 1986.

Amin, Galal A. "Migration, Inflation and Social Mobility: A Sociological Interpretation of Egypt's Current Economic and Political Crisis." In *Egypt Under Mubarak*, ed. Charles Tripp and Roger Owen, pp. 103–21. London: Routledge, 1989.

Amin, Galal A., and Elizabeth Awny. "International Migration of Egyptian Labour: A Review of the State of the Art" (manuscript report). International Development Research Centre, Ottawa and Cairo, September 1984.

Ammar, Hamed. *Growing Up in an Egyptian Village*. New York: Octagon Books, 1966.

Anker, Richard, and Martha Anker. "Measuring the Female Labour Force in Egypt." *International Labour Review* 128 (1989): 511–20.

Ansari, Hamied. *Egypt: The Stalled Society*. Albany: State University of New York Press, 1986.

Assaad, Ragui. "The Employment Crisis in Egypt: Trends and Issues" (unpublished). American University in Cairo, January 1989.

Assaad, Ragui, and Leyla Neyzi. "Locating the Informal Sector in History: A Case Study of the Refuse Collectors of Cairo." Paper presented at the Social Science Research Council's Workshop on the Informal Sector of the Economy in the Middle East, Munich, 28–31 July 1986.

Atiya, Nayra. *Khul-Khaal: Five Egyptian Women Tell Their Stories*. Syracuse, N.Y.: Syracuse University Press, 1982.

Ayubi, Nazih N. M. *Bureaucracy and Politics in Contemporary Egypt*. London: Ithaca Press, 1980.

Badr, Mahmoud et al. "Small-Scale Enterprises in Egypt: Fayoum [Fayyum] and Kalyubiya [Qalyubia] Governorates—Phase One Survey Results." Michigan State University Rural Development, Working Paper no. 23 (1982).

Baer, Gabriel. *Egyptian Guilds in Modern Times*. Jerusalem: Israel Oriental Society, 1964.

Baker, Raymond William. *Egypt's Uncertain Revolution Under Nasser and Sadat*. Cambridge: Harvard University Press, 1978.

————. *Sadat and After*. Cambridge: Harvard University Press, 1990.

Bates, Robert H. "Macropolitical Economy in the Field of Development." In *Perspectives on Positive Political Economy*, ed. James E. Alt and Kenneth A. Shepsle, pp. 31–54. New York: Cambridge University Press, 1990.

Barakat, Halim. "The Arab Family and the Challenge of Social Transformation." In *Women and the Family in the Middle East: New Voices of Change*, ed. Fernea, pp. 27–48. Austin: University of Texas Press, 1985.

Beinen, Joel, and Zachary Lockman. *Workers on the Nile*. Princeton: Princeton University Press, 1987.

Berry, Sara S. "From Peasant to Artisan: Motor Mechanics in a Nigerian Town." African Studies Center, Working Paper no. 76 (Boston: Boston University, 1983).

Bianchi, Robert. "The Corporatization of the Egyptian Labor Movement." *Middle East Journal* 40 (Summer 1986): 429–44.

———. "Egypt's Infitah Bourgeoisie," *MERIP* 142 (Summer 1986): 429–44.

———. *Interest Groups and Political Development in Turkey*. Princeton: Princeton University Press, 1984.

———. *Unruly Corporatism*. New York: Oxford University Press, 1989.

Bibars, Iman M. Diaa el Din. "Women's Political Interest Groups in Egypt." Master's thesis, American University in Cairo, 1987.

Bill, James A., and Carl Leiden. *Politics in the Middle East*. 2d ed. Boston: Little, Brown, 1984.

Binder, Leonard. *In a Moment of Enthusiasm: Political Power and the Second Stratum in Egypt*. Chicago: University of Chicago Press, 1978.

Birks, J., and C. Sinclair. "Aspects of International Migration in the Arab Near East: Implications for USAID Policy" (mimeo). United States Agency for International Development Report, May 1979.

———. "The Socio-Economic Determinants of Intra-Regional Migration." Paper presented at the ECWA Conference on International Migration in the Arab World, Nicosia, Cyprus, 11–16 May 1981.

Boissevain, Jeremy. *Friends of Friends: Networks, Manipulators and Coalitions*. Oxford: Basil Blackwell, 1974.

Booth, John A., and Mitchell A. Seligson. "Images of Political Participation in Latin America." In *Political Participation in Latin America*, vol. 1, *Citizen and State*, ed. Booth and Seligson, pp. 3–33. New York: Holmes and Meier, 1978.

Botman, Selma. *The Rise of Egyptian Communism, 1939–1970*. Syracuse, N.Y.: Syracuse University Press, 1988.

Bromley, Ray. *The Urban Informal Sector: Critical Perspectives on Employment and Housing Policies*. New York: Pergamon, 1979.

Brown, Nathan J. *Peasant Politics in Modern Egypt*. New Haven: Yale University Press, 1990.

Bryant, Coralie, and Louise G. White. *Managing Development in the Third World*. Boulder, Colo.: Westview, 1982.

Cantori, Louis J., and Peter Benedict. "Local Leadership in Urban Egypt: Leader, Family and Community Perceptions." In *Local Politics and Development in the Middle East*, ed. Louis J. Cantori and Iliya Harik, pp. 46–59. Boulder, Colo.: Westview, 1984.

Central Agency for Planning, Mobilisation, and Statistics. *Egyptian Fertility Survey (1980)*. 4 vols. Vol. 1, *Survey Design*; vol. 2, *Fertility and Family Planning*; vol. 3, *Socio-Economic Differentials and Comparative Data from Husbands and Wives*; vol. 4, *Statistical Tables*. Cairo: CAPMAS, 1983.

———. "Family Budget Research by Sample in Egypt: The Combined Results of the Four Cycles 1974–75." Cairo: CAPMAS, September 1978.

———. *Preliminary Results of the Population, Housing and Establishment Census of 1986*. CAPMAS: Cairo, June 1987.

Castells, Manuel, and Alejandro Portes. "World Underneath: The Origins, Dynamics, and Effects of the Informal Economy." In *The Informal Economy: Studies in*

Advanced and Less Developed Countries, ed. Alejandro Portes, Manuel Castells, and Lauren A. Benton, pp. 11–37. Baltimore: Johns Hopkins University Press, 1989.

Charmes, Jacque. "Méthodologie et resultats des enquêtes sur le secteur non structuré en Tunisie." In *Etudes sur l'emploi aux Antilles et en Tunisie: Sous-emploi, secteur non structuré, migrations*, ed. J. Charmes, H. Domenach, and J. P. Geuganant, pp. 51–129. Institut national de la Statistique et des Etudes Economiques, no. 54 (August 1982).

Chazan, Naomi. "Patterns of State-Society Incorporation and Disengagement in Africa." In *The Precarious Balance: State and Society in Africa*, ed. Naomi Chazan and Donald Rothchild, pp. 121–48. Boulder, Colo.: Westview, 1988.

Chmielewski, Piotr. "The Public and the Private in Primitive Societies." *International Political Science Review* 12 (1991): 267–80.

Cloudsley, Anne. *Women of Omdurman: Life, Love and the Cult of Virginity*. London: Ethnographica, 1984.

Committee on Population and Demography. *The Estimation of Recent Trends in Fertility and Mortality in Egypt*, no. 9. Washington, D.C.: National Academy Press, 1982.

Conge, Patrick J. "The Concept of Political Participation: Toward a Definition." *Comparative Politics* 20 (January 1988): 241–49.

Cooper, Marc N. "State Capitalism, Class Structure, and Social Transformation in the Third World: The Case of Egypt." *International Journal of Middle East Studies* 15 (November 1983): 451–69.

———. *The Transformation of Egypt*. Baltimore: Johns Hopkins University Press, 1982.

Cornelius, Wayne A., and Felicity M. Trueblood, eds. *Latin American Urban Research*, vol. 5, *Urbanization and Inequality: The Political Economy of Urban and Rural Development in Latin America*. Beverly Hills: Sage, 1975.

Danforth, Sandra C. "The Social and Poltiical Implications of Muslim Middle Eastern Women's Participation in Violent Political Conflict." In *United Nations Decade for Women World Conference*, ed. Naomi B. Lynn, pp. 35–54. New York: Haworth Press, 1984.

Dareer, Asma el. *Woman, Why Do You Weep?* London: Zed Press, 1982.

Davis, Susan S. *Patience and Power: Women's Lives in a Moroccan Village*. Cambridge, Mass.: Schenkman, 1978.

Dekmejian, R. Hrair. *Egypt Under Nasir: A Study in Political Dynamics*. Albany: State University of New York Press, 1971.

De Soto, Hernando. *The Other Path: The Invisible Revolution in the Third World*. Foreword by Mario Vargas Llosa. Translated by June Abbott. New York: Harper and Row, 1989.

Dwyer, Daisy. *Images and Self-Images: Male and Female in Morocco*. New York: Columbia University Press, 1978.

Early, Evelyn A. *Baladi Women of Cairo: Playing with an Egg and a Stone*. Boulder, Colo.: Lynne Rienner, 1993.

———. "Getting It Together: Baladi Egyptian Businesswomen." In *Arab Women: Old Boundaries, New Frontiers*, ed. Tucker, pp. 84–101. Bloomington: Indiana University Press, 1993.

Economist Intelligence Unit (EIU). "Egypt." *Country Profile Reports* (1986–87): 8–9.

Economist Intelligence Unit (EIU). "Egypt." *Country Profile Reports* 4 (1988).

"Egyptian Income Tax Modernization Project: Hard to Tax Groups" (mimeo). Cairo: U.S. Agency for International Development, n.d.

"Egyptian Income Tax Modernization Project: The Transfer from a Schedular Tax System to a Global Income Tax" (mimeo). Cairo: U.S. Agency for International Development, n.d.

Eickelman, Dale F. *The Middle East: An Anthropological Approach*. Englewood Cliffs, N.J.: Prentice-Hall, 1981.

Elshtain, Jean Bethke. *Public Man, Private Woman: Women in Social and Political Thought*. Princeton: Princeton University Press, 1981.

Esposito, John L. *Women in Muslim Family Law*. Syracuse, N.Y.: Syracuse University Press, 1982.

———, ed. *Voices of Resurgent Islam*. New York: Oxford University Press, 1983.

Fahmi, Hoda. "Divorcer en Egypte: Etude de l'Application des Lois du Statut Personnel." CEDEJ, *Dossier* 3 (1986).

Farah, Nadia. "The Egyptian Women's Health Book Collective: Our Bodies, Ourselves." *Middle East Report* 173 (November–December 1991): 16–17.

Fergany, Nadar "A Characterisation of the Employment Problem in Egypt." In *Employment and Structural Adjustment: Egypt in the 1990s*, ed. Handoussa and Potter, pp. 25–56. Cairo: American University in Cairo Press, 1991.

Fernea, Elizabeth Warnock. "The Family." In *Women and the Family in the Middle East: New Voices of Change*, ed. Fernea, pp. 25–26. Austin: University of Texas Press, 1985.

Folbre, Nancy. "The Black Four of Hearts: Toward a New Paradigm of Household Economics." In *A Home Divided: Women and Income in the Third World*, ed. Daisy Dwyer and Judith Bruce, pp. 248–62. Stanford, Calif.: Stanford University Press, 1988.

———. "Cleaning House: New Perspectives on Households and Economic Development." *Journal of Development Economics* 22 (1986): 5–40.

Foweraker, Joe. "Popular Movements and Political Change in Mexico." In *Popular Movements and Political Change in Mexico*, ed. Joe Foweraker and Ann L. Craig, pp. 3–22. Boulder, Colo: Lynne Rienner, 1990.

Garton-Ash, Timothy. *The Magic Lantern: The Revolution of '89 Witnessed in Warsaw, Budapest, Berlin, and Prague*. New York: Random House, 1990.

Geertz, Clifford. *The Interpretation of Cultures*. New York: Basic Books, 1973.

———. *Local Knowledge: Further Essays in interpretive Anthropology*. New York: Basic Books, 1983.

Gellner, Ernest. "Patrons and Clients." In *Patrons and Clients in Mediterranean Societies*, ed. Gellner and Waterbury. London: Duckworth, 1977.

Gellner, Ernest, and John Waterbury, eds. *Patrons and Clients in Mediterranean Societies*. London: Duckworth, 1977.

Goldberg, Ellis. *Tinker, Tailor, and Textile Worker: Class and Politics in Egypt, 1930–1952*. Berkeley: University of California Press, 1986.

Goldschmidt, Jr., Arthur. *Modern Egypt: The Formation of a Nation-State*. Boulder, Colo.: Westview, 1988.

Goodwin, Jeff, and Theda Skocpol. "Explaining Revolutions in the Contemporary Third World." *Politics and Society* 17 (1989): 489–509.

Gordon, Joel. *Nasser's Blessed Movement: Egypt's Free Officers and the July Revolution*. New York: Oxford University Press, 1992.

Graziano, Luigi. *A Conceptual Framework for the Study of Clientelism*. Western Societies Program, Occasional Paper no. 2. Ithaca, N.Y.: Cornell University, 1975.

Guindi, Fadwa El. "Veiling Infitah with Muslim Ethic: Egypt's Contemporary Islamic Movement." *Social Problems* 28 (1981): 465–85.

Gusfield, Joseph R. "Social Movements and Social Change: Perspectives of Linearity and Fluidity." *Research in Social Movements, Conflict and Change* 4 (1981): 317–39.

Hall, Margorie, and Ismail Bakhita Amin. *Sisters Under the Sun: The Story of Sudanese Women*. London: Longman, 1983.

Halpern, Manfred. "Choosing Between Ways of Life and Death and Between Forms of Democracy: An Archetypal Analysis." *Alternatives* 12 (1987): 5–35.

———. *The Politics of Social Change in the Middle East and North Africa*. Princeton: Princeton University Press, 1963.

Handoussa, Heba. "The Burden of Public Service Employment and Remuneration: A Case Study of Egypt" (monograph commissioned by the International Labour Office). Geneva: ILO, September 1988.

———. "Crisis and Challenge: Prospects for the 1990s." In *Employment and Structural Adjustment: Egypt in the 1990s*, ed. Heba Handoussa and Gillian Potter, pp. 3–21. Cairo: American University in Cairo Press, 1991.

Hankiss, Elemér. "The 'Second Society'": Is There an Alternative Social Model Emerging in Contemporary Hungary?" *Social Research* 55 (1988): 13–42.

Hanna, Milad M. "Real Estate Rights in Urban Egypt: The Changing Sociopolitical Winds." In *Property, Social Structure and Law in the Modern Middle East*, ed. Ann Elizabeth Mayer, pp. 189–211. Albany: State University of New York Press, 1985.

Hansen, Bent, and Samir Radwan. *Employment Opportunities and Equity in a Changing Economy: Egypt in the 1980s, A Labour Market Approach*. Geneva: International Labour Office, 1982.

Hart, Keith. "Informal Income Opportunities and Urban Employment in Ghana." *Journal of Modern African Studies* 11 (1973): 61–89.

Hassan, Nawal Mahmoud. "Beyond Western Paradigms of Development: A Pragmatic Response to Popular Housing." In *Development, Change and Gender in Cairo: A View from the Household*, ed. Diane Singerman and Homa Hoodfar. Bloomington: Indiana University Press, forthcoming.

———. "Report on Survey of Families in Gamaliyya." Cairo: Centre for Egyptian Civilisation Studies and the Higher Institute of Social Work, 1979.

———. "Social Aspects of Urban Housing in Cairo." *MIRMAR* (1985): 59–61.

Hatem, Mervat. "Egypt's Middle Class in Crisis: The Sexual Division of Labor." *Middle East Journal* 42 (Summer 1988): 407–22.

———. "The Enduring Alliance of Nationalism and Patriarchy in Muslim Personal Status Laws: The Case of Modern Egypt." *Feminist Studies* 12 (Spring 1986): 19–43.

Havel, Václav. "The Power of the Powerless" In Václav Havel et al., *The Power of the Powerless*, ed. John Keane, pp. 23–96. Armonk, N.Y.: M. E. Sharpe, 1985.

Hellman, Judith Adler. "The Study of New Social Movements in Latin America and the Question of Autonomy." *LASA Forum* 21 (Summer 1990): 7–12.

Hendriks, Bertus. "Egypt's New Political Map: A Report from the Election Campaign." *MERIP* 147 (July–August 1987): 23–30.

Henry, Stuart, ed. *Can I Have It in Cash?: A Study of Informal Institutions and Unorthodox Ways of Doing Things*. London: Astragal Books, 1981.

Al-Hibri, Azizah, ed. "Women and Islam." *Women's Studies International Forum* 5 (1982).

Hijab, Nadia. *Womanpower: The Arab Debate on Women at Work*. Cambridge: Cambridge University Press, 1988.

Hill, Enid. *Mahkama! Studies in the Egyptian Legal System, Courts and Crime, Law and Society*. Cairo: American University in Cairo Press, 1979.

Hinnebusch, Jr., Raymond A. *Egyptian Politics under Sadat: The Post-Populist Development of an Authoritarian-Modernizing State*. Cambridge: Cambridge University Press, 1985.

Hoodfar, Homa. "Household Budgeting and Financial Management in a Lower-income Cairo Neighborhood." In *A Home Divided: Women and Income in the Third World*, ed. Daisy Dwyer and Judith Bruce, pp. 120–42. Stanford, Calif.: Stanford University Press, 1988.

———. "The Political Economy of Low-income Households in Contemporary Cairo." Paper prepared for the Population Council's MEAwards Workshop on Research on Cairo Households, Cairo, June 1988.

———. "Survival Strategies in Low-income Households in Cairo." *Journal of South Asian and Middle Eastern Studies* 13 (Summer 1990): 22–41.

———. "Survival Strategies in Low-income Neighbourhoods of Cairo, Egypt." Ph.D. diss., University of Kent, 1988.

Hoodfar, Homa, and Fatma Khafagy. Seminar on Women and Migration. The Population Council, Cairo, 23 January 1986.

Hopkins, Nicholas S., ed. "The Informal Sector in Egypt." *Cairo Papers in Social Science* 14 (Winter 1991).

Hopkins, Nicholas S., and Saad Eddin Ibrahim, eds. *Arab Society: Social Science Perspectives*. Cairo: American University in Cairo Press, 1985.

Hosken, F. P. "Women and Health: Female Circumcision." *WIN News* 4 (1982).

Howard-Merriam, Kathleen. "Egypt's Other Political Elite." *Western Political Quarterly* 34 (March 1981): 174–87.

Huntington, Samuel, and Joan Nelson. *No Easy Choice: Political Participation in Developing Countries*. Cambridge: Harvard University Press, 1976.

Hussein, Mahmoud. *Class Conflict in Egypt, 1945–1970*. Translated by Michel and Susanne Chirman et al. New York: Monthly Review Press, 1973.

Hyden, Goran. *Beyond Ujamaa in Tanzania: Underdevelopment and an Uncaptured Peasantry*. London: Heinemann, 1980.

Hyland, A. D. C., A. G. Tipple, and N. Wilkinson, eds. *Housing in Egypt*. University of Newcastle-upon-Tyne, School of Architecture Housing Course, Working Paper no. 1 (1984).

Ibrahim, Barbara. "Family Strategies: A Perspective on Women's Entry to Labour Force Participation in Egypt." *International Journal of the Family* 11 (1981).

Ibrahim, Saad Eddin. "Anatomy of Egypt's Militant Islamic Groups: Methodological Note and Preliminary Findings." *International Journal of Middle East Studies* 12 (1980): 423–53.

———. *The New Arab Social Order: A Study of the Social Impact of Oil Wealth*. Boulder, Colo.: Westview; and London: Croom Helm, 1982.

Ikram, Khalid. *Egypt: Economic Management in a Period of Transition*. Baltimore: Johns Hopkins University Press, 1980.

———. "Meeting the Social Contract in Egypt." *Finance and Development* 18 (September 1981): 30–33.

International Labour Office (ILO). *Statistical Sources and Methods*. 3 vols. Vol. 3: *Economically Active Population, Employment, Unemployment and Hours of Work Household Surveys*. Geneva: ILO, 1986.

———. *Year Book of Labour Statistics (1987)*. 47th ed. Geneva: ILO, 1988.

Ismail, Ellen T. *Social Environment and Daily Routine of Sudanese Women: A Case Study of Urban Middle-Class Housewives*. Berlin: Dietrich Reimer Verlag, 1982.

Jansen, G. H. *Militant Islam*. New York: Harper and Row, 1979.

Joseph, Suad. "Family as Security and Bondage: A Political Strategy of the Lebanese Urban Working Class." In *Arab Society: Social Science Perspectives*, ed. Hopkins and Ibrahim, pp. 241–56. Cairo: American University in Cairo Press, 1985.

———. "Working-Class Women's Networks in a Sectarian State: A Political Paradox." *American Ethnologist* 10 (February 1983): 1–22.

Kagitcibasi, Cigdem, ed. *Sex Roles, Family and Community in Turkey*. Indiana University Turkish Studies Series, no. 3. Bloomington: Indiana University, 1982.

Kamphoefner, Kathryn. "Voices from the Bottom: Women of Cairo View Literacy." Ph.D. diss., Northwestern University, 1991.

Kandiyoti, Deniz. "Introduction." In *Women, Islam and the State*, ed. Kandiyoti, pp. 1–21. Philadelphia: Temple University Press, 1991.

Keddie, Nikki R. "Problems in the Study of Middle Eastern Women." *International Journal of Middle Eastern Studies* 10 (1979): 225–40.

Keddie, Nikki R., and Beth Baron, eds. *Women in Middle Eastern History: Shifting Boundaries in Sex and Gender*. New Haven: Yale University Press, 1991.

Kepel, Gilles. *Muslim Extremism in Egypt*. Berkeley: University of California Press, 1986.

Kennedy, John G. "Circumcision and Excision in Egyptian Nubia." *Man* 5 (June 1970).

Khalaf, Samir. *Lebanon's Predicament*. New York: Columbia University Press, 1986.

Kharoufi, Mostafa. "The Informal Dimension of Urban Activity in Egypt: Some Recent Work." *Cairo Papers in Social Science* 14 (Winter 1991): 8–20.

Khayat, Abdul Aziz. "Association of Sexes in Islam." Reprint from the International Islamic Centre for Population Studies and Research, al-Azhar University, Cairo, n.d.

Khlat, M., and S. Halabi. "Modernization and Consanguineous Marriages in Beirut." *Journal of Biosocial Science* 18 (1986): 489–95.

Khouri-Dagher, Nadia. "The Answers of Civil Society to a Defaulting State: A Case Study Around the Food Question in Egypt." Paper presented at the annual meeting of the Middle East Studies Association, Baltimore, 15–17 November 1987.

———. "Food and Energy in Cairo: Provisioning the Poor." Cairo: United Nations University, Food-Energy Nexus Programme, 1986.

———. "La Survie Quotidienne au Caire." *Magreb-Machrek* 110 (October–November–December 1985): 53–68.

Khoury, Philip S. "Abu Ali al-Kilawi: A Damascus Qabaday." In *Struggle and Survival in the Modern Middle East*, ed. Edmund Burke, pp. 179–90. Berkeley: University of California Press, 1993.

Lesch, Ann Mosely. "Egyptian Labor Migration: Economic Trends and Government Policies." *UFSI Reports* 38 (1985).

Lesch, Ann Mosely. "The Impact of Labor Migration on Urban and Rural Egypt." *UFSI Reports* 39 (1985).

Lesch, Ann Mosely, and Earl L. Sullivan. "Women in Egypt: New Roles and Realities." *UFSI Reports* 22 (1986).

Levine, Daniel H. "Religion, the Poor, and Politics in Latin America Today." In *Religion and Political Conflict in Latin America*, ed. Levine. Chapel Hill: University of North Carolina Press, 1986.

Lightfoot-Klein, Hanny. *Prisoners of Ritual: An Odyssey into Female Genital Circumcision in Africa*. Binghamton, N.Y.: Harrington Press, 1989.

Lomnitz, Larissa Adler. *Networks and Marginality: Life in a Mexican Shantytown*. Translated by Cinna Lomnitz. New York: Academic Press, 1977.

Mabro, Robert. *The Egyptian Economy, 1952–1972*. Oxford: Oxford University Press, 1974.

MacLeod, Arlene Elowe. *Accommodating Protest: Working Women, the New Veiling, and Change in Cairo*. New York: Columbia University Press, 1991.

———. "Hegemonic Relations and Gender Resistance: The New Veiling as Accommodating Protest in Cairo." *Signs* 17 (Spring 1992): 533–57.

———. "The Intersection of Household and Workplace: Cairo's Lower-Middle-Class Women and the Double Bind." Paper prepared for the Population Council's MEAwards Workshop on Research on Cairo Households, Cairo, June 1988.

Maier, Charles S. "Introduction." In *Changing Boundaries of the Political: Essays on the Evolving Balance Between the State and Society, Public and Private in Europe*, ed. Maier, pp. 1–26. New York: Cambridge University Press, 1987.

Mainwaring, Scott. "Urban Popular Movements, Identity, and Democratization in Brazil." *Comparative Political Studies* 20 (July 1987): 131–59.

March, Kathryn S., and Rachelle L. Taqqu. *Women's Informal Associations in Developing Countries: Catalysts for Change?* Boulder, Colo.: Westview, 1986.

Martin, JoAnn. "The Women's Touch: Patterns in Mexican Women's Political Participation" (unpublished paper). Berkeley: University of California Anthropology Department, n.d.

Mazumdar, Dipak. "The Urban Informal Sector." Staff Working Paper no. 211. Washington, D.C.: International Bank for Reconstruction and Development, 1975.

Mernissi, Fatima. *Beyond the Veil: Male-Female Dynamics in a Modern Society*. Cambridge, Mass.: Schenkman, 1975.

———. *Doing Daily Battle: Interviews with Moroccan Women*. Translated by Mary Jo Lakeland. New Brunswick: Rutgers University Press, 1989.

Al-Messiri, Sawsan. "The Changing Role of the Futuwa in the Social Structure of Cairo." In *Patrons and Clients in the Mediterranean Societies*, ed. Gellner and Waterbury. London: Duckworth, 1977.

———. *Ibn al-Balad: A Concept of Egyptian Identity*. London: E. J. Brill, 1978.

Meyer, Günter. "Socioeconomic Structure and Development of Small-Scale Manufacturing in Old Quarters of Cairo." Paper presented at the annual meeting of the Middle East Studies Association, Baltimore, 15–17 November 1987.

Middle East Economic Handbook. London: Euromonitor Publications, 1986.

Migdal, Joel S. *Strong Societies and Weak States: State-Society Relations and State Capabilities in the Third World*. Princeton: Princeton University Press, 1988.

———. "Strong States, Weak States: Power and Accommodation." In *Understand-*

ing Political Development: An Analytic Study, ed. Weiner, Huntington, and Almond, pp. 391–434. Boston: Little, Brown, 1987.

Mitchell, Richard P. *The Society of Muslim Brothers*. London: Oxford University Press, 1969.

Mitchell, Timothy. "America's Egypt: Discourse of the Development Industry." *Middle East Report* 169 (March–April 1991): 18–34.

———. "The Limits of the State: Beyond Statist Approaches and Their Critics." *American Political Science Review* 85 (March 1991): 77–96.

Moore, Barrington. *Privacy: Studies in Social and Cultural History*. Armonk, N.Y.: M. E. Sharpe, 1984.

Moore, Clement Henry. "Money and Power: The Dilemma of the Egyptian Infitah." *Middle East Journal* 40 (Autumn 1986): 634–50.

Nader, Laura. "The Subordination of Women in Comparative Perspective." *Urban Anthropology, and Studies of Cultural Systems and World Economic Development* 15 (Fall–Winter 1986): 377–97.

Nadim, Nawal al-Messiri. "Family Relationships in a 'Harah' in Cairo." In *Arab Society: Social Science Perspectives*, ed. Hopkins and Ibrahim, pp. 212–22. Cairo: American University in Cairo Press, 1985.

———. "The Relationship Between the Sexes in a Harah of Cairo." Ph.D. diss., Indiana University, 1975.

National Bank of Egypt. "The Taxation System in Egypt." *Economic Bulletin* 37 (1984).

National Specialized Councils. *The Economics of Savings of Egyptians Working Abroad*. Cairo: Arab Center for Research and Publishing, 1983.

Nelson, Cynthia. "Biography and Women's History: On Interpreting Doria Shafik." In *Women in Middle Eastern History: Shifting Boundaries in Sex and Gender*, ed. Keddie and Baron, pp. 310–33. New Haven: Yale University Press, 1991.

———. "Public and Private Politics: Women in the Middle Eastern World." *American Ethnologist* 1 (1974): 555–64.

———. "The Voices of Doria Shafik: Feminist Consciousness in Egypt from 1940–60." Paper presented at CEDEJ Conference, "D'un Orient L'Autre," Cairo, April 1985.

———. "Women and Power in Nomadic Societies in the Middle East." In *The Desert and the Sown: Nomads in the Wider Society*, ed. Cynthia Nelson, pp. 43–60. Berkeley, Calif.: Institute of International Studies, 1973.

Nelson, Joan. *Access to Power: Politics and the Urban Poor in Developing Nations*. Princeton: Princeton University Press, 1979.

———. "Political Participation." In *Understanding Political Development: An Analytic Study*, ed. Weiner, Huntington, and Almond, pp. 103–59. Boston: Little, Brown, 1987.

El-Nowaihi, Mohamed. "Changing the Law on Personal Status in Egypt Within a Liberal Interpretation of the Shariʿa." *Middle East Review* 11 (Summer 1979): 40–49.

Oldham, Linda, Haguer El Hadidi, and Hussein Tamaa. "Informal Communities in Cairo: The Basis of a Typology." *Cairo Papers in Social Science* 10 (Winter 1987).

O'Donnell, Guillermo. "Tensions in the Bureaucratic-Authoritarian State." In *The New Authoritarianism in Latin America*, ed. David Collier, pp. 285–318. Princeton: Princeton University Press, 1979.

Oweiss, Ibrahim M. "Egypt's Informal Economy." Paper presented at the 24th annual meeting of the Middle East Studies Association, San Antonio, Texas, 10–13 November 1990.

Oxhorn, Philip. "The Popular-Sector Response to an Authoritarian Regime: Shantytown Organizations Since the Military Coup." *Latin American Perspectives* 18 (Winter 1991): 66–91.

Pateman, Carole. "The Civic Culture: A Philosophic Critique." In *The Civic Culture Revisited*, ed. Almond and Verba, pp. 57–102. Boston: Little, Brown, 1980.

———. "Feminist Critiques of the Public/Private Dichotomy." In *Public and Private in Social Life*, ed. S. I. Benn and G. F. Gaus, pp. 281–303. London: Croom Helm, 1983.

———. "Removing Obstacles to Democracy: The Case of Patriarchy." Paper presented at the International Political Science Association, Ottawa, Canada, October 1986.

Peattie, Lisa, and Martin Rein. *Women's Claims: A Study in Political Economy*. New York: Oxford University Press, 1983.

Perlmutter, Amos. "Egypt and the Myth of the New Middle Class." *Comparative Studies in History and Society* 10 (October 1967): 46–65.

Petry, Carl F. "Class Solidarity versus Gender Gain: Women as Custodians of Property in Later Medieval Egypt." In *Women in Middle Eastern History: Shifting Boundaries in Sex and Gender*, ed. Keddie and Baron, pp. 122–42. New Haven: Yale University Press, 1991.

Portes, Alejandro. "Latin American Class Structures: Their Composition and Change During the Last Decades." *Latin American Research Review* 20 (1985): 7–39.

Portes, Alejandro, and John Walton. *Labor, Class, and the International System*. New York: Academic Press, 1981.

Post, Erika. "Egypt's Elections." *MERIP* 147 (July–August 1987): 17–22.

Posusney, Marsha Pripstein. "Irrational Workers: The Moral Economy of Labor Protest in Egypt." *World Politics* 46 (October 1993): 83–120.

"Private Voluntary Organizations in Cairo Governorate: A Profile." Unpublished report prepared for the Neighborhood Urban Services Project of USAID/Cairo by Wilbur Smith and Associates in association with the Public Administration Service and the Engineering and Geological Consulting Office (Cairo, June 1984).

Przeworski, Adam. "Marxism and Rational Choice." *Politics and Society* 14 (1985): 379–409.

"Public Policy and the Economics of Housing." *The Housing and Construction Industry in Egypt*. Interim Report Working Papers 1979–80, Cairo University–Massachusetts Institute of Technology Technological Planning Program, Cambridge, Mass., 1980.

Rassam, Amal. "Toward a Theoretical Framework for the Study of Women in the Arab World." In UNESCO, *Social Science Research and Women in the Arab World*, pp. 122–38. London and Dover, N.H.: Frances Pinter (publisher for UNESCO), 1984.

Raymond, André. *Artisans et Commerçants au Caire au XVIIIe Siécle*. Damascus, 1973–74.

Reynolds, Nancy Young. "Discourses of Social Change: An Analysis of the 1985 Personal Status Law Debate in Egypt." Honors thesis. Harvard University, 1989.

Rizk, Soad Kamel. "The Structure and Operation of the Informal Sector in Egypt." In *Employment and Structural Adjustment: Egypt in the 1990s*, ed. Handoussa and Potter, pp. 167–88. Cairo: American University in Cairo Press, 1991.

Roy, Delwin A. "The Hidden Economy in Egypt." *Middle East Studies* 28 (October 1992): 689–711.

Rugh, Andrea B. *The Family in Contemporary Egypt*. Syracuse, N.Y.: Syracuse University Press, 1984.

Ruskay, John. "Expanding Noninstitutional Mass Political Participation: The Role of Voluntary Groups in the Egyptian Revolution of 1919." Ph.D. diss., Columbia University, 1977.

El-Saadawi, Nawal. *The Hidden Face of Eve: Women in the Arab World*. London: Zed Press, 1980.

El-Saaty, Hassan. "The New Aristocracized and Bourgeoisized Classes in the Egyptian Application of Socialism." In *Commoners, Climbers and Notables*, ed. C. A. O. van Nieuwenhuijze, pp. 196–204. Leiden: E. J. Brill, 1977.

Sabah, Saadia. "The Interface Between Family and State." In *The Political Economy of Morocco*, ed. William Zartman, pp. 117–40. Boulder, Colo.: Westview, 1987.

Sabbah, Fatna A. *Woman in the Muslim Unconscious*. New York: Pergamon, 1984.

El-Safty, Madiha. "Sociological Perspectives on Urban Housing." *Cairo Papers in Social Sciences* 6 (June 1983): 1–8.

Saleh, Saneya A. W. "The Changing Political and Social Status of Women in Egypt." Paper presented at the Mid-Decade Conference for Women, Copenhagen, July 1980.

"Saudis Suffer High Cost of Marriage." *Los Angeles Times*, 21 September 1986.

Sayed, Hussein A. A., and S. Attia Shadia. "Some Demographic and Family Planning Characteristics at the Governorate Level: Egypt 1984." Paper presented at the annual meeting of the Cairo Demographic Centre, Cairo, 12–15 December 1987.

Sayigh, Rosemary. "Encounters with Palestinian Women Under Occupation." In *Women and the Family in the Middle East: New Voices of Change*, ed. Fernea, pp. 191–208. Austin: University of Texas Press, 1985.

———. *Palestinians: From Peasants to Revolutionaries*. London: Zed Press, 1979.

———. "Roles and Functions of Arab Women: A Reappraisal." *Arab Studies Quarterly* 3 (Autumn 1981): 258–74.

Scott, James C. *Domination and the Arts of Resistance: Hidden Transcripts*. New Haven: Yale University Press, 1990.

———. "Everyday Forms of Resistance." In *Everyday Forms of Peasant Resistance*, ed. Forest Colburn, pp. 3–33. Armonk, N.Y.: M. E. Sharpe, 1989.

———. *The Moral Economy of the Peasant: Rebellion and Subsistence in Southeast Asia*. New Haven: Yale University Press, 1976.

———. *Weapons of the Weak: Everyday Forms of Peasant Resistance*. New Haven: Yale University Press, 1985.

Seligson, Mitchell A., and John A. Booth, eds. *Political Participation in Latin America*. 2 vols. New York: Holmes and Meier, 1978, 1979.

Sen, Amartya. "Gender and Cooperative Conflicts." In *Persistent Inequalities: Women and World Development*, ed. Irene Tinker, pp. 123–49. Oxford: Oxford University Press, 1990.

Shaaban, Bouthaina. *Both Right And Left Handed: Arab Women Talk About Their Lives*. London: Women's Press, 1988.

Shaarawi, Huda. *Harem Years: The Memoirs of an Egyptian Feminist, 1879–1924.* Edited and translated by Margot Badran. New York: Feminist Press, 1987.

Shafiq, M. M. "Egyptian External Migration." *Proceedings of the Organization of Egyptian Labour Migration Conference,* vol. 1. Cairo: January 1984.

Shanawany, Haifaa. "A Socio-Demographic Approach to the Study of Greater Cairo." *Egyptian Population and Family Planning Review* 2 (December 1969): 77–100.

Shorter, Frederic. "Cairo's Leap Forward: People, Households, and Dwelling Space." *Cairo Papers in Social Science* 12, no. 1 (Spring 1989).

———. "The Creation of 'Manshiet Nasser' Out of Cairo's Demographic Growth" (unpublished paper). Cairo: Population Council, 1988.

Shorter, Frederic C., and Huda Zurayk, eds. *Population Factors in Development Planning in the Middle East.* New York: Population Council, 1985.

Siltanen, Janet, and Michelle Stanworth. "The Politics of Private Woman and Public Man." *Theory and Society* 4 (1984): 91–118.

Simon, Dagmar. "Dayas in Urban Health Care: Activities, Problems, and Prospects for the Future." Master's thesis, American University in Cairo, 1981.

Singerman, Diane. "Politics at the Household Level in a Popular Quarter of Cairo." *Journal of South Asian and Middle Eastern Studies* 13 (Summer 1990): 3–21.

———. "The Recent Phenomenon of Rape in Egypt: January–March 1985" (unpublished paper). Department of Anthropology, Sociology, and Psychology, American University in Cairo, May 1985.

———. "Where Has All the Power Gone? Women and Politics in Popular Quarters of Cairo." In *Reconstructing Gender in the Middle East: Tradition, Identity, and Power,* ed. Shiva Bilaghi and Fatma Müge Goçek. New York: Columbia University Press, forthcoming.

Sivan, Emmanuel. *Radical Islam: Medieval Theology and Modern Politics.* New Haven: Yale University Press, 1985.

El-Sokkari, Myrette Ahmed. "Basic Needs, Inflation and the Poor of Egypt, 1970–1980." *Cairo Papers in the Social Sciences* 7 (June 1984).

Springborg, Robert. *Family, Power and Politics in Egypt: Sayed Bey Marei-His Clan, Clients, and Cohorts.* Philadelphia: University of Pennsylvania Press, 1982.

———. *Mubarak's Egypt: Fragmentation of the Political Order.* Boulder, Colo.: Westview, 1989.

———. "Patterns of Association in the Egyptian Political Elite." In *Political Elites in the Middle East,* ed. George Lenczowski, pp. 83–108. Washington, D.C.: American Enterprise Institute for Public Policy Research, 1975.

Stacy, Margaret, and Marion Price. *Women, Power and Politics.* London: Tavistock, 1981.

Staudt, Kathleen. "Public Women, Private Policies, and Development: A Review Essay." In *United Nations Decade for Women World Conference,* ed. Naomi B. Lynn, pp. 55–68. New York: Haworth Press, 1984.

Stauth, Georg. "Gamaliyya: Informal Economy and Social Life in a Popular Quarter of Cairo." *Cairo Papers in Social Science* 14 (Winter 1991): 78–103.

Stauth, Georg, and Sami Zubaida, eds. *Mass Culture, Popular Culture, and Social Life in the Middle East.* Boulder, Colo.: Westview; Frankfurt: Campus Verlag, 1987.

Stowasser, Barbara F. "Women's Issues in Modern Islamic Thought." In *Arab*

Women: Old Boundaries, New Frontiers, ed. Tucker, pp. 3–28. Bloomington: Indiana University Press, 1993.

Sullivan, Dennis J. "Islamic Society vs. Secular State: Political and Economic Development in Egypt." Paper presented at the annual meeting of the American Political Science Association, Atlanta, 31 August–3 September 1989.

Sullivan, Earl L. *Women in Egyptian Public Life*. Syracuse, N.Y.: Syracuse University Press, 1986.

Tadros, Helmi R., Mohamed Feteeha, and Allen Hibbard. "Squatter Markets in Cairo." *Cairo Papers in Social Science* 13 (Spring 1990).

Taylor, Charles. "Interpretation and the Sciences of Man." In *Understanding and Social Inquiry*, ed. Fred R. Dallmayr and Thomas A. McCarthy, pp. 101–31. South Bend, Ind.: University of Notre Dame Press, 1977.

Tekçe, Belgin, Linda Oldham, and Frederic Shorter. *A Place to Live: Families and Child Health in a Neighborhood in Cairo*. Cairo: American University in Cairo Press, 1994.

Thorne, Barrie, and Marilyn Yalom, eds. *Rethinking the Family: Some Feminist Questions*. New York: Longman, 1982.

Tucker, Judith E. *Women in Nineteenth-Century Egypt*. Cambridge: Cambridge University Press, 1985.

———, ed. *Arab Women: Old Boundaries, New Frontiers*. Bloomington: Indiana University Press, 1993.

United Arab Republic. *Egyptian Women: A Long March from the Veil to Modern Times*. Cairo: Ministry of Information, State Information Service, 1975.

———. *The Role of Women in the United Arab Republic*. Cairo: Ministry of National Guidance, 1967.

Vatikiotis, P. J. *Nasser and His Generation*. New York: St. Martin's, 1978.

Verba, Sidney, and Norman Nie. *Participation in America: Political Democracy and Social Equality*. New York: Harper and Row, 1972.

Von Sivers, Peter. "Life Within the Informal Sectors: Tunisia and Egypt in the 1970s." In *Mass Culture, Popular Culture, and Social Life in the Middle East*, ed. George Stauth and Sami Zubaida, pp. 243–57. Boulder, Colo.: Westview, 1987; Frankfurt: Campus Verlag, 1987.

Waterbury, John. *Commander of the Faithful: The Moroccan Political Elite—A Study in Segmented Politics*. New York: Columbia University Press, 1970.

———. *Egypt: Burdens of the Past / Options for the Future*. Bloomington: Indiana University Press, 1978.

———. *The Egypt of Nasser and Sadat: The Political Economy of Two Regimes*. Princeton: Princeton University Press, 1983.

———. "Patterns of Urban Growth and Income Distribution in Egypt." In *The Political Economy of Income Distribution in Egypt*, ed. Gouda Abdel-Khalak and Robert Tignor, pp. 335–37. New York: Holmes and Meier, 1982.

Watson, Helen. *Women in the City of the Dead*. Trenton, N.J.: Africa World Press, 1992.

Weiner, Myron. "Political Participation: Crises of the Political Process." In *Crises and Sequences in Political Development*, by Leonard Binder et al., pp. 159–204. Princeton: Princeton University Press, 1971.

Weiner, Myron, Samuel P. Huntington, and Gabriel Almond, eds. *Understanding Political Development: An Analytic Study*. Boston: Little, Brown, 1987.

Wikan, Unni. *Life Among the Poor in Cairo*. Translated by Ann Henning. London: Tavistock, 1980.

———. "Living Conditions Among Cairo's Poor—A View from Below." *Middle East Journal* 39 (Winter 1985): 7–26.

Wolin, Sheldon S. "Max Weber: Legitimation, Method and the Politics of Theory." *Political Theory* 3 (August 1981): 401–24.

Wood, C. "Equilibrium and Historical-Structural Perspectives on Migration." *International Migration* 16 (1982).

World Bank and International Finance Corporation. *World Tables, 1988–89: From the Data Files of the World Bank*. Baltimore: Johns Hopkins University Press, 1989.

Zaytoun, Mohaya A. "Earnings and the Cost of Living: An Analysis of Recent Developments in the Egyptian Economy." In *Employment and Structural Adjustment: Egypt in the 1990s*, ed. Handoussa and Potter, pp. 219–57. Cairo: American University in Cairo Press, 1991.

Zubaida, Sami. "Islam, the State and Democracy: Contrasting Conceptions of Society in Egypt." *Middle East Report* 179 (November–December 1991): 2–15.

Zurayk, Huda. "Women's Economic Participation." In *Population Factors in Development Planning in the Middle East*, ed. Shorter and Zurayk, pp. 3–58. New York: Population Council, 1985.

Zurayk, Huda, and Frederic Shorter. "The Social Composition of Households in Arab Cities and Settlements: Cairo, Beirut, Amman." *Regional Papers*. Cairo: Population Council, 1988).